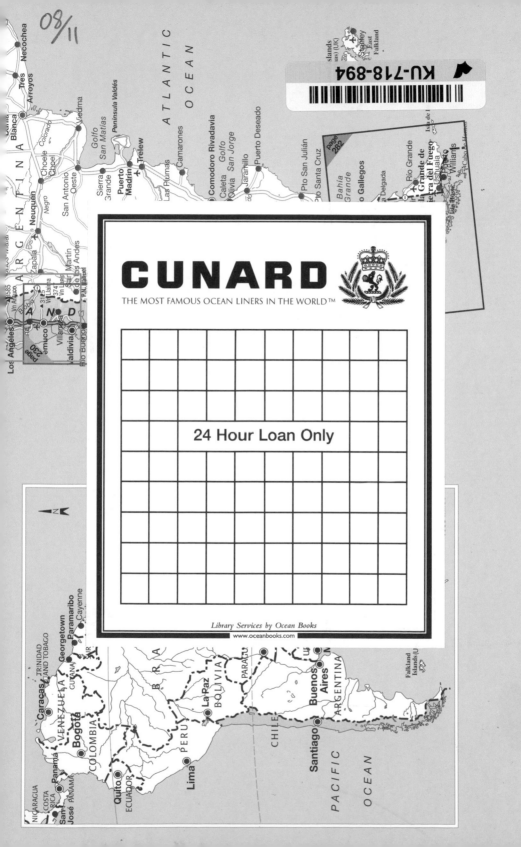

INSIGHT GUIDES
CHILE
& EASTER ISLAND

APA PUBLICATIONS L
Part of the Langenscheidt Publishing Group

✳ INSIGHT GUIDE

CHILE
& EASTER ISLAND

Editorial
Managing Editor
Rachel Lawrence
Art Director
Ian Spick
Picture Manager
Steven Lawrence
Series Manager
Rachel Fox

Distribution

United States
Langenscheidt Publishers, Inc.
36–36 33rd Street 4th Floor
Long Island City, NY 11106
orders@langenscheidt.com

UK & Ireland
GeoCenter International Ltd
Meridian House, Churchill Way West
Basingstoke, Hampshire RG21 6YR
sales@geocenter.co.uk

Australia
Universal Publishers
1 Waterloo Road
Macquarie Park, NSW 2113
sales@universalpublishers.com.au

New Zealand
Hema Maps New Zealand Ltd (HNZ)
Unit 2, 10 Cryers Road
East Tamaki, Auckland 2013
sales.hema@clear.net.nz

Worldwide
**Apa Publications GmbH & Co.
Verlag KG (Singapore branch)**
38 Joo Koon Road, Singapore 628990
Tel: (65) 6865 1600.
apasin@singnet.com.sg

Printing

Insight Print Services (Pte) Ltd
38 Joo Koon Road, Singapore 628990
Tel: (65) 6865 1600.

©2010 Apa Publications GmbH & Co.
Verlag KG (Singapore branch)
All Rights Reserved

First Edition 1991
Fifth Edition 2009

CONTACTING THE EDITORS
We would appreciate it if readers
would alert us to errors or out-
dated information by writing to:
**Insight Guides, P.O. Box 7910,
London SE1 1WE, England.
Fax: (44) 20 7403 0290.
insight@apaguide.co.uk**
NO part of this book may be reproduced,
stored in a retrieval system or transmitted
in any form or means electronic, mechanical, photocopying, recording or otherwise, without prior written permission of
Apa Publications. Brief text quotations
with use of photographs are exempted
for book review purposes only. Information has been obtained from sources
believed to be reliable, but its accuracy
and completeness, and the opinions
based thereon, are not guaranteed.

www.insightguides.com

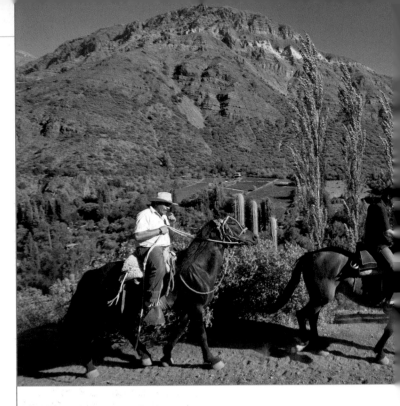

ABOUT THIS BOOK

The first Insight Guide pioneered the use of creative full-color photography in travel guides in 1970. Since then, we have expanded our range to cater for our readers' need not only for reliable information about their chosen destination but also for a real understanding of the culture and workings of that destination. Now, when the internet can supply inexhaustible (but not always reliable) facts, our books marry text and pictures to provide those much more elusive qualities: knowledge and discernment. To achieve this, they rely heavily on the authority of locally based writers and photographers.

How to use this book

Insight Guide: Chile and Easter Island is structured to convey an understanding of the country and its people as well as to guide readers through its attractions:

◆ The **Best of Chile** at the front of the guide helps you to prioritize what you want to do.

◆ The **Features** section, indicated by a pink bar at the top of each page, covers the natural and cultural history of the region and includes illuminating essays on indigenous peoples, outdoor activities, viniculture, and the arts.

◆ The main **Places** section, indicated by a blue bar, is a complete guide to all the sights and areas worth visiting. Places of special interest are coordinated by number with the maps. A list of recommended restaurants is included at the end of each chapter.

◆ The **Travel Tips** listings section, with a yellow bar, provides full information on transportation, hotels,

LEFT: horseback riding in the Maipo Valley.

Chile, revised the History, Features, and Places sections, building on work she did on previous versions of the book. She thoroughly updated the Travel Tips section and she also wrote the features on The Chilean Trail and Fruit-laden Lands, and compiled the Best of Chile.

Other contributors whose work is retained from previous editions include **Mike Gonzalez**, senior lecturer in the Department of Hispanic Studies at Glasgow University; **Jane Letham** and **Mark Thurber**, who run Inti Travel in Quito, Ecuador; salsa expert **Shannon Shiell**; and ethnomusicologist **Jan Fairley**. The following Santiago-based journalists contributed their inside knowledge of Chilean life: **Claudio Alvarez**, information editor for the daily newspaper *PubliMEDIA*; **Mark Mulligan**, a *Financial Times* correspondent now working in Madrid; freelance journalist, **Patrick Nixon**; and **Marta Infante**, editor of the Chilean adventure sports magazine *Outdoors*.

The principal photographer was Abe Nowitz, ably assisted by his father Richard, but many other talented photographers contributed their work, including **Eduardo Gil**, **Helen Hughes**, **Daniel Bruhin**, **Gunther Wessel**, and **Andreas Gross**.

The text was proofread by **Sue Pearson** and the index was compiled by **Helen Peters**.

activities from culture to shopping to sports, an A–Z section of essential practical information, and a handy Spanish phrasebook. An easy-to-find contents list for Travel Tips is printed on the back flap, which also serves as a bookmark.

◆ The **photographs** are chosen not only to illustrate the Chilean landscape, and the beauty of its cities, nature reserves, and beaches, but also to convey its cultural diversity.

The contributors

This new edition was commissioned and edited by **Rachel Lawrence**, and builds on previous versions edited by **Tony Perrottet** and **Natalie Minnis**, and written by **Tim Frasca**, **Lake Sagaris**, **Patricio Lanfranco**, **Imogen Mark**, **Malcolm Coad**, and **Rebecca Gorman**.

Ruth Bradley, a British journalist who lives and works in Santiago de

Map Legend

▬ ▪▪	International Boundary
▬ ▬ ▬	Regional Boundary
▬•▬	National Park/Reserve
▬ ▬ ▬	Ferry Route
✈ ✈	Airport: International/Regional
🚌	Bus Station
❶	Tourist Information
🕈 † ⴕ	Church/Ruins
†	Monastery
∴	Archaeological Site
🏰 🏚	Castle/Ruins
☾	Mosque
✡	Synagogue
∩	Cave
👁	Statue/Monument
★	Place of Interest
⌓	Crater

The main places of interest in the Places section are coordinated by number with a full-color map (e.g. ❶), and a symbol at the top of every right-hand page tells you where to find the map.

Contents

LEFT: Puyehue National Park in the Lake District.

Maps

THE BEST OF CHILE: TOP ATTRACTIONS

From the world's driest desert and virgin ice fields to the mysterious ancient statues of Easter Island, here is a rundown of Chile's most spectacular attractions

△ It may be the driest place on earth, but the **Atacama Desert** is rich in natural and geological treats as well as indigenous history. Don't miss the El Tatio geysers and their stunning display of geothermal energy as they thrust columns of steam into the cold morning air. *See pages 195–8.*

▷ **Valparaíso's ascensores** (funiculars) may look rickety but are, in fact, quite safe and afford spectacular views of the bay. One of the most curious is the *Ascensor Polanco*, which rises vertically through the heart of the hill up to a suspended walkway. *See page 177.*

▽ The undisputed queen of Chile's national parks, **Torres del Paine** lies at the southern tip of the Andes mountain chain. It can only be visited comfortably in the southern hemisphere summer (Dec–Mar), but it offers exhilarating walks amid scenery of unparalleled beauty. *See pages 290–2.*

△ There are few places where it is possible to be so alone as on the windswept island of **Tierra del Fuego** at the tip of South America. You're more likely to see *guanacos* and, in the woods, beavers than other people. *See pages 299–305.*

△ One of Chile's most prestigious red-wine growing areas, the **Colchagua Wine Valley** retains its old rural traditions, alongside state-of-the-art wineries and boutique hotels. During the *vendimia*, or grape harvest, which takes place between early March and mid-April, there are numerous festivals. *See page 104.*

△Chile's **southern fjords** with their inlets, islands, glaciers, and dense forests, are a transport engineer's nightmare, but the boats that ply the channels are a nature lover's dream. *See page 331.*

▽ Look down into the molten lava of **Volcán Villarrica**, listen to its tectonic rumblings and sniff the sulfur; the crater of the conical snow-capped volcano is a relatively easy one-day hike from Pucón, and a sight that few will ever forget. *See page 234.*

◁ With its mysterious stone statues and Polynesian roots, **Easter Island** is 2,000km (1,240 miles) away from the nearest inhabited land, farther than any other island in the world. *See pages 308–25.*

▽ **La Moneda**, in Santiago, is still the seat of government, although no longer the president's home. This is the palace that Chilean air force fighter planes bombed during the 1973 military coup; its courtyards are open to the public. *See page 144.*

◁ The **churches of Chiloé** are known for their unusual wooden architecture and often stand alone by the sea where they were built by Jesuit missionaries during the colonial period. Some of them have been listed as World Heritage sites *See pages 255–65.*

THE BEST OF CHILE: EDITOR'S CHOICE

Vast national parks, world-class rafting, and thermal springs are all waiting to be experienced in Chile, as well as great wines and exotic fruits. Here, at a glance, are the editor's top tips for making the most of your visit

BEST NATIONAL PARKS

● **Lauca** At the heart of this national park on the border with Bolivia, the Chungará Lake lies at 4,500 meters (14,760ft) above sea level against a backdrop of snow-capped volcanoes and teeming with bird life, including flamingos. *See page 200.*

● **Nevado Tres Cruces** Overshadowed by Ojos del Salado, the world's highest volcano, this national park is off the beaten track but includes several Andean lakes and part of the spectacular Salar de Maricunga salt flat. *See page 191.*

● **Vicente Pérez Rosales** Founded in 1926, this vast national park, at the eastern end of Lago Llanquihue, has some of the most beautiful countryside in the Lake District and is dominated by the Volcán Osorno. *See page 245.*

BEST ADVENTURE SPORTS

● **White-water rafting** From the Maipo River near Santiago to the Futaleufú River in the far south, Chile's fast-flowing mountain rivers are prized by rafters, both for their scenery and their range of difficulty. *See pages 120–1.*

● **Surfing** The pick of Chile's surfing beaches is Punta de Lobos in Central Chile, but there are also plenty of good beaches in the north. *See page 124.*

● **Mountain biking** The Carretera Austral in Aisén is the ultimate goal of mountain bikers in Chile but the Lake District offers many less challenging, but equally beautiful, routes. *See page 124.*

● **Sea kayaking** A kayak is a great way to explore the Patagonian fjords, and the inlets and remote islands of Chiloé. *See page 123.*

● **Mountaineering** Climbers from around the world visit Chile, attracted by peaks like Aconcagua, the Ojos del Salado volcano, and the "towers" of Torres del Paine. *See page 344.*

● **Paragliding** Although paragliding is practiced at many places along the coast of central Chile, Iquique in the north is by far the most popular center. *See page 124.*

ABOVE: snow-capped volcano in Parque Nacional Lauca. **LEFT:** kayaking on Lago Grey.

BEST FOOD AND WINE

● **Fruit** Chilean restaurants only too rarely serve the fresh fruit that is one of the country's joys, whether peaches and apricots in summer, grapes in fall, or custard apples (*chirimoyas*) in winter. *See page 94.*

● **Seafood** Kingclip (*congrio*) and sea bass (*corvina*) from Chile's cold coastal waters, tuna fish from Easter Island, lobster from the Juan Fernández islands, and king crab (*centolla*) from Punta Arenas are just some of the seafood not to be missed in Chile. *See page 93.*

● **Carmenère** Unique to Chile, this is the country's signature wine, the equivalent of Argentina's Malbec. Lighter than Cabernet Sauvignon, it is suitable for drinking on its own as well as with a meal. *See page 102.*

● **White wines** Although Chile is better known for its red wines, it also produces some excellent Sauvignon Blanc and Chardonnay wines. Look out for those from the Casablanca Valley. *See page 103.*

ABOVE: fresh fish caught off Easter Island.

BEST HISTORICAL SITES

● **Pukará de Quitor** Three km (2 miles) from San Pedro de Atacama, this 12th-century fortress is where the native peoples made their last stand against Pedro de Valdivia and the invading Spaniards. *See page 203.*

● **Socoroma** On the colonial pack route from the Potosí silver mine down to Arica, this Aymara farming village has cobbled streets and a 17th-century church.

● **Cerro Alegre and Cerro Concepción** These two hills in Valparaíso, overlooking the bay, are where English and German immigrants made their home during the port's economic heyday. *See page 176.*

● **Chiflón del Diablo mine, Lota** Former miners describe the grueling life at the coal face as they guide visitors down this old mine under the sea. *See page 224.*

BEST HOT SPRINGS

● **Puritama** At these springs, northeast of San Pedro de Atacama, you can wallow in steaming pools or take a natural shower under one of the waterfalls, while looking out over the Atacama Desert. *See page 198.*

● **Baños de Colina** There are no facilities at these hot springs in the Andes above Santiago, but the smooth, natural pools on terraces carved into the mountainside are a wonderful place from which to contemplate the moonscape scenery. *See page 164.*

● **Cauquenes** In the foothills of the Andes, 28km (17 miles) east of Rancagua, these waters have been venerated since pre-Hispanic times. The cathedral-like building with its individual stone baths is open to visitors as well as guests at the excellent hotel. *See pages 216–7.*

● **Tolhuaca** In the eastern part of the beautiful Tolhuaca National Park, these open-air hot baths, with an intense smell of sulfur, are off the beaten track and quite rustic, but very attractive.

● **Puyehue** Both the mud baths at the luxury Termas de Puyehue Hotel or the nearby Aguas Calientes hot springs are renowned for their curative powers. *See page 244.*

LEFT: ruins in the Atacama Desert.
RIGHT: the Baños de Colina.

BIENVENIDOS

Chile's politics have kept the country in the international headlines, but it's the well-developed infrastructure, spectacular scenery, and welcoming people that appeal to visitors

Squeezed between the Andes and the Pacific, this spaghetti-like strip of land was affectionately tagged "the thin country" by Nobel Prize-winning Chilean poet Pablo Neruda. It is never more than 355km (221 miles) wide, and its coastline extends over 4,300km (2,700 miles). Within its borders are the world's driest desert, lush expanses of forest, and a spectacular array of glaciers and fjords. And, stretched directly along the Pacific "ring of fire," Chile has over 2,000 volcanoes, of which around 60 have erupted in the last 500 years.

This wild geography hasn't stopped Chile from becoming one of the continent's most developed nations. Travelers are often surprised by the efficiency of Chile's banking system, transportation, and services, but behind the affluent surface are social and economic imbalances waiting to be redressed. Chileans are predominantly mestizos – the descendants of mainly Spanish immigrants and indigenous peoples – although there are pockets of pure-blooded Mapuches, as well as direct descendants of German, Swiss, and other immigrants. Indeed, the feeling of Chile's cities and the manners of Chileans are strongly European. Their reputation for legalizing and business acumen has earned them the somewhat facetious label of the "English of South America."

But it is the country's political history that has done most to push it into the world's view. In 1970, Chile elected a socialist government, then, in 1973, it suffered a bloody military coup. For the next 16 years of dictatorial rule under Augusto Pinochet, Chile's freedom became an international cause célèbre, which was revived in 1998 when the ex-dictator was arrested in London on charges of crimes against humanity. However, since 1990, four center-left democratic governments have presided over a period of political stability and, for the most part, high economic growth.

The traditional hospitality of Chileans, noted by travelers since the 18th century, is even more evident today. After years of dictatorship, Chileans have welcomed the influx of foreigners who come to enjoy its invigorating Andean atmosphere as a sign of international integration. ❏

PRECEDING PAGES: Torres del Paine; young lovers in one of Santiago's many parks; watching the sunset from Cerro San Cristobal in Santiago. **LEFT:** strolling through the capital's Bellavista neighborhood. **ABOVE:** summertime fun in Valparaíso.

EARTH, FIRE, AND ICE

From searing desert heat to sub-Antarctic chills, with volcanoes, lakes, and geysers along the way, the natural world makes its presence strongly felt in Chile

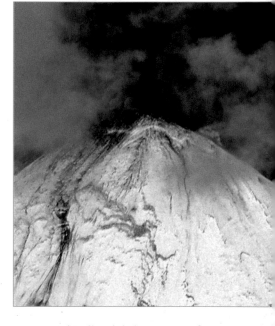

Chile must be a top candidate for the world's strangest geographical layout. In spite of the country's relatively small landmass (756,000 sq km/292,000 sq miles), its 4,300-km (2,700-mile) coastline makes it seem enormous. Though the country is never more than 355km (221 miles) wide, a trip from Arica in the north to the port of Punta Arenas in the far south covers the same distance as New York to Los Angeles or Paris to Tehran. Parts of Chile are so narrow that in some areas the Andean peaks of its eastern border can be seen from the Pacific beaches.

The Pan-American Highway, which runs down the country's spine, connects every imaginable climatic zone: it crosses vast expanses of total desert, an agricultural valley the size of California's, and a province of mountain lakes and volcanoes. Farther south, car ferries and the

"Such a country should be called an island," wrote the 20th-century Chilean geographer Benjamín Subercaseaux referring to Chile's unique geographical position, "even though its borders do not strictly fit the definition."

Carretera Austral highway – actually a dirt road – connect Chiloé, the continent's second-largest island, to hundreds of kilometers of scarcely inhabited fjords and islands. A spectacular glacier field then divides these from the sheep farms of Chilean Patagonia, which is only accessible by road from Argentina.

LEFT: a guanaco in Patagonia. **RIGHT:** Volcán Llaima, one of Chile's most active volcanoes.

Geographically, Chile has a sense of separateness and forbidding boundaries. Its northern desert, the Atacama, is one of the driest places on earth. The Andes, which form the 4,000-km (2,500-mile) frontier with Argentina, rise in sharp grades on the Chilean side, from sea level to as high as 7,000 meters (23,000ft) in little more than 100km (60 miles).

Chile's far southern tip points towards the polar ice of Antarctica. The country's western coastline faces the Pacific, the broadest ocean in the world and one of Chile's south-sea possessions, Easter Island, is the most isolated bit of inhabited land on earth, a thousand kilometers away from any other inhabited island. Perhaps it is this geographical isolation that causes Chileans to reflect so obsessively on themselves, to examine their national character and their prized idiosyncrasies, and to lay claim to myriad faults and virtues.

From lush valleys to dry desert

In the semi-arid Norte Chico (Little North), irrigation has extended Chile's agricultural heartland north to the dusty valley town of Copiapó. Here, the many mountain rivers maintain a year-round flow, fed by seasonal rains and Andean snows. Despite the blistering sun, there is considerable humidity and minimal tempera-

the fascinating remains of lost civilizations.

Chile's capital city, Santiago, is located at the country's latitudinal mid-point, next to the steep Andean foothills. The city, with a population of 6 million, is surrounded with a lovely but unfortunately placed set of smaller hills that trap its heavy air pollution. In this central region and along the coast, rains come sporadically from May to October, while the summer months of January to March are almost uniformly cloudless and hot.

The Central Valley has abundant agriculture with ample rivers, fed by the melting Andean snows. The famous wine grapes and other fruit

ture change, making the region excellent for irrigated farming. Tropical fruit, especially *papaya* and *chirimoya* (custard apples), is commercially grown. The region's ideal atmospheric conditions for astronomical work have led to the construction of important observatories in the hills near La Serena.

The vegetation ends where the Norte Grande (Great North) begins. The extreme north of Chile, annexed from vanquished Peru and Bolivia after the 19th-century War of the Pacific (see page 41), does not at first glance seem worth the trouble. Among the brown, barren hillsides and parched Atacama Desert are places where no rain has ever been recorded. But for the visitor, this barren region is fertile in geological spectacle and

A RICH MINERAL VEIN

The tangible wealth of Chile's north lies beneath the Atacama Desert; its apparently barren surface conceals rich mineral deposits. Nitrates for fertilizer were once the basis of Chile's economy and two ghost towns still stand testimony to the industry's former glory (see page 201). Today, it is copper that drives the Chilean economy and the Escondida mine, controlled by BHP Billiton, is the copper mine with the largest production in the world. Silver and gold are also present in commercial quantities, while salt is exported for human consumption and industrial use, and attention is increasingly turning to the potential of the desert's lithium reserves.

such as peaches, nectarines, apples, pears, kiwis, and cherries, flourish in the intense, dry heat.

Towards the chilly south

Farther south in the Lake District, year-round precipitation keeps the landscape green, but limits farming to the cultivation of more traditional grains and the rearing of animals. An active volcano belt provides picturesque landscapes (most of Chile's active volcanoes are in this area), but also can disrupt the lives of villagers with dangerous clouds of toxic particles. Twelve great lakes, including the continent's fourth-largest, Lago Llanquihue, give the area its dominant

remote zones on the continent. Foreign trout fishermen fly to the provincial capital of Coyhaique to fish in the pure streams and lakes of the region. The road sweeps past beautiful Lago General Carrera and basks in the microclimate around Chile Chico, ending in the 300-inhabitant frontier town of Villa O'Higgins.

The furthest tip of Chile is accessible only by boat, plane, or via a long detour overland through Argentina. This inaccessibility seems to make Magallanes all the more exciting for many visitors, who come to explore the vast wilderness of Parque Nacional Torres del Paine, with its relatively tame wildlife, accessible glaciers, and

characteristic – even the high Andean plateaux in this region are strewn with large lakes.

Where the lakes meet the Pacific Ocean, the coastal mountain range becomes a 1,000-island archipelago with Isla Chiloé at its head. The Chilote people's folklore and the island's unique stilted buildings are renowned throughout Chile. Rainfall of over 4,000mm (157in) annually is registered in Chiloé and its satellite islands, giving Chile both precipitation extremes, with the Atacama Desert at the other end of the scale.

The Carretera Austral, an unpaved road from Puerto Montt, allows access to one of the most

trademark mountain peaks. Punta Arenas, with just over 120,000 inhabitants, is the southernmost city of its size in the world. Temperatures rarely rise above 10°C (50°F) in this gusty port, which is almost perpetually shrouded in cloud.

Farther south lies Tierra del Fuego, the "land of fire", whose name was inspired by the smoke from the fires of its now-extinct indigenous tribes. South America's largest island forms the main part of this forbidding archipelago, which Chile shares with Argentina. (Chile nearly went to war with Argentina here in the late 1970s, until the Vatican sponsored peace negotiations.) Beyond Tierra del Fuego lies the considerably harsher territory of Antarctica, a large part of which Chile claims. ❑

LEFT: the Valley of the Moon in northern Chile.
ABOVE: Parque Nacional Lauca.

DECISIVE DATES

PREHISTORIC TIMES

13,000–10,000 BC

A group of mastodon hunters settle in the area now known as Monte Verde, near modern Puerto Montt.

PRE-COLUMBIAN CULTURES

c.1450

The Incas, led by Tupac Yupanqui, make their way down from Peru and conquer northern Chile, but fail to subdue the Araucanian tribes in the south.

EUROPEAN CONQUEST AND SETTLEMENT

1520

The Portuguese explorer Ferdinand Magellan becomes the first European to glimpse Chile as he sails through the straits that are later named after him.

1533

Inca rule ends when they are defeated by Spanish conquistador Francisco Pizarro.

1536

Pizarro's comrade Diego de Almagro travels from Cuzco to Copiapó and then on to the Aconcagua Valley in search of gold.

1541

Pedro de Valdivia sets off to conquer Chile and founds Santiago.

1550–1

Valdivia establishes the settlements of Concepción, Valdivia, Villarrica, and several other cities.

1553

Valdivia is killed by the native Mapuches, led by Lautaro, near Concepción.

1557–61

A new governor, called García Hurtado de Mendoza, re-establishes Spanish rule in Concepción and founds Osorno and Cañete.

1599

A major uprising by indigenous tribes wipes out all Spanish settlements south of the Biobío river in the Central Valley region.

17th Century

Ranching becomes Chile's primary export trade, with large estates (*haciendas* or *latifundas*) employing bonded mestizo peasants to replace *encomiendas* as European diseases reduce the native population.

18th Century
Around 20,000 Spaniards emigrate to the new colony.

1740
Chile loosens its bonds with the Viceroyalty of Peru, seat of the Spanish American Empire, as direct trade is permitted with Spain and other colonies in the New World.

1750
Chile is permitted to mint its own coins.

INDEPENDENCE FROM SPAIN
1808
The French emperor Napoleon invades Spain, dethroning King Ferdinand VII.

1810
Leading Chilean citizens force the Spanish governor in Chile to resign and, following the example of Spanish cities, select a ruling junta in the name of King Ferdinand.

1811
The first Chilean National Congress gathers, swearing loyalty to the Spanish king.

1812
Following a coup d'état, the Carrera government proposes that the Spanish king should recognize Chile's constitution and sovereignty and establishes democratic rule.

1813
Spain invades Chile.

1814
Chilean nationalists are beaten at Rancagua, and their leaders flee to Argentina.

1817
The nationalists, led by Bernardo O'Higgins, defeat the Spanish forces with the help of Argentine hero General José de San Martín. O'Higgins is appointed Supreme Dictator.

1818
Chilean independence is declared. The nationalists win a decisive victory over the royalist forces at the Battle of Maipú.

GROWTH AND STABILITY
1823
Slavery is abolished.

1829–30
A lengthy period of "Conservative Republic" is ushered in under Diego Portales.

1839
The first Chilean bank notes go into circulation.

1840s
Prosperity grows as more silver is found in the north, Chilean farmers supply Californian gold-diggers, and Magallanes is founded to take advantage of European trade routes.

PRECEDING PAGES: *Presence of Latin America* by Jorge González Camarena. FAR LEFT TOP: copper Moche mask. FAR LEFT BOTTOM: Tupac Yupanqui. LEFT TOP: onetime comrades Francisco Pizarro and Diego de Almagro. TOP: nineteenth-century coin. ABOVE: worker in a silver mine. LEFT: the Battle of Maipú, 1818.

1843
The University of Chile is founded in Santiago.

From 1848
German settlement is encouraged, as immigrants flee the revolutions in Europe, bringing European political and revolutionary ideas to Chile. Work begins on Chile's first railroad, from Copiapó to Caldera.

1850s
Guano is discovered, putting the area north of Coquimbo into dispute with both Peru and Bolivia.

1860
Free primary education is introduced.

1876–8
Flooding in the south and drought in the north lead to famine. Agricultural problems combined with a fall in the demand for silver lead to an economic crisis.

1879
Chile declares war on Bolivia and Peru.

1881
Last uprising of Chile's indigenous peoples. The rebellion is quashed by the army and the territory of the Mapuches is declared state property.

1883
Peru cedes Tarapacá, Tacna, and Arica to Chile.

1884
Bolivia cedes Antofagasta to Chile.

1891
Civil war breaks out over the issue of presidential powers. After defeat, President José Manuel Balmaceda commits suicide.

THE 20TH CENTURY

1907
The massacre of striking mine workers at Santa María de Iquique ends a period of intense union activity.

1912
The Chilean Socialist Workers' Party is founded.

1918
The invention of synthetic nitrates makes Chile's "desert gold" obsolete.

1925
A new constitution separates church and state.

1926
Economic and political crises bring army officer Carlos Ibáñez to power. He creates a powerful state system.

1929
The Wall Street Crash and world depression lead to political instability.

1931
Ibáñez resigns and goes into exile.

1932
Arturo Alessandri returns to power, ushering in a period of economic recovery and political stability.

1945
Chilean poet Gabriela Mistral is awarded the Nobel Prize for literature.

1949
Women win the right to vote.

1952
Carlos Ibáñez is elected president and returns to power.

1964
Eduardo Frei leads the Christian Democrat Party to power with US support.

1970
The leftwing coalition Popular Unity, led by Salvador Allende, scrapes to victory as Chile's first Socialist government.

1971
The Allende government nationalizes the copper mines as part of a sweeping reform program. Chilean poet Pablo Neruda wins the Nobel Prize for literature.

1973
The Allende government is overthrown in a violent military coup, ending in the suicide of Allende in Santiago's Moneda Palace, which brings General Augusto Pinochet to power. Thousands are tortured and murdered during his regime.

1980
A new Constitution stipulates a referendum on continued military rule in 1988.

1982–3
Chile's economy nosedives, sparking off strikes and protests.

1986
An attempt to assassinate Pinochet fails.

1988
Fifty-four percent of voters reject Pinochet's regime in a referendum.

1989
Christian Democrat Patricio Aylwin is elected President as the country returns to democracy. General Pinochet stays on as Army commander-in-chief.

1990s
Prosperity increases rapidly, although income distribution remains extremely unequal.

1991
The National Commission on Truth and Reconciliation establishes military guilt in violating human rights, but few of the perpetrators are punished.

1994
Christian Democrat Eduardo Frei, son of 1960s President Frei, is elected to head the Concertación, the center-left government coalition.

1998
Pinochet retires as army commander in chief. Later that year, he is detained during a visit to London on human rights charges filed by a Spanish judge and is held under house arrest until March 2000 when he is released on grounds of ill health.

FAR LEFT TOP: mining nitrate in the desert. FAR LEFT MIDDLE: Salvador Allende. FAR LEFT BOTTOM: Gabriela Mistral. ABOVE: news of General Pinochet's death. LEFT: anti-Pinochet graffiti during the 1988 referendum. RIGHT: President Bachelet.

2000
Ricardo Lagos, a Socialist, is elected to head the Concertación's third term.

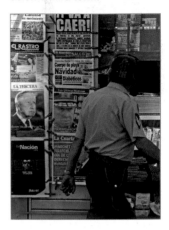

2002
Pinochet is declared mentally unfit to stand trial in Chile and retires from public life until his death in December 2006.

2006
Concertación candidate Michelle Bachelet, a Socialist, is elected as Chile's first woman president.

2007
Chile is invited to apply for accession to the Organization for Economic Co-operation and Development (OECD).

THE WILD FRONTIER

Prehispanic Chilean society was as diverse as the latitudes it covered, which helped the southern tribes to repel invasions by the Incas as well as the Spanish

Chile was never a top priority for South America's explorers or colonizers. The Incas made their way down from Peru in the mid-15th century, less than 100 years before the Europeans arrived, when Tupac Yupanqui defeated the northern tribes and established Inca rule as far south as present-day Santiago.

The native Atacameño and Diaguita cultures, which had thrived in the northern deserts for centuries, were fairly organized societies compared with the Araucanians farther south. Both of the northern groups were farmers. They grew beans, maize, potatoes, and coca, using irrigation techniques that suggest they had a central authority strong enough to impose rules on their small societies. They kept llamas, wove cloth and baskets, made and decorated pots, and traded with each other and with the peoples in Peru. The Atacameños mummified their dead while the Diaguitas took their wives to the grave with them. Little more is known about their civilizations, though their numbers were estimated to be about 80,000.

Unconquered tribes of the south

Beyond present-day Santiago, the Incas ran into serious opposition. The Araucanian tribes, who numbered around 1 million in total, lived from the River Aconcagua down to Chiloé. There were three main groups, all speaking the same language, but with significant cultural differences.

The Picunches (men of the north) lived in the fertile Central Valley between the Aconcagua and Biobío rivers. They grew most of the same crops as the Diaguitas and Atacameños to

LEFT: ancient Atacameño tapestry. RIGHT: Atacameño mummy in the Museo Gustavo Le Paige.

the north, but with much less effort required in their temperate climate and well-watered soil. The Picunches lived in small, generally peaceful, self-sufficient family groups, and were no match for the Incas when they arrived.

It was the less submissive Mapuches (men of the land), the Huilliches (men of the south) and, to a lesser extent, the nomadic Pehuenches, Puelches, and Tehuelches, whom the Incas called "the rebel peoples." The Mapuches lived precariously in the area between the Itata and Toltén rivers, farming temporary clearings in the dense forests and moving on once the land was exhausted. The Huilliches lived in the same way between the Toltén and the island of

Chiloé. The Incas gave up on these loosely grouped nomads, who did not recognize a central authority or understand any form of tribute. They set their frontier at the River Cachapoal, near Rancagua, and left the rest of the Araucanians to themselves.

The Incas interfered little with the customs and practices of the peoples that they colonized, as long as they paid tribute, in gold, and provided labor. Inca rule lasted less than 40 years. An internal power struggle developed, and the Inca garrisons were withdrawn from Chile back to Cuzco in present-day Peru. The quarrel ended with their defeat at the hands of the Spanish conquistador Francisco Pizarro and the demise of their empire.

The Spaniards' conquest begins

The first European to see Chile was the Portuguese explorer Ferdinand Magellan, who sailed through the straits which took his name on November 1, 1520. He only glanced at the new territory as he sailed up its coast. Next to arrive was Pizarro's comrade Diego de Almagro, who made his way over the cordillera from Cuzco in 1536 with a couple of hundred men and high hopes of treasure. They reached Copiapó, where the native people received them peacefully

THE INCA TRAIL

The lasting contribution of the Incas' short-lived rule in Chile was the "Inca Trail," a series of paths which reached as far south as Talca. There were three routes, one along the coast, one through the desert, and one over the altiplano (high plain) and along the Andes. They were later used by the Spanish explorers to access their base in Peru and, although less developed for trekking than the famous Inca Trail in southern Peru, some stretches have now been incorporated into the Sendero de Chile trail *(see page 125)*. One of the most spectacular routes starts at the Chilean-Peruvian-Bolivian border and runs 14km (8 miles) to the tiny Andean town of Visiri.

enough, and then traveled on to the Aconcagua Valley. All the time the Spaniards scouted about in vain for the fabulous gold mines of which the Incas had spoken.

A solitary captain and 80 men were sent down to the Magellan Straits, but they returned, having got no further than the River Itata, with terrifying tales of ferocious natives. Spirits sank, and Almagro's men resisted his proposal to stay and colonize the new territory. Returning empty-handed to Peru in 1537, Almagro tried to take on Francisco Pizarro for control of the Andes. He lost the civil war that ensued and paid for the uprising with his life.

The reward for one of Pizarro's backers was Chile. Pedro de Valdivia set off to subdue the southern territory. He was to take for himself and his followers any land he found. But Almagro's unfruitful trip had discouraged fortune-seekers, and Valdivia had a hard time finding recruits. Eventually he set off with only a dozen others, and his faithful mistress, Inés de Suárez.

As Valdivia had hoped, many other marauder-explorers joined him on the way. There were 150 in the motley band when they reached the River Mapocho in the Central Valley, and decided to make their first settlement. This was Santiago, founded on February 12, 1541.

Press-ganged into service, the local Mapuches waited for a few months and then rebelled. On September 11 a local chief, Michimalongo, attacked the settlement while Valdivia was away. Inés de Suárez, in a chainmail jacket, fought alongside the men in a day-long battle. By the

> Inés de Suárez, born in Spain in 1507, is reported to have met Pedro de Valdivia in Cuzco in 1538 where she had traveled in search of her soldier husband. Her life is the subject of a book by Isabel Allende, Inés del Alma Mía.

end of it, the Spaniards stood, triumphant, on the burned-out site, but all of their belongings – food, seeds, even clothes – were destroyed.

Despite living in hunger and scarcity, Valdivia fell in love with the new land, and he wrote to the king with great enthusiasm: "This land is such that life here cannot be equaled. It has only four months of winter... and the summer is so temperate and has such delicious breezes that men can walk all day in the sun and not suffer for it. It is abundant in grass, and can support any kind of cattle or livestock and plants that you can imagine; there is plenty of beautiful wood for building houses, great quantities of wood for fuel for heating and working the rich mines. Wherever you might dream of finding them, there is soil to sow, materials for building and water and grass for the animals, so that it seems as if God had created everything so that it would be at hand."

Death by gold

Gradually the Central Valley Mapuches were subdued. Valdivia handed out parcels of land to

LEFT: one of the last Inca strongholds in Chile.
RIGHT: Inés de Suárez defends Spanish battlements.

his followers, along with groups of Mapuches bonded to labor in *encomiendas*. Theoretically, that made the Spaniards trustees charged with the care and conversion of the local population. In fact they became feudal estates, with the native people simply enslaved labor to work the land or pan for gold.

In 1550 Valdivia founded Concepción, and a year later, Imperial, Valdivia, Villarrica, and Angol. In each settlement, Valdivia left 50 or 60 men to build the "city" with the help of the subdued Mapuches. But his troops were stretched thin. At the end of 1553 he left Concepción with only 50 men. The fort at Tucapel, when they

reached it on Christmas Day, was a smoking ruin. As they surveyed the wreckage, the Mapuches attacked. Valdivia and his men fought back, but by dusk most of them were dead, including Valdivia. He was tied to a tree, legend has it, and forced to swallow molten gold.

The victor was Lautaro, who had worked for the Spaniards before going off to fight against them. He was said to be the first Mapuche to realize that the Spaniard and his horse, which was a creature completely unknown to the native Chileans, were two separate animals. Lautaro advanced on Santiago, but was knifed by a traitor on the night before the planned attack. Morale fell, and smallpox decimated his men. Santiago was saved. With Valdivia's death, three rivals fought to succeed him as governor, until in 1557, Peru sent a new governor, García Hurtado de Mendoza. He re-established Spanish rule in the area around Concepción, restored the city and subdued the Mapuches in the region. Two new cities, Osorno and Cañete, were founded. His period as governor, up to 1561, marks the end of the period of conquest.

But the war with the native people of Araucania was far from over, and the Spaniards, fighting as a part-time citizens' army, were ill-equipped to win it. At the end of the 16th century, another governor, Martín García Oñez de Loyola, lost his life in a major native uprising. The settlements

south of the Biobío were wiped out, and the northern bank of the river became the frontier of the Spaniards' territory. By then, the colony numbered about 5,000 Europeans.

Life on the wild frontier

War with the Araucanians was a background noise for the whole of the next century, and most of the one that followed. There were periodic uprisings and massacres, and the governor of the territory was based permanently down on the frontier in Concepción. By this time the colonizers had recognized that there were no rivers of gold or fabled silver cities in Chile, and that wealth needed to be tilled from the land or dug from the mines. Native people, or mixed-

race mestizos were put to work, and before long the new territory was exporting wheat, copper, leather, and wine.

But the Spanish authorities sent from Madrid could not impose law and order. A sinister and unscrupulous figure, Doña Catalina de los Ríos y Lisperguer, known as *la Quintrala*, reflected the worst aspects of the colony in the 16th century. An upper-class lady, she is credited with poisoning her father, cutting off the ear of one of her lovers, arranging a tryst with another and then having him murdered while she watched. "Lower" beings such as servants were killed or mutilated according to her whims.

Many members of the Church set no better example. Chroniclers recorded open fights between members of the Augustinian and the Franciscan orders. Gambling was a passion in the

> Fights over gambling debts between clergymen became such a problem in 16th-century Chile that the bishop banned them from entering public gambling houses, or from having packs of cards in their own homes.

new colony, and the main entertainment for men. Clothes were of prime importance for society women, and for some men too – the richer and more ostentatiously embroidered, the better.

Cultural influences

By the late 17th century Chile was becoming more civilized. The influence of the French Bourbons (now rulers of Spain) brought French culture and manners to the distant colony. Governor Cano de Aponte arrived in his new domain in 1720 with "twenty-three boxes of furniture and dishes, a clavichord, four violins, a harp and various Andalusian tambourines, as well as fifteen mules loaded with fine clothes."

The Jesuits brought over architects, engineers, pharmacists, weavers, painters, and sculptors. They also collected the best library in the colony – 20,000 volumes by the mid-18th century. Chile was already on the way to becoming the prosperous and highly Europeanized country that would later be seen as an example to the more turbulent emerging nations of Latin America. ❏

LEFT: Pedro de Valdivia.
RIGHT: the foundation of Santiago.

INDEPENDENCE AND PROSPERITY

Once independence had been won from Spain, there was no stopping the new republic, and Chile soon became one of the strongest economies in the Americas

S pain tried to keep its colonies free of foreign influences. It banned the entry of books printed outside Spain and prohibited printing presses within the colonies. But colonials still traveled to Europe, picking up "subversive" books, and new ideas.

The French Revolution and the revolt of the British colonies in North America in the late 18th century set conflicting examples. The excesses of the French rebels could be held up as an awful warning. But the sober, enterprising North Americans were rather an encouragement to their southern neighbors.

In the first 13 years following independence, Chile tried five different constitutional formulas and went through 11 changes of government.

As it turned out, it was the ambitions of Napoleon that led to the independence of the Spanish colonies. When the French emperor invaded Spain, he forced the abdication of the king, Ferdinand VII, and placed his own brother, Joseph Bonaparte, on the Spanish throne. In Spain itself, there was immediate resistance. In each city the leading citizens set up a junta to govern in the name of the deposed king. Soon, the local bodies delegated power to a central junta in Seville.

A new Congress

According to the Spanish governor in the American colonies, the junta in Seville represented authority while the true king was absent.

LEFT: *The Vision of San Martín.* RIGHT: foot soldier in Chile's revolutionary army.

But many colonials felt they shared the same status as the Spanish cities, and that they should have the right to elect their own authority, subject only to the king.

In Chile that was what they did. The inept Spanish governor was persuaded to resign in favor of a native Chilean, Don Mateo de Toro Zambrano. The next step was to form a ruling junta, as the Argentines had done. In Chile the governor called a *cabildo abierto*, a formal meeting of the leading citizens. They gathered on September 18, 1810 and chose a junta, which swore undying loyalty to the Spanish king.

Their first act was to secure the defense of their new nation. An infantry battalion was formed, along with two cavalry squadrons and more artillery. Envoys were sent to buy arms in England and Argentina. The junta also decreed free trade with all nations, hoping to boost the state's income from customs duties.

Finally, it convoked a National Congress, which was to be representative and also to guarantee that there were no abuses of power – two radical new notions that had infiltrated from Europe and the United States. The voters were people who "by their fortune, work, talent, or qualities enjoy consideration in the parts where they reside, being older than 25 years." They elected deputies who "for their patriotic virtues,

September 4, 1811, Juan José and José Miguel stormed the Congress at the head of a mob and presented a list of "the people's demands." It was a coup d'état. A cowed Congress agreed to sack some of its most conservative members and set up an executive junta. After that, the reforms came faster, but still not fast enough for the Carreras. José Miguel forced Congress to set up a new junta, with himself at the head, and in December 1811, dissolved the Congress.

The Carreras had their sights set on Chile's independence, but they were in a minority. One of their first acts was to acquire a printing press and put a radical priest called Fray Camilo Hen-

talents, and acknowledged prudence may have merited the esteem of their fellow citizens."

The selection of the deputies went ahead in early 1811. The first National Congress gathered on July 4 and, once again, its members swore loyalty to the Spanish king. A majority of its members were conservative landowners, who wanted only a minimum of reforms. But an energetic elite wanted radical change.

A radical coup d'état

The first to make a bid for the leadership of the nation were the Carreras. Three brothers – José Miguel, Juan José, and Luis – and one sister, Javiera, came from a wealthy Santiago family. But their ideas were extreme for the day. On

ríquez in charge of it. He began publishing revolutionary ideas about popular sovereignty in a weekly paper, *La Aurora de Chile*.

In 1812, the government promulgated a new Constitution. Formally, this still recognized the Spanish monarch, but it proposed that the king should in turn recognize Chile's own Constitution and sovereignty. The new Constitution also established the rights of the individual, and set limits on the powers of the government, which was now to be elected by the people. This was a drastic change from being ruled by a monarch.

Most of José Miguel Carrera's compatriots, especially among the aristocracy, were not ready for such revolutionary gestures, and did not like either the man or his ideas. But before they could get together to do anything about him, the Spaniards took a hand.

The wars of independence

On March 26, 1813, Spain invaded the Chilean Central Valley, using officers from Peru and 2,000 men recruited among royalists in Valdivia and Chiloé. They took Talcahuano and Concepción, and started to move north. Carrera took command of the army and organized the defense of the capital, together with another military leader, Bernardo O'Higgins.

O'Higgins was another product of the ruling elite. He was the illegitimate son of a former

governor, Ambrosio O'Higgins, an Irishman who had emigrated via Spain and Peru to Chile, where he became one of the most effective governors. An affair with a lady of Chillán, Doña Isabel Riquelme, produced Bernardo, who was sent to Lima and then England for education.

Back in Chile, O'Higgins was elected a deputy to the Congress. He then distinguished himself as a military leader, and took over command of the army in 1813 from the more impetuous José Miguel Carrera. But by the end of the year the war was going badly. A truce was negotiated. Both sides were exhausted.

LEFT: Bernardo O'Higgins, who led Chile to independence. **ABOVE:** clergymen, early 19th century.

In March 1814, the Treaty of Lircay was signed. But the Carrera brothers and their troops rebelled and took the government again. O'Higgins set off to overthrow the new regime, but before he and the Carreras clashed the news came that a new royalist army had disembarked at Talcahuano. Divided and unprepared, the patriots met them at Rancagua on October 1, and were soundly beaten. O'Higgins and the Carreras all fled together to Argentina.

Spain back in charge

Ironically, it was the Spanish reconquest which finally convinced the Chileans that independence was their only option. The Spaniards tried to turn the clock back to 1810. Every reform the patriot governments had made, from allowing free trade to abolishing slavery, was annulled by the royalists.

> Avenida Libertador General Bernardo O'Higgins, the main east–west road through Santiago, is named after Chile's independence hero and his name crops up in streets, squares, and statues around the country.

There was direct persecution of patriots. Many were sent into internal exile – one group was banished to a cave on the Juan Fernández Islands. Nationalists in the public prison in Santiago were shot. The rest of the citizenry had to prove their loyalty to the Crown. Patriot public servants lost their jobs, others, their property. Heavy fines were exacted from all wealthy citizens. Chileans were not allowed to travel without permission, or carry arms. Public festivals were banned, a very unpopular move, and the gaming houses were closed.

Meanwhile, the remains of the patriot army, led by O'Higgins, had joined forces with the Argentine General José de San Martín and spent the next two years in Mendoza preparing to invade. A spy network kept the patriots in touch with sympathizers in Chile. Its leader was Manuel Rodríguez, a young lawyer who helped form guerrilla bands to harass the Spaniards. Rodríguez became a national folk hero; the tales of his clever disguises and narrow escapes from the Spaniards passed into legend. On one occasion he took refuge in a Franciscan monastery and, disguised in a monk's robes, showed his pursuers around the convent to prove he was not there. Another time he dressed as a beggar and politely helped the Spanish governor to alight from his carriage. Even if they were not all true, the stories helped to keep up people's spirits.

Triumph for the nationalists

By 1817, O'Higgins and San Martín were ready, and their 3,600-strong "army of the Andes" crossed the mountains. On February 12, they defeated royalist troops at Chacabuco, then entered Santiago in triumph, welcomed by vast crowds of Chileans.

patrolled the coasts of Peru, disrupting the enemy's supplies. At the end of the year, the navy took Valdivia, which was one of the few remaining royalist strongholds in Chile.

On August 20 1820, the army of the Andes, now mainly composed of Chileans but led by the Argentine San Martín, set off for Peru. With the fall of Lima and the final defeat of the Spanish, Chile's independence was assured.

Tribulations of the new republic

Once independence was secure, the Chileans had to work out how to replace two and a half centuries' rule by an absolute monarch with a

The first job was to set up a new government. O'Higgins was named *director supremo*. On January 1, 1818, the new regime declared the independence of Chile. But there was still fighting to be done. The royalists counter-attacked with a new force from Peru, and took Talca. The patriots soon recovered and inflicted a final defeat on the Spaniards at the Battle of Maipú on April 5, 1818. That settled Chile's future.

But O'Higgins continued to fight for the independence of the rest of South America, not least because Chile would never be secure while the royalists held Peru. A navy was formed under Lord Cochrane, a Scot, with ships begged and borrowed from all parts, and mostly foreign officers and sailors. In 1819, the new force

republic. Most of the trial Constitutions and reforms introduced were received quite peacefully but were not always popular. In 1823, O'Higgins ran into determined opposition from the landowning aristocracy. He was forced to resign and went back to Peru, where he lived the rest of his days dreaming of return. He eventually died in 1842, but his body was not brought back to Chile until 1869.

The other revolutionaries fared worse. Two of the Carrera brothers were shot by the Argentines in 1818; then José Miguel, too, was shot, in Mendoza three years later. A secret society, known as the *Logia Lautarina*, formed originally by O'Higgins and San Martín in 1815, was said to have given the orders for their executions.

Only Javiera Carrera survived and returned to Chile after the downfall of O'Higgins.

Manuel Rodríguez, who had been closer to the Carreras than to O'Higgins, presented a problem for the new government. He was a headstrong, popular leader. O'Higgins tried to

> Diego Portales argued that Latin America was not ready for democracy: "When morality has been established, then comes a true liberal government, free and full of ideals, in which all citizens can take part."

send him into gilded exile in the United States as a diplomat. Rodríguez refused, and ended up first in prison and then, in 1818, shot – "while trying to escape," said the official report.

But most of the decade was taken up with the struggle between conservative landowners and the Church against the Chilean liberals, who were strong in the towns, and among the intellectual elite. The liberals hung on to the government until 1829, when they lost control of Santiago and the administration.

Finally, in 1833, the conservatives were able to impose an authoritarian model of government that lasted until the next century. On paper, the president was all-powerful and Congress was a mere sideshow. It sat for only four months of the year, while the president could veto laws, and had personal representatives in each province. The president could also veto electors, giving him enormous influence over the election of congressmen and of his successor.

Conservative values

The real leader of the conservative movement, though he never ran for president and preferred to rule from behind the throne, was Diego Portales, best-known until then as a businessman.

Like other leaders of the independence movement, he was committed to liberal ideas in the abstract but argued that, in practice, Latin America was "not ready" for democracy. It was never made clear when the transition would take place or under what circumstances what came to be called the "enlightened despotism" would end.

LEFT: Valparaíso, one of the world's busiest ports by the late 19th century. **RIGHT:** southern market town in the 1860s.

While the Congress was writing the new Constitution, Portales was busy imposing the authority of the central government. He himself was minister for the interior, foreign affairs, the army, and the navy. He purged the army of its rebel leaders and reorganized the military academy: officers were to return to the professional, non-political status they held before independence. To encourage this, Portales reinstated a system of local militias, directly loyal to the government.

A successful campaign stamped out banditry in the countryside. Economic and financial reforms reduced the size of the army and the civil service and brought in better bookkeeping

and fiscal controls. Such was Portales's influence in these years that in 1833 the British consul wrote home that "Every measure of the government originates with him (Portales) and no state body dares carry out any order without his express approval..."

Portales was murdered by political opponents in 1838. The organizational model he had established, however, lasted for nearly a century. By and large, the deeply conservative Chilean bureaucracy was better-organized and less corrupt than others in the region – on the other hand, Portales's expressed desire to extend democracy to Chilean society as a whole would only be fulfilled much later and in the wake of major social conflicts.

Stability and prosperity

Chile developed through the 1800s in largely stable conditions, though violence and social unrest erupted in the 1850s as the undemocratic manner of selecting presidents came into dispute. Reforms of the electoral system in the early 1870s temporarily resolved the issue.

Throughout most of the 19th century, a strong state oversaw an economic growth concentrated in overseas trade and copper and silver exports. Like its neighbor Argentina, Chile encouraged European immigration; in the south, for example, German immigrants came to control some of the larger and most profitable estates, while Euro-

pean dominance of trade ensured that the British and French occupied key positions elsewhere in the economy. The British led the shipping business. In 1825, 90 British ships called at Valparaíso compared with 70 from the US. Fifteen years later, the number of British vessels had doubled, while the number from the US continued to fall. By 1875, Britain took 70 percent of Chile's exports and sold it 40 percent of its imports.

Market forces

Much of Chile's growth came from copper exports. In 1826, 60 tons were shipped out of the country; by 1831, that was up to 2,000 tons, and by 1835, it was 12,700. By 1860, copper represented 55 percent of all Chile's exports. How-

ever, copper sales taught Chile about the dangers as well as the benefits of joining the world economy. The industrial revolution in Britain had boosted demand for copper in the 1830s. But industrial slumps in Europe in the 1850s and 1870s hit Chile hard. From then on, the daily price of copper on the London Metal Exchange became a national obsession.

Another problem that Chile faced in this period was the cost of being so far from its markets. In the 1840s, Chile found a profitable new market for its wheat and flour in California, at the height of the gold rush. Its exports leapt more than 70-fold in three years. But by 1854 the North American farmers were back on top, and Chile's sales slumped. When the gold rush started in Australia a little later, Chilean farmers could not compete in price with their Californian rivals. For the rest of the century there was a steady flow of migrants from the countryside and its decreasingly profitable farms, to the towns and the mining centers of the north.

Rail, cables, and banknotes

Transportation was a problem internally. The first railway line was planned in 1845, from Copiapó to the little port of Caldera. An energetic North American, William Wheelwright, organized the finances from the private sector and by 1851 the first 81km (50 miles) were inaugurated. Another line from Valparaíso to Santiago was finished in 1863. A telegraph line linked the main port with the capital in 1852; by 1876 there were 48 national lines, and one each to Argentina and Peru. In 1853, Chile introduced postage stamps, just 13 years after Britain.

Getting a banking system organized was a major task. There was a physical shortage of coins and paper money – the first banknotes began to circulate in 1839. In the mining sector the owner-entrepreneurs started to use their own trade bills as a form of exchange, and to coin lead tokens to pay their workforce. Their logical next step was to set up a bank. By 1850, there were 60 operating, including the Banco de Chile. The government regulated their currency issues, but did not produce its own.

Already by the 1840s, contemporary chroniclers were writing about the effects of a period of stability and prosperity. There were fine new houses in Santiago, such as the Palacio Cousiño, as well as two theaters, a school of painting, and several literary magazines.

In 1843, the University of Chile was founded for research and debate. The Instituto Nacional was the only higher-education center, but there were schools for music and art. In 1860, primary education was made free and a state responsibility. At this date only 17 percent of the population was literate, but 60 years later the figure had risen to a creditable 50 percent.

War with the neighbors

In the first half of the 19th century, the northern desert area close to the Peruvian and Bolivian borders had attracted little attention. But from the 1850s onwards, deposits of natural fertilizers (guano and nitrates) were discovered there. Guano became a major source of income for Peru, and Chile and Bolivia disputed deposits along the coast north of Coquimbo. By 1874 Peru and Chile had agreed for both to exploit the guano, but the labor was mostly Chilean.

In 1878, new disputes broke out, this time over nitrate deposits. In 1879, Chile occupied Antofagasta, which until then was Bolivian territory. When it discovered that Peru and Bolivia had a secret defense pact, Chile declared war on both its neighbors. The ensuing War of the Pacific resulted in Chile gaining a future source of

wealth, nitrates, and its best-loved national hero, Captain Arturo Prat. Today, his statue graces the plaza of even the smallest village, and the day of his death, May 21, is a national holiday.

The Chilean army marched to the Peruvian capital, Lima. Peru had to sue for peace; the Treaty of Ancón, signed in 1883, gave Chile Tarapacá and the towns of Arica and Tacna for a 10-year period. Bolivia ceded Antofagasta in 1884, thereby losing its only exit to the sea. Since then, successive Bolivian governments have pressed the Chileans to give them even just a strip of coast for a port. Peru eventually resigned its claim to Arica in exchange for Tacna in 1927.

LEFT: Arturo Prat, a national hero. **ABOVE:** mineworkers became the backbone of Chile's union movement.

Nitrate boom and bust

One result of the war with Peru was that Chile now controlled the nitrates deposits of the north. Taxes from the new nitrates mines were the primary source of income for the Chilean state for many years thereafter.

The man who made the most money out of nitrates, however, was not a Chilean but an Englishman, John Thomas North. During the War of the Pacific, he bought up cheap title deeds to some of the best nitrates deposits. Then, back in England, he raised money on the stock market to work the mines. "Chile saltpeter" caught the British public's imagination. The shares sold like hot cakes, and North became a famous figure. "He's the most important man in England at the moment," wrote one of his competitors, "with the possible exception of [Prime Minister] Gladstone."

However, by the 1890s the nitrate bubble had burst. There was overproduction and, as a result, prices plummeted. Then, early in the 20th century, a cheaper substitute was invented. Attempts to cut production failed, the price went on falling, and the industry declined, until by the 1930s only a handful of offices were still producing. Once-bustling camps and villages such as Humberstone still stand today, now deserted and ghostly witnesses to Chile's past (see page 201).

Power struggle and civil war

The power struggle between president and Congress had been muted during the 1860s and 1870s by a series of mild-mannered presidents and minor reforms. However, the key issue remained – the president's power to elect the Congress that he wanted.

Congress was not much more than a debating society, although it could block effective government. Presidents played off party factions against each other to buy support. By the end of the century the factions, now more like organized parties, were becoming harder to pacify with crumbs of power.

DEATH OF A HERO

The story of Arturo Prat's death is in the best naval tradition of heroic defeats. His ship, the Esmeralda, was trapped in the Bay of Iquique by the two biggest battleships of the Peruvian fleet, the Huascar and the Independencia. Prat refused to surrender and his ship resisted the enemy fire for two hours, until the Huascar rammed it. Sword in hand, Prat leapt into the Huascar with a handful of men, and was cut down. The Peruvian commander, Admiral Grau, was gentlemanly enough to send back the captain's sword and a letter he had written to his wife. It earned him equally generous treatment when the Chileans captured the Huascar later that year.

Under President José Manuel Balmaceda, the issue came to a head. Balmaceda faced a factious Congress, made some politically inept appointments, and reacted to criticism by trying to assert his presidential powers. He finally lost his majority in Congress. When he tried to rule without it, and refused to convoke a special session to approve the military budget, the navy rebelled. Congress and the rebels organized an army and defeated government troops at the battles of Placilla and Concón, seizing Santiago. Balmaceda took refuge in the Argentine embassy, where he committed suicide. ❑

ABOVE: Santiago shopping arcade, late 19th century.
RIGHT: the navy rebellion at Valparaíso in 1891.

A CENTURY OF UPHEAVALS

From democracy to military rule and back to democracy –
the 20th century saw extraordinary reversals in Chile's
political, social, and economic arenas

The civil war of the 1890s tilted the balance of power in favor of the Congress and against the presidents, who were reduced to refereeing the fights for cabinet posts among the parties. But by this time there were new actors on the political scene. The railways had made travel easier and the towns were growing, and with them a new cultural and social life. A new middle class was organizing in the recently founded Radical Party. A strong force within it were the freemasons, whose lodges were political debating centers.

A new working class was forming, too. Industry had grown up in the early and mid-century in specific centers – everything from biscuit and pasta factories in Valparaíso that supplied passing ships, to breweries started by German settlers in the south. The new railways needed workshops, and the growing towns needed textiles, shoes, soap, and furniture. Business boomed, as did the numbers of urban artisans.

It was getting ever harder to scratch a living in the countryside, so many peasants were drawn to the nitrate mines of the north. Once there, they were often trapped, earning low wages paid in tokens that could only be exchanged for goods in the company store. Schools, a police force, and courts were practically non-existent. Alcohol was easier to come by than water in the northern mining camps of the pampas.

Birth of the trade unions

It was in these harsh conditions that the modern Chilean trade union movement was born,

LEFT: Santiago's Paseo Ahumada in the 1930s.
RIGHT: lumberjacks take strike action.

evolving out of the early mutual aid societies. The miners formed the basis for Chile's early political movements, anarchist at first and later socialist. One figure stands out in that early history of working-class organization. Luis Emilio Recabarren, a former print worker, traveled the country as a union organizer. He got an audience among the miners for his political message by publishing newspapers which carried news from other parts of the country. They helped the immigrants isolated in the pampas to keep in touch with their homes, and also provided a means of communication between groups of workers in the cities, the mines, and the countryside, who until then had been isolated from one another. In 1912, Recabarren founded the Chilean Socialist Workers' Party. After the Russian Revolution in 1917, it was the basis of the Chilean Communist Party.

Recabarren traveled to Russia, and met Lenin and Trotsky, as well as trade union and political leaders from across the world. He was elected to the Chilean parliament twice during this period, though he was never allowed to take his seat. Although he was a key figure in the early history of the Chilean left, Recabarren's relationship with the Communist Party was always difficult. Political difficulties may well have been the cause of his suicide in 1928.

Chilean flag, and surrounded by the flags of other nations. They were the strike committee... All eyes were fixed on them just as all the guns were directed at them. Standing, they received the shots. As though struck by lightning they fell, and the great flag fluttered down over their bodies."

Most thought that was the end of the incident. But, said the witness, "There was a moment of silence as the machine guns were lowered to aim at the schoolyard and the hall, occupied by a compact mass of people who spilled over into the main square... There was a sound like thunder as they fired. Then the gunfire ceased and

Desert slaughter

The massacre at Santa María de Iquique, a remote mining town in northern Chile, has come to symbolize the struggle of Chile's mineworkers in the early 1900s. In 1907, the miners went on strike for better pay and conditions. When an envoy was sent from central government to speak with them, the miners and their families gathered in the town center to hear what he had to say. Four-and-a-half thousand of them were crammed into the local school, and 1,500 more were in Plaza Manuel Montt. An eyewitness gave a chilling account of what happened as squads of soldiers began to appear in the plaza.

"On the central balcony... stood 30 or so men in the prime of life, quite calm, beneath a great

the foot soldiers went into the school, firing, as men and women fled in all directions."

The army general later reported that there had been 140 victims. The eyewitness quoted

> In 1969, the musician Luis Advis composed a famous oratorio based on the tragedy at Santa María de Iquique. which he performed and recorded with his folk music group, Quilapayún (see page 83).

talked to doctors and others involved, and estimated the figure at 195 dead and 390 wounded. Others reported many more.

Social inequalities

Experiences like these, combined with the organizing work of Recabarren, laid the foundations of Chile's strong trade union tradition. At one stage, before and during World War I, sections of the ruling classes gave some consideration to the implementation of basic social welfare legislation – the nitrates industry, after all, was booming as a result of the war. But the discovery of artificial nitrates had a powerful impact on Chile, putting a swift end to the boom, and all such proposals were shelved.

Agriculture was stagnant, dominated by huge landed estates whose owners lived either in town or in Europe, and had little interest in raising productivity or modernizing. Import figures for 1907 show the ruling class's priorities: 3.7 million pesos were spent on importing agricultural and industrial machinery, while 6.8 million went on the purchase of French champagne, jewels, silk, and the latest perfume from Paris. As tax revenues from nitrates declined and the foreign debt grew, increasing numbers of ordinary Chileans found themselves without work or the possibility of it, and facing poverty and collapsing living standards.

Power struggles

In conditions of growing social conflict, there often emerge leaders who claim to bridge the conflicting interests of all social classes. In Chile, that "figure above society" was Arturo Alessandri, the son of an Italian immigrant.

Typically, his rhetoric was nationalistic and deliberately vague, enabling him to appeal to different sections of Chilean society at the same time. His election to the presidency in the early 1920s did not give him the power over Congress he aspired to, and in deepening conditions of crisis he turned to the younger and more restless sections of the army.

The result was a military coup in 1928, which gave military caudillo Colonel Carlos Ibáñez del Campo dictatorial powers. His models were Mussolini and Spain's José Primo de Rivera, and he was a fierce critic of the traditional political structures, especially the parties, some of whose leaders he "invited" to leave the country. But he was even more fiercely anti-Communist, and had Communists and union leaders

LEFT: nitrate workers, Antofagasta. **RIGHT:** Arturo Alessandri, who had two shots at leadership.

arrested and deported. It was a return to authoritarianism such as Chile had not seen since the years of Diego Portales.

In a sense, the coup brought an end to a system of power which had observed the democratic rules but within a limited framework, in which power was simply exchanged between sections of the ruling classes. Chile has a reputation for a long democratic tradition; yet this was pushed aside in the 1920s, as it would be again in the 1970s, with considerable ease.

Ibáñez set about creating a powerful state sector of the economy, establishing the national airline and the daily government newspaper *La*

Nación, which still exists today although with a minute circulation. This was an attempt to shift resources into new areas of the economy, placing them under national control and overcoming the resistance of the traditional ruling classes, using the state as an instrument of economic control.

Recession and social unrest

This was a bad time to be increasing state expenditure. With the Wall Street Crash in 1929 and the world recession that followed, the Chilean economy went into a crisis. Nitrate sales had long been declining, and now the expanding copper industry was also hit as the Great Depression squeezed its markets. There was widespread unemployment and social unrest.

The government set up an emergency employment program, and printed money to pay for it. Inflation rose, and so did the protests.

Ibáñez was forced to resign. He left for exile in July 1931, but his elected successor was promptly overthrown by a military-civilian junta. In June 1932, a "Socialist Republic" was installed by Colonel Marmaduque Grove. Grove belonged to a group of radical young officers whose aim was to bring about a redistribution of wealth, particularly through land reform, that would set the economy to work again. The new republic lasted only 100 days, however, before Grove was exiled to Easter

Island and Arturo Alessandri returned with a draconian program in October 1932. He purged the army of dissident elements, clamped down on trade unions, banned strikes, and closed down the opposition press.

Although Grove's social experiment had achieved very little, some proposals had reached the statute book: 40 years later, President Salvador Allende would begin to implement some of the changes that Grove had envisaged.

Recovery and reform

By the late 1930s, economic activity had resumed as the United States economy began its recovery under the Roosevelt New Deal. A new Chilean government, elected in 1938, offered a program of mild economic and social reform. Headed by a Radical, Pedro Aguirre Cerda, it enjoyed the support of both the Communist and the Socialist parties, but disputes later broke the alliance. Aguirre Cerda's elected successor, another radical, quickly outlawed the Communists.

The radicals boosted the state sector of the economy substantially, with a steel industry and a nationwide electrification program. But in the countryside, government intervention had a negative effect. Strict price controls on farm produce meant that the landowners had little incentive to invest and produce more. Public opinion was beginning to sense that farming would simply never take off under ruling-class ownership and that the only hope was to take away the

> During World War II, and later in the Korean War, the US government bought copper from US-owned copper companies in Chile at a special low price, which meant a substantial loss of tax revenues for the Chilean state.

land and give it to those who could produce.

The other conflict that began to loom was the ownership of the copper mines. The main deposits had always been owned and worked by US corporations. Control of such a major source of national wealth was bound to become an issue.

The caudillo returns

By the late 1940s, party infighting and petty corruption had again paved the way for a "strong man." Carlos Ibáñez was returned to power by the electorate in 1952, demanding "a fundamental change of direction," and brandishing a symbolic broom with which he would sweep away politicking and corruption. He had the support of a redoubtable figure, María de la Cruz and her Feminine Party of Chile – women got the vote, finally, in 1949 and promptly strengthened the conservative forces.

Ibáñez had the personal charisma to get himself elected, but no organized support. He tried to get the Constitution reformed to give more power to the presidency, failed, and sat out the rest of his term in political impotence. In 1958, Arturo Alessandri's son, Jorge, succeeded the old general, elected almost entirely on the strength of his father's name. Since then, no president from the political right has been elected in Chile.

The Christian Democrats

The center and the left were now grouped in two easily definable camps. In one were the Socialist and the Communist parties – full-blooded Marxist-Leninists who talked of armed struggle to overthrow "the bourgeois state," but who were actually engaged in building up their electoral strength to win it by peaceful means.

Their rival, proposing very similar reforms in, for example, land ownership and nationalization of the copper mines, was the Christian Democrat Party. It developed in the 1930s out of a movement started by a group of young Catholics from the Conservative Party, initially with vaguely Fas-

Christian Democrat Party was the first of its kind in Latin America to get into government, in 1964, with a good deal of North American financial support. The following year they won a solid majority in Congress, with party leader Eduardo Frei Montalva becoming the first president in Chilean history to have at least theoretical control over both the executive and the legislature.

Success went to their heads, and they boasted that Christian Democrats would govern for the next 30 years (like their Italian counterparts). However, the Frei government made two powerful enemies: the old landowning class, who opposed its attempt at land reform, and the

cist leanings, who called themselves the Falange Nacional. By the end of the 1950s their ideas had been modified to Christian socialism and they were growing rapidly among both the middle and working classes. They had strong links to the Catholic Church and a comparably strong anti-Communist message. There was not a vast difference between the programs of the two camps.

In the early 1960s when the influence of the Cuban revolution was sweeping through Latin America, the Christian Democrats throughout the region appeared to many people to be the best answer to the Marxist threat. The Chilean

military, who felt underpaid and unappreciated. An army general, Roberto Viaux, led an uprising in 1969 to protest against their conditions.

The old political right, which had helped vote Frei into office, now withdrew to reform itself into a new party, the Nationals. Tensions within Frei's own party led to a split in 1969, and his left-wingers, who felt that the reforms had not gone far enough, went off to join the Marxists.

The Allende years

In 1970 a left-wing coalition known as Popular Unity put forward as their candidate a middle-class doctor turned socialist senator, Salvador Allende. Allende won his fourth attempt at the presidency by a paper-thin margin (36.3 percent).

LEFT: Turri Clock, Valparaíso. **ABOVE:** Dr Salvador Allende. **RIGHT:** General Augusto Pinochet.

One of the first electoral promises he honored was to give every poor child in Chile a pair of shoes, and to provide free milk in schools.

But the new government faced formidable enemies in the United States. President Nixon's government pumped in approximately US$8 million in covert financing over the next three years to boost the opposition and to help, for example, to keep the anti-Allende publishing group *El Mercurio* in business.

At home the government had some early successes. In 1971, it got all-party support in Congress for the nationalization of the copper mines. But Allende's decision not to pay compensation

in small factories reacted by taking over their workplaces. Neighborhood committees set up their own retail networks, bringing goods direct from the factories. By this time the opposition had convinced itself that Allende was out to install a full-blooded Marxist state. The far left of Allende's own Socialist Party encouraged this view – ironically, the Communists were moderators in the unruly coalition, committed to a "peaceful road to socialism."

The tanks roll in

In March 1973, despite the growing chaos, the government won an increased majority (44 per-

to the North American owners sparked an official US boycott of non-military aid and credits for Chile. The US government also tried to ban Chilean copper from world markets.

Social discontent

The political tension grew. When Fidel Castro visited Chile in November 1971, upper- and middle-class women held the first "march of the empty saucepans" to demonstrate against food and other shortages. A year later, the shortages were even worse and truck owners went on strike following a government proposal to create a state transportation system.

Doctors, shopkeepers, and bus owners joined in, and industrialists staged lockouts. Workers

cent) in the parliamentary elections. The opposition decided that it could not wait until the next presidential elections, which were sched-

> US Secretary of State Henry Kissinger condemned Allende's reform program, saying that he did not see why the US should stand idly by "and let a country go Communist due to the irresponsibility of its own people."

uled for 1976. In late August, Congress declared the government unconstitutional. Days later, on the morning of September 11, tanks rolled into the streets of Santiago, and the military took over the radio stations and announced a curfew, calling on President Allende to resign.

Besieged in the presidential palace with only a few advisers, Allende refused to resign. Photographs from the palace show him in a helmet and armed with a machine gun given to him by Fidel Castro, and the popular image remains of Allende fighting to the end. In his final broadcast to the nation, he ordered his supporters not to resist, yet he himself refused an offer of a safe conduct to the airport and exile. Allende's doctor testified that he died by his own hand, alone, in the ruined palace which the air force had bombed.

Pinochet who would emerge over the following two years as its undisputed head. And it was he who was largely responsible for the violence that

> The Italian film Il Postino *was based on the novel* Ardiente Paciencia, *by Chilean novelist Antonio Skármeta, which depicted the weeks following the 1973 Pinochet coup.*

followed the coup. The military took power quickly, pursuing and detaining all those who had led the trade unions, popular organizations,

Pinochet's rise to power

The Chilean coup sent shock waves around the world. For some, the 1970 elections had proved the possibility that social change could occur peacefully, gradually, and via the ballot box. That hope now lay in ruins. Chile's reputation as a haven of democracy in a subcontinent given to resolving its political problems by violent means had now lost its legitimacy – in fact, military intervention had been a feature of 20th-century political life in the country.

Though the coup was led by a junta of the heads of all the armed forces, it was Augusto

LEFT: the bombing of the presidential palace, during the 1973 coup. **ABOVE:** demonstrations against Pinochet.

student groups, and cultural movements most identified with the Allende regime.

The descent into brutality

The particularly brutal murder of the singer Víctor Jara *(see page 83)* came to symbolize thousands of other, equally violent deaths, as the foreign journalists who were herded into the National Stadium together with Jara and other suspected left-wingers to suffer beatings and torture, would later testify. Thousands of people were murdered, many more were tortured, and hundreds of thousands went into exile to escape persecution or, in some cases, in search of work as factories, government institutions, schools, and universities were reopened under direct military control.

All opposition activity was banned. The last demonstration in Chile for some 10 years was the funeral of Chile's great poet Pablo Neruda, who died just two weeks after the coup. The 3,000 mourners who marched between ranks of soldiers through the streets of Santiago shouted slogans against the military and carried placards bearing the names of Neruda and Allende. Thereafter there would be no more public expressions of hostility to Pinochet until the 1980s.

Initially, churches provided refuge for those who could not find asylum in foreign embassies. From its formation in 1976, the Vicariate of Solidarity, organized by the Catholic Church,

helped the victims of repression to find legal aid and became a focus for protests against the human rights abuses that continued in the years following the coup.

Free-market economics

By 1977 it was clear that Pinochet's regime had its own economic as well as political agenda. The crude anti-Communism of the earlier years now combined with a new economic philosophy of neo-liberalism, or complete openness to the world market – ideas advocated by Milton Friedman and a group of his Chilean acolytes known as the "Chicago boys" (see page 57). The low-wage open economy that they advocated, with its savage reductions in public spending, would become

familiar throughout Latin America from the 1980s onwards. But Chile was its first test case.

In the late 1970s, the new economic philosophy seemed in its own terms to have succeeded – there was a consumer boom and foreign firms were investing heavily. New exports such as wine and fruit were beginning to find markets abroad, and the electrical goods assembled by poorly paid Chilean workers for US-based corporations were sold throughout Latin America.

The other side of the coin was the deepening poverty of a majority of the population, but this was concealed behind a curtain of repression while the "Chilean miracle" was celebrated. Thus only 25 percent of those who voted in the 1978 referendum dared to defy Pinochet as he concentrated more and more power in his own hands. The 1980 Constitution consolidated Pinochet's power and control over Chilean life.

Crisis and disintegration

The years 1982–3 brought a crisis in the Chilean economy which threatened to drive down even further the living standards of the majority, as well as to end the boom of the previous decade. In 1983 trade unions again began to call strikes, and there was widespread protest as the gross domestic product (GDP) collapsed. All political organizations remained illegal, and most of the left-wing groups had been destroyed after the coup. In this new climate of protest, however, they began to reorganize.

The Communist Party had taken a moderate line under Allende, and had argued after 1973 that the coup happened because things had gone too far too fast in the Allende years. The party now turned in a radical direction as a new generation of young people joined its ranks. By 1985, the creation of the Manuel Rodríguez Patriotic Front marked a commitment to armed struggle, which culminated in the failed attempt to assassinate Pinochet in 1986.

Thereafter the old enemies came together in a series of agreements to build a joint campaign for a "No" vote in Pinochet's 1988 plebiscite, which was designed to confirm him in power for another eight years at least. In the event, and to the dictator's evident surprise, 54 percent of the Chilean people voted "No."

Elections followed in 1989, amid intense negotiations at a number of levels. The pace and direction of the return to democracy had to be agreed on by businessmen and trade unionists,

Christian Democrats, and Communists who supported the "No" campaign – people whose purposes were very different. The hopes for a peaceful transition led the campaign into a series of talks with Pinochet. While he yielded the presidency, and formal authority, it could hardly be said that he relinquished power.

The end of the party for Pinochet

The 1980 Constitution remained in force; the judiciary was dominated by Pinochet's appointees; a block of senators would continue to be nominated directly by the armed forces, giving them a controlling voice in parliament; the

about the "disappeared" and the human rights abuses that had occurred under his rule, there would be neither revenge nor restitution.

As a result, Chile remained a deeply unequal society, in which the transition to democracy left virtually intact the previous distribution of wealth and power as well as the political influence of those around Pinochet. The memories of the 1973 coup and its aftermath were sufficiently fearsome for the suggestion of renewed military intervention to silence any complaints.

Thus it was that Pinochet could display such absolute confidence and certainty when, in March 1998, he retired as commander-in-chief

financial gains Pinochet had made as president would remain untouched. Pinochet stayed on until 1998 as head of the army and, while a commission of investigation would seek the truth

> An official report published in 2004 revealed that at least 27,000 people were tortured under the Pinochet dictatorship, in more than 1,100 detention centers, and that this systematic policy was financed out of the fiscal budget.

LEFT: campaigning for a "No" vote to Pinochet.
ABOVE: socialist supporters march through Santiago in the closing weeks of a turbulent century.

of the army, at the age of 82. He had already been named *senador vitalicio* – a senator for life – and in this capacity was given effective immunity from prosecution for crimes against human rights committed in Chile during his regime, for which there were some 200 cases pending in the Chilean courts.

It was with the same confidence that he left for Britain in September 1998 for medical treatment. Pinochet's period in power had largely coincided with the governments of Margaret Thatcher in Britain, and her relationship with him had always been cordial and admiring – as had US President Ronald Reagan's with them both.

In the meantime, a series of cases had been brought before courts elsewhere on behalf of the families of Pinochet's non-Chilean victims. Among the cases pending was one brought before a Spanish court by a team of lawyers including Joan Garcés, ex-adviser to Allende. While Pinochet was in London, the Spanish Justice Ministry initiated extradition proceedings with Britain, and he was placed under house arrest. An extraordinary chain of events was set in motion, as the House of Lords in London confirmed by a majority that he had a case to answer under international law, and later overturned their own ruling when it was revealed that one of the Law Lords had links with the human rights group Amnesty International. Meanwhile,

journalists and commentators began to revisit the experience of Chile in 1973, while those Chileans still in their countries of exile even after 1990 emerged in demonstrations.

In March 2000, the British Home Secretary agreed to the release of Pinochet on the grounds of ill health, opening the way for his return to Chile. The local courts later removed his immunity from prosecution, but then declared that the former dictator was unfit to stand trial.

Forced to resign his Senate seat and, subsequently, further discredited by the revelation of secret multimillion-dollar bank accounts held abroad in his name and those of family members, the former dictator gradually disappeared from public life and died in December 2006.

Social progress

The center-left Concertación coalition, which took office in March 1990 under Christian Democrat Patricio Aylwin (1990–4) and is now in its fourth term under President Michelle Bachelet, largely maintained the dictatorship's free-market economic policies. For example, privatized industries were not returned to the state, despite evidence that some had been sold to Pinochet supporters at bargain prices.

However, the different Concertación governments have emphasized social welfare policies while, under their leadership, Chile has also recovered the international integration denied to it under Pinochet because of repudiation of his dictatorship's human rights violations. In recent years, Chile has signed free-trade agreements with export markets that include the United States, the European Union, and China.

The poverty rate which was running at almost 40 percent in 1990 dropped to less than 14 percent in 2006, thanks mainly to the trickle-down effect of strong economic growth but also to active social policies. Spending on education – which had been starved of financing during the dictatorship, partly because of its fear of the sectors' unions – has tripled since 1990, and access, although not yet attainment, has increased dramatically. Today, seven in 10 university students are the first generation in their family to receive higher education.

A reform of healthcare, launched under President Ricardo Lagos (2000–6), seeks to ensure universal access to timely and low-cost attention for a growing number of important illnesses. Similarly, the country's housing deficit has been substantially reduced, and current government efforts focus on increasing the standards of the social housing built by private companies with state support.

These achievements were recognized in 2007 when Chile was invited to apply for membership of the Economic Co-operation and Development (OECD) – only the second Latin American country after Mexico. At the time of writing, only one issue, Chile's rules on bank secrecy, remains to be resolved, making it likely that it will be formally accepted before the end of President Michelle Bachelet's government in March 2010.

Impatience for change

The election of Michelle Bachelet in 2006, a socialist and the country's first woman president, was a sign of demand for change and helped to unleash its public expression. Whilst Chile's per capita income had been rising since 1990, income distribution had shown little improvement, resulting in impatience for faster progress, especially amoung young people facing an unemployment rate over twice the national average.

Only a matter of months after she took office, marches and sit-ins organized by secondary schoolchildren in support of better state education mushroomed into the largest show of civil defiance since the Pinochet days. The movement was another symptom of the maturing of Chilean democracy – with no memory of the Pinoc-

the two seats. Designed to promote consensus government, the system guarantees that, in most constituencies, the government and opposition coalitions will each take one of the seats.

This not only means that the political parties, in practice, "designate" their representatives in Congress, it also deprives minority parties outside the two main coalitions, such as the Communist and Humanist parties, of any chance of obtaining a seat. A reform bill was presented to Congress by the Bachelet government in early 2007 but will have, at best, a difficult passage in the face of the vested interest of incumbent members of Congress in maintaining the existing system.

het dictatorship, today's schoolchildren do not have their parents' fears for its potential fragility.

There is, however, also broader demand for a deepening of democracy. A constitutional reform implemented in 2005 eliminated the Senate seats reserved by Pinochet for the armed forces, but Chile's electoral system, also introduced by his 1980 Constitution, is seen as a major barrier to more effective political participation.

Under this system, each constituency returns two representatives to each house of Congress, with the party or coalition that comes second only needing a third of the vote to take one of

LEFT: military parade on the anniversary of the coup.
ABOVE: Michelle Bachelet, Chile's first female leader.

Reward for virtue

One of the complaints of Chile's schoolchildren in 2006 was the government's decision to save part of its revenues from record copper prices. The international economic crisis has, however, vindicated its "tightfistedness." With savings of some US$20 billion, or just over 10 percent of GDP, it has been able to finance fiscal stimulus measures without recourse to borrowing.

The government's prompt response to the crisis has put new wind in the sails of former president and son of Eduardo Frei Montalva, Eduardo Frei Ruiz-Tagle. As the Concertación's likely nominee for the 2009 presidential elections at the time of writing, it remains to be seen how he will fare against his opponent, Sebastían Piñera. ❏

ECONOMIC PROGRESS

After two decades of sustained economic growth and social progress, Chile is arguably Latin America's most developed country, but income inequality remains high

For almost 17 years after the 1973 coup, Chile was ruled by a military dictatorship, committed to crushing even the most limited aspirations for social reform. Its recipe was free-market policies and the "trickle-down effect" – the theory that wealth created by the private sector would flow down and benefit the workers. These policies were imposed by a military dictatorship in a country without a Congress, without a free press, and with restricted labor organizations – ideal, if abnormal, conditions for such an experiment. The "scientists"

Fees at Chile's top private schools, at around US$500 per month, are cheap by international and even Latin American standards, but are almost ten times the per-pupil subvention received by state schools in Chile.

were economists, most of whom had studied at the University of Chicago, at the feet of Milton Friedman, the guru of free-market economics. They were dubbed the "Chicago boys."

They made some bad mistakes, even on their own terms. In the late 1970s, the Finance Ministry fixed Chile's exchange rate for more than two years, and lifted controls on bank-lending. When the peso finally had to be devalued, there was a near-fatal bank crash. As a result, the state had to bail out most of the private banks, but many companies went bankrupt, mortgage repossessions soared, and an economic recession followed, lasting until the mid-1980s. The

high unemployment and economic hardship of this period were key factors in mounting discontent with the dictatorship.

An example to the world

But Chile weathered the storm, and by the late 1980s was able to show better-balanced books and a flourishing economy with a growing export sector and a lot of interest from foreign investors. It now had a model that other countries in the region were being encouraged to copy, not least by their bankers.

In the 1980s, a leading "Chicago boy," Joaquín Lavín, who became mayor of Santiago's Las Condes district in the 1990s and, in 2000, narrowly

LEFT: World Trade Center, Santiago.
RIGHT: consumer culture in the capital.

lost the presidential election, wrote a book about the changes he saw in Chile. Called *The Silent Revolution*, it was a paean of praise for the economic model, and it became a bible for many businesspeople and right-wing politicians. Lavín wrote enthusiastically, for example, about the new fruit export business, which developed during the military government; and he picked out the region of Copiapó in northern Chile as a prime example of a place where workers were making good money in a new, modern industry.

This was an area where the military government was sure that it would win a majority of votes in 1988, when it held a national plebiscite

touching each other; a modernizing tendency for an elite which is more and more integrated into the international world; and a tendency towards the ever-increasing impoverishment of a majority, which relies increasingly on state help."

He highlighted the fate of the lowest-income groups living in makeshift, overcrowded homes on the outskirts of the capital, the non-existence of worker rights, and high unemployment among young people (which remains a problem today).

Tempering the military legacy

Once democracy was restored in 1990, one of the new government's challenges was to attempt to

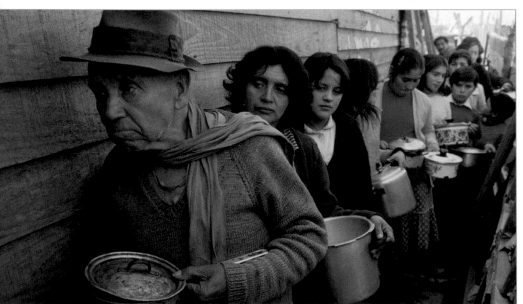

to vote President Pinochet another eight years in power. But here, and throughout the rest of Chile, the majority of voters apparently felt that "the economy may be doing fine but I'm doing badly," and the dictatorship was defeated.

The other side of the coin

The other side of Lavín's Chile was presented by Eugenio Tironi, a left-wing sociologist. In answer to Lavín's *Silent Revolution*, he published a book called *The Silence of the Revolution: the Other Side of Modernization*, in which he described the negative social effects of the dictatorship's economic policies. He wrote about the phenomenon of "two Chiles" – "a society in which two groups coexist practically without

reduce the huge gap between the very rich and the very poor, without upsetting Chile's healthy balance of payments and finances. The new center-left government, led by President Patricio Aylwin (1990–4), accepted the main tenets of the macroeconomic policies of the "Chicago boys." Even the Socialist Party admitted that "the market has the main role in assigning resources" and that a mixed economy with "all forms of property" is the best recipe for sustained growth.

With the grudging assent of the right-wing political parties, the Aylwin government raised corporate and income taxes to finance improvements in health and education. These had been squeezed of resources by the "Chicago boys," for whom state-run enterprises were anathema.

The new government also battled some fairly timid labor reforms through Congress to help improve wages and working conditions, and

Chile's small, open economy is vulnerable to weaker international growth; in late 2008, the price of copper – its largest export – dropped far more rapidly than in any previous cycle.

give the unions more strength to defend their members. These were much more controversial than the tax increases. The business community

well as launching major school and criminal justice reforms, President Frei, a civil engineer by profession, concentrated on projects like improving roads and airports (usually through private concessions), and on privatizing ports and water companies. These reforms vastly improved infrastructure – laying the foundations for the international-standard highways seen in Chile today – and increased productivity as the key to competitive exports and sustained future growth.

President Ricardo Lagos (2000–6) headed the Concertación's third government. A moderate socialist, he sought to combine economic growth with greater social justice and to extend

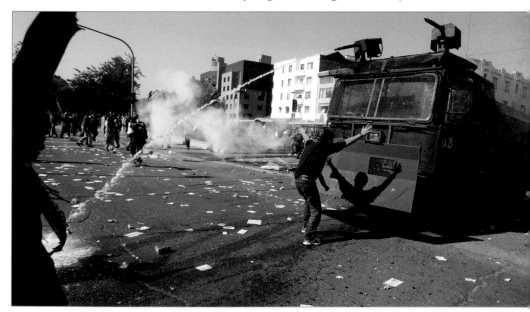

insisted that low wages for miners, forestry, and industrial workers were crucial, if Chile's exports were to remain competitive in world markets. However, labor leaders argued that, without stronger unions, the workforce had no defense against routine abuses such as permanently renewable short-term contracts.

Improvements to infrastructure

President Eduardo Frei, a son of the 1960s Christian Democrat president, succeeded President Aylwin in 1994, heading a government of the same center-left coalition, the Concertación. As

LEFT: queues for food in the 1980s. **ABOVE:** police and demonstrators clash during a Labor Day rally.

the benefits of increased prosperity not only to the urban poor, but also to provincial Chile. Despite slower economic growth from 1999 through to 2003, owing mainly to the weakness of international export markets, his government, for example, introduced unemployment insurance and embarked on a major reform of public and private health services in a bid to increase their efficiency and to achieve greater equality of access to care.

A national census, carried out in 2002, revealed a radical improvement in material welfare since the previous census a decade earlier. By 2002, 96 percent of Chile's homes had access to electricity, up by a fifth on 1992, and 91 percent had drinking water, representing an increase of more than a quarter. Similarly, 82 percent had a refrigerator, as compared with 55 percent in 1992, while 79 percent had a washing machine, as compared with 48 percent a decade earlier.

Unsatisfied demands

Since 1990, Chile's exports, the main driver of its small economy, have diversified, helped by free-trade agreements with most of the world's main markets. Copper, of which Chile is the world's largest producer, still accounts for the bulk of exports, but the forestry, fruit, wine, and salmon industries, which barely existed 20 years ago, are now also major exporters, and other

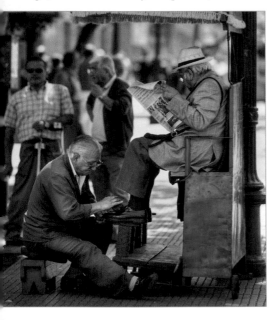

Chilean products, like olive oil, are starting to gain recognition in international markets.

At the same time, Chile has earned a reputation for macroeconomic and political stability, helping it to attract the foreign investment that has played a key role in financing its growth. However, for many Chileans, eager for a larger slice of the economic pie, their democratically chosen governments did not live up to expectations. Although poverty has dropped to a third of its level in 1990, income distribution has improved little while, after 20 years of democracy, Chileans have become far more confident of their rights, and inclined to demand them.

Pent-up demands played a crucial role in the election of Chile's current president, Michelle Bachelet, a socialist. During her 2005 election campaign, she drew attention to the extreme inequality of income distribution, promising greater social protection, a fairer society, and a larger say for voters in decisions that affect their lives. Early in her government, she reformed the private pension (AFP) system, introduced by the Pinochet dictatorship, to improve pensions for the poor and women and reduce the commissions charged by fund administrators.

On the threshold of development

On many indicators, Chile is very close to becoming a developed country. Its per capita income of almost US$11,000 is still far from those of the world's industrialized countries but is similar, for example, to that of Portugal in the mid-1990s and the United Nations Development Programme (UNDP) defines Chile as having a high level of human development, on a par with countries that include Hungary, Poland and Slovakia.

> In mid-2009, Chile opened South America's first terminal for the import of liquefied natural gas (LNG), in response to restrictions imposed by Argentina on the export of natural gas through pipelines across the Andes.

With its tradition of careful fiscal management and sound public policies, Chile is, moreover, well-placed to address its remaining development challenges. The catch, however, is that these are in many ways the most difficult ones, with inequality as the most important.

According to a government survey in 2006, the richest tenth of Chileans take 38.6 percent of national income to the 1.2 percent of the poorest tenth. This inequality is, moreover, also reflected in other spheres and, for example, life expectancy and, particularly, infant mortality show clear income-related differences.

The key to improvements lies in education. With pupil attainment closely correlated to family income, this is identified as one of the main factors in locking in inequality, but change in this area will necessarily be slow and its impact measured in generations, rather than years. ❑

LEFT: shoeshine man on the Alameda, Santiago's main street. **RIGHT:** the Santiago Stock Exchange.

THE CHILEANS

In a land where the "melting pot" has well and truly melted, social hierarchies are still firmly in place. But fascinating contradictions remain, and change is in the air

For centuries lonely travelers have made brief visits to Chile that have stretched into lifetimes. Maybe that's because the Chileans are among the most contradictory and intriguing of Latin America's peoples. They are inherently careful and cautious – quite unlike their more effusive and spontaneous Argentine neighbors. Yet it was Chile that, in 1970, elected the socialist government of Salvador Allende, beguiled by its promise of radical economic and social change, an experiment that ended in the tragedy of the 1973 military coup.

> Eighty-seven percent of the Chilean population lives in cities and 40 percent of the total population is to be found in Greater Santiago.

And the contradictions have continued. Chile is – as Isabel Allende points out in her nostalgic autobiographical book *Mi País Inventado* (My Invented Country) – the end of the line and about as far away as you can get from the world's main consumer markets. Yet, over the last 20 years, it has used international trade to build one of Latin America's most successful economies.

Chileans take great pride in this achievement and in their modern economy, and are avid users of the Internet and eager foreign travelers. Yet – another contradiction – the country remains an island of social conservatism that critics sometimes dub "Victorian Chile." Until recently, it was one of only a handful of Western countries not to have a divorce law.

PRECEDING PAGES: chess players in Santiago's main square. **LEFT:** young *Chilena*. **RIGHT:** street art.

For most of its history, Chile was cut off from the rest of the world by the Andes mountains in the east, the Atacama Desert in the north, the Pacific Ocean on the west, and the Strait of Magellan and Antarctica in the south. Even during its period as a Spanish colony, Chile was on the periphery, an isolated outpost that looked towards the empire's center of operations in Peru.

Isabel Allende, in fact, describes her home country as an island. And that is key to understanding not only Chile's social conservatism, but also many other aspects of the national character, including a fierce pride in all things Chilean. She advises foreign visitors "not to question the wonders they will hear about the country, its wine, and its women, because the foreigner is not allowed to criticize; for that, there are 15 million Chileans, who do it all the time."

Chile's roots

Chileans are primarily mestizo, the product of unions between the country's original peoples, especially the Mapuches of the south, and the Spanish colonizers. Chileans' great admiration for patriotic symbols, like the Spanish conquistadors and the great Mapuche guerilla fighters, is the source of another striking contradiction. They idolize both the conquerors and the natives who resisted them.

black hair, and tend to be short and stocky. Skin color in Chile is, in fact, synonymous with class – the whiter your skin, the higher your class.

There are still many Aymara and other native communities high up in the northern Andes or on the border with Bolivia, while some 200,000 Mapuches *(see page 75)* continue to live around the southern city of Temuco. Reduced to small patches of land, generally of poor quality, the Mapuches suffer from many of the ills of native peoples throughout the Americas. Those who haven't moved to the cities usually live in large extended families, cultivating wheat, corn, potatoes, and vegetables.

In the wealthy areas of Santiago and luxury vacation spots in southern Chile, shopping centers and resorts often have names of native origin. However, the native peoples themselves mostly live in poverty, whether it be in traditional rural communities or in the cities to which many have migrated. In addition, urban Chileans know surprisingly little about the country's indigenous cultures. In fact, they are likely to tell you they were "poor," especially by comparison with the Inca and Aztec cultures, and not really worthy of interest.

Physical beauty in Chile, as in many other Latin American countries, is associated with being tall, thin, and fair. By contrast, the Mapuches are brown-skinned with strikingly

A NEW MIDDLE CLASS

The La Florida district of southern Santiago, with its gleaming new malls and fast-food restaurants, is typical of Chile's burgeoning middle class. Families tend to be small – two or three children at most – and both parents usually work. Money is tight and consumer borrowing, mainly through store cards, high, but these families are buying their own homes and are ambitious for their children. The Maipú district in the southwest of the city is treading the same road, although at a slightly lower income level, and the same phenomenon can also be seen in provincial cities to which the main department store chains and supermarkets have gradually expanded.

Others combine farming with traditional handicrafts: woven ponchos, woodcarvings, handmade ceramic pots, and baskets can make a significant contribution to family economies, along, increasingly, with rural tourism projects.

New arrivals

A mixed bag of surnames bears testimony to the variety of settlers who followed the Spanish to Chile and eventually formed small foreign enclaves within the larger population. Ethnic groups include the Germans, immigrants from the former Yugoslavia, and, more recently, the Spanish (exiled during the Civil War), the Arabs, the Italians, and the Jews.

The German "colony" has played an important although sometimes ambivalent role in Chilean society (see page 240). In the 18th century Ambrosio O'Higgins decided that the solution to Chile's perennial problem of colonizing the lush but harsh territory of the Lake District was to import people from Europe. This idea was not implemented until the 19th century, when a presidential adviser, Vicente Pérez Rosales, began the task of recruiting Germans. In 1853, they founded the city of Puerto Montt on the shores of the Gulf of Reloncaví.

By 1860, more than 3,000 immigrants had built homes along Lago Llanquihue, and in Osorno, Río Bueno, La Unión, and as far north as Valdivia. By 1900, 30,000 German colonists had cleared the native forests, planted crops and created small towns. Today, German surnames are still common, as is the language, and the area is famous for its sausages, cakes, and pastries. Many small farmhouses offer *küchen* to passers-by.

British immigrants were also important in the nitrates industry and the construction of railroads, as well as in shipping and banking, particularly in the port of Valparaíso. Chileans have a great admiration for the British and like to call themselves the "English of South America" in reference to their phlegmatic temperament and lack of "tropical" excitability.

In 1998, that admiration faced a tough test among Pinochet supporters when the former dictator was arrested in London, where he liked to indulge in the pleasure of having tea with Margaret Thatcher (a bond built during the

Falklands War when Chile provided discreet support to British troops). For a brief time, whisky was outlawed as a socially acceptable drink in these circles, but the general's supporters often returned from trips to visit him in London with conspicuously new Burberrys and, once the general was safely home, the incident was soon forgotten.

A small country

When one lives in Chile, one quickly realizes that in spite of the huge distances from north to south, it's a small country as far as the people are concerned. The same surnames crop up

again and again in Chilean history – even today, a person's surname can help or hinder a career.

Chilean politics are rife with influential families wielding power publicly or behind the scenes, generation after generation. Even the democratic Congress, which was elected in December 1989 after 16 years of military rule, was full of the brothers, sisters, sons, and daughters of past and present leaders.

And although Santiago has a population of over 6 million, it's common to bump into friends and acquaintances, even if you haven't been there very long. That is partly because the people you'll meet tend to frequent just a few areas of the city, mainly in the Las Condes and Providencia districts.

LEFT: pupils at a fee-paying school. **RIGHT:** today's young people have very different expectations to their parents' generation.

Newspapers also reinforce the small-town feeling. *El Mercurio*, the grande dame of the Chilean press, has a large section of social pages – at weekends, they take up more space than international news – in which the same faces appear time and time again in events that range from the opening of art exhibitions to embassy cocktail parties.

That is also a reflection of the closely knit nature of the Chilean political, business, and intellectual elite. Most of its members went to the same private schools and to the same universities, live in the same neighborhoods, and even take holidays in the same places.

cura, while Las Condes and Providencia are upper-middle-class territory, and nearby La Reina and Ñuñoa are popular with less conventional but successful professionals. The west of the city and the densely populated southern outskirts are where most of the working class lives.

Over the last 20 years, increasing prosperity has gone a long way to reduce poverty – although it has made little dent on the country's extremely unequal income distribution. By 2006, the poverty rate had dropped to 13.7 percent (2.2 million people), down from 38.6 percent in 1990. Shantytowns, once common on

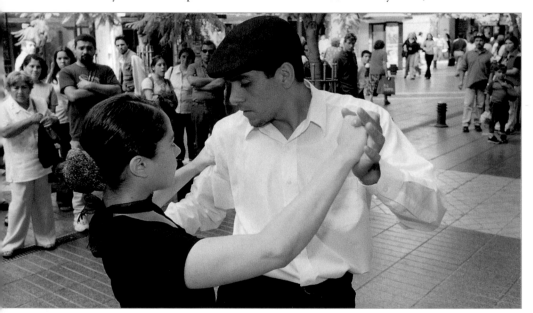

It was this privileged upper class that felt most threatened by the reforms promised by the Popular Unity's experiment with socialism in the early 1970s and reacted with the violence that finally culminated in the military coup. For them, democracy was acceptable only so long as it did not upset the status quo – that is, the unequal social order.

If you're in Santiago long enough, you'll soon realize that the city is unusually segregated. There are virtually no areas in which different classes live side by side, and a person's home address is an almost fail-safe guide to social extraction. The moneyed elite, who have gradually moved out towards the mountains, now tend to live in La Dehesa or Vita-

the periphery of large towns and cities, have gradually been eradicated and replaced by state-subsidized housing, often taking the form of

> *Twenty-six percent of Chileans are under 15 years of age, but the country is aging fast. According to the 2002 National Census, over-60s are the fastest-growing age group and make up over 11 percent of the population.*

the large and bleak apartment blocks that you'll see alongside any of the main roads into the city. These are cramped affairs but do, at least, have all the basic services.

Winds of change

Beneath this rigid surface, social change is afoot in Chile, even if not apparent at first sight. The prosperity of the 1990s, when GDP almost doubled, laid the foundations of a new middle class. Materially ambitious, it apes the consumer habits of the moneyed elite, but has little time for their social conventions.

The development of this new class was temporarily halted in the late 1990s, when the Asian financial crisis brought high unemployment to Chile, and is again expected to suffer as a result of the 2008 international meltdown. It is, however, a long-term trend that resurges as

thing that was unheard of, and would have been considered shameful in the 1990s.

The Catholic Church

In a national census in 2002, 70 percent of Chileans identified themselves as Roman Catholics. A much smaller number attend Mass regularly, but the country's exceptionally conservative Catholic Church is still very powerful.

The Opus Dei and the Legionaries of Christ, two bastions of conservatism within the Catholic Church, are strong and very active in Chile. They control private schools and universities and have a great deal of influence in the busi-

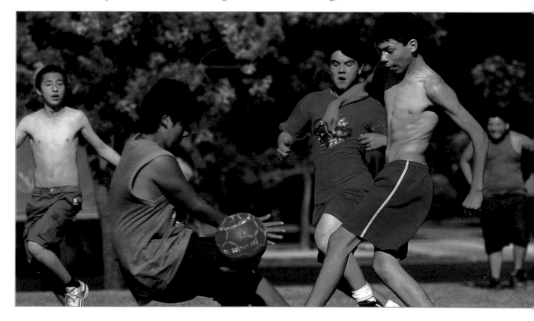

soon as economic growth picks up again.

Young people, both from this new middle class and from the moneyed elite, are another important force for change. More open to new ideas than their parents, they avidly follow American soaps on cable television, and their lifestyle has changed enormously since democracy was restored.

Ten years ago, most young people lived at home until they married. Today, they are marrying later and frequently move out to live on their own as soon as they have secured a job. And, increasingly, couples live together, some-

ness community and the media. Until recently, the center-left government coalition was loath to flout the Church because of the debt of gratitude it feels for the protection that some priests provided for the victims of the dictatorship's human rights abuses.

That helps to explain why divorce was not legalized in Chile until mid-2004 and then only in the teeth of fierce opposition from the Church. Previously, an ad hoc annulment system existed, based on the fiction that a marriage was invalid due to some administrative irregularity. However, that required the consent of both parties.

Abortion, even when a mother's life is at risk, is illegal in Chile, although many abortions do in fact take place, either in expensive private

LEFT: young dancers in Santiago. **ABOVE:** as across Latin America, soccer is hugely popular in Chile.

hospitals, where they are disguised as some other operation, or in unregulated backstreet clinics. And, although the morning-after pill is now available on prescription, there was a great fuss when it was introduced.

Gay people also still have a hard time in Chile. Although tolerance reigns among young people, few gays come out, mostly for fear of hurting their families, or of being discriminated against at work.

Chilean families

In keeping with Catholic morality, Chileans set a high value on the traditional family, or at least

The only difference is that Chileans are more discreet or, depending on your point of view, more hypocritical than in many other countries. Foreigners planning to settle in Chile are often given a piece of advice that sums up local lore: behave as badly as you like, just don't make the mistake of talking about it.

Girls in Chile nowadays get just as much schooling as boys and tend to perform slightly better. Similar numbers of girls and boys go on to university, and female university students are more likely to graduate than their male peers. According to the United Nations Development Program, only 36.6 percent of women in Chile

claim to. Most like to think they're very attached to their families; certainly, families play a major role in the weekly rituals of visits, telephone calls, and Sunday lunches.

However, Chileans are no more or less faithful to their partners than in other countries. In general, the machismo of Chilean men is less obvious than that of other Latin American males. However, while subtle, it remains pervasive. For generations it was customary for men to have two families – one with their wife and one with their mistress. And today, the outskirts of cities are full of motels (some without so much as a sign to identify them) dedicated to renting beds, by the hour or the night, to couples desperate for a little sexual recreation.

MEATY GATHERINGS

One of the most cherished social events among all age groups is the *asado* – a huge steak or roast cooked over hot coals, not to be compared with the rather squalid (at least to Chileans' eyes) hamburgers and hot dogs that you might find at North American or Australian barbecues. This ceremony usually occurs either in someone's backyard or in a park. While the men compare recipes and worry about how the meat is shaping up, the women prepare huge tomato, potato, and other salads. Everyone drinks abundant quantities of red wine, and the meal ends with sweet desserts or whatever fruit is in season (or both).

were economically active in 2006, as compared with 61.3 percent in Colombia, 56.7 percent in Brazil and 40.2 percent in Mexico.

Moreover, in Chile, relatively few women reach positions of power either in the private or public sector. Under President Ricardo Lagos, five out of 15 ministers in his first cabinet were women, up from three out of 21 under his predecessor, President Eduardo Frei, and President Michelle Bachelet, Chile's first woman president, has further improved the balance. However, in the present Congress elected in December 2006, only 18 of the 120 lower-house seats are occupied by women, and just two women sit in the 38-seat Senate. Similarly, few women occupy board seats in large companies and, in general, women who work earn an estimated fifth less than men.

A hard-working country

Chile has worked hard for its economic success, and expatriate businesspeople posted to Chile are often surprised by the long hours put in by their Chilean staff. Schools start at eight in the morning, so many parents, after dropping their children off, are in the office by half past eight and usually stay there until at least seven. Nor do Chileans indulge in long lunches – unless business is being discussed, an hour is the norm.

Overseas executives frequently complain that they find it embarrassingly difficult to head for home at half past five, or whatever is their usual time. That is perhaps also one reason why so few Chilean women work, despite the availability of domestic service.

Chileans are often very late for social appointments, but for business meetings, they are rarely more than 10 minutes behind schedule. And, in one of the keys to Chile's success in attracting foreign investment, they are reliable. Their word is their bond, and corruption, although it certainly exists, is scarce by Latin American and even international standards. In many neighboring countries, taxi drivers will happily tell you the amount of the bribe expected for different traffic offenses; in Chile, an attempt to bribe a policeman is more likely to get you arrested.

Chile's economic success is the source of some irritation among neighboring countries. Immigration, particularly from Peru, is common, with

LEFT: couples tend to marry later in modern Chile.
RIGHT: many families have only two or three children.

immigrants often taking jobs as, for example, live-in maids, that most Chileans now shun.

Folk traditions

Scratch any Chilean, no matter how urban or sophisticated in appearance, and you'll find someone superstitious and sentimental about the country's folklore. September is the best month for observing Chile's folk traditions, as Chileans dust off their ponchos and handkerchiefs and get ready to celebrate Independence Day on September 18.

For children, the traditional pastime is kite flying; for adults, it's lots of *chicha* (fermented

grape juice) and empanadas (savory turnovers); and for just about everybody it means at least one visit to the *fondas*, eucalyptus-roofed shelters that suddenly crowd empty lots, turning them into improvised dance halls.

The *cueca* is Chile's official national dance, and September is also the best time to catch a glimpse of everyone from the national president down, strutting their stuff and doing some serious flirting as men, women, and children stomp the floor in the traditional one-two rhythm, twirl their handkerchiefs, and generally go after each other in what is supposed to be a stylized imitation of mating chickens. You'll also see *cumbias*, *corridas*, rock, and jive, since cultural influences from more northerly countries are also strong.

Each of Chile's various regions has its own version of the *cueca*, and there's also a kind of class division between the *cueca patronal* (boss's *cueca*), characterized by the women's elegant dresses and men's colorful ponchos and shiny black boots with silver spurs, and the *cueca campesina* (peasant's cueca), whose performers are far more simply dressed and go barefoot. The dance's formal gestures and rather strict stereotyping between the aggressive, strutting male and the shy, fluttery female have changed over the years, and young people's versions of the dance often challenge more traditional versions. Chile's folk traditions are more than skin

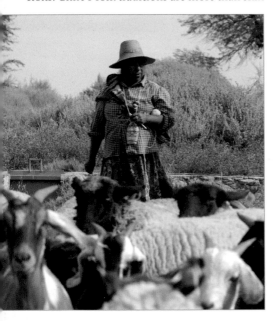

deep. They include a wide variety of folk music, which varies from the Andean music of the altiplano (high plain) prevalent in the north, to the music of Chiloé towards the south, and various ethnic songs and dances, particularly of Yugoslavian origin, around Punta Arenas.

Payadores are grassroots poets and musicians, who engage each other in witty, passionate poetic duels whenever they meet. This may be during a barbecue in the Andes mountains or in a smoky city café.

Folk traditions include stories about each region's original inhabitants, be they human, ghostly, godly, mythical, or immortal. Popular beliefs have blended with grassroots medical knowledge to create different kinds of faith

healers. *Mal de ojo* (evil eye) is still considered a common cause of stomach and other health problems, and the person most equipped to cure it is still the *curandera*, whose knowledge of herbal – and magical – medicine works more frequently than skeptics might care to believe.

Maybe it's not surprising that in a country of such intense geological activity, earthquakes are central to Chileans' mentality. Popular wisdom has it that every (democratic) government in Chile gets welcomed into office by an earthquake – an act of God which was conspicuously absent after the 1973 military coup.

Inside information

Chileans generally like foreigners and treat them well, but foreigners here remain so all their lives. Unlike some other New World coun-

> *According to the United Nations Development Program, life expectancy in Chile reaches 78.3 years as compared to 75.6 years in Mexico, 74.8 years in Argentina and Mexico, and 71.7 years in Brazil.*

tries, where the population consists mainly of immigrants, it often takes several generations for a family of foreign origin to become accepted as Chileans.

Perhaps the best source of behind-the-polite-smile information about Chileans are Chilean writers. Chile may be a small country, but when it comes to literature it's a giant. Two Nobel prize-winning poets, Gabriela Mistral (1945) and Pablo Neruda (1971), have plumbed Chileans' contradictions and aspirations through their work, which is widely available in English translation.

Chilean novelists have participated in the "boom" in Latin American literature. José Donoso, Jorge Edwards and, more recently, Ariel Dorfman, Isabel Allende, Poli Délano, and Antonio Skármeta, have explored Chilean events and psychology in books with universal appeal, enhanced in many cases by prolonged experience abroad. Allende's books are all available in English either through inclusion in anthologies or translation of full books. ❑

LEFT: Aymara goatherd. **RIGHT:** folk music and traditions are an important part of Chilean culture.

THE MAPUCHES

They were unconquered until the late 19th century. But now the native people of the Araucanía struggle to maintain their culture in cities as well as in their homelands

The Mapuche people, in their myriad mythologies, believe in a perfect balance between the positive and negative forces present in every act. Ngenechen, the positive god, represents the forces of life, creation, and love. His counterpart is Wekufu, god of death and destruction. It is in these terms that the Mapuches understand the meeting of European and American cultures 500 years ago.

For Native Americans and their descendants, the arrival of Christopher Columbus meant the destruction of the delicate balance of forces which had until then sustained their culture, their way of life, their language, their habitat, and their religion. Wekufu's spirit threw its mantle over the world's boundaries, leaving Ngenechen unable to keep up his end of the balance.

The Spanish passion for gold overwhelmed the "love of God" or "loyalty to the Crown" that they used as excuses to commit abuses against indigenous peoples. The Mapuches, living in the continent's extreme south, were not exempt from this treatment. But their reaction was a long and often successful resistance to the theft of their lands and the violation of their traditions.

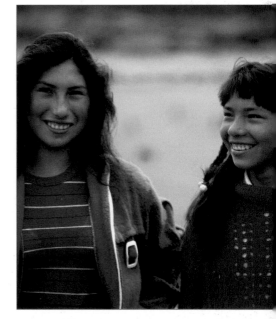

A hierarchical society

The Mapuches, or "people of the earth," were used to living from the earth's fruits and from hunting. They lived in scattered settlements from the Aconcagua Valley in the north, as far south as the Island of Chiloé. They also inhabited most of what is now Argentine Patagonia.

The Mapuches had, and still have today, a relatively hierarchical society based on family

LEFT: playing the *kultrun*. **RIGHT:** Mapuche girls in the Araucanía region.

structures. Women played a major role in the mystical and mythological aspects of society. Only they were allowed to communicate

> Only a fifth of Mapuches speak or understand Mapudungun as compared to 81 percent of Easter Island's Rapu Nui people; however, in the case of the Mapuches, that means over 200,000 people, against 1,800 Rapu Nuis.

directly with the gods, and their functions were distributed according to the type of forces they represented. The gods of life, for example, would communicate with women called the *Machi*; those of death, with the *Kalku*. Music always accompanied their rituals, particularly percussion instruments like the *kultrun* and the *trompe*, and wind instruments like the *trutrucas* and wooden whistles. Oratory skills were of prime importance to the Mapuches and their language, Mapudungun, reached truly poetic heights as it captured extensive images within its sounds.

Freedom-lovers

During the first 100 years of war between the Mapuches and the Spanish the northern limit of their territories was reduced to the River Biobío,

a border that remained for more than 300 years. The cross and the sword could not defeat the lances of the naked-chested Mapuches, and the Spanish Crown was finally forced to negotiate. It recognized borders and established trade and transport agreements between the territories.

Many historians who defend the Spanish cause speak of the Mapuches as belonging to a "military race" or being a "fierce people." Nevertheless, the testimony of friars who accompanied the Conquest indicates that the Mapuches were peaceful and friendly. It became convenient for pro-Spanish historians to paint the Mapuches as "ferocious warriors" in order to justify their side's defeat. But the Mapuches are and were a peaceful, humble people, dedicated to their land and

their traditions. The reasons for the long struggle are to be found not so much in their "warrior virtues" as in a profound dignity and immense love for their land and their freedom.

Their devotion to their own cultural values led the Mapuches to acts of great heroism and impassioned resistance. They quickly learned about their enemy and its weapons, and developed the tactics necessary to defend themselves.

Perhaps the most striking reason for the Spaniards' inability to conquer the Mapuches was that, unlike the Incas and Aztecs, they had no central authority. Their political and economic organization was based on the family. The family head was the polygamous *cacique* (pronounced "ka-see-kay"), or *lonko*. He could have as many as 10 wives, forming an extended family group of up to 500 members.

> When the Conquest started, the Mapuches believed the Spanish attacker and his horse were one creature, unbeatable, a god which had come to conquer them.

The *lonko* developed his prestige through the accumulation of wealth and the wise advice that he gave to youths inclined to fight among themselves. Faced with a warlike situation, the Mapuches chose a *toqui* as their leader, and their peacetime authority was the *ulmen*. Both were chosen for their gifts for public speaking and their decision-making abilities.

Alliances between *caciques* were established to develop economic activities like the gathering in of breeding stock, hunting, and fruit collection, and the benefits were shared among the participating members.

This loose organization meant that the Spanish could not seize control through capture of a single political leader. The Mapuches didn't have villages to harass and destroy. While they weren't nomads in the strict sense of the term, they lived in *rucas* or huts, which they moved from place to place according to need.

Lautaro the liberator

When the Spanish began their advance they were fast and efficient, but when the Mapuches realized that these horseback attackers were only human they began to develop unique military strategies to defend their land. Lautaro, a Mapuche who was barely 20 years old, escaped from the Spanish camps where his intelligence had caused him to be trained as the page of the conquistador Pedro de Valdivia. He was chosen as *toqui*, leader of the *caciques*, to lead the war against the invaders.

Lautaro – who now knew the language, weapons, tactics, and weaknesses of the enemy – taught his warriors to ride. They became better horsemen than the Spaniards. He also developed two combat tactics which today are recognized as the beginning of guerrilla warfare in this continent. The first was "mounted infantry" where each rider also carried along a foot soldier holding

campaigns, he reached the gates of Santiago.

During Lautaro's northward push, many Yanaconas, another indigenous people who had until then formed part of the Spanish troops, joined Lautaro's forces. One of these betrayed Lautaro, killing him while he rested in his tent the night before the great assault on the capital. This was a terrible blow to the Mapuches, who decided to retreat southward, where they continued to defend "their" border for 300 years.

The last uprising

The last general uprising of Chile's indigenous peoples took place in 1881. This time it was

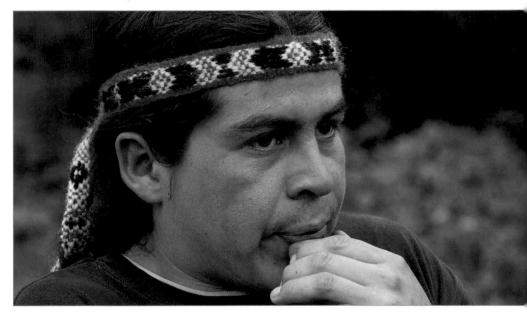

onto the horse's tail. This allowed rapid movement of large parties of fighters. The second and more devastating tactic was the constant replacement of squadrons: each group fought ferociously for 15 to 20 minutes before being replaced. The Spanish soldiers labored under their heavy armor, and finally yielded to the waves of native fighters who, fresh and rested, gave them no respite.

These tactics led to enormous victories for Lautaro, who not only killed Pedro de Valdivia himself, but also secured for his people all the southern territories, burning and destroying the Spanish forts until, after four years of victorious

---

LEFT: a Mapuche *cacique* on horseback.
ABOVE: playing a traditional wooden whistle.

directed against what was now the Chilean Republic, which was doing everything possible to take over the southern lands. Mapuche *huer-*

> Lorenzo Colimán, a 19th-century Mapuche lonko *lamented his people's loss of freedom:* "What we've achieved with the civilization they say they have given us is to live squeezed together like wheat in a sack."

quenes, messengers specially educated for eloquence and good memories, began to travel through mountains and valleys, bearing knotted red cords around their wrists. Every day they undid one knot. When these were all gone, the *caciques* simultaneously attacked the forts, towns, and missions of the Chileans – an impossible attempt given the superiority of the army's weaponry, but another example of the Mapuche's dedication to their independence and freedom. The army, fresh from its victories in a war against Peru and Bolivia, suffocated the bloody rebellion, and from then, the Mapuches became farmers of small, individual plots.

Integration and adaptation

Throughout the 1880s, the indigenous territories shrank. A decree made Araucanía (the

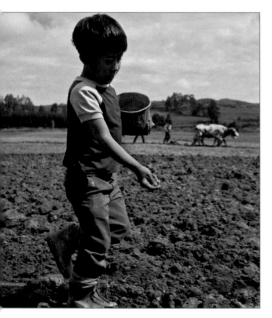

Mapuche territory) property of the state, and a colonization process began in which the native people received very little for their land. Along with this, a process of cultural transformation began. It was a time of fear, disease, hunger, and loss of identity, as the Mapuches became an ethnic minority within Chilean society.

The 20th century saw three reactions to this process. The first, encouraged by missionaries, was to press for the total integration of the Mapuches into Chilean society. Education and evangelization would "absorb" the Mapuche culture. This later became the policy of the 1973–90 Pinochet dictatorship, which decreed an Indian Law that allowed the Mapuches to split their collectively held land into small

farms with individual titles. With no access to credit or technology, many were forced to sell their land to wealthy landowners. The second reaction was a modified form of integration which, in 1914, inspired one group of Mapuches to develop a special school which taught Spanish but valued indigenous cultural traditions.

The third was to reject any integration and seek to recover their stolen lands and culture. The first attempts were led by Manuel Aburto Manquilef, a descendant of *caciques*, who mobilized huge numbers of Mapuches in search of their own identity. This movement insisted that the central problem was the seizure of the Mapuche lands. Its activists revived the rites and traditions of the *malones* (meetings to listen to dreams and predict the future) and *machitunes* (collective

> The educational gap between Chile's indigenous and non-indigenous people is closing only slowly; in 2006, indigenous people had an average 8.7 years of schooling, compared to 10.3 years for non-indigenous people.

prayers to the gods). It organized many congresses and made the native voice heard in Santiago.

One of the great merits of this group was its ability to find allies within other social movements of the period. Its leaders had the vision to recognize that the problem wasn't simply between Mapuches and *huincas* (the name that the Mapuches gave to the Spanish invader), but rather between the wealthy and the poor. This led to the Mapuches' own struggle being more generally recognized as one of the social problems of the 1930s.

The Workers' Federation of Chile (FOCH) became the Mapuches' mouthpiece in Santiago, helping them to participate in mainstream politics through the Democratic Party and eventually through elected representatives in the House of Deputies. However, under the Pinochet dictatorship, Mapuche organizations were heavily repressed, and many native people were arrested and "disappeared."

An Indian Peoples Law was passed by the new democratic government, but failed to live up to the expectations of the Mapuches who, in the 1990s, found a new enemy – the expanding forestry industry. As well as occupying land claimed by Mapuche communities, the industry has deprived them of access to the woods that are their traditional source of fuel, medicinal plants, and food.

Another focus of protest in the 1990s was the construction of the vast Ralco hydroelectric dam on the upper reaches of the River Biobío. The reservoir, which began to be filled in mid-2004, flooded land belonging to some of the last remaining communities of Pehuenches, a branch of the Mapuches.

The border lands today

In a national survey in 2006, 1,060,786 people (7 percent of the population) identified them-

poverty rates, with a fifth of the population below the poverty line.

Considerable progress has been made since 1990 in taking basic services, particularly electricity, to indigenous communities, and in improving roads. However, the intensely proud Mapuches – who consider themselves the "true Chileans" – resent their lack of political status. Chile is the only Latin American country that does not afford its indigenous minorities constitutional recognition, and no Mapuches – or, indeed, members of other ethnic groups – sit in Congress. Moreover, their lack of say, even at a local government level, in decisions that

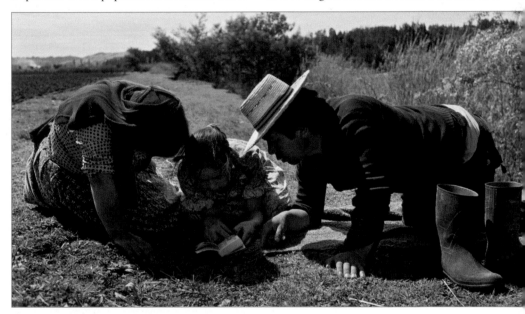

selves as belonging to one of its nine indigenous peoples, of which the Mapuches are by far the largest (87 percent). Many Mapuches have migrated to the cities, particularly Santiago, where they often form tight-knit communities, notably in the La Pintana district of southern Santiago, and keep their traditional customs alive. In a recent initiative, the national health service has, in some of these areas, begun to offer Mapuche remedies to treat minor ailments.

However, some 450,000 Mapuches still live in communities south of the River Biobío and Araucanía has one of the country's highest

affect their lives also means that too many well-intentioned government initiatives have failed dismally to achieve their objective.

A few radical Mapuche organizations remain active, and violence occasionally flares up in Araucanía, directed mostly against forestry companies or local *huinca* farmers. Most communities, although they do not directly support these organizations, defend their methods as a useful tactic in the struggle for greater recognition.

The fire in Chile's south has not yet gone out. The spirits of Ngenechen and Wekufu still wander, caressing *canelo* trees and araucaria pines – the Mapuches' sacred trees. They still seek a balance between life and death, and good and evil. And justice. ❑

LEFT: the Mapuche's battle to regain stolen land continues. **ABOVE:** outdoor education.

A CULTURAL RENAISSANCE

After contributing to the downfall of the Pinochet dictatorship, the arts in Chile have blossomed and diversified under democracy

The moving simplicity of Violeta Parra's voice, accompanied by a lone guitar, echoes through each of her recordings, bearing testimony to the inspiration of a woman who sang to life, but succumbed to death. Her song *Gracias a la Vida* (Thanks to Life) – composed, ironically, after one of her suicide attempts – is one of Latin America's best-loved songs. Violeta Parra's influence marked the development of popular music in Chile from the 1960s onwards and her offspring have continued to play a prominent role in the arts.

Violeta was born in Chillán in the south of Chile in 1917. Her family was poor, but artistically prolific. It produced not only Violeta, but also her brother Nicanor (Chile's "anti-poet" and a many-time Nobel candidate) and Roberto, the creator of a new style of *cueca* (Chile's national dance) and the author of *La Negra Ester* (Black Esther), the play seen by the largest number of people ever in Chile's history.

A tragic star

Violeta received little recognition during her lifetime, either from critics or the public. Her work was characterized both by the incomprehension with which it was met, and by the irrepressible creativity seen both in her music and her tapestries, which have been exhibited in the Louvre art gallery in Paris. The appreciation of her work outside Chile led Violeta to settle in France for two years, a period during which she toured Europe. But, in 1965, she returned to Chile, where, apparently overwhelmed by frustration, isolation, and an ill-fated love affair, she committed suicide in 1967, depriving the country of one of its most lucid voices.

But her legacy and quest to rediscover Chile's musical roots, which she revitalized with lyrics protesting against social injustice, lived on. She was followed by a generation of singer-composers, led by Víctor Jara, who continued her work and whose influence is still very present in the music of Chile today.

Amid the social upheaval of the 1960s, Jara and other artists, including Angel and Isabel Parra (children of Violeta), Patricio Manns, and the Inti-Illimani and Quilapayún groups, gave birth to a new type of music: *La Nueva Canción Chilena* (Chilean New Song).

PRECEDING PAGES: colorful street mural in Santiago. **LEFT:** street theater. **RIGHT:** Violeta Parra.

Their rebellious songs were in stark contrast to the romantic melodies of the radio singers who then dominated popular music in Chile, imitating the ballads and twist of their American contemporaries and even using English names. This harsher music was not only a perfect soundtrack for the changes taking place in Chile in the early 1970s, but also became the official music of President Salvador Allende's Popular Unity government. So much was this the case that one of Víctor Jara's songs was used each day to start the transmissions of the state television channel. And both Quilapayún – with *El Pueblo Unido* (The People United) as the battle hymn of the

After the 1973 coup

The seizure of power by the armed forces meant the death or exile of the icons of the New Song movement. Inti-Illimani and Quilapayún were performing in Europe at the time of the coup, but Víctor Jara was immediately arrested, brutally tortured, and shot in the Estadio Chile (Chile Stadium), now known as Estadio Víctor Jara. Angel Parra also suffered at the hands of the dictatorship, first as a prisoner in the National Stadium and then in the Chacabuco concentration camp. Los Jaivas emigrated to Argentina and, later, France, where they were joined by Quilapayún and Illapu, a group that

Popular Unity coalition – and the Parra family were a staple part of government ceremonies.

The 1970s saw the emergence of a new strand of the New Song movement when a younger generation took the elements and instruments of Latin American folklore and merged them with rock music. The result was revolutionary, and *Todos Juntos* (Together), sung by Los Jaivas, became a symbol to an entire generation – so much so that, in 1999, when Chileans were asked to vote for their favorite song with which to greet the new millennium, this was the title they chose. Together with Los Blops and Congreso, they formed a generation whose careers in Chile were cut short by the military coup of September 11, 1973.

GRACIAS A LA VIDA

Gracias a la vida, que me ha dado tanto
Me dio dos luceros, que cuando los abro
Perfecto distingo, lo negro del blanco
Y en el alto cielo, su fondo estrellado
Y en las multitudes, la mujer que amo.

Thanks to life, which has given me so much
It has given me two eyes, which, when I open them
I can clearly distinguish black from white
And in the infinite sky, its starry depths
And in the crowds of people, the woman I love.

– Violeta Parra

had become famous thanks to their song *Candombe para José* (Candombe for José).

This exile had unanticipated consequences for Chilean music. Awakening the sympathy of the countries where they were granted asylum, these groups sang songs of protest against General Augusto Pinochet to an international audience. As a result Inti-Illimani, for example, sold more than a million records in Italy alone. But while their music was acclaimed abroad, cultural repression reigned in Chile as the military attempted to stamp out any hint of ideological opposition. Records made during the Popular Unity government were banned.

However, the growing discontent felt by many Chileans found an echo in the work of exiled artists, which was smuggled into the country, and the New Song movement was kept alive as a vehicle for expressing – between the lines – opposition to the dictatorship. Groups such as Schwenke y Nilo, Huara, and Sol y Lluvia peppered their songs with contemporary references that escaped the military's grasp.

In the 1980s, in France, Los Jaivas launched *Las Alturas de Macchu Picchu* (The Heights of Macchu Picchu), a conceptual album that set to music the words of Chilean poet Pablo Neruda. The acclaim with which this album was received was such that the group was allowed to return to Chile to perform at massively attended concerts.

It was at this time that Los Prisioneros, from San Miguel, a working-class district of Santiago, made its appearance. Mixing punk, rock, and techno music with the angry lyrics of its vocalist, Jorge González, the trio was a phenomenon in its own right. Despite the efforts of the dictatorship, the band became a reference point for an entire generation as cassettes were passed from hand to hand. Los Prisioneros also opened the way for many new bands, which took their place in the late 1980s, when Los Prisioneros broke up.

The end of the most brutal period of the dictatorship gradually permitted the return of exiled musicians, who became influential in the protest movement that, in 1988, culminated in the "No" vote against General Pinochet (*see page 52*).

Into a new era

The return of democracy brought with it a new generation of musicians. Los Tres, a band from Concepción in southern Chile, led by Alvaro Henríquez and including a grandson of Violeta, were in the forefront of this generation. Mixing the rockabilly of Chuck Berry with the lyrics of Roberto Parra, Los Tres – the first Chilean group to record an unplugged session for MTV – gave new popularity to the *cueca*, freeing it from the stigma it had acquired when harnessed to the dictatorship's efforts to foster patriotic support. The band broke up in 2000 but staged a return in early 2007, with a series of mass concerts and a new album.

By dint of combining pop with Anglo-Saxon aesthetics, another Chilean band, La Ley, suc-

cessfully launched an international career. However, after receiving the highest accolades ever achieved by a Chilean band, the group, led by Beto Cuevas, split up in 2005.

In the 1990s, other rhythms also became popular in Chile. These included hip hop, which, thanks to the group Tiro de Gracia and its album *Ser Humano* (Human Being), led the local sales rankings for a time. However, more recently, despite the appearance of interesting bands like Makiza, hip hop has retreated to working-class neighborhoods and dropped out of the rankings.

Funk also became an established taste with Chancho en Piedra, which remains one of Chile's most popular bands, while pop was revitalized by

LEFT: a guitarist pays tribute to Víctor Jara on the anniversary of the military coup. **RIGHT:** Víctor Jara.

the appearance of Lucybell, a band whose dark lyrics and aesthetics combined with meticulous sound production carried it to success not only in Chile, but also in Mexico.

However, since 2000, Chilean music has again returned to its roots. The appearance of groups like Los Bunkers, a young rock quartet from Concepción influenced both by 1960s British rock and protest songs, and the return of Los Tres have led a revival of traditional folkloric music, while pre-dictatorship music has also become popular among young people. Up-and-coming bands venerate and pay homage to "old" musicians, with covers of

record labels and prefer to produce their own albums. Examples of this trend include musicians like Gepe and Leo Quinteros and bands such as Sinergia and Saiko. In addition, some of the country's established groups have abandoned the main record labels in favor of smaller labels and have tended to focus on markets like Mexico in preference to the small domestic market, where a platinum album is one that has sold only a little over 20,000 copies.

A moving image of Chile

Filmmaking in Chile dates back to the early 20th century, when Salvador Giambastiani and

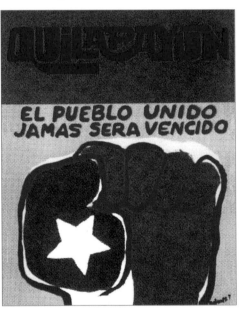

songs by Violeta Parra and Víctor Jara frequently included in new albums and recitals, while their pictures – the image of pure and rebellious talent – are a common sight at concerts and demonstrations.

Another interesting phenomenon is the appearance of more commercial bands and soloists, invented by producers or brought to prominence through TV shows. Designed to appeal to adolescents, they include Kudai, a mixed quartet formed by adolescents that has been successful around Latin America, and the singers who came to fame through Rojo, a program broadcast by TVN, the state television channel.

The new millennium also brought with it a new class of independent musicians who shun

his wife, Gabriela von Bussenius, made the 1919 documentary *Recuerdos del Mineral de El Teniente* (Memories of the El Teniente Mine), and, in 1926, Pedro Sienna, an actor, producer, and director, made the film *El Húsar de la Muerte* (The Hussar of Death), about the life of Manuel Rodríguez, one of the heroes of Chile's independence from Spain (*see page 37*). Other films made in this early period include *Sueño de Amor* (Dream of Love), in which Chilean pianist Claudio Arrau played the role of Franz Liszt.

In the 1940s, local film production received state support and a number of memorable films were made, including *La Dama sin Camelias* (The Lady without Camellias) by José Bohr while, in the 1960s, it received a new injection of life when the University of Chile set up its Department of Experimental Cinema, again with state support. *Ayúdeme Usted Compadre* (Help Me, Mate), a film

> "A country without documentary films is like a family without a photo album." Patricio Guzmán, director of The Battle of Chile, *the prize-winning documentary about the Allende years.*

by Germán Becker that was seen by a then record 370,000 people, and Raúl Ruiz's *Tres Tristes Tigres* (Three Sad Tigers) correspond to this period.

was executed by a firing squad. Littín's film was a success both with spectators and critics.

During the Popular Unity government, only nine films were produced, despite state incentives. It was in this period that Raúl Ruiz made *Palomita Blanca* (White Dove) – although it was not screened until 1993 – and Patricio Guzmán, a documentary-maker who has recorded much of Chile's recent history, made *El Primer Año* (The First Year).

After the military coup, many filmmakers were forced into exile, while those that remained in the country mostly made commercial advertising. Nonetheless, seven full-length films were

In 1970, Miguel Littín directed one of Chile's most famous films, *El Chacal de Nahueltoro* (The Jackal of Nahueltoro). This recounts the true story of a man who, while under the influence of alcohol, murdered his partner and children. The incident caused considerable public commotion at the time, not only because of the brutal nature of the crime, but also because of the murderer's fate. A man of virtually no education, he changed dramatically while in prison, acquiring schooling and reformed attitudes. However, despite this, the courts showed no mercy and he

FAR LEFT: Roberto Márquez of Illapu in concert.
LEFT: poster for the protest group Quilapayún.
ABOVE: rappers performing at an open-air concert.

shot in Chile between 1973 and 1985. These include *Julio Comienza en Julio* (Julio Begins in July) by Silvio Caiozzi.

A fertile time

In the 1990s and, particularly, since 2000, film production has boomed. Initially, films tended to focus on political issues, such as *La Frontera* (The Frontier) by Ricardo Larraín, about the relegation to remote areas of the country used by the dictatorship to punish its opponents. However, an increasing number of films have gradually sought to depict the everyday life of Chileans.

Examples of this type of film include *Johnny Cien Pesos* (Hundred-Peso Johnny) by Gustavo Graef-Marino, based on the true story of a hold-up in Santiago that went amiss and ended with hostage-taking, *Historias de Fútbol* (Football Tales) by Andrés Wood, and *La Sagrada Familia* by Sebastián Lelio. This movement also produced *Taxi para Tres* (Taxi for Three), directed, written, and produced by Orlando Lübbert, which received the best-film award at the San Sebastián Film Festival in 2001.

More recently, films made in Chile have also begun to mirror changing attitudes towards sex and, by challenging taboos, have helped to push back the frontiers of public discussion. The success of *El Chacotero Sentimental* (The Sentimental Teaser), based on a radio phone-in in which

that their friendship attempts to bridge, and of how the 1973 military coup took advantage of this gulf and prized it further open.

Although social comedy remains the most popular genre in Chile, the range of films produced has expanded enormously in recent years. It now goes from vampire stories, like *Sangre Eterna* (Eternal Blood), and thrillers such as *Angel Negro* (Black Angel) – both by Jorge Olguín – to martial arts films, like *Kiltro* (starring Chile's first action hero, Marko Zaror, who worked as a stuntman for American actor Dwayne "The Rock" Johnson in his 2003 film, *The Rundown*) and cartoon productions.

young listeners talked about their sex life, and *Sexo con Amor* (Sex with Love), seen by a record 990,000 spectators, are a clear sign that Chileans are avid to see themselves portrayed on the screen with their behavior, and its virtues and defects, stripped naked.

However, by far the most important film of recent years was *Machuca* (2004). Directed by Andrés Wood, this tells the story of the friendship of two 11-year-old boys, one from a prosperous neighborhood of Santiago and the other from a nearby shantytown, who meet towards the end of the Popular Unity government as a result of a Catholic school's social integration program. The two boys and their homes – divided by the city's river – are a reflection of a yawning social divide

Te Recuerdo Amanda

Te recuerdo Amanda, la calle mojada
corriendo a la fábrica, donde trabajaba Manuel
La sonrisa ancha, la lluvia en el pelo
no importaba nada, ibas a encontrarte con el
con el, con el, con el...

I think of you Amanda, in the wet street
running toward the factory, where
Manuel worked
With a broad smile, the rain in your hair
Nothing mattered, you were meeting up with him,
with him, with him, with him...

– Víctor Jara

Chile on stage

The theater in Chile has survived in the face of constant difficulties. Its inventiveness allowed it to survive the dictatorship and even to serve as a channel for veiled criticism, particularly by the Ictus group. But, since the return of democracy, it has taken on a new lease of life, thanks to initiatives like Teatro a Mil (Theater for a Thousand Pesos). Because of its accessible price and its focus on comedies and other plays with a ready appeal, this annual event draws an audience far wider than that of traditional theater productions.

La Troppa, a group formed by actors Juan Carlos Sagall, Jaime Lorca, and Laura Pizarro

pher, he studied for six years at the Théâtre du Soleil in France before returning to Chile to found the Gran Circo Teatro, which mounted many memorable productions. He is most remembered as the director of *La Negra Ester*.

Over the past few years, theater companies have also branched out into more commercial productions, often starring soap-opera television actors. Such plays tend to be put on in new and more comfortable theaters (some of which are to be found in shopping malls). Local versions of plays, such as *The Vagina Monologues* and *The Gronholm Method*, which have been successful in other countries, have also become common.

achieved acclaim both in Chile and Europe with original and innovative productions, like *Pinocchio*, and *Gemelos* (Identical Twins).

Local playwrights, such as Ramón Griffero, Marco Antonio de la Parra, Egon Wolff, Juan Radrigán, and Benjamín Galemiri, regularly have plays on show and, as audiences become better acquainted with the theater, are expanding the range that is on offer.

Perhaps the most venerated figure of Chilean theater is Andrés Pérez, who died of Aids in 2002. A director, playwright, dancer, and choreogra-

If proof of the Chileans's avid interest in the arts were required, this was abundantly provided when France's Royal De Luxe street theater

> One of the few Chilean playwrights to have triumphed abroad is Ariel Dorfman, whose La Muerte y la Doncella *(Death and the Maiden)* was made into a movie in 1994 by Roman Polanski, starring Sigourney Weaver.

company took its *Little Giant* to Santiago in 2007. The performance lasted three days and its final procession was followed by 300,000 people – an all-time record for an event of this type. ❏

LEFT: scene from *Machuca*. **ABOVE:** Roman Polanski and Sigourney Weaver on the set of *Death and the Maiden*. **RIGHT:** The *Little Giant* in Santiago.

A TASTE OF CHILE

Chile, the home of the potato and the strawberry, used to be known for its bland fare. That is now changing as the country rediscovers the indigenous origins of its cuisine

Pablo Neruda's *Oda al Caldillo de Congrio* (Ode to Conger Eel Soup) is a recipe in verse that lingeringly savors each step in making this rich and fragrant soup from the "giant eel with snow-white flesh." Flavored with potatoes, onion, and garlic, this is one of Chile's most traditional and best-loved dishes. The poet was mistaken on one count: *congrio* isn't – despite the common belief in Chile – an eel at all, but a fish known internationally as kingclip. But Neruda's ode – as do the many others he wrote about the simple joys of Chilean food – makes no mistake about the satisfying pleasure of a steaming bowl of *caldillo*, especially on a cold winter day.

Congrio, with its springy white flesh, is also popular *frito* (fried), when it is traditionally served with *ensalada chilena* (a salad of sliced tomato and blanched onions). "If you visit Chile without trying *congrio frito*, you haven't really been there," warns Chilean chef Carlo von Mühlenbrock.

In Santiago, the Mercado Central, the city's old fruit and vegetable market by the River Mapocho, is a good place to try *congrio*. At the main restaurant, Donde Augusto, you'll find excellent *caldillo* and *congrio frito* at modest prices, as well as *corvina* (sea bass) and a variety of the shellfish that flourish in the cold Antarctic waters that are carried up the Chilean coast by the famous Humboldt Current.

Another of the treats not to be missed in Chile is the *cordero* (lamb) that is raised in the far south of Chile around the Magellan Strait. It has a special taste attributed to the sea winds

that feather the grass with salt, and to the fact that, in this area's virtually virgin pastures, the land is free of herbicides and insecticides. Unfortunately, though, lamb is not very popular in Chile (most of the Magellan lamb goes straight for export) and, except in Patagonia, it tends only to be served in more expensive restaurants.

Chile is also famous for its farmed salmon which, over the past 20 years, has developed into a major export industry. Salmon is rarely absent from a restaurant menu in Chile and is widely considered to have a more pleasant, less strong taste than that of Norwegian or Scottish salmon. It has, however, become the target of international criticism for the industry's heavy

---

PRECEDING PAGES: *cazuela.* **LEFT:** fine dining at a vineyard. **RIGHT:** traditional Mapuche cooking.

use of antibiotics (although stringent pre-harvest tests control residue levels) and its poor environmental practices.

Chile's fresh fruit is also not to be missed if you visit in spring or summer. Too infrequently served in restaurants – on the grounds that fruit is not a "real" dessert – it is a delight. If you visit the Sernatur tourist office on Santiago's Providencia Avenue, you'll find an excellent fruit and vegetable market just around the back of the building.

In summer, the roads are lined with stalls offering the pick of the season: blackberries, plums, strawberries, peaches, apricots, cherries, melons, kiwis, and, as autumn approaches, the

– before spreading to the Andean altiplano where the Spanish conquistadors found it in the mid-16th century. Even today, the potato forms a staple part of the islanders' diet as, for example, in *milkao*, a traditional flat bread made with grated potatoes that are fried in lard. And, on the smaller islands of the archipelago, many varieties have survived, some with graphic names like the long thin black potato that is known as *mojón de gato* (cat's dung).

It is, therefore, all the more surprising that only one standard variety of potato is generally sold in Chilean supermarkets or served in the country's restaurants. But that is changing; a

famous Chilean grape, sweet and luscious. And, during a winter visit, don't neglect to try the *chirimoyas* (custard apples), a sweet and fragrant fruit grown mostly around La Serena, and best eaten just with a dressing of freshly squeezed orange juice.

In Chile, it is hard not to miss the *paltas* (avocado pears) that have also become an important export. They are excellent and will turn up in nearly all your salads, on most hamburgers and, in mashed form, on *completos* (hot dogs).

Indigenous roots

Some scientists believe that the potato originated in Chile, probably on the island of Chiloé 13,000 years ago – although Peru disputes this

firm called Papas Arcoiris (Rainbow Potatoes), based in Puerto Varas, and other small farmers have begun to rescue and market varieties that did not previously reach consumers.

> The translation of the names for Chilean fish can be confusing. Corvina *is sea bass and,* unlike bacaloa de profundidad *(Patagonian tooth fish), a type of cod often referred to as sea bass abroad, is not in danger of extinction.*

Carlo Von Mühlenbrock is one of the leaders of a new generation of Chilean chefs who have rebelled against the international, and frequently undistinguished, fare that was until recently standard in most Chilean restaurants. "Restaurant owners used to think that local dishes weren't chic; they scorned them as rustic and not sophisticated enough," he recalls. But that is also changing. Until a few years ago, most Chileans had never heard of *merkén*, a Mapuche seasoning. However, thanks to research by von Mühlenbrock and other like-minded chefs, it is now a common feature of restaurant menus. A red spicy paste that the Mapuches spread on bread or use to liven up stews, it is made from red chili peppers – traditionally smoked by being hung above the cooking fire in Mapuche homes – which are then ground to a powder with cilantro (coriander) seeds, garlic, and salt, and mixed with water when needed.

Another popular addition to restaurant menus are *piñones*, the fruit of the monkey puzzle tree, and the staple diet of the Pehuenches, the branch of the Mapuches who live in the Andes mountains. The Pehuenches use *piñones* to make bread, or simply eat them boiled, much like chestnuts, which they resemble in taste, although not in their long, thin shape. Today, you can find *piñones* served as a garnish alongside a piece of meat.

Beans and sweetcorn

The Chilean word for beans – *porotos* – is believed to originate from the language of the Quechua people of the Andes, but beans were also an important part of the Mapuche diet.

Beans are popularly eaten in Chile as a rich summer soup known as *porotos granados*. This is made from shelled haricot beans, pumpkin, onion, and sweet corn, seasoned with basil, and is usually eaten with chopped tomatoes and chili pepper but, in the countryside, sometimes comes with a beefsteak (*bifstek*) on top. *Porotos con riendas* – literally, beans with reins – is a bean stew with spaghetti added, a typically rural dish that is rather despised by urban Chileans. But there is wisdom in the hearty mixture; recent research has shown that it an ideal mix of readily-digested proteins.

Sweetcorn, which is known as *choclo* (the Quechua name for corn) is also used in many other Chilean dishes, but the most famous are

humitas and *pastel de choclo*. *Humitas* are the Chilean equivalent of the tamales found in many other Latin American countries, with the difference that they contain only mashed corn – no meat, as is often the case in other countries – and are always wrapped in corn leaves and not, for example, banana leaves. *Humitas* are usually served with *ensalada chilena* and finely chopped chili pepper, although some Chileans prefer to eat them with sugar.

Pastel de choclo has a minced-meat base that includes quarters of hard-boiled egg, olives, and sometimes a piece of chicken, and is covered with a mashed corn layer. It is, in fact, much like

a cottage pie, with corn replacing the potato. Raisins are often added to the meat base, and sugar is sometimes sprinkled over the corn top before it is put in the oven to brown.

The popular *empanada* – a savory pastry turnover – is found in most Latin American countries, although the name varies, and has a definite Spanish origin. In fact, it traces its roots back to the hollowed-out loaf of bread in which European farmworkers used to carry their midday meal to the fields.

In Chile, it is most commonly filled with *pino* – the same mixture of minced meat, onions, hard-boiled egg, olives, and raisins that is used in *pastel de choclo*. In this version, it is baked in the oven, but there is also a tasty fried version, with

LEFT: raspberries and blueberries – one of Chile's most profitable exports. **RIGHT:** *choclo* (sweetcorn).

a flakier pastry, that is filled with cheese. On the coast, *empanadas de mariscos* – filled with shellfish and, typically, the rosy-fleshed *macha* razor clam – are a popular alternative.

> The 19th-century traveler Edward Revel Smith described the cazuela as "the best dish that can be had in Chile, and one which, I believe, can be had nowhere else."

Another Chilean favorite, *cazuela*, is a winter dish. It starts with a meat *(carne)* broth in which

the middle of a rustic, checked table-clothed room, complete with a guitar-playing *huaso* (horseman). This is a good place to try a *prieta*, a Chilean blood sausage. If you simply order a *parrillada*, you'll get meat grilled (possibly at the table). It is also quite common to order pure entrails if you like them.

Post-Conquest influences

Chileans consider – with some justification – that their cuisine is a poor relation to Peruvian and Mexican cuisines, undeniably the most varied and interesting in Latin America. The difference, says Carlo von Mühlenbrock, is explained

potato, pumpkin, corn, and peppers are cooked. The dish arrives at the table as a sea of steaming soup, with large vegetable and meat islands, under which a bed of rice is discovered. As well as beef, this is often made with chicken or turkey and, in the latter case, is sprinkled with *chuchoca* (milled corn that is similar to Italy's polenta). This is a very hearty meal and is usually cheap.

While not considered as fine as Argentine meat, Chilean cattle produce very creditable steaks, which are served up in restaurants known as *parrilladas*. The *parrilladas* cook every type of meat over a charcoal grill – anything from a steak to a sausage or chop. In some of the *campesino* (farming) areas, you can find great cheap *parrilladas*, usually with a big fire in

largely by the lack of post-Conquest influences in Chile. The lack of the African influence that is so clear in Peru reflects the fact that few black slaves were taken to Chile, and those that were did not, except in the far north, survive its harsher climate. And the Chinese immigration that, in Peru, merged with the local cuisine, to produce the *chifa* cuisine, was virtually absent in Chile.

In addition, argues von Mühlenbrock, Chilean society was less permeable to outside influence, perhaps partly because of its difficulty in establishing control over Mapuche lands. That also explains, he says, why there are so few regional variations in Chilean food. "An empanada is an empanada from Arica to Punta

Arenas because that's the way Chileans wanted it to be," he notes.

In fact, only two post-Conquest influences have played a significant role in the development of Chilean food – Italian and German cuisine. Italian immigration into Chile was small, but pasta is a common main course in restaurants and homes, a custom probably learned through Argentina, where Italian immigration was far more important and pervasive than in Chile.

The German influence is seen most strongly in the Lake District of the south, which is where most settlers from Germany arrived in the 19th

Ligua, cakes of sponge or meringue filled with *manjar*. La Ligua is just off the PanAmerican Highway traveling north around an hour and a half out of Santiago, and the *dulces* are well worth the detour, although they can also be acquired in bakeries in Santiago.

Globalized tastes

In recent years, as prosperity has increased with economic growth, more and more Chileans have had the opportunity to travel abroad and, much as occurred in Britain in the 1960s and 1970s, this has been reflected in the incorporation of new ingredients on supermarket shelves,

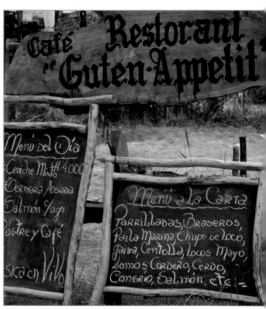

century. This may explain the importance that cabbage now has in the Mapuche diet, and it is certainly reflected in the widespread use of the word *küchen* to describe any sort of fruit tart.

Küchen is, in fact, one of the few traditional sweet pastries in Chile. However, in the sweet line, *manjar* is very popular. Similar to Argentina's *dulce de leche* (which literally translated means sweet milk), *manjar* is traditionally made by slowly boiling up a mixture of milk and sugar, flavored with a vanilla pod, until it thickens and turns a light caramel brown. By far the best way to sample *manjar* is in *dulces de La*

the appearance of new ways of using traditional Chilean ingredients and, above all, a greater variety of restaurants.

> The Emporio Nacional with branches at Bellavista 0360 and in the Galería Drugstore on Providencia, is one of the best places to buy Chilean gourmet specialties, including some of the best of the country's cheeses.

Today, most supermarkets, at least in prosperous areas of Santiago, have a section devoted to the materials for preparing Japanese and Thai dishes as well as Peruvian and Mexican food.

LEFT: traditional *parrillada*. **ABOVE:** *postre* (dessert).
ABOVE RIGHT: a German café in the Lake District.

Whether it is wasabi, rice vinegar, or lemon grass that you want, the chances are that you will be able to find it.

Chinese restaurants and take-aways, long common in Chile, have been joined by ubiquitous sushi bars, some more authentic than others. Chilean salmon is the staple ingredient of rolls that – to the surprise of foreigners – often also include *palta*. The number of Indian restaurants, although still small, has also increased.

Putting a new spin on Chilean fish, many restaurants now also serve *ceviche*, a Peruvian specialty of raw fish cooked in lemon juice. In fast-food restaurants too, the influence of globalization

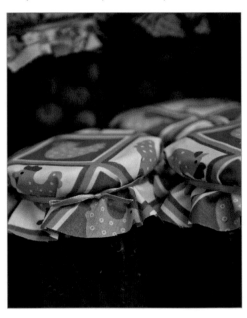

is clear – you'll be just as likely to find tacos and burritos as hamburgers and chips and, in line with a growing concern about obesity, salads.

A day of dining

Breakfast is *desayuno*. In most *residenciales* this will simply be bread with jam and butter (*mermelada y mantequilla*) and coffee or tea. Coffee will almost certainly be instant. *Café con leche* (with milk) is milky coffee; if you want just a little milk, ask for *un café cortado*. Tea-lovers should prepare themselves for a challenging time in Chile. Asking for a cup of tea usually gets you a tea bag in a cup of hot, but not necessarily boiling, water. Beware, also, of asking for milk with your tea. This will almost certainly be warm and

often in a larger quantity than you anticipated.

A fuller breakfast can be ordered anywhere that serves *desayuno* (though rarely before 9am). Eggs and toast (*huevos con tostadas*) should be no problem. Fried eggs are *huevos fritos*, scrambled are *revueltos*, poached are *pasados*, hard-boiled are *huevos duros*, and soft-boiled are *a la copa*.

Lunch (*almuerzo*) is served after 1.30pm and can run until around 4pm. Set lunches (*colaciones* or *menú del día*) are usually very good value, and give you the opportunity of trying something typical without having to know what to order. As a starter, you'll be served something like tomatoes, cooked beans, and cheese, before a main

dish of perhaps *porotos granados* (bean stew) or *pollo con arroz* (chicken with rice), and then there may be a little *postre* (dessert). Tea or coffee, or a soft drink, is usually part of the deal.

> Chile has recently begun producing olive oil and has won a number of international prizes. The flavor varies from fruity and mild to very strong. At some restaurants, oil seasoned with merkén is served with bread for dipping.

In Chile, late afternoon, between 5 and 7pm, is somewhat confusingly the time for *onces* (elevens). These usually include tea, coffee, sandwiches, and cakes, to bridge the gap between lunch and dinner, which is rarely eaten before 9pm. The name is said to come from the British custom of having "elevenses," a late-morning snack. An alternative theory is that this used to be the time when the man of the house would sneak off for a peaceful drink of *aguardiente*, the local firewater, the name of which contains 11 letters.

As in most Latin American countries, dinner *(cena)* isn't served until after 8.30pm, and usually runs on until late. If you don't drink coffee after dinner, try an *aguita*, a fresh herb tea found everywhere.

shellfish to eat, or buy them from artisan fishermen trading on quaysides or beaches.

Water contamination in Santiago's market-garden region has been cleared up, and serious food-borne illnesses like cholera, typhoid fever, and hepatitis have been virtually eradicated. Raw salads and strawberries (traditionally a hazard because they grow near the ground) now represent no danger at all. The exception is *berros* (watercress), which harbors a nasty parasite, and should be avoided everywhere, unless you can be sure it was grown under hydroponic conditions.

Although coffee-drinking habits have evolved in recent years, instant coffee is still ubiquitous

Health issues

Health-conscious travelers may find Chileans' liberal use of sugar and salt quite disturbing. In this case, the phrases *sin sal* and *sin azúcar* (without salt/without sugar) should be slipped into your vocabulary.

The only really serious food-related health hazard is *marea roja* (red tide), a toxic alga that infects shellfish and can be fatal. Restaurants are perfectly safe because of strict controls on the transport of products from the areas, mostly in the south of Chile, where infections occur. However, you should not gather your own

FAR LEFT AND LEFT: cold cuts and preserves.
ABOVE: catching up over a pitcher of *cerveza*.

in Chile, especially in cheaper restaurants where, after dinner, you may be asked to spoon instant into your cup, which the waiter will then fill with hot water. To avoid a surprise, specify that you want *café café* or *café de grano*, the two usual terms for real coffee.

Vegetarians used to have a hard time in Chile, but that is changing. Santiago now has a number of vegetarian restaurants, such as El Huerto, or its lower-priced La Huerta sister-restaurant, in the Providencia district, and La Chakra organic café in Las Condes *(see listings, page 157)*, and the same is true of most other cities and large towns. In addition, most restaurants carry a small selection of vegetarian alternatives. ❏

FRUIT OF THE VINE

Immensely popular worldwide, Chilean wines are still seen as new and exotic, yet they are made from grapes with an ancient European pedigree

Chileans have been making fine wines for more than a century, and have probably boasted about them for almost as long. Their great selling point, as every Chilean schoolchild knows, is that the best wine is produced from vines which can trace their ancestry straight back to cuttings brought over in the middle of the 19th century from France by some enlightened Chilean vineyard owners.

Before that era, the Spanish conquistadors had grown vines, legend has it, by planting the pips of the raisins they had brought over with them from Spain. This was the origin of what is known as *país*, or "native" wine, the equivalent of California's "mission" wine. Winemaking was also an essential part of the activities of the Jesuit missionaries, who settled in the country throughout the 18th century.

French roots

A century later, an affluent landowner, Don Silvester Ochagavía, decided to improve the quality of his vines and went to France. It was a timely visit, as Ochagavía brought back cuttings not long before a plague of the dreaded phylloxera beetle began to chew away at the roots of the parent stock in Europe, and nearly destroyed the wine industries in France, Italy, and Germany.

The European growers saved their vines by eventually grafting tougher, beetle-resistant American stock onto them. But while the European vineyards were being replanted, several out-of-work French enologists went to Chile, together with their vines, to give technical advice on planting and wine-making.

LEFT: Casa Blanca Valley. RIGHT: grapes have been cultivated in Chile since the nineteenth century.

The phylloxera blight never reached Chile, cut off as it is from the rest of the world by natural barriers – the Pacific Ocean, the Atacama Desert, and the Andes. So Chilean vineyard owners boast that their vines grow naturally, ungrafted, from original European stock. Wine buffs argue about whether this makes any difference to the wine's taste. It certainly does make a difference to the economics of the industry, because ungrafted vines can go on producing for three or four times longer than the grafted stock that now dominates in Europe.

Señor Ochagavía brought cuttings of Cabernet Sauvignon vines, which is now the most common type used for red wine (*vino tinto*). It is usually produced as a 100 percent unblended wine, though it is sometimes blended with Merlot grapes, or occasionally with Malbec. At around the same time, someone – it is not known who – also brought cuttings of Carmenère from its Bordeaux homeland. The plant and its wine are similar to Merlot, but with subtle differences – so subtle, in fact, that until the late 1990s, when a sharp-eyed (or nosed) Frenchman spotted it, it was marketed as Merlot. DNA testing proved that it was Carmenère, and it has become a Chilean signature because of its rarity value. White wine comes from Chardonnay grapes and from Sauvignon Blanc.

Local consumption of wine, however, has been dropping steadily since the 1970s, although there is a strong wine-drinking culture among the middle and wealthy classes. Even so, beer and fizzy drinks have become far more popular, and wine consumption is well below that of other European wine-producing countries and much less than neighboring Argentina.

Modernizing for export

In the 1980s, the future looked bleak for wine producers. However, some of the bigger enterprises decided to test their reputations by trying to sell in a big way to the outside world. That

Señor Ochagavía brought his cuttings of the Sauvignon Blanc vine from Bordeaux rather than the Loire Valley, and the flavor is softer and less pungent than the Loire Valley variety.

Changing tastes

By the 19th century, Chilean wine growers already had the best vines and an excellent place to grow them – the long Central Valley, with its ideal temperate climate, hot sunny days and cool nights, and the right type of soil for the vines to flourish. But it is only since the late 1980s that they have really begun to make consistent top-quality wines that sell successfully in Europe, the United States, and Asia, and are even making inroads into the giant Chinese market.

meant changing the heavy, full-bodied wines – with the strong tannin taste that Chileans were used to – and going for the lighter and fruitier unblended wines (*varietales*) that are popular in

> At the beginning of the 1970s, the average Chilean drank 50 liters (106 pints) of wine a year; by 2000, this figure had dropped to 15 liters (32 pints), in favor of beer and soft drinks.

the United States and Europe. That called for investment in new equipment. For example, red wine was traditionally matured in big, old casks of *rauli*, the native oak, which masks the taste of fruit. The vineyards that decided to go for export markets had to import very expensive small casks, made from French oak, each of which lasts for only three or four years before it has to be replaced.

The investment for making good white wine was even larger, since white wine needs more careful handling. The grapes have to be picked in the cool hours of the morning, not in the heat of a summer afternoon. It's also important to pick them when they are not too ripe, or the wine will lack acidity, at least for non-Chilean tastes.

Vineyards have installed computerized pneumatic grape presses, which don't crush pips, and

been the production of Sauvignon Blanc in valleys close to the sea, which gives them a different bouquet and flavor.

Wine producers

The bigger producer-exporters are Concha y Toro and its subsidiary, Santa Emiliana, and Santa Rita, which also owns Viña Carmen. However, Chile has some 150 wineries and a wealth of small boutique-style vineyards, such as Miguel Torres and Los Vascos, which produce mainly for export.

Most of the winemaking areas are located in the Central Valley to the south of Santiago. To the

stainless-steel tanks, in which the temperature of the fermenting juice can be rigidly controlled.

More recently, in a bid to broaden their range of exports, wine producers have begun to experiment with new varieties. They now produce some Malbec – the flagship wine of Argentina's Mendoza province just across the Andes – and have had considerable success with Pinot Noir, a light red wine, in the cooler valleys where most of Chile's white wines are grown. New white wines, such as Viognier, Riesling, and Gewürztraminer, have also begun to appear, although the main change in white wines has

north, some wine is produced, for example, in the Limarí Valley but most of the vines are for growing table grapes, with the exception of the *pisco*, a pink Muscatel-like variety which is distilled to make the spirit of the same name (*see page 190*).

The Valle del Elqui, near the pretty northern town of La Serena, is the most famous *pisco* area. Two main brands are distributed nationally, but if visiting the valley or La Serena it is worth tasting and shopping around for local brands, which have the finest taste and smell of ripe grapes.

Visiting vineyards

The *vendimia*, or grape harvest, takes place between early March and mid-April – the farther south the vineyard, the later the picking

LEFT: filling wine barrels at Viña Veramonte.
ABOVE: Viña Mar, in the Casablanca Valley.

starts. By far, the largest festival takes place in Santa Cruz, in the Colchagua Valley, 178km (110 miles) south of Santiago. It includes a craft fair and concerts as well as wine-tastings. There are also other festivals in the nearby towns of Curicó and San Fernando, and, in the north, in the Limarí valley, the last area where wine is produced before the Atacama Desert begins.

The Colchagua Valley also offers organized tours of its vineyards. Starting in Santa Cruz, they range from a half-day tour to a two-day package that includes an overnight stay in the Santa Cruz Plaza Hotel (tel: 02-209 600). Bookings for the wine tour can be made through the

tors can ride the train – hauled by a refurbished 19th-century steam engine – through the Colchagua Valley, stopping off to visit state-of-the-art wineries and taste their wares (tel: 02-470 7403).

Public visits to most vineyards in the off-season are usually limited to the bottling plant and the original cellars. This kind of tour takes only about an hour, so you might plan a visit as part of a day out in the countryside around Santiago. Tastings are usually included in the tour, and most wineries have added elegant sales rooms and, in some cases, restaurants.

The closest to Santiago – indeed, now almost swallowed up by the city – is **Cousiño Macul**

hotel or directly with the Ruta del Vino (Wine Route) office in Santa Cruz (tel: 72-823 199). Santa Cruz can easily be reached by taking the train to San Fernando and a *colectivo* from the

> *In 2008, Chile's wine exports reached almost US$1.4 billion. The industry's largest markets are the UK (US$206 million in 2008) and the US (US$193 million), where it is facing increasing competition from Argentinian wines.*

station. A century-old railway line linking San Fernando with the coast has been reopened and renamed "Tren del Vino" (the Wine Train). Visi-

winery, one of the oldest in Chile. Grapes have been grown there since vines were planted by its first owner, Juan Jufré, one of the conquistadors who came with Pedro de Valdivia. The winery has been in the Cousiño Macul family since 1856, and the person most responsible for its development was the daughter-in-law of the first Cousiño, Doña Isidora Goyenechea, who had the cellars built and brought over an enologist from Bordeaux to produce quality wine. A leafy oasis on the outskirts of Santiago, it is well worth a visit. Tel: (02) 351 4175.

Concha y Toro, which is by far the biggest single wine producer and exporter, has its plant located in the direction of the Cajón del Maipo, about an hour's drive southeast of Santiago or a short taxi ride from the Puente Alto subway station. A tour of the plant and old family estate might be included in a weekend trip to the mountains, but requires a booking. Tel: (02) 476 5680.

Santa Rita, near Paine just off the Pan-American Highway south of Santiago, has a lovely little Precolombian Museum and, with its excellent restaurant, makes a pleasant day trip from Santiago. Booking is advised, particularly for the restaurant. Tel: (02) 362 2594 or, at weekends, (02) 362 2590.

Viña Undurraga is near Melipilla, about an hour's drive toward San Antonio, and could be combined with a visit to the resorts of Algarrobo or Las Cruces, or the port of San Antonio. Tours run daily starting at 10am. Again, booking is advisable. Tel: (02) 372 2850.

> *Wine growing in the Casablanca Valley only started a little over 20 years ago. Its "discovery" is generally attributed to pioneer Pablo Morandé, who was looking for a cooler place for white grapes.*

Another happy hunting ground for wine lovers is the Casablanca Valley, between Santiago and Valparaíso. This is where Chile's best white wines are produced and visits or an overnight stay can be organized through the Casablanca Valley Wine Producers Association (tel: 032-274 3933). Some of the vineyards also have excellent restaurants, making the valley a favorite excursion for *santiaguinos* on a sunny Sunday.

The **Casas del Bosque**, just outside the town of Casablanca, offers tours all year round but, during the vendimia, also allows visitors to participate in the harvest, cutting grapes and learning more about the process that follows. Lunch is available at its Tanino restaurant (snacks only on Monday). Tel: (032) 377 9431.

Viña Indómita. The restaurant of this vineyard is a favorite with *santiaguinos* and it also offers tours. Tel: (032) 275 4400.

On the western edge of the Casablanca Valley, **Viña Matetic** not only produces some very interesting wines, it also has a stunningly designed restaurant that is widely acclaimed for

the quality and creativity of its food, and a guest house. Tel: (09) 8920 2066.

Trying and buying

Wine buffs might enjoy a visit to the **Restaurant Camino Real**, on Santiago's pleasant wooded Cerro San Cristóbal, where you can sample a range of wines at about US$2 a glass. The restaurant is open from 12.30am–4pm and 8–11pm. If you arrive unannounced, there will be no expert on hand to comment on or recommend wines. But if you want to take sampling more seriously, you can make an appointment and arrange for a private tasting session (tel: 02-232 1758).

If you want to take some Chilean wine home, try one of the big supermarkets chains, such as Jumbo or Líder, in upmarket areas of Santiago such as Providencia, Las Condes, Vitacura, or Avenida Kennedy. These stores offer large wine selections at good prices. But, if you want expert advice, you'd be better off in one of the specialized wine shops in the El Golf area. El Mundo del Vino, in Isidora Goyenechea, is one of the best, and the staff are generally well informed. El Mundo del Vino also sells some cheap and very useful inflatable plastic sheaths for wine bottles that allow them to be safely carried in bags that go in the hold of a plane, now that they are not allowed in hand baggage. ❑

FAR LEFT AND LEFT: Viña Undurraga. **RIGHT:** wine tours usually include an opportunity to sample the produce.

WILD CHILE

Chile's wide range of climatic zones gives it an unusually diverse flora and fauna – but sadly, much of it is endangered

With the world's driest desert in the north and the continent of Antarctica in the south, it is not surprising that Chile's climate is divided into extremely different zones and that its wildlife varies tremendously. Add to this the country's huge extension of ocean (the 320-km/200-mile territorial limit is almost the width of Chile at its widest point) on the west and the lofty Andes on the east, and you have a world of differences packed into one long strand of a country.

Chile's wilderness areas hold few dangers for the intrepid camper or hiker. There are no bears in the mountains, no poisonous snakes, and only two kinds of poisonous spider (the corn spider or *araña del trigo*, with a red splash on a black body, and the brown corner spider, *araña del rincón*, found in houses), which you're unlikely to run into. Way up in the mountains there are wildcats and pumas, but they usually avoid people.

Unfortunately, while Chileans are generally proud of the numerous species endemic to their country, many of these are in danger of extinction, including the world's smallest deer, the *pudú*, and the *huemul*, the large, royal-looking deer which appears on the Chilean coat of arms. On Chile's island territories (Easter Island and particularly the Juan Fernández Islands) are species that, developing in isolation, have formed their own unique gene pools.

The far north

The soils of Chile's northernmost desert regions are dry, and the climate is harsh, but the coastal

PERILOUS PENGUINS

Chile has nine species of penguin, the largest of which is appropriately called the emperor. These penguins can grow as tall as 1.2 meters (4ft), and are characterized by a yellowish-orange patch on both sides of their chests. They live in colonies of up to 5,000.

The most common species is the Magellanic penguin, which nests in sandy burrows in colonies of up to several thousand birds. If frightened, it hastens back to its burrow making a braying call like a donkey. Though seemingly tame, these penguins have been known to bite. Be warned if you see one pointing its beak towards you and hissing.

PRECEDING PAGES: llamas near Volcán Licancábur, San Pedro de Atacama. **LEFT:** the elusive puma.
RIGHT: tiny Darwin's frogs.

areas teem with seals and all kinds of birds: seagulls, pelicans, petrels, penguins, and *jotes* (vultures). High up in the Andes, disguised among the low shrubs and rocks, is the occasional herd of *huemules* deer, hard to find but protected (at least in theory) in the national parks. Parque Nacional Lauca *(see page 200)* is the only area in Chile where the *huemul* is easily spotted at dawn or dusk, maybe hiding amongst the *queñoa* trees.

Chilean flamingos can be seen picking bugs out of the mud around altiplano lakes. The Andean flamingo and the James flamingo are also often seen in the salt marshes south of

chas are quite easy to spot as they run around, popping out from behind rocks during the day.

High in the altiplano (over 4,500 meters/ 14,800ft) is one of the world's last reserves of wild chinchilla. The French naturalist Claude Gay described the chinchilla as "one of Chile's most beautiful animals" and said they were easily tamed. They live in extensive caves dug under the ground, and come out only at night, so their eyes are extremely sensitive to the light. The chinchilla is an endangered species: in the early 20th century, an average of 350,000 chinchilla skins were exported per year. According to Chile's Committee for Defense of Flora and Fauna (CODEFF),

Parque Nacional Lauca. Conservation groups are working to protect flocks from collectors who gather the eggs to sell as food.

At least 150 other bird species have been noted in the park, one of the most obvious being the giant coot, a turkey-sized bird that builds huge nests up to 2.4 meters (8ft) wide, floating or resting on piles of stones in water.

Mountain cats, wild ducks, *ñandúes* (rheas), owls, eagles, and condors also add life to the dry landscape of Chile's far north, at 3–4,000 meters (9,800–13,000ft) above sea level. The *vizcacha* or Andean rabbit is endemic to the Andes. Its fluffy tail, tufted ears and long whiskers give it a rabbit-like appearance, but this rodent is actually a relative of the chinchilla and guinea pig. *Vizca-*

CAMELID SPOTTING

Visitors to Chile will almost certainly spot a few camelids on their travels, but few will be able to say with certainty whether the wooly creatures are llamas, guanacos, vicuñas, or alpacas. Here's how to tell them apart and impress your travel companions.

The guanaco and llama are the largest of the camelids. The guanaco has rust-colored fur with a dark head and tail, while the vicuña has creamier-colored fur. Alpaca and llama may be a combination of black, grey, white, rust, or cream, the alpaca being slightly smaller and with a fatter, often shorter neck. Alpacas have short, straight ears, while llamas have longer, curved ears.

these wild chinchillas are particularly important because most existing animals have been born and bred in captivity, with the resulting damage to gene pools which results from excessive inbreeding. These last, wild chinchilla are key to the renewal of breeding animals and have been studied by professors at the University of Chile.

In the broad plains formed between the coastal and Andean mountain ranges can be found the occasional hollow covered with the only sparse grasses capable of resisting the extreme saltiness of the soil. Climbing slightly higher into the mountains, around 2,200 meters (7,200ft) above sea level, cacti appear, accompa-

with gentle, timid and very curious personalities… They're very sociable and live in herds of many females with one male… They're hunted for their edible flesh and because exceptionally strong lassos can be made from the skin of their neck… Their only form of defense is spitting at people who try to come near them: at the slightest provocation they lay their ears back and fling saliva mixed with other matter which doesn't cause the least damage."

Toward the Norte Chico

South of Parque Nacional Pan de Azúcar (see page 191) there is enough humidity to permit

nied by birds, some insects and lizards – the main life forms capable of surviving in the area.

The camelids

All over the northern territories and in many parts of the south are herds of the animals most closely identified with (and arguably best adapted to) the extreme conditions of the altiplano: llamas, vicuñas, guanacos, and alpacas. All relatives of the camel, these four species are hard to tell apart, though the llama and alpaca are long-haired (and valued for their wool).

Claude Gay described guanacos as "animals

the growth of a large variety of cacti, many of which are valued abroad. Over the years ruthless hunting has reduced the herds of guanacos and the number of *vizcachas* and chinchillas as well. Colorful beetles of all kinds are noteworthy throughout this region.

Thorns, shrubs, and small trees, along with wild flowers like the Cordilleran violet and chamomile, give way to the forests of Fray Jorge and Talinay, full of trees more commonly found further south (particularly the *canelo* and *olivillo*). The vegetation hums with abundant insects, including dragonflies, butterflies, and beetles, which in turn sustain a sizeable population of lizards and non-poisonous snakes. Wild donkeys live in the Andean foothills.

LEFT: Andean condors. **ABOVE:** penguin family, Otway Sound, Magallanes.

From this region down toward Santiago, the climate, while still dry, is considerably more generous toward plants and animals. The climate in these regions is among the most pleasant in the world. The average temperature for the area is around 14°C (57°F) all year round, and mists blown off the ocean condense on the coastal mountains, ensuring sufficient moisture to support a wide variety of flowers, trees, and other vegetation necessary to maintaining animal life. However, the landscape pays dearly for those years when the moisture is not sufficient: huge dunes have formed and have begun to creep steadily into formerly fertile areas, turn-

ing them into semi-deserts, which may be virtually impossible to recover.

In these more temperate regions, sea swallows and cormorants join the bird species more common farther north, and farther inland there are thrushes, turtledoves, and partridges along with the other species named above. Wasps, scorpions (although their sting is painful, it is not dangerous), *tábanos* (horseflies), and both black and large hairy spiders form part of the anthropod population, while frogs and toads join the lizard and snake community.

The central region

From the early days of the Spanish Conquest, Chile's fertile Central Valley region, where Santiago is located, became the principal area of settlement and agriculture. As a result, the main animals of the area are people.

As you travel farther south, the landscape changes and with it the animals which inhabit it. In the lush forests which cover a large part of the southern region are rabbits, hares, *coipo* and mice, wildcats, and other small animals. The *coipo*, a sort of Chilean beaver, is hard to see in the wild because it usually only comes out at night. Many of the animals which formerly populated the coast have been virtually wiped out by indiscriminate hunting, particularly the different species of seal which once thrived in the area.

Birds with names such as *huairavo, piquero, pollito de mar, pinguera, chucao, run-run*, and *becacinas* populate the forests, and the lizards are joined by four-eyed toads, the cowboy toad and different kinds of frogs. One of the more unusual is the Darwin's frog. It lays eggs, which

PUMAS – LIONS OF THE MOUNTAINS

Chileans who live in the mountains frequently see pumas (*felis concolor*, but popularly known as *leones* – lions), particularly in winter. Pumas rarely attack people, however, unless they are cornered. The presence of guanaco may indicate that pumas are nearby, as these animals are a key part of their diet. Guanaco skeletons found in remote areas often have dislocated necks, which is a sign of the work of this powerful mountain lion. Pumas also feed on hares, *vizcachas*, and *huemules*, attacking domestic animals only occasionally.

Despite this, hunting has seriously reduced their numbers. In 1980 the government banned the hunting of pumas; in response, many sheep farmers have since switched to raising cattle as their sheep were being increasingly ravaged by pumas.

A solitary animal, the puma reaches maturity at two or three years of age, and usually has two kittens per litter. Pumas and their relatives are found throughout Chile, particularly in the mountainous areas of the Lake District and Tierra del Fuego. Indeed, they are among the few animal species found throughout the Americas, all the way from Canada right down to the Strait of Magellan. This elusive creature grows up to 1.5 meters (5ft) in length and stands 63cm (2ft) at the shoulder. It has a light-brown coat with a white muzzle, and is hard to see, but sightings of its human-fist-size footprints are fairly common.

are then swallowed and tended by the male, who, upon their maturation, "gives birth" through the mouth to the young tadpoles.

The insect community includes a fascinating beetle, the *madre de la culebra* (snake's mother), which is a couple of centimeters or more in length, with long claws. Praying mantis, colorful "stink bugs" of a bright metallic blue, and different kinds of butterflies also thrive under the trees – although they, like all species, have been affected by the wholesale cutting and burning of Chile's native forests and have not adapted well to foreign species like the lodgepole pine, which have been used for reforestation in some regions.

cat, but they live in the wild, surviving on partridge, hare, rabbit, mice, and birds.

The Lake District

Between Lago Vichuquén and the coastal village of Llico is the Reserva Nacional Laguna Torca, where graceful black-necked swans crowd the lake, feeding on aquatic plants and laying their eggs on floating nests. Upon hatching, the white offspring climb onto their parents' backs. Along the coast, colonies of penguins and swamp cormorants can be seen.

Farther south, the climate becomes increasingly damp and rainy, and the species change

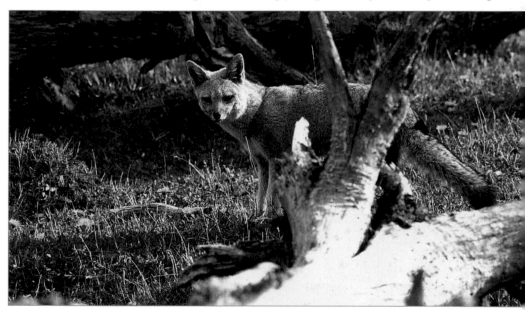

Long-tailed snakes (which look very similar to North American garter snakes) and short-tailed snakes feed on mice, toads, and small birds. They're about 8cm (3in) long at birth and can grow to 2 meters (7ft). They are not poisonous.

Condors inhabit the high peaks of the cordillera, and Chile's mountain forests also provide homes for wild ducks, mountain partridges and tricahue parrots. *Felis colo colo* (mountain cats), which are peculiar to Chile, are an altogether unnerving sight – their physical appearance is exactly that of the marmalade domestic

---

LEFT: flamingos in flight, Magallanes. **ABOVE:** the *culpeo* (Chilean fox).

somewhat as a result. However, considerable deforestation in the area has severely cut back on what would otherwise be a numerous population of wild animals. There are still some foxes, *pudús*, wildcats, and pumas, but they tend to concentrate as far from human inhabitants as they can get, and are very difficult to spot.

The *pudú*, a tiny reddish deer which is endemic to Chile, lives in thickets in the densely forested areas between Chillán and Isla Chiloé, and is almost impossible to spot in the wild. Also found in this region is the *llaca*, the only marsupial left in the southern Andes. It spends its life in the trees and feeds on fruit and insects. In winter it goes into a state of semi-hibernation, just lazing around in the trees.

Chile's smallest and rarest fox is the Darwin's or chilote fox. The destruction of its natural habitat has put it in danger of extinction. It has, however, been sighted on Isla Chiloé and in the forests north of Osorno.

The Lake District is home to one of the world's largest beetles, the stag beetle, which grows as long as 9cm (3½in) and lives in the oak and *coigüe* forests of this southern region. Woodpeckers and hummingbirds are common in the forests of the region, especially near wild fuchsia (bleeding hearts). Dolphins appear in the coastal areas, where whales were once hunted virtually into extinction.

Magallanes and Tierra del Fuego

High up in the most isolated southern parts of the Andes are small herds of *huemules*, which are virtually extinct, and now protected in Chile's national parks. In Chile's southernmost region, sea lions can also be sighted along with seals and dolphins. Beavers (introduced from abroad), muskrat and *coipo* are also common here, along with petrels, albatross, cormorants, and other seabirds. Foxes, guanacos, pumas, and skunks roam the pampas of Tierra del Fuego.

Magellanic penguins can be seen in colonies at the Otway Sound, situated 60km (37 miles) north of Punta Arenas, and on the island

RESOURCEFUL REPTILES

Chile's varied landscapes are home to 76 species of lizard and six species of snake. Unlike most Chilean wildlife, reptiles are common throughout the country – except in the Magallanes region in the south. Many of these species are endemic to Chile. The history of their development has been extremely difficult to trace, but the sparse evidence available indicates that lizards go back about 70 million years in Chile.

Chilean lizards live in the desert, on the coast, in tropical forests, in the heights of the Andes, and on the Patagonian and southern steppes. Some lizards have been found at altitudes of up to 4,900 meters (16,000ft). These species live in underground burrows and have evolved special adaptations for keeping warm by absorbing more radiation from the sun.

Some lizards reproduce by laying eggs, while others give birth to live young. Sizes range from 10cm (4in) from nose tip to tail, and up to half a meter (1½ft) long, as is the case with the Chilean iguana.

Lizards play a key role in the ecology, living on flies, crickets, locusts, and other insects, thus controlling the insect population. Many birds and several species of Chile's snakes in turn live on the lizards. None of the species found in Chile are dangerous: lizards generally prefer to get away if approached by humans and will only bite when there is no alternative.

nature reserve of Monumento Natural Los Pingüinos, near Punta Arenas. Magellanic penguin skins were once heavily sought after by indigenous people in the area for food and clothing, and penguin eggs provided an important source of food.

Other birds scouring the beaches and fishing the coastal-shelf waters include blue-eyed cormorants, pintado petrels, wandering albatross, brown skuas, pink-footed shearwaters, chinstrap penguins, gulls, oyster catchers, and steamer ducks.

Within the chilly Antarctic waters, the delicate food chain depends first on marine zooplankton (arrow worms, microscopic crus-

food chain are seals (Weddell, elephant, Ross, and leopard), fur seals, and sea lions, which, with their thick blubber and fur, are all well

> Avoid contact with field mice or their droppings if camping or staying in rural cabins as some mice carry hantavirus. Cases are few and far between but the virus, which causes a form of pneumonia, can be fatal.

adapted to the cold Antarctic water. Unfortunately, hunting in the 20th century reduced

taceans and shrimp-like krill). These zooplankton thrive in the nutrient-rich Antarctic water and feed the ecosystems of the continental shelf. Small marine species in the area depend on marine zooplankton for survival. There are hundreds of endemic mollusks, starfish, sea urchins, sponges, jellyfish, and other marine species that have adapted to the extreme temperatures and harsh conditions.

A little higher on the food chain are an estimated 25 species of octopus and squid, along with five fish families. Toward the top of the

FAR LEFT: the Chilean southern ringed kingfisher.
LEFT: a giant red-headed woodpecker.
ABOVE: a *vizcacha* makes itself cozy.

their populations, but an international treaty now protects them.

The Weddell seal is the deepest diver, reaching depths of 600 meters (1,968ft), with the ability to hold its breath for over an hour. Fish, shellfish, and squid make up the bulk of the seal's diet, but the leopard seal will also feed on penguins and other seals.

The blue whale, 20–30 meters (66–98ft) long and weighing over 100 tons, consumes about 40,000kg (88,000lbs) of zooplankton each day. Orcas (killer whales) also inhabit the waters of southern Chile. They are particularly fond of eating sea lions, tossing them into the air with their tail fins to stun them before moving in for the kill. ❑

ADVENTURE ACTIVITES

Chile's great outdoors is unusually tempting, and there are many ways to enjoy it, whether on skis, on a surfboard, in a boat, or on foot

With over one third of the nation's population living in the capital Santiago, it is easy to find somewhere in Chile to get away from it all. But Chile offers more than remote and pristine wilderness. Its dramatic, untamed, and highly varied landscape makes it a land of adventure.

The options are as varied as the country's many geographical zones. In the north, the vast empty desert can only be crossed in a four-wheel drive. The heart of the Andes must be reached either on foot or on horseback. There are volcanoes to be climbed and rivers to be rafted, while the glacier-riddled islands of the southern archipelago can often only be visited on organized boat trips.

The season for adventure tourism is summer: November to March. This is when the weather stabilizes, save on the Andean high plain at the northeastern border with Bolivia, where electric storms are common. Do not expect rain in the Atacama Desert, even in the foothills – some parts only see rain every 30 to 50 years. From there to Santiago, rain rarely falls between October and March.

The spectacular Alpine and coastal wilderness of southern Chile attracts visitors from October through April. The town of Pucón is a good base from which to organize hikes, climbs, river rafting, mountain biking, and horseback riding into the nearby national parks of Huerquehue and Villarrica.

Chile's many volcanoes offer treats for hikers, while thrill-seekers scale the sheer rock faces of Patagonia, whose main attraction is Parque

Nacional Torres del Paine. Here are great opportunities to hike or go horseback riding past towering granite spires and azure lakes, amid roaming guanaco and *ñandú* (rheas).

Northern jeep excursions

The Chilean Norte Grande offers a wide selection of geological phenomena and archeological sites, from ancient civilizations to the remains of early 20th century nitrate-mining "ghost towns" *(see page 201)*. However, vast distances between sites and roads that are often barely distinguishable tracks make traveling difficult. Some sites are very hard to find so a good option is to pay for a driver or an organized excursion in a four-wheel-drive

PRECEDING PAGES: rafting on the Maipo river.
LEFT: reaching the Torres del Paine. **RIGHT:** paraskiing in the Valle Nevado.

vehicle. Tours can be arranged in Arica Iquique, Calama, and San Pedro de Atacama.

The main rule of thumb in the desert is never to leave the road unless you know exactly where you are going. It can take hours of pushing and shoving in the blazing sun to free a vehicle stuck in the sand. It is also important to take a large supply of fresh water along. Even up in the mountains where it is possible to find streams, a high mineral content often makes the water brackishly saline and generally undrinkable.

The desert can be very cold after the sun goes down, especially if there is a wind. In fact, it will probably be freezing should you arrive early in

places hiring horses or organizing treks, either in Santiago or in the south. Riding skills are not required either, as, given the terrain, most of the trip is a walking tour. The guides for these trips are *arrieros*, men who run cattle herds over the Andes or take them up to pasture after the spring snows melt. Many have learned the trails from their fathers and grandfathers before them. Their tales, related around the campfires as the beef sizzles on the spit, are worth learning Spanish to understand, and there is usually a musician to liven up the evenings.

Some excursions include visits to lagoons, which are not marked on road maps, such as

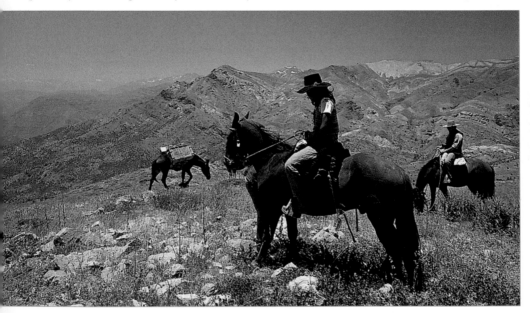

the morning to see the El Tatio geysers or the wildlife around Lago Chungará. Take warm clothing even if it seems a ludicrous prospect in the cloying heat of the desert. Prepare also for the effects of altitude if you are embarking on a trip to El Tatio or the high altiplano. Headaches are likely, so take aspirin along with you. Queasiness is also a symptom. Altitude problems can strike unexpectedly, and rest is the best remedy. In serious cases sufferers should immediately return to lower levels.

Horseback riding

Exploring the many nooks and crannies of the high Andes from the back of a horse is not as difficult as you might think, and there are many

Laguna Negra and the twin Lagunas del Yesillo, whose surfaces support floating blocks of snow. *Piuquenes* (wild geese) make their nests in the lake that bears their name. The atmosphere is so dry and clear it seems you could see to the end of the world if the snow-capped peaks were not blocking your vision. And the overwhelming silence of the cordillera makes modern metropolitan life seem very distant.

White-water rafting

The River Futaleufú, southeast of Chaitén, in Aisén, is Chile's white-water paradise. Depending on the water level, the river's rapids are rated grade 4+ on the international scale of 1 to 6, while upstream, the Inferno Canyon and Terminator sections can reach grade 5+, and this is not a trip to be attempted by anyone but expert kayakers with guides. Shorter excursions on other rivers, such as the Claro, Palena, or Petrohué, are not quite as wild as the Futaleufú, but every bit as exciting, and can be easily arranged. Relaxing day trips floating down stretches of the River Trancura can be organized in Pucón; the upper reaches of the river are stunning, with a backdrop of high volcanoes, while in the lower part, it becomes calmer, but "bouncy."

Climbing a volcano

Chile has 55 active volcanoes, and some of them can be climbed. The Llaima and Villarrica volcanoes are the most active in Chile, with a record of 10 eruptions each during the last century (Llaima erupted as recently as 1994). A

> The River Biobío in central Chile used to be one of the most exciting rivers in all the Andes. However, following the construction of the vast Ralco hydroelectric dam, only the rapids on its very upper reaches remain.

strong eruption in these volcanoes or in the nearby peaks of Quetrupillán, Lanín, or Mocho-Choshuenco can cause a chain reaction in the area. This is what happened in the mid-17th century – the Mapuches tell of how they were forced to move out of the area because of the extensive volcanic activity. The age of the forests – not more than 250 years old – in the valleys between Freire and the mountains confirms the folk memory. More recently, in 1971 the town of Coñaripe was buried below a terrifying slide of mud, ash, lava, and tree trunks caused by volcanic activity; while the last time a lava flow reached the banks of Lago Villarrica was 1908.

If you care to take on one of these roaring giants, agencies in Pucón organize hiking tours right up to the very crater of Volcán Villarrica (2,840 meters/9,320ft). Walking up the conical mountain takes you through one of the centers of the Pacific "Ring of Fire," surrounded by volcanic peaks. Here and there are emerald and sapphire lakes. Sometimes you hear some of the dark, hidden underground groans of Mother

Earth, and feel a few tremors and shakes. To stare down the 100-meter (330-ft) drop into the crater of hellishly boiling molten lava is a sight that few will forget. Here, the subterranean noises reach a roar and the stench of sulfur can be almost overpowering.

The ascent of the western face of Volcán Villarrica takes around four hours, thanks to a ski-lift that cuts the climbing distance. The descent of the volcano takes about three hours. The climb is strenuous, but anyone who is in reasonable health and physically fit should be able to make it. It is also possible to ascend other volcanoes such as Osorno, near Lago Llanqui-

hue. The ascent of this particular volcano, however, is quite a bit more difficult and requires climbing gear.

It is also possible to climb Ojos del Salado, the world's highest volcano, in the heart of the Atacama Desert, surrounded by green lagoons that are home to colonies of flamingos. Although a period of acclimatization is needed, the ascent is not difficult, and there are two mountain shelters on the route.

Sailing the southern channels

There are a number of boats that visit the archipelagos of southern Chile. In many cases, small short-distance vessels are rather lacking in safety measures and have a tendency toward danger-

---

LEFT: a horseback trek in the River Maipo Canyon.
RIGHT: white-water rafting.

ous overcrowding during the peak season. The calmest parts of the day for navigation tend to be early morning and sunset. On these journeys, it is a good idea to take your own life jacket and water, and a sleeping bag to put over the bare mattresses or reclining chairs on the freighters.

> There are an ever increasing number of cruises to Antarctica, most of which include opportunities to land on the Antarctic Peninsula. With its albatrosses, petrels, and penguin colonies, this is a birdwatchers' paradise.

lar scheduled freighters on rather spartan voyages between Puerto Montt and Puerto Chacabuco, or through the windswept Golfo de Penas to Puerto Natales.

Cruceros Australis (tel: 02-442 3110; www.australis.com) operates the comfortable *Mare Australis* and *Via Australis* ships that navigate the Patagonia Channels from Punta Arenas to Ushuaia in Argentina, passing through the Strait of Magellan and the Beagle Channel and its glaciers at the very southern tip of Chile. On the way back, it visits Isla Magdalena, which is inhabited by 40,000 breeding pairs of Magellanic penguins from October through March.

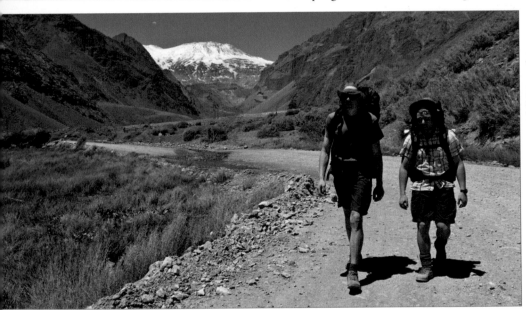

Other recommended items include woolen pants, socks, and a heavy sweater or fleece jacket. Rubber boots are best for going ashore. Stops are often made in pristine, uninhabited environments and where the clear, unforested land tends to be marshy at the water's edge. Here, birds which have no fear (or knowledge) of humans will sometimes hop onto your shoes, to pull at the laces, presumably mistaking them for hefty worms.

The most luxurious cruise boats are those of Skorpios (*see page 331*) for trips from Puerto Montt to Laguna San Rafael by way of the Northern Ice Field, or from Puerto Natales to Puerto Edén, visiting the glaciers of the Southern Ice Field. Navimag (*see page 331*) runs regu-

Camping in the sodden south

For those who wish to camp on the banks of the fjords, beware of the large differences between low and high tide in the area. Grass-covered islands in the rivers, which are common at the inland extremes of fjords, can gradually disappear at high tide, particularly around the time of the full moon. More than one camper in the Cahuelmo fjord has had to keep warm in the thermal tubs carved into the hillside after he and all his gear were soaked at 2am, when the full moon's tide came in. Short, yellow, wild flowers with bunches of tiny concave petals mark the highest tide level.

When camping in dense forest it is worth bringing a machete to clear the site. Ferns and the gigantic leaves of the *nalca* vie with the native bamboo *quila* and towering trees for ground space. Hanging, flowering vines twist up trunks bearded by thousands of varieties of multicolored lichens. Where the forest canopy allows sufficient light, one finds native blue *calafate* and red *murtilla* berries growing.

Tours are available that pass the small hamlets of Isla de Chiloé, through the Guaiteca Archipelago, to return through inland fjords passing the great San Rafael glacier. This enormous field of ice calves, with bomb-like explosions, into Laguna San Rafael. The melting icebergs become top-heavy and roll over, to expose the most incredible translucent shades of lavender, powder blue, or emerald green, like floating jewels.

> A good source of information and guides is the Federación de Andinismo in Santiago (see page 344), whose members often organize expeditions for both professionals and amateurs.

Hiking in Torres del Paine

Several companies offer trekking excursions in the most beautiful national park in the country, Parque Nacional Torres del Paine, created in 1959 and declared a Biosphere Reserve by Unesco in 1978.

The park itself is centered around the amazing "towers" and "horns" of rock, sculpted by glaciers, which point heavenward like daggers ripping at the sky's fluffy white belly. Here, the visitor will not only see some of the most incredible and beautiful Chilean landscapes, but will also experience everything that comes under the title "weather" – from cloudless skies to deafening thunderstorms, often in a time lapse of only 24 hours.

While there are log-cabin refuges along the trails, the distances between them are sometimes a hike of as many as seven to eight hours. For those visitors wishing to hike alone, a tent is a necessary precaution, as weather conditions can slow the hiker down, and rivers can swell, making it necessary to postpone a crossing. Garbage must be taken with you – abandoned garbage is often the only sign that one is not the first explorer to set foot in this unblemished, primeval territory.

LEFT: hiking in Monumento Natural El Morado.
RIGHT: snowboarding at Antillanca, near Osorno.

Sea kayaking

The fjords and majestic mountains of northern Patagonia make a spectacular backdrop for sea kayaking. The Canal de Dalcahue (Dalcahue Channel) is a good area for beginners to practice before heading out to the other islands off Isla de Chiloé. Altué Expediciones *(see page 343)* organizes sea kayaking trips that last from two to nine days. Around the Golfo de Ancud (Gulf of Ancud), in northern Patagonia, particularly Hornopirén and the fjords of Comau, Quintupeu, and Cahuelmo on the eastern side, are glacial valleys, thermal hot springs, and temperate rainforests, with dolphins, sea lions, and penguins.

Fishing

Wild rainbow and brown trout and six species of Pacific salmon may be the reward for a fishing expedition anywhere in the south of Chile. Four- to 8lb (2–3.5kg) trout are a rule rather than an exception. Some say that the trout are so abundant you have to keep the smaller fish from jumping into your boat with a stick – which may or may not be another fisherman's tale. Contact local hotels or travel agencies for organized excursions.

Skiing and snowboarding

Chile has some of best long ski runs in the world. Most runs are at altitudes of around 3,000 meters (9,843ft), and there is an abundance of natural snow, particularly "champagne" snow blown in from the Antarctic storms. Resorts stretch from just north of Santiago all the way to Patagonia. Portillo, near Santiago, is one of the most famous ski resorts in South America. Valle Nevado, also near Santiago, is a modern resort built in 1988 and the seat of snowboarding world cups. Heli-skiing, paragliding, and parascending are also available here. The best time to visit is June to October (*see page 167*).

Termas de Chillán, situated 80km (50 miles) east of Chillán on the slopes of Volcán Chillán (3,122 meters/10,243ft) is famous for its ther-

explore Easter Island, but it's probably best to bring your own bike if you want to go any distance in Chile. If you go biking in the desert north, where trails pass through the salt flats, national parks, and indigenous villages, it's essential to carry water supplies. The Carretera Austral often attracts cyclists along its unpaved road.

Surfing

Many spots along the coast of Chile are acquiring a worldwide reputation as surfing centers, with good conditions virtually all year round. Powerful reef breaks near Iquique and Arica in the north attract big crowds.

mal springs. There are plenty of groomed runs, but if you want to get away from the crowd, it is easy to find virgin powder runs.

To reach the extreme runs, you can either hike up the mountain or go for the easy (and pricey) option and take a helicopter. A special park has been set up for snowboarders to show off their freestyle moves. Other attractions at the resort are snowmobile and helicopter tours. After a long, hard day on the snow, you can relax in the thermal baths. The season runs from June to September only.

Mountain biking

There are endless places to go biking, particularly in southern Chile, and this is one way to

Farther south, the water becomes colder and a 3x2 wetsuit will be needed.

From the Santiago region the coastal shelf is more abrupt, and swell conditions pretty consistent. Pichilemu, a popular beach resort just south of Santiago, has become internationally known as a surfing center.

Paragliding

The fast-growing sport of paragliding (*parapente*) has also caught on in Chile. A hardcore of paragliders soar through the sky near Santiago or launch themselves off the ski slopes at resorts like Antillanca in the south. There are paragliding schools in many different seaside resorts, but particularly in Iquique in the north. ❏

The Chilean Trail

The creation of the Sendero de Chile has opened up a network of hiking trails through some of Chile's most spectacular scenery

One of Chile's main attractions is its variety of landscapes – from the vast, windswept expanses of the altiplano (high plain) and salt flats of the north to the lush virgin forests of the south. The only catch is that much of the most beautiful scenery is far off the beaten track and not easily accessible, but, for those visitors who like walking, biking, or horseback riding, there is a solution – the Sendero de Chile (Chilean Trail).

The trail, on which work started in 2003, is one of a number of projects being developed ahead of Chile's celebration of the 200th anniversary of its independence in 2010. It currently consists of 35 separate segments – selected as particularly representative of some of Chile's most unique scenery – that will gradually join up. Ultimately, it will comprise over 8,500km (5,300 miles) of paths, making it the longest hiking trail in the world.

Joining the trail

A convenient place to join the Sendero de Chile is the Mahuida Park in the La Reina district of eastern Santiago. From there, it is possible to walk or cycle 8km (5 miles) along the foothills of the Andes with a magnificent view of the city spread out below. Just south of Santiago, another segment starts from the Termas de Cauquenes *(see page 216)* and climbs steadily 26km (16 miles) alongside a small river to the Portezuelo de las Nieves Hill (1,850 meters/6,070ft).

Longer segments of the trail to be are to be found in the north of the country and the far south. In the north, to the east of the port of Iquique, two separate stretches, both of some 100km (62 miles), run through salt flats as they weave their way beneath snow-capped volcanoes, following a route once used by the Incas. The first starts in Colchane, a town with a bus service from Iquique, while the other can be joined at the Coposa salt flat, close to the road from Iquique to the Collahuasi copper mine.

LEFT: coming down to earth gently on a paraglider. **RIGHT:** trails all over Chile will join up to create the Sendero de Chile.

In the far south, a segment of a similar length stretches from Palena, near the border with Argentina, south to the beautiful Lago Verde (Green Lake), passing through dense forests and rolling grasslands against a backdrop of mountains and glaciers. This part of the trail, which crosses several rivers with abundant fish, can only be covered on horseback and in summer (November to March).

In a token to Chile's island territories, small segments of the trail also exist on Easter Island and Robinson Crusoe Island. The 8-km (5-mile) stretch on Easter Island is suitable for trekking and horseback riding.

Use of the trail is free, except when it passes through a national park (where the normal entrance fee is charged). In national parks, camping facilities are normally available, and, because the project has been developed in close collaboration with the communities along its path, some of these offer basic accommodations as well as an opportunity to pick up provisions. However, elsewhere, visitors are literally on their own – except for the company of the wildlife and the unparalleled scenery.

The Chilean trail is being developed jointly by the National Commission for the Environment (Conama) and the National Tourism Service (Sernatur). Further information can be found at www.senderodechile.cl (in Spanish) or by contacting Conama on (02) 240 5611. ❑

THE SKILLS AND THRILLS OF THE RODEO

The horse is the star of Chile's national sport, demonstrating skills of patience and agility, with the help of its close companion, the *huaso*

The stocky Chilean horse, or *corralero*, is the inseparable companion of the horseman, or *huaso*. This working pair still dominates in the movement of stock in the Chilean countryside. The *huaso* and his horse are also the protagonists in one of Chile's national sports – the rodeo.

Most rodeos are held between September and May. The most famous is the Chilean Championship, held at the end of March in Rancagua, in the Central Valley. In a semicircular arena, or *medialuna*, a pair of riders and their mounts attempt to chase and maneuver a steer to a padded section of wall. Here it must be stopped and held by direct horse-to-steer body contact. The curved shape of the corral means the horse must learn to gallop sideways, an extremely difficult task. The *huasos* must work in close, fast coordination, one chasing the steer, the other hemming it close to the wall. This exercise produces spectacular shows of horsemanship, with horses spinning about on their back legs, changing direction, rearing, and galloping as they track the steer about the ring. Riders earn *puntos buenos* (good points) or *puntos malos* (bad points) depending on where they hit the steer, if brute force is used (the rougher, the more bad points), and their appearance.

ABOVE: unlike Australian and American rodeos, in Chile there is no roping or riding of wild beasts, although the animal still gets knocked about somewhat.
BELOW: at the end of the rodeo, the prize-giving takes place. The horses rest, but the winning *huaso* is in for a long night of dancing and feasting.

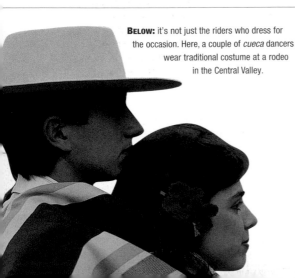

BELOW: it's not just the riders who dress for the occasion. Here, a couple of *cueca* dancers wear traditional costume at a rodeo in the Central Valley.

DANCING WITH THE DEVIL

After the excitement of a rodeo, a hearty meal of beef and beans is knocked back with red wine. Then out from the pockets come the handkerchiefs for the *cueca*, Chile's national dance. The *cueca* is an integral part of the event, and a *huaso* is not roundly accomplished if his Cuban-heeled boots don't do a coordinated stomp.

To begin the *cueca* (pronounced like "quaker"), the man first advances toward his female partner in a courting fashion. She, keeping her distance, establishes the pattern of pursuer and pursued. Folklore has it that the dance is inspired by a rooster stalking a hen. As the courting continues, both partners hold their handkerchiefs aloft and flick them about as they step in a smooth, shuffling manner. The dance must be accompanied by festive music and a crowd of clapping onlookers, spurring the man on in his hot pursuit.

The *cueca* produces such a high-spirited response that Chileans believe even the devil himself can't help but uncrumple his scarf and join in with a young *señorita*.

HT: appearance is so important
huasos may have their sombrero
ed beside the ring, to ensure a
rim during the
petition.

ABOVE: a *huaso's* Cuban-heeled boots sport large spoked spurs, ensuring a melodic jangle when he walks. He also wears finely plaited, tasseled leather leggings.
BELOW: a well-stocked *talabartería*, or saddlery, will offer an impressive selection of hand-made leather tack and carved wooden stirrups.

PLACES

A detailed guide to the entire country, with
principal sites clearly cross-referenced to
specially drawn maps

Despite its elongated shape, Chile is one of the easiest
countries in South America to travel around. Domestic
flights connect the country's major cities; modern
passenger buses run to almost every minor town (and depart
punctually every time), and passenger boats link remote locations in the far south.

Almost all travelers flying into Chile arrive in the bustling
capital of Santiago. At the country's midway point, Santiago is
the logical base for exploring. Just a 90-minute drive away is the
capital's colorful port city, Valparaíso, while neighboring Viña del Mar is
one of Chile's most popular beach resorts. Irregular flights from Santiago
also reach the Juan Fernández Islands, famous as the temporary home of
the Scottish sailor whose experiences inspired the novel *Robinson Crusoe*.

The landscape north of Santiago becomes progressively drier as it
extends toward the hauntingly beautiful Atacama Desert. Many travelers
fly directly to Calama, support town for the spectacular Chuquicamata
copper mine, before heading for the oasis village of San Pedro de Atacama. In the vicinity are ancient pre-Columbian ruins, thermal springs,
salt flats, and dramatic geyser fields.

Most of Chile's vineyards are located south of Santiago in
the lush Central Valley. Farther south, beyond the River
Biobío, lies Chile's most famous attraction, the Lake District,
with its spectacular rivers, volcanoes, forests, and lakes. The
fishing port of Puerto Montt marks the end of the Lake
District. South of this point, the landscape becomes wilder
and travel more unpredictable, although boat cruises
through the southern archipelago are popular. Aisén is a vast area of
woods and glaciers opened up over the past 25 years by the Carretera
Austral road. Then come the sheep plains of Magallanes and Parque
Nacional Torres del Paine. At the southernmost tip of Chile is the windswept island of Tierra del Fuego, shared with Argentina.

Chile's most remote outpost is Easter Island, 3,800km (2,360 miles) west
of the mainland. This mysterious speck of land covered with ancient statues continues to attract and intrigue visitors from all over the world. ❑

PRECEDING PAGES: Atacama Desert; Puerto Varas; Valle de la Luna. **LEFT:** Volcán
Osorno. **ABOVE LEFT**: sign for a volcano trek. **ABOVE RIGHT**: cacti in northern Chile.

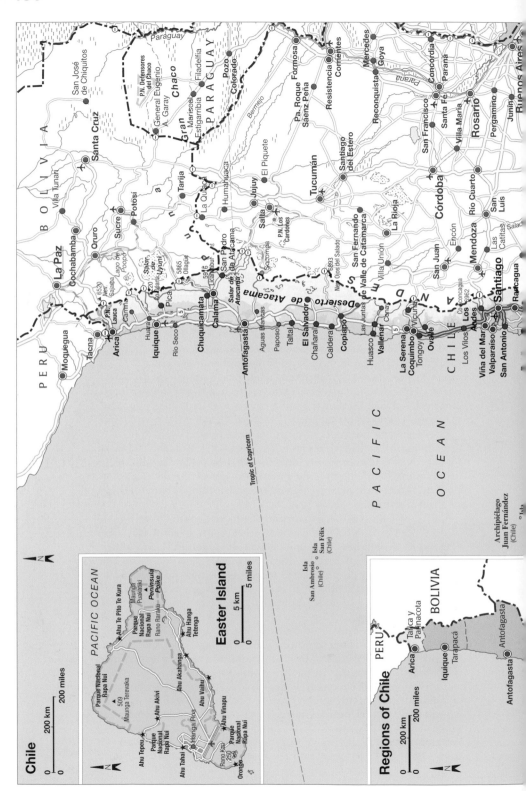

Chile

0 200 km
0 200 miles

Easter Island

PACIFIC OCEAN

Ahu Te Pito Te Kura

Maunga
Puakatiki
▲
Peninsula
Poike

Parque
Nacional
Rapa Nui

Rano Raraku

Ahu Hanga
Tetenga

Ahu
Akahanga

Ahu Vaihu

Ahu Vinapu

Parque
Nacional
Rapa Nui

Ahu Tahai

Hanga Roa

Rano Kau
250
Orongo

Ahu Tepeu

Parque Nacional
Rapa Nui

509
Maunga Terevaka

Ahu Akivi

0 5 km
0 5 miles

Isla
San Ambrosio
(Chile)

Isla
San Félix
(Chile)

Regions of Chile

0 200 km
0 200 miles

PERU

Tacna y
Parinacota

Arica

BOLIVIA

Iquique

Tarapacá

Antofagasta

Antofagasta

PACIFIC OCEAN

SANTIAGO

Elegant colonial architecture, bustling pavement cafés, and colorful street performers give Chile's capital city a cosmopolitan feel

Map on page 142

Santiago

Main Attractions
PALACIO DE LA MONEDA
CERRO SANTA LUCÌA
PLAZA DE ARMAS
MUSEO CHILENO DE ARTE PRECOLOMBINO
MERCADO CENTRAL
MUSEO NACIONAL DE BELLAS ARTES
CERRO SAN CRISTÓBAL
BARRIO BELLAVISTA

PRECEDING PAGES: Andean backdrop. **LEFT:** Bellavista. **BELOW:** taking in the view.

W hen Chilean children draw or paint, in the background there is almost always a stylized line of snow-capped mountains. In Santiago, it is easy to see why. Rising immediately alongside the city, the Andes are a constant presence, albeit a shadowy one in the city's habitual smog, but still engraving themselves on the minds and subconscious of *santiaguinos* from birth. For the visitor, they not only impress with their beauty (above all when bathed in the rose-colored light of a clear sunset), but also serve a very practical purpose: it is hard to lose your bearings in Santiago.

So long, that is, as the smog does not cloud your vision. Air pollution is a serious problem in Santiago, whose streets are often clogged with motor traffic. The pollution is worsened by the city's almost windless location between the Andes and nearby hills, making one wish fervently that the Spanish conquistador Pedro de Valdivia had been forewarned about the internal combustion engine before siting Santiago here in 1541. But this is the only real drawback to a gently attractive and unpretentious city, whose people, though less effusive than others in Latin America, are friendly and always ready to welcome foreigners. Endowed with an ideal Mediterranean, or Californian, climate it is a pleasant place to visit at any time of year.

Santiago is also one of the most manageable capitals in Latin America

for the first-time visitor. It is a big city but, standing in the compact few blocks and narrow streets of its center, it's hard to believe you are at the heart of a conurbation of 6 million people. The city's sprawling extension gives it a feeling of spaciousness, despite the mountains; only in the center is there much of the sense of pressure and density characteristic of most cities of this size. The rest is residential suburbs: leafy avenues and sophisticated shopping malls in the plush *barrio alto* (high neighborhood), and vast swathes of

well-tended middle-class neighborhoods and poor working-class areas – labyrinthine networks of tiny adobe and wooden dwellings, and bleak state-subsidized apartment blocks.

A European touch

Many visitors are struck by the European feel of Santiago, with its tidy grass verges and elegantly fading colonial buildings, but after three decades of free-market economics, the North American influence is more apparent in newly developed areas of the city. The old buildings of the city center were built by European architects, inspired by Paris and Rome, but the smoked glass and marble of the new *barrio alto* offices transport the visitor to Chicago or Houston rather than a European capital.

Getting around the city is easy. A brief glance at a map – there's an excellent A to Z booklet that comes with the Santiago phone book, as well as those you can pick up at bookshops and kiosks – will reveal just how straightforward the city is. You're almost bound to enter the city along

the **Avenida Libertador General Bernardo O'Higgins**. This broad avenue, named after the Chilean-Irish independence hero and father of the republic, has been the city's main thoroughfare since a fork of the River Mapocho was filled in before independence to create it. It is known universally as "the Alameda" (a word of Arab origin meaning an avenue with trees and spaces for recreation).

If you enter Santiago on the old road from the airport, rather than taking the ring road or the new Costanera Norte highway, your first main point of reference will be the imposing wrought iron of the **Estación Central**, the city's only remaining functioning railway station. Surrounded by the hue and cry of one of the city's most popular and active commercial sectors, the station is well worth a look.

The heart of Santiago

The ugly concrete telecommunications tower run by the company Entel announces the beginning of the city center proper. A block farther on, the Alameda broadens, and the low form of

The Entel telecommunications tower – one of the city's less attractive landmarks.

BELOW: watching the world go by in Bellavista.

the presidential palace, **La Moneda Ⓐ**, rises to the left. La Moneda, so called because it was originally designed by the Italian architect Joaquín Toesca as the country's mint, was built between 1788 and 1805. Between 1846 and 1958, Chile's presidents lived there, sharing the premises with the mint until 1929. Squat by comparison with the high ministerial buildings around it (Toesca designed it low to resist earthquakes), many consider La Moneda one of the finest examples of colonial public buildings in the sub-continent.

The building's tragic international fame came with the military coup led by General Augusto Pinochet on September 11, 1973, when much of its interior was destroyed by rocketing from Air Force Hawker Hunters and its image, smoke and flames belching from its northern side, leaped onto the world's front pages and TV screens. It was here that the deposed president, the socialist Dr Salvador Allende, committed suicide during the onslaught.

The newly restored palace was re-inaugurated in 1981 as the seat of gov-ernment. The patios of the palace are open to the public (daily 10am–6pm; identification document required), and free guided tours of some of the beautifully restored rooms, with their prime collection of Chilean painting, can be arranged by appointment (tel: 02-690 4000).

Around La Moneda

In front of the palace's main entrance, in the **Plaza de la Constitución**, former presidents Jorge Alessandri and Eduardo Frei, the father of President Frei who was elected in 1993, and Salvador Allende stare at each other from their pedestals on opposite sides of the square. The plaza was remodeled by General Pinochet, who built underneath it a complex network of meeting rooms, offices, an emergency war room, and a television studio for making broadcasts to the nation, all known popularly as *el bunker* – the entrances are visible on three sides of the square. On the west side of the plaza is what was the luxury **Hotel Carrera** and is now the Ministry of Foreign Affairs. It was from the upper stories of the Car-

BELOW: the former National Congress building.

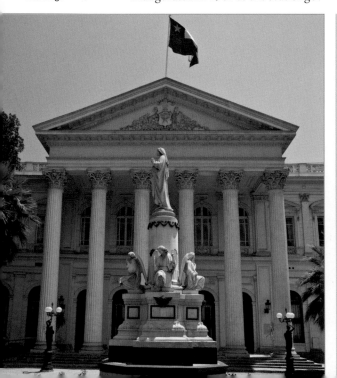

Urban Transformation

Over the last 50 years, Santiago has grown from a compact city of 2 million inhabitants to one that, with a population of 6 million, has spread east up the Andes foothills, creating the prosperous residential districts of La Dehesa and Lo Barnechea. To the north, new housing estates with large gardens, favored by middle-class families with young children, have also sprung up on what was once agricultural land. The working-class districts of southern Santiago have expanded all the way up to Puente Alto, a former country town that has become a major dormitory with its own subway link to the city center. New business centers have also appeared and, although many banks still have their headquarters in downtown Santiago, other businesses have moved to the more fashionable El Bosque and El Golf districts.

rera that the bombing of La Moneda during the 1973 coup was filmed.

On the south side of the palace is the **Plaza de la Ciudadanía**, inaugurated in 2006, and one of a number of projects planned with a view to Chile's celebration of the bicentenary of its independence in 2010. Underneath the esplanade, with its glistening expanses of water, lies the **Centro Cultural Palacio de la Moneda**, a beautifully designed arts center, all three levels of which have natural light. As well as exhibition rooms, it houses a collection of Chilean films, which are shown regularly in its cinema, and an excellent craft shop (www.ccplm.cl; daily 9am–9pm; exhibitions daily 10am–7.30pm; charge).

Across the Alameda is the Plaza O'Higgins, flanked by the headquarters of the armed forces and the Carabinero police. Every day at 10am, a green-uniformed, jackbooted detail of the Carabinero palace guard, a special unit whose members are selected for their height, marches from the Carabinero HQ to La Moneda in an impressive changing-of-the-guard ceremony.

Buildings of the colonial era

Continuing along the Alameda, past the **Banco del Estado** on the left (believed to have been the largest building in Latin America on its completion in 1945), is the **Club de la Unión**, Latin America's oldest and plushest gentleman's club, membership of which is still a much-prized goal for Chile's male conservative elite. The building, inaugurated in 1925, is lavishly decorated inside in Louis XIV and XV, Gothic, and other European styles. All the club's tableware was specially imported from France, Spain, and England, and it has an excellent collection of Chilean art.

Opposite, on the southern side of the Alameda is the yellow-washed central campus building of the **University of Chile ⓑ**. The building, begun in 1863, was designed by Lucien Henault, one of the contracted French architects who founded the neoclassical style which dominated Chilean public architecture of the time and hence much of the profile of Santiago's city center. Outside is a statue of the university's founder, the Venezue-

Santiago's efficient Metro system provides a cheap and easy way to get around the city.

BELOW: underground art: Centro Cultural Palacio de la Moneda.

lan exile Andrés Bello, one of the continent's great intellectual figures of the 19th century.

Back on the north side of the Alameda, beyond Calle Bandera, is the **Paseo Ahumada**, a busy pedestrian walkway that bisects the city center from north to south. This is the natural entry to the center, to which we'll return shortly. Meanwhile, on the other side of the Alameda again, is one of Santiago's best-known landmarks: the red-washed colonial church of **San Francisco ❻** (daily, closed Sun 2–6pm), the oldest in the capital. Franciscan friars built the first church on this site in 1572 to house the "Virgen del Socorro" (the Helpful Virgin), which Pedro de Valdivia himself brought to South America, firmly attached to his saddle. The original adobe church was destroyed by an earthquake in 1583 and replaced by a stone church, the nave of which survives, that was completed in 1612. The church's distinctive tower was added in 1860. The "Virgen del Socorro," of Italian or Spanish origin, was declared the patron of Santiago by the conquistadors after she was said to have saved them during the first major Mapuche attack in the Mapocho Valley by appearing before them and throwing dirt into the attackers' eyes. Much-venerated, she can still be seen above the church's main altar.

Inside the church, note the wooden ceiling, built in the first half of the 17th century. Its original Mudéjar-style decoration was replaced in a 19th-century neoclassical restoration. The attractive cedarwood choir stalls are the oldest in Chile. The museum in the adjacent Franciscan monastery (Mon–Fri 9.30am–1.30pm and 3–6pm, Sun 10am–2pm; charge) has a fine collection of Chilean and Peruvian colonial art, including 54 large-scale paintings of the life of San Francisco.

Behind the square outside the church is the quaint **Barrio París-Londres**, two short streets named after these European capitals, whose houses, designed as a whole by a group of architects in the 1920s, jumble together imitations of styles ranging from neoclassical to Mudéjar and Gothic. The next structure of note is the **Biblioteca Nacional ❼**, which occupies the main part of a block

BELOW: picturesque Cerro Santa Lucía.

on the northern side of the Alameda. The imposing building, in late 19th-century French style, opened in 1924 and houses one of Latin America's largest national libraries and archives, with a reading room open to the public and free concerts, talks, and film shows (Mon–Sat, closed Sat pm; free guided tours can be arranged by appointment; tel: 02-360 5288).

Landmarks of character

Beyond the Biblioteca is one of Santiago's most curious and historically significant sites, the **Cerro Santa Lucía E**. It was here, on what was then a rocky outcrop known by the indigenous people as Huelén (Pain), that Pedro de Valdivia and his 150 men first encamped, and Valdivia decided to found the city. He renamed the *cerro* (hill) after the saint of the date on which he reached it, December 13, 1540. In August 1834, Charles Darwin stayed for a week in Santiago and climbed the "little hillock of rock," noting the striking view. A plaque on the hill commemorates his visit. In 1872, the great historian and intend-

ant of Santiago, Benjamín Vicuña Mackenna, began to transform the hill into the baroque maze of pathways, gardens, fountains, and squares which it is now.

Together with the **Parque Forestal** by the River Mapocho, the Cerro is one of the city's best-loved venues for lovers and strollers. There is a lift on the west side, on Calle Santa Lucía.

At the foot of the Cerro, on the Alameda, is a fine mural in homage to Gabriela Mistral, representing the poet herself and the main themes of her work. A few yards farther on, a smooth rock is set in the skirt of the hill, engraved with an extract of a letter sent by Pedro de Valdivia to Emperor Charles V in 1545, extolling Chile's climatic virtues.

The Cerro marks the end of the city center as such, and the start of the last stretch of the Alameda. On its north side is the vast and, to many, hideous **Diego Portales building F**, erected in record speed and constructivist style in 1972 (part of which was destroyed by fire in 2006 and is being rebuilt as an arts center). General Pin-

Gabriela Mistral (1889–1957) was the first person in Latin America to be awarded the Nobel Prize for Literature, in 1945. See also page 190.

BELOW: changing of the guard at the Presidential Palace.

In the Banco de Chile on Ahumada, between Agustinas and Huérfanos, the old wooden cash desks are still in use.

BELOW: stained-glass window in former Bank of Chile building.

ochet's government made it the HQ of the military junta, and now it is the Defense Ministry.

Just across the road stands the Carabineros' church, the small neo-Gothic **Iglesia de San Francisco de Borja**, and in front of it a monument to members of the police force who were killed in the line of duty. Immediately afterwards is the Crowne Plaza Hotel, located opposite one of the city's best art cinemas, the Cine Arte Alameda.

A few meters farther on, the Alameda ends at the junction with Avenida Vicuña Mackenna and the Plaza Italia (also referred to as Plaza Baquedano), centered on the equestrian statue of General Manuel Baquedano, commander of the Chilean army during the War of the Pacific against Peru and Bolivia. This spot marks the end of central Santiago and the beginning of Providencia and the *barrio alto*. It is therefore a good point to retrace your steps and return to the Paseo Ahumada (by metro, three stops to Universidad de Chile). In the Universidad de Chile station, the giant murals *(see picture, page 152)* are by Chilean painter Mario Toral.

Shopping and business

If the Alameda is the center's main thoroughfare for motor traffic, Ahumada is the pedestrian hub. Everyone – shoppers, businesspeople, and street artists – seems to converge there. Business gossip is exchanged in cafés like the Haiti, where miniskirted young women serve *expresos* and *cortados* (black and white coffee) with glasses of mineral water. Crowds press past the Paseo's many and varied shops, banks, department stores, and well-stocked newspaper kiosks.

To the left of Ahumada is the *barrio cívico*, a few blocks built in the 1930s around La Moneda in rigorously utilitarian style. This area holds the **Intendencia** (corner of Moneda and Morandé), the **Stock Exchange** (Calle La Bolsa, just behind the Club de la Unión), the **Banco del Estado**, the **Central Bank**, and most government ministries.

Uptown from Ahumada, three blocks along Calle Agustinas, is the 17th-century church of **San Agustín**, site of an interesting wooden crucifix above the northern altar carved in Peru in 1613 (daily, closed Sun pm). Beyond the church is the **Teatro Municipal** . Designed and restored by French architects – its original plans were approved by Charles Garnier, the architect of the Paris Opera – the theater opened in 1857. Housing the city's symphony orchestra and ballet and opera companies (all of them considered among the finest on the continent), the theater has played host to artists from Sarah Bernhardt to Plácido Domingo, who appeared there in 1990. Opposite the theater is perhaps the city's finest example of the influence of late 19th-century French architecture: a house built by the millionaire wine-producing family of French origin, the Subercaseaux, now occupied by the Air Force Officers' Club and a bank.

Street life and sacred art

Ahumada ends in the **Plaza de Armas** , the city's historic center. Originally traced out by Pedro de Valdivia in 1541, it takes its name from the weapons held in the fort built in the square to shelter the first settlers at night. Thereafter, the plaza was used for all public activities from troop parades and religious processions to hangings. It is always a hive of activity: shoe-shiners, portrait painters, and pentecostal preachers ply their trades while chess players gather on the bandstand on the eastern side of the Plaza.

The **Cathedral** ❶ (daily, closed Sun pm), on the west side of the plaza, is the fifth on the site. Its predecessors were destroyed by earthquakes in 1552, 1647, and 1730, while the first was burned down in an attack by native people shortly after Pedro de Valdivia built it. Work on the present building began in 1747, but the final design was by Joaquín Toesca, who was brought from Italy for this task, moving on later to La Moneda (*see page 144*) – though the twin towers were not added until 1899 by another Italian, Ignacio Cremonesi. The cathedral's internal decoration bears the somewhat heavy imprint of the Bavarian Jesuits who created much of it, although some of their work, and important local handicraft adornments, were destroyed by clumsy restoration carried out by Cremonesi. Those buried in the cathedral

Many stores in the city center stay open until 7.30pm.

BELOW: the city's historic Cathedral on the Plaza de Armas.

Fresh fish on sale in the Mercado Central.

BELOW: Natural History Museum.
BELOW RIGHT: mid-morning coffee.

include the four Carrera brothers, partners and rivals with O'Higgins in the country's liberation from Spain (*see page 36*), and Diego Portales (*see page 39*), considered by many as the founder of Chile's 19th-century conservative state. After the Conquest, the land along the northern face of the plaza was owned by Pedro de Valdivia, who lived in a house on the site now occupied by the **Correo Central** (central post office). In 1541, however, the house was burned down in an attack by native people; later, Valdivia sold the land to the Royal Treasury in order to finance further expeditions south. Two centuries later, the post office site saw the city's first, and reputedly magnificent, theater. Chile's first stamps, printed in England, were sold here in 1857 and the present building was finished in 1902.

Palaces and museums

Next door to the Correo Central is the Palacio de la Real Audiencia, now the **Museo Histórico Nacional** (Tue–Sun 10am–5.30pm; charge, except Sun), which was inaugurated in 1808 to house the sessions at which the Spanish Crown's representatives heard local reports and dispensed justice. This purpose was short-lived, however, and two years later the building was used for the swearing-in of the first revolutionary government junta. The first Congress met here, and the palace was the seat of government until President Bulnes moved to La Moneda in 1846. The museum, which contains some 12,000 pieces from prehistory until the 1930s, moved there in 1982 and is well worth a visit.

The last building along the plaza's northern edge is the **Municipalidad** or Town Hall (Mon–Fri 9am–2pm). Formerly the Palacio Consistorial, it was designed by Toesca for the colonial *cabildo* and opened in 1790. The facade was replaced in the 1800s by the present neoclassical design, and restored again after the 1985 earthquake. High on the facade, and in the wrought ironwork above the entrance, you can see the red lion coat of arms granted to the city by the Spanish Crown after the first *cabildo* met. In front is an equestrian statue of Pedro de Valdivia donated by Chile's Spanish community in 1986.

On Calle Merced, at the southeast corner of the square, is the striking red-washed **Casa Colorada**. Built in 1769, this is the best-preserved colonial house in the city. It was the residence of the president of the first revolutionary junta, Mateo de Toro y Zambrano and, for a time, of Lord Thomas Cochrane, the maverick Scottish admiral hired by O'Higgins to command naval operations against Spain. Now it houses a tourist office and the **Museo de Santiago ❶** (Tue–Sat 10am–6pm, Sun 10am–2pm; charge, except Sun), dedicated to the history of the capital. This has didactic models of the city, but few real exhibits. Plaza de Armas has two pavement cafés, neither of which serve very good coffee but, behind the Casa Colorada, there is a small plaza, sheltered from the city noise, with a restaurant that is a good place for a coffee or light lunch.

Two blocks westward, the excellent **Museo Chileno de Arte Precolombino ❿** (Bandera 361; www.precolombino.cl; Tue–Sun 10am–6pm) occupies what used to be the Real Aduana (Customs House). Access is by way of an arcade built through the building on the corner. This museum is widely recognized as the best and most important in Santiago. Immediately west are the Law Courts, and across Calle Compañía is the neo-classical grandeur of what was the pre-1973 Congress Building. Previously, this was the site of the Jesuit headquarters (hence the name of the street, after the Compañía de Jesús), until they were expelled from the country in 1766, and later of a church which burned down in 1863, at the cost of 2,000 lives. Also close by is the curious but sadly run down **Palacio de la Alhambra** (Compañía 1340; Mon–Fri 11am–2pm and 5–8pm), begun in the 1860s and later transformed into a miniature copy of the famous Mudéjar palace of the same name in Granada, Spain, complete with mock-Arab furniture made in Paris.

Wrought-iron splendor

Back in the Plaza de Armas, if you're feeling hungry and like seafood, you can do no better than walk north along

BELOW: inside the huge wrought-iron Mercado Central.

The water fountains in the Plaza la Avación, near the Salvador metro station in Providencia, are sometimes lit up with a dazzling array of colors.

BELOW: the colorful Universidad de Chile metro station.

Calle Puente (the continuation of the Paseo Ahumada) to the **Mercado Central** (daily until 5pm). This, together with **La Vega**, on the other side of the River Mapocho, is the city's central market. Bustling with the character of such markets around the world, both the interior and the exterior of this elegant structure are worthy of attention. Designed in Chile but built in England, the market was inaugurated in 1872 by Vicuña Mackenna as the site of a national exhibition to celebrate the thrusting and confident economy of the time. It is full of cheap eating places, and above all *marisquerías* where cheap and abundant portions of Chile's remarkable seafood are served, considered by many the best in the world.

Here, too, is the fine, copper-roofed shell of what used to be Santiago's second railway station, the **Estación Mapocho**. Opened in 1912, and designed by another of Chile's leading French architects, Emile Jécquier, this once served as the terminus for trains arriving from the coast, but it is now an arts and convention center.

An artistic park

The Parque Forestal, which is generally referred to by Chileans as their Bois de Boulogne, was laid out by the French landscaper Georges Dubois in the late 19th century. The idea was to make use of the wasteland left over after the canalization of the Mapocho in its now characteristic stone course. Looking at the generally narrow flow of the Mapocho (a name which in Mapuche means "river which loses itself in the land," in reference to its partially subterranean course west of Santiago), it is hard to believe that it is capable of swelling suddenly with torrents of melting snow or rain from the Andes. In the past, flooding caused several disasters and was dealt with first by wide stone embankments, or *tajamares*, built by the Italian architect Toesca, then by the present channel.

Planted with varieties of native and imported trees, the park contains several small squares and monuments to figures such as Columbus, Bach, the god Pan, and the seminal Nicaraguan modernist poet, Rubén Dario (opposite Merced 230), who wrote his most

Public Transport Moans

In 2007, a new bad word entered the Chilean vocabulary – Transantiago. This is the name of an ambitious public transportation system launched in the capital in February 2007. Designed to rationalize the city's complex spider web of bus routes, reducing road congestion and air and sound pollution, it instead resulted in long queues for overflowing buses, the virtual collapse of the Metro, the city's subway, and enormous public anger. As new bus lanes have been built and the number of buses has increased, service standards have gradually improved but not enough to prevent a shift to car use, defeating one of Transantiago's key aims. And Santiaguinos still haven't forgotten the misery it caused and are only too happy to explain Transantiago's iniquities – at length.

important work, *Azul*, while exiled in Chile in the 1890s.

Halfway along the park, close to the northern tip of the Cerro Santa Lucía, is the **Museo Nacional de Bellas Artes** Ⓜ (Tue–Sun 10am–6.50pm; charge, except Sun), the country's principal art gallery. Designed by Jéquier as an approximate copy of the Petit Palais in Paris, it owns a rich collection of contemporary and past Chilean art, although sadly little is on permanent display, as well as hosting visiting exhibitions. The University of Chile's collection of Chilean art from the first half of the 20th century is housed in the **Museo de Arte Contemporáneo** in renovated premises in the back part of the building (Tue–Sat 11am–7pm, Sun 11am–6pm; charge). Farther east still is the extraordinary **Palacio Bruna**, another turn-of-the-20th-century mansion designed in part by one of Chile's leading poets, Pedro Prado, who studied architecture without ever graduating. It is now occupied by the National Chamber of Commerce.

Shortly before you reach the *palacio*, a few steps backtracking along Calle Merced takes you to Calle José Victorino Lastarria and the pleasant **Plaza Mulato Gil de Castro** Ⓝ. The **Museo de Artes Visuales** (Tue–Sun 10.30am–6.30pm; charge) in the plaza holds a small but choice private collection of Chilean painting and sculpture from the 1960s onwards. The adjoining **Museo Arqueológico de Santiago** is also worth a visit (Tue–Sun 10.30am–6.30pm; charge except Sun). Nearby is the **Biógrafo** art cinema. The Parque ends with the extravagantly symbolic **Fuente Alemana**, representing Chile and its wealth of natural resources. This monument was presented by the country's German community in 1910 for the first centenary of Independence, and its fountains serve as an impromptu bathing pool for schoolchildren. Note, too, the strange Art Deco house, complete with mythological beast, at Merced 84.

Elevated views

We are now back at the **Plaza Italia**, shadowed on the left by the looming shape of the **Cerro San Cristóbal**,

The CTC telephone company's tall corporate building on Plaza Italia is designed in the shape of a cellphone.

BELOW: the Museo Nacional de Bellas Artes.

TIP

The government tourist
service, Sernatur, has
its main office in the old
Providencia fruit and
vegetable market
(Providencia 1550).

which was named after St Christopher, the patron saint of travelers, by the Spanish because of the landmark it offered to travelers. To reach the Cerro, cross the river by the **Pío Nono bridge** and proceed past the 1930s pile of the University of Chile's Law School up Calle Pío Nono. At the far end is the entrance to the **Parque Metropolitano**, the park containing the Cerro's attractions. You can tour the Cerro completely by car, a minibus service, or on foot. But a more picturesque route is to ascend by the 60-year-old funicular (Mon–Fri 10am–8.30pm, closed Mon am), following in the footsteps of Pope John Paul II, who rose to bless the city during his 1987 visit in his bullet-proof "pope-mobile."

Perched halfway up the hill is the **Zoo** (Tue–Sun 10am–5pm, until 6pm in summer; charge), and at the top there are lookout points and the **Santuario de la Inmaculada Concepción** (Shrine of the Virgin Mary). In front of the nearby chapel is a tree from the Basque town of Guernica, planted by Chile's Basque community. The 14-meter (46ft) high statue of the Virgin, dating from

1908, is frequently the focus of religious ceremonies.

From here you can take a 10-minute ride in the Swiss cable-car (Mon 2.30–8pm, Tue–Fri 12.30–8pm, weekends 10.30am–8.30pm), opened in 1980, along the length of the Cerro and linking the hills to the end of Avenida Pedro de Valdivia, in Providencia, with an optional stop on the way at the Tupahue gardens and public swimming pool. Other attractions in the park include cafés, restaurants, Chilean and Japanese gardens, a wine-sampling center and exhibition (Camino Real), and another open-air swimming pool.

Tickets can be purchased for part or all of the round trip at the foot of the funicular and at the end of the cable-car. This trip is particularly worthwhile for its view of the snow-capped Andes if you happen to be in Santiago in winter, after a day of rain has washed the city's air clean of smog.

From Plaza Italia, you can also take the metro (Line 5, southbound) to visit the **Museo Interactivo Mirador** (Sebastopol 90, La Granja), an interactive science museum that children enjoy enormously (daily 9.30am–5.30pm, open until 6.30pm in summer, closed Mon pm; charge). From the Mirador metro station, *colectivos* (communal taxis) run to the door of the museum. The visit is also an opportunity to get a glimpse of one of Santiago's working-class suburbs.

Artists' quarter

The area between the Cerro and the Mapocho is called **Bellavista**, which is the closest Santiago gets to a bohemian barrio. This is a mixed residential and artistic neighborhood with lots of charm and interest. Nobel poet Pablo Neruda had one of his houses, **La Chascona**, here *(see page 174)*. This house is now open to the public (Fernando Márquez de la Plata 0192; Tue–Sun 10am–6pm; charge).

Bellavista's main streets, apart from Pío Nono, are Purísima, running paral-

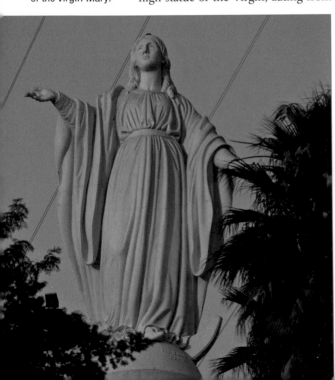

BELOW: the Shrine of the Virgin Mary.

lel, and Antonia López de Bello, cutting across laterally. A great variety of restaurants are scattered through the barrio. There are also several theaters, and at night there is considerable street life, with musicians, and handicrafts sold from the pavement. Calle Bellavista itself has a string of more tourist-oriented shops specializing in Chile's national stone, lapiz lazuli.

Bellavista is skirted along the Mapocho by Avenida Santa María, the fast route uptown to the wealthy neighborhoods of **Las Condes**, **Vitacura**, **La Dehesa**, and **Lo Curro**. The last is home to the huge and unmistakable modernistic presidential residence built by General Pinochet, but never occupied after the scandal it produced; now it is the army's country club. Along the way, Santa María crosses under the Américo Vespucio loop road, which from here provides a rapid freeway connection around the north of the city to Arturo Merino Benítez airport – a useful way of avoiding the city center for trips between the airport and the upper *barrio alto*.

Embassies and ice creams

Across the river from Bellavista, Avenida Providencia runs uptown from the Plaza Italia. In Plaza Italia, the Telefónica building has a ground-floor art gallery that puts on excellent exhibitions (daily 10am–8pm; free). Several squares cluster around the point at which the Alameda becomes Providencia, with monuments to several historical figures, including the Cuban independence leader José Martí and the hero of Chile's Independence War, Manuel Rodríguez. Between Providencia and the river is the long Parque Balmaceda, with children's amusements and the Café Literario, a bookstore and coffee shop.

Avenida Providencia continues on through the shopping and residential area into Avenida Apoquindo, its continuation under another name, now the site of some of the city's most modern office blocks. This is also a good place from which to walk towards Avenida Isidora Goyenechea, the heart of the El Golf neighborhood where, on Sundays, there is a small antiques market in Plaza Perú. ❑

Waiting tables in a Bellavista café.

BELOW: bohemian Bellavista.

RESTAURANTS, CAFÉS, AND BARS

Restaurants

Prices are per person for a three-course meal, not including drinks.

$ = under US$15
$$ = US$15–25
$$$ = US$25–35

El Centro

Blue Jar
Almirante Gotuzzo 102
Tel: (02) 696 1890
www.bluejar.cl
$$$
An oasis of good food in crowded downtown Santiago; closed at weekends.

Cívico
Centro Cultural Palacio de la Moneda
Plaza de la Ciudadanía
Tel: (02) 671 4260
www.civicochile.cl
$$$

This relatively new restaurant, which specializes in meat, is expensive, but quiet. In summer, it provides a welcome respite from the hot pavements above.

Donde Augusto
Mercado Central
Calle Puente
Tel: (02) 672 2829
$$
Fish and shellfish served in downtown Santiago's fruit and vegetable market from early morning through to late afternoon; crowded, but well worth a visit.

Fulano Zutano Mengano
Agustinas 1352
Tel: (02) 290 5700
$$
Simple but imaginative international dishes; a favorite of officials from all the nearby government offices. Mon–Fri, lunch only.

Parque Forestal/ Lastarria

Café de las Artes
Monjitas 404
Tel: (02) 632 3017
$
Ideal for a coffee or light lunch after visiting one of the nearby museums. Also open every night until 11pm.

Café Escondido
Rosal 346C
Tel: (02) 632 7356
$$
This bar, hidden at the end of a small street, is the perfect place for a quiet drink in the evening.

Emporio La Rosa
Merced 291
Tel: (02) 638 9257
$
Seating is a problem at lunch time but this is a great place to buy a snack to eat in the nearby park or one of the ice creams for which it is famous.

Kintaro
Monjitas 460
Tel: (02) 638 2448
$
One of Chile's first Japanese restaurants continues to turn out good food at very moderate prices.

El Txoko Alaves
Mosqueto 485
Tel: (02) 638 2494
$$
Local regulars and tourists mix happily in this Spanish restaurant and the service is just as friendly whether you order a full lunch, or dinner, or just a glass of wine and some tapas.

Bellavista

Galindo
Dardignac 098
Tel: (02) 777 0116
www.galindo.cl
$$
Hearty Chilean food in an old adobe house.

Muñeca Brava
Malinkrodt 170
Tel: (02) 732 1338
$$
Decorated with props from movies, this is a Bellavista classic, serving international and Mexican food.

Patio Bellavista
Pío Nono 40–50
Tel: (02) 777 4582
www.patiobellavista.cl
$–$$
A lively restaurant and arts and crafts center located in the heart of Bellavista, with options ranging from Italian and Peruvian food to sushi. There is also an Irish pub.

Il Siciliano
Dardignac 0102
Tel: (02) 737 2265
$$
Emulating an Italian trattoria from the 1930s, this restaurant has a great atmosphere.

Providencia

Aquí Está Coco
La Concepción 236
Tel: (02) 235 8649
$$$
One of the best places in the city to sample Chile's wonderful fish.

Astrid y Gastón
Antonio Bellet 201
Tel: (02) 650 9125
www.astrydygaston.com
$$$
Excellent Peruvian food in one of the city's most acclaimed restaurants; booking recommended.

Bar Liguria

This traditional bar has three branches in Providencia:
Avenida Providencia 1373
Tel: (02) 235 7914
Avenida Pedro de Valdivia 047
Tel: (02) 334 4346
Avenida Luis Thayer Ojeda 019;
Tel: (02) 231 1393
www.liguria.cl
$$
Liguria bars get packed so you may have to wait for a table. All serve meat and pasta, but try the famous *mechada* (beef) sandwiches.

Le Flaubert

Orrego Luco 0125
Tel: (02) 231 9424
$$
A quiet bistro; the perfect place for a French-style light lunch or afternoon tea. The garden at the back is lovely in summer.

El Huerto

Orrego Luco 054
Tel: (02) 233 2690
www.elhuerto.cl
$$
Good vegetarian food, with a cheaper version, La Huerta, next door.

El Toro

Santa Beatriz 280
Tel: (02) 235 5012
$$
Tasty Mediterranean food, a good wine list, and a great atmosphere. Also has a branch in Bellavista (Loreto 33).

Plaza Nuñoa

Bigas

Jorge Washington 164
Tel: (02) 453 6901
$
Restobar with a great terrace for a drink and some tapas or a simple meal.

La Tecla

Dr. Johow 320
Tel: (02) 274 3603
$

One of the stalwarts of nightlife around Plaza Ñuñoa, La Tecla specializes in pizzas and pancakes. Cheap and very cheerful.

El Bosque

Café Melba

Don Carlos 2898
Tel: (02) 232 4546
$$
Run by a New Zealander, this restaurant is popular with gringos; a great place for breakfast, lunch, or just a coffee.

La Chakra

Avenida Mariano Sanchéz Fontecilla 534
Tel: (02) 234 2138
$
On the other side of Avenida Apoquindo from the main El Bosque area, this small café serves vegetarian, mostly organic, food as well as selling organic produce. The homemade lemonade with mint is delicious.

Happening

Avenida Apoquindo 3090
Tel: (02) 233 2301
www.happening.cl
$$$
This local branch of an Argentine restaurant serves great meat; fast service.

Pinpilinpausha

Isidora Goyenechea 2900
Tel: (02) 233 6507
www.pinpilinpausha.cl
$$$
Excellent Spanish food is served at this traditional restaurant.

La Sal

Avenida Vitacura 2911
Tel: (02) 233 6312
$$
International menu which offers excellent value for money.

Vitacura

Borde Río

Avenida Monseñor Escrivá

de Balaguer 6400
www.borderio.cl
$$–$$$
This upmarket restaurant complex has some of Santiago's most fashionable restaurants, including Zanzibar and Le Due Torri, in a lovely setting by the river.

Europeo

Alonso de Córdova 2417
Tel: (02) 208 3603
$$$
Perhaps Santiago's best restaurant and one of its most expensive; the right place for a real splurge.

Le Fournil

Avenida Vitacura 3841
Tel: (02) 228 0219
$
A French bread shop that also serves light meals; the quiches are excellent.

La Mar

Nueva Costanera 3922
Tel: (02) 206 7839
$$$
Opened recently by the owners of Astrid y Gastón *(see opposite)*, this restaurant specializes in Peruvian-style fish. The *ceviches* (fish "cooked" in lemon juice) are excellent.

Mestizo

Avenida Bicentenario 4050
Tel: (09) 7477 6093
$$$
A stylish restaurant overlooking a park; in summer, the terrace is a great place for a drink while the sun sinks behind the hills.

Parque Arauco

Avenida Kennedy 5413
Tel: (02) 299 0500
www.parquearauco.cl
This shopping mall's open-air boulevard has over 20 restaurants, including branches of some of the best in the city, and is open on Sunday night when most other places are closed.

Puerto Fuy

Nueva Costanera 3969
Tel: (02) 208 8908
$$$
Fashionable and expensive restaurant serving excellent, imaginative dishes.

LEFT AND RIGHT: Santiago is home to many excellent restaurants, including the renowned Astrid y Gastón.

SANTIAGO EXCURSIONS

The countryside around Santiago is perfect for day trips, with numerous outdoor activities possible, from wallowing in hot mud to wine tasting, and skiing to sunbathing – and all amid gorgeous surroundings

Santiago

On an average day the jagged peaks of the Andes loom mistily over the eastern end of Santiago, a distant yet overbearing presence. In fact, you can travel within a day, by car or bus, far up into the mountains beside the winding course of the **Río Maipo**. This rushing torrent sweeps the loose earth of the mountains downstream toward the rich agricultural plains of Chile's central valley region, pouring itself finally into the Pacific, 4km (2½ miles) south of San Antonio. The Maipo Valley, or **Cajón del Maipo**, is a popular weekend venue for *santiaguinos* anxious to escape the relentless pace of the city streets for a few hours of fresh air and relaxation.

For the sedentary, the canyon offers an easy but visually seductive drive towards the mountains' heart; and for the more active, depending on the season, there are plenty of opportunities to swim (in open-air pools), ride horses, picnic, hike, camp, or cabin overnight. The river is too rough for regular canoeing or kayaking, but agencies like Cascada Expediciones *(see page 344)* offer raft rides all year round. You must be over 10 years old (or more, depending on the time of year and river conditions) and know how to swim.

There's also a surprising variety of wonderful country restaurants, with varied menus that include traditional Chilean foods, espresso coffee, and *küchen* that would be a credit to any German pastry chef. The delicious home cooking draws heavily on the canyon's almond, walnut, and cherry orchards. The canyon's economic base depends largely on tourism, but prices tend to be reasonable and the Chilean flavor of the area remains distinct.

Homemade produce

Driving up the winding road, especially on weekends, you'll see white flags and small tables by the roadside, piled with round breads of more than 30cm (1ft) in diameter. The white flags mean someone is selling something they've prepared in their kitchen: bread

Main Attractions
SAN JOSÉ DE MAIPO
MONUMENTO NATURAL EL MORADO
BAÑOS DE COLINA
PIRQUE
POMAIRE
ISLA NEGRA
FARELLONES

PRECEDING PAGES: Monumento Natural El Morado. **LEFT:** fresh cherries. **BELOW:** roadside fruit vendor.

Traditional basket-weaving uses designs and techniques that have been around for hundreds of years.

cooked in ashes, often in the traditional ovens of baked mud; jams made with local walnuts, almonds, and berries; fresh honey; the ubiquitous empanadas, as common in Chile as the hamburger is in the United States. The sight of the sellers' bread with *chicharrones* (fried pork skin) evokes nostalgic enthusiasm from most Chileans, especially those who have spent part of their childhood in the country.

Toward the summer's end (February), you may be lucky enough to have a prickly pear, or *tuna*, fall at your feet. This visually unappealing fruit should be handled carefully, to avoid the prickles. When peeled, it will yield a mouthful of melon-like flesh, full of pips small enough to swallow. Prickly pears are as common as apples in Chile, where they droop like large, green teardrops on cactus arms. *Tunas* are particularly popular crushed and blended into refreshing juices, with the pips filtered out.

Exploring the lower Andes

Strung out along the road are stopping points affording spectacular views of the canyon itself, as well as small towns and villages, campgrounds, parks, and an obelisk marking the site where, in 1986, the Manuel Rodríguez Patriotic Front (a Marxist guerrilla group) staged a daring ambush of General Augusto Pinochet's cavalcade, which almost put an end to his dictatorial rule.

As you pass through **La Obra** you will be able to see craftspeople working at the roadside with the pale-pink stone that characterizes the area and is popular for terraces and other building projects. A few kilometers before La Obra is the sales room of the Cavas del Maipo winery; visits by appointment (tel: 02-871 1508). Just past La Obra is **Las Vertientes**, a small town with a gorgeous swimming pool surrounded by grass and flowers, where you can spend the day swimming and sunbathing.

Silver boomtown

San José de Maipo ❶, *c.*25km (16 miles) from Santiago, is the canyon's main town, founded in 1792 after silver deposits were discovered in the surrounding area. The town's buildings are constructed in the adobe and straw common to the region. This is a pleasant place to stretch your legs, enjoy the fresh air, and absorb some of the tranquility of a traditional Andean town. On the outskirts of San José, a narrow gravel road sheers off from the main highway and begins climbing up to **Lagunillas** ❷, a ski resort perched on a mountain peak, overlooking an immense bowl formed by part of the cordillera. Good nerves and a head for heights are required for this trip, but it is worth it, especially during the ski season.

A New Age retreat

If you prefer to continue along the canyon, you will pass through the towns of **El Toyo** and **El Melocotón** before reaching **San Alfonso** ❸. This village sits in a generous hollow, which was carved through the Andes by the river itself. The people who live around the village are a curious mixture of old country-dwellers and New Agers attracted by the area's spectacular natural setting, the peace, and the proximity to Santiago.

La Cascada de las Animas (Waterfall of Souls), a camping and picnic ground, captures this peculiar mix. It has a circular swimming pool and handmade cabins built with local materials, and belongs to a family who once owned most of the land on which the town now sits. The sons and daughters of the original *latifundista* have established a community based on New Age ideals and sensitivity to the natural environment. The result is that the park and campgrounds are maintained extraordinarily well, and the trail rides (usually over weekends and for week-long periods) provide an excellent opportunity to explore some of the remoter areas of the Andes. Other activities offered by the community include guided walks and rafting on the river. For more information or to reserve a cabin, tel: (02) 861 1303.

For the less adventurous or for those with less time, the Hostería Los Ciervos serves meals in a garden lined with lush, well-kept plants and, if the weather is cold, has a cozy dining room with the purple abundance of a bougainvillea visible through a window.

San Alfonso is a good stopping and turning point for a leisurely day. However, it's also possible to start early in the morning from Santiago and head

In the villages around Santiago you can find all sorts of handmade souvenirs, from pottery to pencils.

BELOW LEFT: zip-lining in the Maipo Valley.
BELOW: en route to the Monumento Natural El Morado.

TIP

The Reserva Nacional Río Clarillo, one of the closest to Santiago, is 23km (14 miles) south-east of Pirque on a tributary of the Maipo River. Buses leave from the Bellavista de La Florida metro station.

straight up the canyon 70km/44 miles to **Lo Valdés** ❹, although the last 14km/9 miles on a gravel road may be difficult in winter. The road passes the rather run-down hot springs of **Baños Morales** and continues up past a checkpoint (the Chile–Argentine border is near), to the **Refugio Alemán**, a comfortable inn with a good restaurant, a spectacular view of snowy peaks, and a deep natural pool, surrounded by fossils from the period when the Andes were under the sea. Baños Morales is also the entry point to the **Monumento Natural El Morado**, where a three-hour hike through majestic scenery will take you to the San Francisco glacier. The park is administered by CONAF, the national park service, and basic camping facilities are available.

A further 11km (7 miles) on are the **Baños de Colina**, hot springs which are open to the public from September to April, where the water reaches temperatures as high as 60°C (140°F). The drive (feasible only in summer) takes you through a spectacular moonscape, completely different from the rest of the canyon, and the baths themselves

are arranged in smooth, natural pools on terraces carved into the mountainside. At the source, hot water steams out of natural caves into the hottest bath, which in turn jets into pools farther and farther down. The farther away from the source the pool is, the more bearable the temperature. In the second pool, you can rest your elbows on the edge and gaze down the valley at the mountains' extraordinary shades of gray, green, and subtle pinks, as your body soaks in warm, sulfurous luxury.

On the Argentine frontier

Another alternative is to turn left at **San Gabriel** ❺ (before El Volcán) and follow the **Río Yeso** to the Yeso dam, high up in the Andean cliffs. You'll have to stop at a control on the way and leave your identification at the checkpoint, because this is a pass to Argentina. The round trip from Santiago is 170km (106 miles), 65km (40 miles) of it on a dirt road, so it's a good idea to carry a picnic lunch.

To return it's possible to retrace your steps as far as El Toyo and then cross the River Maipo and follow the other side of the canyon back down to the Las Vertientes bridge. Here you can cross and retrace your path to Santiago, or carry on through **Pirque** ❻, a picturesque country town with a public sales and tasting room of Concha y Toro, Chile's largest wine producer. You can tour the huge vats where wines are stored and matured and peer through the gloom and dust into the "devil's locker room" where one of the company's top wines, *Casillero del Diablo*, is aged. The original country estate and family mansion can be seen from the road, surrounded by the smaller cottages of the vineyards' workers. The main house, which appears on some of the labels, was built around 1875, at roughly the same time that the French landscape designer Gustavo Renner was designing the surrounding park.

A car gives the most flexibility for traveling up and down the canyon, allowing plenty of time for visiting

BELOW: relaxing in the Baños de Colina.

anything which catches your fancy. However, buses run regularly from Santiago up the canyon, some of their routes ending in San José de Maipo or San Alfonso. Take Line 5 of the metro to the Bellavista de la Florida station and, from there, catch the frequent MB72 bus (one-way fare approximately US$1) or a *colectivo* (collective taxi) for around US$2.50. During January and February there is also a daily bus up to Baños Morales (weekends only in winter). To visit Pirque, take Line 4 of the metro to Puente Alto and a *colectivo*.

A village of potters

It is easy to catch a bus from Santiago that will drop you off at the crossroads to **Pomaire** ❼, a town where clay pottery is the sustaining activity for almost the entire population. The road to the town, about a half-hour's walk from the highway, stretches between an avenue of trees and green fields.

In 1985, an earthquake razed the original adobe homes, and they have mostly been replaced by simple wood houses. The reddish clay once common in the town is now virtually exhausted,

and the raw material for the pottery is mostly imported from other parts of the country, but the magic of this small village is still potent.

Designs are primarily traditional, including *miniaturas* – small figures inspired by country stories and religious beliefs – decorative work, and, perhaps most beautiful, the utilitarian ovenproof clay pots of all shapes and sizes, ideal for many Spanish and Chilean dishes. A shapely, sensual parade of vessels are displayed for sale, with names like *pailas*, *fuentes*, *tinajas*, *maceteros*; all are considerably more enticing than the one English word that sums them up: pot.

You can easily spend an enjoyable morning or afternoon wandering up and down Pomaire's two main streets, trying in vain to resist the temptation of taking at least a *chanchito* (a peculiarly Chilean pig pot) or an old worn-out clay shoe, back to your homeland to hold plants or trinkets. Tucked in between the potteries are small plant stores and greenhouses, along with restaurants offering traditional Chilean fare such as empanadas and *cazuela*, a stew made with a variety of vegetables

The town of Pomaire is known for its clay pottery and there are numerous stores selling pots in all shapes and sizes, as well as other objects.

BELOW: *cazuela* pots in Pomaire.

and containing a piece of beef, chicken, or, most traditionally, turkey.

Down to the Pacific

If you're traveling by bus, the round trip to and from Pomaire is probably enough for a good, full day. If you're using a car and you don't mind driving back to Santiago after dark, you have the option of carrying on to **Isla Negra** ❽ on the coast. Returning from Pomaire to the new Autopista del Sol (Highway of the Sun), continue along this stretch until just before San Antonio, where you turn north to head toward the popular seaside resorts of **Cartagena**, **Las Cruces**, and **El Tabo**. (Be careful to take the old coast road, rather than the tolled highway.) Cartagena was one of the resorts that became popular in the early 19th century, with the arrival of the railway from Santiago.

Isla Negra, a little farther up the coast from all three, has a special quality. It is unclear whether this is because Pablo Neruda, one of Chile's most influential poets, chose to live there, or whether he chose to live there because it is so special. Neruda's favorite house (see page 174) overlooks a particularly rough stretch of Isla Negra's beach, where the waves crash against humped rocks rising abruptly out of the white sand like children's castles. You can easily lose an hour or two, hunched on the humped rocks, gazing out over the restless, changing landscape that cast its spell on so much of Neruda's work.

From here it's a short trip back down the coast to **San Antonio** ❾, a working port with the grime of hard labor in evidence and fishing boats moored in the harbor. There are several good restaurants in San Antonio, but the *picadas*, as the Chileans call them, are right on the harbor itself: these are where the fishing people themselves like to eat. Here you'll get huge platefuls of your favorite shellfish or fish dish, with a fresh Chilean salad, rice, or French fries, at very reasonable prices.

If you're looking for slightly more comfortable surroundings, then try the Juanita (Antofagasta 261), which serves all of Chile's most traditional fish dishes at very affordable prices. The drive back to Santiago takes about an hour and a half, all on the Autopista del Sol. ❏

BELOW: shellfish in a San Antonio *picada*.

RESTAURANTS AND CAFÉS

Cajón del Maipo

Café Vienés
Camino al Volcán 16692, Guayacán
Tel: (02) 861 1109 **$**
Excellent cakes, coffee, hot chocolate, and juices.

Cascada de las Animas
Camino al Volcán 31087, San Alfonso
Tel: (02) 861 1303 **$**
Wholesome Chilean and vegetarian food in a lovely setting.

Hostería Los Ciervos
Camino al Volcán 31411, San Alfonso
Tel: (02) 861 1581 **$**

Traditional Chilean fare; try the *humitas*.

La Vaquita Echá
Ramón Subercaseaux 3355, Pirque
Tel: (02) 854 6025 **$$**
Typical Chilean food in an old adobe house; barbecued meat a speciality.

Pomaire

La Greda
Manuel Rodríguez cnr. Roberto Bravo
Tel: (02) 831 1166 **$**
The vine-covered outdoor dining room is pleasantly shady in summer and, in winter, is warmed with woodstoves.

San Antonio

La Juanita
Antofagasta 261
Tel: (035) 211 928 **$**
Generous helpings of good, simple food at modest prices.

Restorán Logroño
21 de Mayo 274
Tel: (035) 233 621 **$$**
A good place to eat seafood, with an ocean view.

Prices are per person for a three-course meal, not including drinks.

$ = under US$15
$$ = US$15–25
$$$ = US$25–35

Andean Ski Resorts

The ski season in Chile runs from June to October, drawing winter sports enthusiasts from all over the world to its top-class resorts.

There are five ski centers near Santiago: Portillo, Valle Nevado, Farellones, La Parva, and Lagunillas. All of them are located in the same area about 50km (31 miles) from Santiago except Portillo (www.skiportillo.com), which is 164km (102 miles) away, close to the border with Argentina.

Farellones

The road to Farellones winds narrow and steep through the cordillera, following most of the Mapocho River Canyon deep into the Andes. This is an excellent day trip whatever the season, but snow chains are required in winter (they're available for rental where the road begins). Careful driving is essential at any time of year. Access to the road is controlled by the police in winter, and on weekends and public holidays. Drivers are allowed to head up until 2pm, but it's best to start the journey early in the morning. Cars can begin the return descent only after 4pm. Warm clothes are essential, whatever the temperature in Santiago when you leave. Snow usually begins in June and lasts until September.

Farellones provides excellent conditions, and equipment rental and classes can be arranged in the town itself. It has four well-equipped slopes extending to altitudes of 3,333 meters (10,935ft), which are suitable for skiers of variable experience. Both group and private classes are available.

Even if you're not a skier, it's well worth making the trip to Farellones. The view from the road as you ascend higher and higher, the pure sky, the clear air, and the chance to enjoy the Andes from the inside out all make the drive worthwhile.

La Parva

Near Farellones is the hamlet of La Parva, situated at 2,816 meters (9,239ft), with a spectacular view down the valley toward Santiago. La Parva usually enjoys snowy conditions until well into October and you can ski as high as 3,630 meters (11,910ft). See www.laparva.cl for further information.

RIGHT: the ski resorts around Santiago offer some fantastic high-altitude pistes.

Valle Nevado

The turn-off to Valle Nevado, 2km (about 1 mile) before Farellones, takes you 10km (6 miles) deep into the mountains. This modern ski center first opened in 1988 and today attracts both families and daredevil heli-skiers. The resort contains three luxury hotels and a luxury apartment building, providing services as varied as movies, a discotheque, a French restaurant, a gymnasium, a pool room, a sauna, a whirlpool bath, and a snack bar (see www.vallenevado.cl). Stores sell and rent ski equipment and clothing, and there is a day-care center and a medical center equipped for any emergency. The highest point you can ski at is 3,670 meters (12,040ft) above sea level.

Lagunillas

Lagunillas is located 80km (50 miles) southeast of Santiago in the Cajón de Maipo. Run by Club Andino de Chile, this small resort offers skiing and snowboarding. For more information, visit www.skilagunillas.cl (in Spanish).

Skiing in Chile is an expensive activity, and prices of equipment and accommodations are similar to those in European and North American ski resorts.

More information on all of the ski resorts around Santiago can be obtained from the Sernatur Tourist Office in Santiago (tel: 600-7376 2887). Alternatively, visit www.sernatur.cl. ❏

VALPARAÍSO AND VIÑA DEL MAR

The port and its neighboring beach resort are steeped in history, but it's the unusual *ascensores* that scale Valparaíso's hills that will leave a lasting impression

Valparaíso and Viña del Mar may sit side by side on Chile's Pacific coast, but when it comes to urban character, they are worlds apart. One of the first Chilean cities founded by the Spanish in 1541, Valparaíso was Santiago's thriving port for centuries. It is spread along some spectacularly steep hills, with stairways and streets winding up past splendid aging buildings, many built by the British in the 19th century, when the port was virtually run from the City of London.

Viña, on the other hand, is a tourist city of steel, glass, and neon. Traditionally the reserve of the well-off, it is now middle-class territory and a pleasant enough place to relax, but Valparaíso holds the attractions of its wild and varied history. And, although the poverty that followed the opening of the Panama Canal is still apparent, Valparaíso is now being smartened up again, particularly since Unesco declared its historic center a World Heritage Site in 2003.

Arriving in Valparaíso

Three bus companies run a shuttle service to Valparaíso and Viña from the Pajaritos metro station in Santiago, and this is by far the easiest – and cheapest – way to visit them. A car is more of a liability than a help on Valparaíso's steep hills, and there are regular bus and train services between the port and Viña. The 90-minute bus journey from Santiago will take you through the vine-draped Casablanca Valley, where sea breezes help to produce some of Chile's best white wines.

From Santiago you enter **Valparaíso** ❶ along Avenida Argentina. On Wednesdays and Saturdays, this avenue's central walkway becomes a city market, groaning with vegetables and fruit, fresh fish and shellfish, dry goods, and spices. On Sundays it is home to a vast flea market, or *feria persa*.

As you reach Avenida Pedro Montt, a former horserace track, the Congress building rises up imperiously. For

Main Attractions
PLAZA DE LA VICTORIA
MUSEO A CIELO ABIERTO
LA SEBASTIANA
CERRO ALEGRE
CERRO CONCEPCIÓN
ASCENSOR POLANCO
PARQUE NACIONAL LA CAMPANA

PRECEDING PAGES:
Cerro Alegre.
LEFT AND BELOW:
the steep and cobbled streets of Valaparaíso.

some, this is the symbol of the new Chilean democracy, but for most, the exile of Congress to Valparaíso, dictated by the outgoing military government, is just one more reminder of this painful period.

Foundation of a great port

The sea has shaped Valparaíso's history since its foundation, four and a half centuries ago. Before the Spanish arrived, the region was inhabited by the Chango people, who fished the bay and called it Quintil. In 1536, Juan de Saavedra sailed down from Callao in Peru to meet a supply ship for Diego de Almagro's earlier foot expedition to Chile. The bay's beauty flooded him with such nostalgia for his distant homeland that he named it Valparaíso (Paradise Valley) after his hometown in Spain.

In 1547, Pedro de Valdivia, the founder of Santiago and governor of Chile, would find himself here, isolated, impoverished by wars, and discouraged by the lack of news and support from the Crown. With characteristic (and very Chilean) ingenuity,

he called on colonists wishing to return to the more developed northern colonies to load their fortunes (built through the exploitation of gold reserves using native slaves) and themselves onto his ships. About 20 families boarded. On the last night before setting out, under the pretext of a final goodbye banquet in the port, Valdivia set them all ashore where they cheerfully set to consuming wine and meats in huge quantities. But as the feasting reached its height, Don Pedro weighed anchor and set out with the gold, leaving a beach full of furious victims.

Valparaíso went on to become the main port for the growing city of Santiago. This made it a tempting target for pirates, mostly of English or Dutch origin, and the port had to build strong fortifications to repel the attacks, which continued through most of the 16th and 17th centuries. Its defensive towers and forts not only discouraged potential attackers but also acted as a strong stimulus to trade and the warehousing of merchandise. Soon the English stopped raiding and became the largest trading partner of the newly

Valparaíso's importance as a port declined in the early 20th century, when the opening of the Panama Canal meant that boats no longer had to travel round Cape Horn.

independent Chile, buying up large parts of Valparaíso.

Revolutions and riots

Occasionally laid waste by earthquakes and tidal waves, Valparaíso also became notorious for political disturbances. Two of the city's governors died tragically within 20 years of each other. The first was the powerful "kingmaker" Diego Portales, who was shot to death on his way to Quillota in 1837, during a brief military uprising. The other was an army general, killed on September 18, 1859, during a civil uprising at the doors of the La Matriz church, during a religious ceremony giving thanks for Chile's independence.

But, by the early 20th century, the old port had begun to assume its present look. Builders battled the sea for a few extra meters of earth for the *costanera* (coast road) and the railway line. European-style buildings marked the skyline, and the old street of trade became the financial and banking center for all the maritime and port activity. The growing population began to spill out of the city's basic *plan* – as the lower part of the city is called – and the incredible feat of building on the *cerros* (hills) began. Each individual builder found his or her own techniques for fighting gravity and resisting earthquakes, creating a unique city of winding streets, stairways, walks, and lookout points, which began to string together the different hills, each one separated by the abrupt ravines that characterize the area.

To conquer the hilltops, the *ascensores* (funiculars or cable-cars) were introduced, and remain the main form of transport up the city's hills. No visit to Valparaíso is complete without a trip in an *ascensor* – appearances aside, they've proven a secure means for traveling up the hills, while affording spectacular views of the bay.

Exploring the city

The best way to see Valparaíso is on foot, and the best place to start is by the Cathedral on **Plaza Victoria Ⓐ**. General Augusto Pinochet was born in Valparaíso and must have known this square well because he spent his childhood in a nearby (unmarked) house.

Cerro Artillaría is dotted with charming restaurants and cafés, some which have fantastic views over the bay.

BELOW: colorful facades in Valparaíso.

Memories of Pablo Neruda

Chile's most revered poet was an avid collector of books, paintings, shells, wines – and houses, three of which are now open to the public.

A winding street leads to a modest bungalow with a rough stone face that sets it apart from its showy neighbors. But where the inside should begin there's a leafy patio of ladders and stairs leading to rooms of glass scattered among gardens, terraces, and mosaics. This is La Chascona, meaning "woman with tousled hair," on Cerro San Cristóbal in Santiago. Built between 1953 and 1958, it was the home of Chile's most famous poet, Pablo Neruda, who won the Nobel Prize in 1971 and died shortly after the military coup in 1973. He built the house for his lover Matilde Urrutia while he was still married to his second wife, the painter Delia del Carril. Neruda named La Chascona for his lover's rebellious hair. Neruda and Matilde later married.

By the time of his death Neruda had four houses: La Chascona (see page 154), Isla Negra (see page 166), La Sebastiana in Valparaíso (see page 175), and La Quinta Michoacán in Santiago.

Friends called Neruda a spontaneous architect: his houses just grew. "In Isla Negra everything flowers," Neruda wrote. "The sea flowers all year round. Its rose is white. Its petals are salt stars." This is the place where Neruda and Urrutia are now buried, after being moved there in 1992 from Santiago's General Cemetery.

Poetry and politics

Neruda's thirst for life and his love for poetry were tempered by his sensitivity to the poverty around him. He joined the Communist Party in 1943 and was elected senator for Antofagasta and Tarapacá, but was later forced into hiding and then into exile in Argentina and Europe as a result of his opposition to center-right president Gabriel González Videla.

While alive, Neruda dedicated his work to the daily struggles of Chileans. In death, he left his wealth to them. "Neruda didn't collect things in order to hoard them, but rather to share them," said Juan Agustín Figueroa, head of the Neruda Foundation. "He always imagined that his things would become the heritage of the people of Chile."

Upon the deaths of Neruda, Delia del Carril, and Matilde Urrutia, the four houses were to be donated to the Communist Party, for use as cultural centers. But after the 1973 coup, the military confiscated their goods. Military patrols repeatedly sacked La Chascona and La Sebastiana.

This didn't stop Matilde from holding Neruda's wake there, and his funeral became the first march against the military regime. From then until her death in 1985, she and a small group of lawyers, writers, and artists waged silent war against the military's bureaucracy. Matilde spent her last years in La Chascona, repairing the house and organizing Neruda's library, papers, and writings. After her death, the Neruda Foundation published her memoirs and made La Chascona its headquarters. The military confiscated the house in Isla Negra, but Matilde never gave up possession. After a lengthy struggle, the government eventually recognized the Foundation.

Today, visitors can follow a guided tour of La Chascona or stroll around La Sebastiana at their leisure. The Isla Negra house has been turned into a permanent museum by the government. Guided tours can be arranged in advance through the Fundación Pablo Neruda in Santiago (tel: 02-777 8741; www.fundacionneruda.org). ❑

LEFT: Pablo Neruda in the 1940s.

Nothing suggested the prominent role that Pinochet, a mediocre student at the old Sacred Heart School, would play in Chilean history. In the center of the plaza sits the lovely **Neptune Fountain**, a war trophy that was stolen from the Peruvians in 1879.

A block along Calle Condell is the neoclassical **Palacio Lyon** Ⓑ, once the mansion of a wealthy family, that now houses the city's natural history museum and municipal art gallery. At the bottom of Calle Huito, which runs alongside the Palacio, the Ascensor Espíritu Santo (the Holy Spirit Lift), one of the city's 15 funiculars, will carry you up to **Cerro Bellavista** Ⓒ and its **Museo a Cielo Abierto** (Open-Sky Museum), a collection of murals painted on the sides of houses, some of them by leading Chilean artists, although now rather run-down. Along Calle Ricardo Ferrari, you will reach **La Sebastiana**, one of the homes of Chilean poet Pablo Neruda (Tue–Sun, Jan–Feb 10.30am–6.50pm, Mar–Dec daily 10.10am–6pm; charge). Although Neruda actually used this house relatively little, many visitors find it the most attractive of his four homes, partly because they are allowed to wander through it without taking a guided tour, but also because of the spectacular view over the Bay of Valparaíso that Neruda could enjoy from his bed.

Alternatively, from the Palacio Lyon continue along the narrow, curving Calle Condell – on which buses race at great speed, contributing to the air pollution of this lower part of the city – to Plaza Aníbal Pinto, with one of the landmarks of the city's gastronomic history: the old **Bar Cinzano**, a traditional spot frequented by locals where tango and Chilean music are played live. From there, Calle Esmeralda leads to the **Turri Clock** Ⓓ, Valparaíso's equivalent of Big Ben. This is where Avenida Prat, the city's financial heart, begins. The British influences are so obvious here that it's hard to believe you're in a Latin American city. At Cochrane 851 is the **Bar Inglés** (English Bar), a wood-paneled reminder of the city's past.

At the end of Esmeralda you'll find yourself in the open expanse of **Plaza**

An interesting feature of Valparaíso is the numerous murals that decorate the streets of Cerro Alegre.

BELOW: Salvador Allende lives on in Cerro Alegre.

A mural outside the Mirador *restaurant on Cerro Artillería.*

BELOW: the port.
BELOW RIGHT: street off Plaza Sotomayor.

Sotomayor E, overlooked by the gray-washed Naval Headquarters. The plaza is dominated by the Monument to the Heroes of Iquique, who died in a key naval battle in the 19th-century War of the Pacific *(see page 41)*. In a crypt under the monument, naval hero Arturo Prat and his crew are buried (visits to the crypt must be arranged 5 days in advance, tel: 032-252 6643). The handicraft stalls on the nearby pier, Muelle Prat, are tawdry, but this is the departure point for boat trips out into the bay, with a magnificent view of the port's amphitheater of hills. On New Year's Eve, you can enjoy Valparaíso's unique fireworks show on the water: all the ships anchored in the harbor sound their horns together to welcome the New Year.

A prosperous past

To the northwest of the plaza is **Cerro Playa Ancha**, one of the city's largest hills in both size and population. Residents proudly call this the "People's Independent Republic of Playa Ancha." Valparaíso's naval school is here, as well as the hospital, a cemetery and the edu-cation, medicine, and biology faculties of the University of Valparaíso. A walk around Playa Ancha is also a reminder of the port's better days of fine but unostentatious buildings that populated the hill, little by little. Walking down the Paseo 21 de Mayo gives the city's best view of the bay and the whole port area. In the distance you can see Viña del Mar.

In Caleta El Membrillo, a restaurant run by the Fishermen's Co-operative, serves up a variety of local specialties, in particular, fantastic shellfish and fish which, eaten with a glass of wine, give the sensation of a perfect world. However, this is definitely a place to keep a close eye on your possessions.

From Plaza Sotomayor, you can also take the Ascensor El Peral (opposite the law courts) to **Cerro Alegre** which, along with neighboring **Cerro Concepción F**, is part of an area declared a World Heritage Site. At the top of Ascensor El Peral is Paseo Yugoslavo, one of a number of similar short promenades that look out over the bay, with the **Museo de Bellas Artes** (Fine Arts Museum) housed in Palacio Baburizza.

This has an excellent collection of Chilean painting and the setting is magnificent but, unfortunately, the museum has been closed for renovation for several years and no date has yet been set for its reopening.

From the Paseo Yugoslavo, it's a short walk down and up again to Cerro Concepción, also accessible by the Ascensor Concepción (close to the Turri Clock). This was the residential area preferred by the British in the late 1800s, and it is still a haven of attractive buildings, broad avenues, and sea views, principally from Paseo Atkinson and Paseo Gervasoni. From there, it's a short walk back down to Plaza Aníbal Pinto.

Both of these hills have become fashionable places for a weekend home, and, as well as tasteful renovation, this has brought a sharp increase in property prices. However, they are full of small, moderately priced restaurants, especially along Almirante Montt, and tiny art galleries of varying quality.

Another side of town

As a general principle, the hills of Valparaíso become poorer the higher you climb. And some are, indeed, very poor. However, during daylight, they are perfectly safe: their people are generally warm and welcoming – much more so than in Santiago – and they will be only too happy to share their love of their city, and its many attractions, with you. And, although the streets twist and turn, it's not easy to get lost, as the sea is always there as the ultimate landmark.

It's worth going up the **Ascensor Polanco**, on the eastern side of Avenida Argentina. This ingenious *ascensor*, built in 1915 and now a National Monument, is a feat of engineering. Reached by a walk through a long, narrow, but well-lit tunnel, it rises vertically through the heart of the hill, before emerging into daylight at the top of a tower that is connected to the hilltop by a suspended walkway. The poverty here is apparent, and the contrast with the monumental Congress, although now muted by new blocks of high-rise apartment buildings, gives some idea of why, when it was built in the late 1980s, the ostentatious Congress building seemed so out of keeping with its surroundings.

In 1834, Charles Darwin climbed Cerro La Campana, east of Valparaíso, which is now a national park. The adjoining Parque Nacional Ocoa is one of the last reserves of the native Chilean palm.

BELOW: the steep hills of Valparaíso.

OPPOSITE: the beach at Viña del Mar.

From here, you can walk north towards **Cerro Barón**, so called because a European baron once built his castle there, and then on to **Cerro Los Placeres**, literally "the hill of pleasures." This hill is virtuously protected by the imposing Castle of Don Federico Santa María, today a university which bears his name.

Valparaíso is a good base for daytrips by car to **Parque Nacional La Campana** and the region's interior cities. Quilpué, Limache, Quillota, and San Felipe are all small towns whose buildings recall colonial times. Plazas and squares full of palm trees, the peaceful, slow pace, and a climate especially kind to the elderly, make these towns particularly agreeable for relaxing.

The glittering resort

Just northeast of Valparaíso is the adjacent resort haven of **Viña del Mar ➋**. Viña is an affluent city, with elegant hotels, a casino, and numerous good restaurants, all set in wide palm-lined avenues. It was born as Valparaíso's seaside resort in the mid-19th century, when the two were connected by railway. In spite of some industrial development (principally textiles, mining, and metal), its major source of income is still tourism. The Cerro Castillo palace, on a hill overlooking the city, is the summer home of Chile's presidents.

If Valparaíso is the city where Augusto Pinochet grew up, Viña is the city that sheltered the remains of Salvador Allende, the Chilean president who committed suicide amid the relentless bombing of the Air Force's Hawker Hunters during the 1973 military coup. His tomb in the Santa Inés cemetery remained unmarked until 1989, but was always covered with fresh flowers placed by admirers. On September 4, 1990, exactly 20 years to the day after he was elected president of Chile, Dr Allende's remains were finally moved to his permanent resting place, in a mausoleum in Santiago's General Cemetery.

Fall is the best time to see Viña, when summer tourists have abandoned it and only its inhabitants remain. Avenida Perú is the perfect place to stroll along the shore, enjoying the sunset. For those with a car, the northbound coastal road is lovely on a clear day. One by one the resorts of Reñaca, Cochoa, Higuerillas, and Concón appear, surrounded by rocky outcrops and reefs where you can see sea lions, pelicans, cormorants, and, with a bit of luck, a penguin looking for the island across from **Cachagua**, a small town 60km (37 miles) north of Viña del Mar. **Concón**, at the mouth of the River Aconcagua, has very good restaurants serving traditional seafood empanadas and tasty fish dishes and sauces.

On your way back to Santiago from Viña, climbing Cerro Agua Santa, you will have a clear view of Valparaíso. If you pass this way in the dark, you can enjoy a view from the crest of the hill of the marvelous firmament of lights of both Valparaíso and Viña. By night the two very different cities can barely be distinguished, blending together in a clandestine love affair. ❏

RESTAURANTS

Valparaíso

Le Filou de Montpellier
Almirante Montt 382, Cerro Alegre
Tel: (032) 222 4663
$–$$
A charming French restaurant serving excellent and inexpensive fixed-price lunches. Open for dinner Thur, Fri, and Sat only.

Hamburg
O'Higgins 1274
Tel: (032) 259 7037
$$
Owned by a former German sailor, this restaurant offers generous portions of mainly hearty Ger-

man dishes. Perfect for getting your energy back after a day exploring the hills of Valparaíso. Credit cards not accepted.

Pasta e Vino
Templeman 352, Cerro Concepción
Tel: (032) 249 6187
$$$
This place on Cerro Concepción is always packed, and for good reason. Booking advised, especially at weekends.

Portofino
Bellamar 301, Cerro Esperanza
Tel: (032) 262 9939
$$$
The place to eat sea-

food with a majestic view of the bay.

Viña del Mar

Hotel del Mar
Avda. San Martín 199
Tel: (032) 284 6100
$$$
This posh hotel, adjoining the casino, has three restaurants; the Savinya is expensive but a good choice for a splurge.

Prices are per person for a three-course meal, not including drinks.
$ = under US$15
$$ = US$15–25
$$$ = US$25–35

EL NORTE CHICO

Chile's "Little North," the area just north of Santiago, is a dry, mostly flat region of wide Pacific beaches, deserted mining settlements, and spectacularly starry night skies

H op on a northbound bus in Santiago and, in just a few hours, the crush and bustle of the city will be replaced by windswept coastal expanses and empty, arid desert.

As most long-distance buses in Chile travel at night, you will probably be treated to views of northern Chile's extraordinarily clear night skies, which are so exceptional that the region has five major observatories. Maybe it's not surprising that this region is also on the map for international UFO-spotters.

Chile's long, skinny north is unofficially split into two regions: for convenience, the southernmost part is known as El Norte Chico (The Little North), and the northernmost part as El Norte Grande (The Great North). This terminology reflects the awe inspired by the extreme conditions and vast extension of the Atacama Desert, beside which the dry scrublands closer to Santiago seem a pale imitation. But both regions are characterized by expansive Pacific beaches and resort towns, and both regions bear the scars of Chile's mining enterprises, with the skeletons of old mines open to visitors (see page 201). The two areas contain petroglyphs and other archeological remains of ancient desert cultures.

The clearest night skies are seen in El Norte Chico, where four of the main observatories, along with several smaller ones, are located. Pisco, Chile's piquant grape brandy, is produced in this region, which was also the birth-place of the Nobel Prize-winning poet Gabriela Mistral.

El Norte Grande, covered in the next chapter (see pages 195–201), is a geological wonderland of geysers, hot springs, salt lakes, strange desert formations, and snow-tipped volcanoes. The abundant remains of the Atacameño cultures, including mummies, textiles, and ancient structures, can also be seen here.

Chile's north is harsher territory than its lush, picturesque south. The north is utilitarian; it provides much of the

Main Attractions
A PISCO DISTILLERY
MONUMENTO ARQUEOLÓGICO
VALLE DEL ENCANTO
VALLE DEL ELQUI
SALAR DE MARICUNGA
LAGUNA VERDE

PRECEDING PAGES: the altiplano.
LEFT: Laguna Verde.
BELOW: El Tololo observatory.

Norte Chico

country's wealth, and has also frequently been used as a dumping ground for the politically inconvenient. Much of the north was annexed by Chile late in the game; in 1884, Chile defeated a confederation of Peru and Bolivia in the War of the Pacific to take control over the flourishing nitrate mines. This "white gold," a key ingredient in the production of fertilizer, provided fabulous wealth for several decades, while copper and silver mining already flourished in the provinces closer to the capital. Later, a vast copper mine was developed at Chuquicamata *(see page 196)*, part of the captured spoils.

The distances from the northern deserts to Santiago and the few transport options available encouraged the idea of a journey north as a sort of banishment – whether it was self-imposed exile in the pursuit of spiritual or material gain, or literally an attempt by others to get the unlucky subject out of the way. The central male character in Isabel Allende's famous novel *The House of the Spirits*, published in 1985, makes his way north early in life to slog out a miserable living in the nitrate mines. He manages to accumulate capital and returns to lay claim for the hand of his chosen fiancée. But he never goes near the north again for the rest of the book.

Bustling cities

Unlike his southern cousin who receives the urban visitor with shy admiration and enormous instinctual hospitality, the northerner must be convinced that the newcomer is worthy of his confidence or even his notice. The cities of the north bustle; those of the south doze. But this does not mean there is no room for friendliness or hospitality here – an initial brusqueness can often be an abrupt opening to further communication, leading to unexpected warmth and humor.

The north is the birthplace of the Chilean left. Away from the moderating influences of intermediate soci forces such as small landowners, p fessionals, and shopkeepers, and the ideological grip of "leading families," the northern laborer was face to face with the company.

Along with this history of class conflict, Chile's north is also associated with military feats and heroism dating from the earliest colonial campaigns against Inca rule. Near San Pedro de Atacama are the ruins of the last stand of the Incas who had ruled the area for less than a century. The great naval battle of Iquique in 1879 was key to the defeat of the Peruvians in the war for control of the desert; it is commemorated in a national holiday every May 21.

Arica, the border city facing Peru, is physically dominated by the El Morro Hill, another famous battle site from the Peruvian War. On the Peruvian side is the site of the La Concepción battle where an entire Chilean battalion was wiped out to the last man rather than surrender. The soldiers are honored in the Santiago metro station Los Héroes. The desert cities of Arica, Iquique, and Antofagasta tend to have a noticeable military presence, being frequently visited by soldiers on leave from lonely outposts in the mountain border stations or local barracks.

Age-old mining traditions

The Diaguitas culture moved into the El Norte Chico region from across the Andes around AD 900 and flourished until the Inca conquest 500 years later, quickly followed by the arrival of the Spaniards. Ceramic work of this group is considered among the best in the Americas, and the black-and-white geometric designs on a red base are widely copied in Chilean decoration. Both La Serena and Ovalle have anthropological museums with excellent artifacts. Mineral smelting and the need for domestic fuel wiped out most native woods throughout the desert. The ore grade in the early mines was always at least 25 percent and could reach 50 or 60 percent. (Modern large-scale copper mining works with ore with a copper content of only 1 or 2 percent.)

Driving north from Santiago, the Central Valley vegetation soon disappears, to be replaced by hardy thorn trees. Signs of inhabitants become fewer and fewer, and lands are no

A graffitied corner of La Serena's lighthouse, El Faro Monumental.

BELOW: the steaming geysers of El Tatio.

A beautiful stained-glass window in a church in Pisco Elqui.

BELOW: rocky coastline near Pichidangui.

longer enclosed in farm plots or ranches. The highway descends to the coast, where a series of popular beach resorts are located, far enough from the capital to retain their small-town dimensions. Long stretches of deserted beach are surrounded by rocky cliffs. Pichicuy and **Pichidangui** ❸ ("pichi" means "little" in the Mapuche tongue) have white-sand beaches with strong surf. At Pichicuy there is a church built on a promontory over the sea. A bird sanctuary with abundant sea life is located in between at the **Los Molles** rock gardens, where underground caverns produce a thunderous roar. Nearby is the **Governor's Chair**, which, at 695 meters (2,280ft), is the country's highest sea cliff, and visible from Valparaíso in good weather.

Copper country

A few kilometers off the highway is the lively tourist town of **Los Vilos**, which is full of rustic seafood restaurants and artisans who carve in *guayacán*, a durable wood once plentiful in the district. The **Bodegón Cultural** (Cultural Warehouse), which opened in 2002 in the restored 19th-century Customs building, holds regular art exhibitions in summer. A sculpture park, created by a local architect on the cliffs, is open to the public and worth a visit.

North of Los Vilos is the Choapa River Valley and the city of **Illapel** ❹, its principal urban center. Illapel, like many northern towns, had a mining boom and bust and has since returned to its original agricultural economy. Some 18th-century construction is preserved, both in the town and on the road to Salamanca, giving an idea of how rural estates were built around a central courtyard. A typical mansion has an adobe first-floor which blocks the heat and a wooden upper floor with balconies surrounding the inner patio. Sometimes the adobe walls are painted brightly.

The entire zone is arid and mountainous but has some surprisingly green valleys and attractive river beaches with excellent trout fishing. It is good for camping off-season when the sun is not so strong. The old north–south road which followed the Inca route, and which predates the Pan-

American Highway, can be taken from Illapel up a severe climb through the narrowest part of Chile, in which the sea is only 80km (50 miles) from the Argentine border. The view from the top just before **Combarbalá ❺** is superb, with views of the snow-topped Andes. The design of the town's central plaza is inspired by the colors and geometrical schemes of the Diaguitas people. *Pirquineros*, independent miners, are plentiful in the zone, where the soil has a reddish tinge due to its copper content. A whitish, marble-like stone particular to the area, called *combarbalita*, is cut and polished by the artisans to make miniature figures.

Petroglyphs and pisco

The next valley to the north is the **Limarí**, with the city of **Ovalle ❻** at its center. The surrounding area is an agricultural zone traditionally dependent on the city of La Serena to the north, but recently the expansion of irrigation has added new lands for export grapes and a burst of unevenly distributed prosperity. Five km (3 miles) southeast of Ovalle is the **Monumento Arque-** **ológico Valle del Encanto** (Enchanted Valley National Monument), which is rich in archeological treasures (daily approximately 9am–6pm; charge). There is evidence of a hunter-gatherer civilization here dating back 4,000 years, though the bulk of the artifacts are from the Molle culture of around AD 700. This idyllic valley contains over 30 petroglyphs – designs carved into rocks – as well as 20 *piedras tacitas*, groups of circular indentations hollowed out of flat rocks in the river bed. The number of petroglyphs that are visible depends on the angle of the sun and late afternoon is a good time to visit.

To the north of Ovalle is the **Recoleta Reservoir**, a popular lake resort. En route, the junction of the Grande and the Hurtado rivers can be seen from a high altitude. Farther toward the cordillera along this route is the **Monumento Natural Pichasca**, with gigantic rock formations and petrified wood. Many of the hamlets in this region, lying along the original north–south route through the mountains, were Inca outposts ruled by a representative of the empire. The town of

TIP

A new tourist observatory, Cruz del Sur, which opened in Combarbalá in 2009, offers talks about astronomy as well as viewing opportunities.

BELOW: petroglyphs in the Monumento Arqueológico Valle del Encanto.

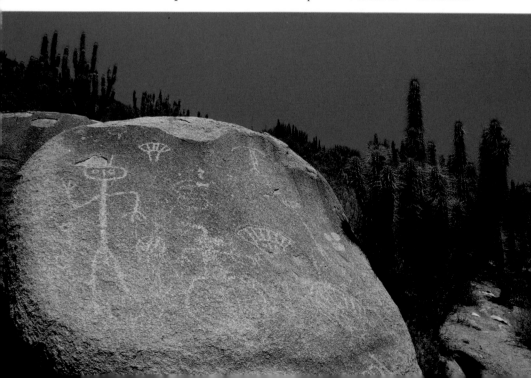

Hurtado is known for its dried fruit, figs, quince jelly, and nuts, as well as its flower farms of dahlias and chrysanthemums. From here, the mountains can be crossed straight north toward Vicuña (*see opposite*) on an unpaved road which offers a panoramic view of both the Andes and the next valley north, the **Valle del Elqui**.

Rare gems

Just southeast of Ovalle is the giant **La Paloma reservoir**, responsible for much of the new agricultural wealth of the region. Planted with stands of trees, it presents a refreshing spectacle in its dry setting. At the end of the difficult gravel road is the small village of **Las Ramadas**, whose nearby hills contain one of the two known lapis lazuli mines in the world (the other is in Afghanistan). This semi-precious blue stone is worked into a variety of pendants, earrings, and decorations, and sold in artisan markets throughout the country.

Back on the Pan-American Highway is a turn-off for **Parque Nacional Fray Jorge**, a dense green forest which is surrounded by near-desert. This concentration of plant life is the result of an almost constant ocean fog which hugs the hillside. In nearby **Tongoy** (town names now begin to be Quechua in origin, rather than Mapuche), the beaches are among the finest in Chile, composed of extremely white pulverized conch shells. Tongoy is also one of the best places to try the local scallops, served in the innumerable beachside restaurants.

City of serenity

The comfortable, slow-paced northern city of **La Serena** ❼ was the first settlement established by Pedro de Valdivia as part of his plan to secure the region for Spain. As such, it became an important hotel center from the beginning of the colonial period to receive travelers making the long trek across the desert. Religious orders also built receiving houses for their missionaries, and the city still has 29 churches; the oldest of these have remarkable stone facades. The discovery of silver in 1825 led to an upsurge of prosperity and a construction boom, though most of the original buildings were superseded

BELOW: San Francisco Church, La Serena.

by an ersatz "Spanish colonial" style imposed in a 1940s urban renewal scheme.

All the landowning families of the Limarí, Elqui, Huasco, Choapa, and Copiapó valleys had their own residence here. La Serena's **Museo Arqueológico** (Tue–Fri 9.30am–5.50pm, Sat 10am–1pm and 4–7pm, Sun 10am–1pm; charge, except Sun and holidays) has an excellent collection of Diaguitas artifacts, and the cemetery provides an ample view of the river valley from above. Along with the tomb of native son and Chilean president Gabriel González Videla and relatives of Gabriela Mistral is a stone honoring officials of the Salvador Allende Unidad Popular government who were shot in the days after the 1973 military coup. González Videla's house on La Serena's main square is a national monument and museum (Mon–Fri 10am–6pm, Sat 10am–1pm; charge).

The sister city of **Coquimbo** is a small port, active mostly at the height of the fruit export season in December and January. Some elaborate woodcarving, the handiwork of foreign carpenters, can still be seen on a few buildings. These craftsmen arrived as the mining industry grew, since local tradesmen did not know how to build on the scale required. Shipped in from abroad were Oregon pine (neither pine nor from Oregon) and a sturdy species of bamboo from Ecuador, which could be planed to form a solid surface. These materials and techniques were used to build the region's churches, most of which have a high central bell tower and have survived severe earthquakes. The city also has a large mosque, donated by the king of Morocco and built by Moroccan workmen.

The starriest skies

The sleepy village of **Vicuña** ❽, east of La Serena in the Valle del Elqui, was the birthplace of Gabriela Mistral (see page 190), and houses a museum of the famous poet (Jan–Feb Mon–Fri 10am–7pm, Sat–Sun 10am–6pm; Mar–Dec Mon–Sat 10am–5.45pm, Sun 10am–1pm; charge). From Vicuña, the road continues up to **Monte Grande**, where she is now buried. This is also Chile's main pisco-producing area, and plants

Chile's two species of carnivorous plant, known as fox's ear, grow between La Serena and Copiapó.

BELOW: vineyard near Vicuña.

BELOW: Cerro Tololo observatory.

can be visited without appointment. The outlying hills of the Valle del Elqui are the haunt of a variety of esoteric movements and guru-led communities, in part, no doubt, due to the great clarity of the night skies and the sensation that, as the title of a book about the zone suggested, *Heaven is Nearer*. North of La Serena, the Pan-American Highway cuts back toward the interior, but a side spur leads to the interesting beaches and fishing villages at **Temblador** and **Chungungo**, the last being the name of a local species of otter.

Bethlehem Steel ran the world's largest iron mine between 1914 and 1954 at **El Tofo**, 10km (6 miles) in from this part of the Chilean coast, and its abandoned remains can still be seen. Also nearby is the Camanchaca Project: here the heavy mist that rolls in from the sea (called *camanchaca*) is captured and condensed on fine netting to provide a water supply. The atmosphere in the mountains here is excellent for astronomical purposes as the air is particularly clear and populated areas are sparse. With 300 nights a year suitable for sky photography, it is one of the Southern Hemisphere's most popular observatory spots (Mount Palomar in the United States has 215). The observatories at **Cerro Tololo**, **La Silla**, **Las Campanas**, and **Gemini Sur** can be seen from the highway, and from Cerro Grande in La Serena. Visits are possible by appointment.

The area just north of La Serena is the transition zone between the transversal valleys, where agriculture is still possible, and the Atacama Desert, where it is frankly inconceivable. The Copiapó is the last river to make its way down from the mountains to the sea. North of here, any mountain flows evaporate into nothing along the way, with the one exception of the River Loa, which flows past the Chuquicamata copper mine (and becomes seriously contaminated). The Andes now divide into two parallel ranges, trapping the melting snows in an interior basin to form enormous salt flats, a phenomenon repeated all the way north into Bolivia. These deposits have great commercial potential for the concentrations of lithium, potassium, and borax as well as being used to pro-

Gabriela Mistral

Vicuña is the birthplace of Gabriela Mistral, one of Chile's greatest poets. An austere rather than popular heroine, Mistral is treated in Chile like the precious mineral commodities that are unearthed from the dry, surrounding hills – a resource to be claimed and honored for its undeniable value, but not in itself a source of joy or pleasure. Awarded the national literary prize six years after winning the Nobel Prize, she was mistrusted as an eccentric during her life and was never one of the darlings of Chile's literary elite. A schoolteacher by profession, she spent much of her life abroad, first in Mexico, where she participated in educational reform and, later in life, as Chilean Consul in different countries.

Her first book of poetry, *Desolation*, was published in New York, the city where she died. The themes of her work are displacement, separateness, and the difficulty of romantic love in a world ruled by a punishing God.

Further up the Valle del Elqui from Vicuña is Monte Grande, the village where Mistral spent most of her childhood under the watchful eye of her elder sister, the local school- and postmistress. The school is now a small, very pleasant museum. Here too, on a rocky outcrop overlooking the valley, Gabriela Mistral is buried.

duce salt for human consumption. In the central plain, followed by the Pan-American Highway, an occasional wet winter brings the desert into flower the following spring. This rare and short-lived display is an unforgettable sight.

Salt lakes and flamingos

Copiapó ❾, the capital of the region, is now a grape-growing zone par excellence, the result of enormous investments in earthmoving and irrigation. As these grapes are the first to ripen and hit US supermarkets around Christmas, they are worth the expense. From Copiapó it is possible to drive eastwards through the desert to the salt flats, an extraordinary trip if correct precautions are taken: wear warm clothes; bring food, water, and petrol; and register your route and the duration of the trip with the local *carabineros* (police).

The **Salar de Maricunga** salt flat is impressive for its setting near the Andes, including the world's highest volcano, Ojos del Salado (6,893 meters/22,615ft), which last erupted in 1956. For a longer stay, the national park service (CONAF) has a very basic guest-house in Parque Nacional Nevado Tres Cruces, a bit farther along the road. Near the Argentine border, the **Laguna Verde** lake is apparently dead, but flamingos live in the salt flat, contentedly picking bugs out of the oily ooze in the rocks. Explorer/conqueror Diego de Almagro used this crossing from Argentina in his ill-fated 1536 journey: he lost most of his men en route in the frigid passes. Legend has it that half-frozen survivors often pulled off a couple of toes along with their boots.

Bahía Inglesa, near Copiapó, is said to be the most beautiful beach of the north, but there are many bathing spots along the Pan-American Highway, which returns to the shore for a long stretch between **Caldera** ❿ and **Chañaral** ⓫. The latter port was severely polluted by wastes from the copper mine at Salvador. Deposits from the copper mine are now diverted to a newly inaugurated desert site, ending 60 years of contamination. Bahía Hedionda (Stinky Bay) takes its name from this unfortunate history. North of Chañaral is the wildlife refuge **Parque Nacional Pan de Azúcar**. ❑

The Museo Mineralógico in Copiapó has one of Chile's largest collections of mineral samples and is a good introduction to the area's geological history.

BELOW: Volcán Licancábur and Laguna Verde.

RESTAURANTS

La Serena

Mercado La Recova
Cienfuegos y Cantournet
$
For a cheap lunch of typical Chilean food, such as *cazuela* (meat and vegetable broth), scout the tiny restaurants and stalls of the Recova market.

La Mia Pizza
Avenida del Mar 2100
Tel: (051) 212 232
$$
Serves international dishes as well as pasta dishes and pizza. Tables outside and sea views make this a pleasant place for a leisurely lunch.

Tololo Beach
Avenida del Mar 5200
Tel: (051) 242 656
$$
Seafront restaurant with a great atmosphere. Serves good seafood at affordable prices.

Valle de Elqui

El Ranchito de Don René
Centenario s/n,
Pisco Elqui
Tel: (051) 451 068
$
Serves simple but delicious Chilean dishes, including barbecued meat.

Vicuña

Restaurant Halley
Gabriela Mistral 404
Tel: (051) 411 225
$$
Typical country fare, including roast goat. There is also a large outdoor dining area under a straw roof.

Prices are per person for a three-course meal, not including drinks:
$ = under US$15
$$ = US$15–25
$$$ = US$25–35

EL NORTE GRANDE

Chile's far north, or "Great North," is an area of
spectacular beauty, with Pacific beaches, deserts,
volcanoes, lakes teeming with wildlife, and the
remnants of ancient civilizations

Santiago

The Atacama Desert is located in the same latitude belt as other deserts in the Southern Hemisphere, whose dominant high-pressure systems prevent storms from moving in. Chile's twin mountain ranges aggravate the situation; no precipitation has been measured in this desert since the Spanish colonization, giving it the title of driest spot on earth. The Altiplanic Inversion occurs around the summer equinox (December 21), when strong evaporation generates sometimes violent rain and hailstorms in the mountains, and the water rushes down the dry gorges. These storms last until March, and serious flooding can make many roads virtually impassable.

The extraordinary dryness is responsible for great archeological treasures, such as the famous Atacama mummies, which predate the Egyptian varieties by several thousand years. All sorts of artifacts are easily preserved, and new finds occur regularly. The excellent Le Paige Museum in San Pedro de Atacama, founded by a Belgian Jesuit, Gustavo Le Paige, has 380,000 objects. A 2,800-year-old site called Tulor has been unearthed nearby (daily 8.30am–7pm; charge).

Water is obviously a major logistical problem, not only for personal use but also to satisfy the enormous demands of modern mining. Huge investments have been made in pipelines to bring Andean waters to the coast or to mining outposts. At the Conchi bridge north of Chiu Chiu (near San Pedro), six pipelines come together. The first known industrial use of solar energy in the world was in a water desalinization plant built in 1872 at Carmen Alto near Antofagasta. Pollution from mining and smelting has been rife, but not all industrial intervention has been a disaster: the River Salado was diverted to Chuquicamata in 1951, removing its unwanted salts from the Loa, which runs all the way to Antofagasta. (Unfortunately, the Loa now has high levels of arsenic.)

Main Attractions

CHUQUICAMATA MINE
VALLE DE LA LUNA
SAN PEDRO DE ATACAMA
EL TATIO GEYSERS
MUSEO ARQUEOLÓGICO
   SAN MIGUEL
PARQUE NACIONAL LAUCA

PRECEDING PAGES:
Reserva Nacional
Las Vicuñas. **LEFT:**
adobe church, San
Pedro. **BELOW:**
Atacama mummy.

Desert metropolis

Antofagasta ❶ is the fourth-largest city in Chile and the most populous of the Atacama Desert. It is still an important port for export of minerals.

However, an alternative port has developed in nearby Mejillones, mostly to relieve road congestion in Antofagasta. Antofagasta's 20km (12-mile) beachfront gives it a fresh, gracious air, despite the unrelieved brown of the hills. A financial dispute and property seizure here in 1879 sparked the War of the Pacific, which ended Bolivian control of the town and lands to the east. This portion of Chile is the widest, measuring 355km (221 miles) from the Andes to the sea.

In Antofagasta, the excellent **Museo Regional** (Tue–Fri 9am–5pm, Sat–Sun 11am–2pm; charge except Sun and holidays) relates local history and includes archaeological exhibits relating to the area's indigenous peoples, but the city has few other attractions for visitors.

Some 13km (8 miles) north of the city is the famous **La Portada**, a huge rock eroded into an arch by the sea. Across a peninsula to the north is the town of **Mejillones** ❷, which started out as the northern railroads' mechanical shop, producing wagons and locomotives. One of the most sheltered bays in the area, it now houses thermal power plants and other heavy industries, as well as port facilities.

Northeast of Antofagasta are two of the world's largest copper mines: Escondida copper mine, controlled by BHP Billiton, an international mining company, and the state-owned **Chuquicamata** mine, or Chuqui as it is fondly known. Together, these two mines produce almost a seventh of the world's copper. The service town of **Calama** ❸ has little to offer besides streets full of cheap bars and strip joints and most travelers stay only overnight to take a tour of the Chuquicamata mine.

The first thing that strikes you in Chuqui is the special trucks that carry the mineral loosened by dynamite explosions from the terraced sides of the vast pit. Their wheels alone are nearly 4 meters (13ft) in diameter, and drivers sit another 2 meters (6ft) above them, reducing all other traffic to Lilliputian status. Regular-sized trucks circulate with flags on long poles in order to alert the big-truck drivers to their presence.

Nearby **Chiu Chiu** was the prehispanic crossroads at the fork of two rivers. It fulfills the stereotype of a desert oasis, a green speck in the midst of a hostile brown sea, and has a 1675 church whose construction borrowed elements of the Atacameño indigenous culture.

The road toward San Pedro de Atacama crosses the Plain of Patience, whose name soon begins to make sense: the landscape between two distant ridges appears not to change at all for miles. An advertised alternative route to San Pedro though the **Valle de la Luna** (Valley of the Moon) is not advised for small cars as sand accumulated on the road can trap them, and this is definitely not a place where you'd want to be stuck.

Center of activity

The oasis town of **San Pedro de Atacama** ❹ is a popular base for explor-

ing the north's most spectacular sights. A dry salt lake, the **Salar de Atacama**, stretches beyond the town to a distant row of snowcapped volcanoes – including Licancábur which, at 5,916 meters (19,410ft), is one of the highest extinct volcanoes in the Andean chain.

San Pedro is extremely popular with backpackers and, although fun, has become a little touristy and can get crowded. It has a restored adobe house on one side of the plaza that is universally called Pedro de Valdivia's residence but is now thought to be prehispanic in construction. Opposite is a 16th-century church, one of the oldest in Chile.

San Pedro's **Museo Arqueológico Gustavo Le Paige** (Mon–Fri 9am–6pm, Sat–Sun 10am–6pm; charge) was founded by the former village priest after whom it is named, it has an unusually wide array of pre-Columbian artifacts, all excellently displayed. However, the museum's most famous exhibits – its collection of ancient mummies of both children and adults, preserved in the dry desert air, with their deliberately deformed skulls – were withdrawn in 2007 at the request of local

The Salar de Atacama covers 750,000 acres and contains Chile's largest deposit of salt.

BELOW: sandboarding in the desert.

indigenous communities who protested about this display of their dead ancestors. The mummies are still stored at the museum while their possible reburial is discussed.

Southeast of San Pedro is the village of **Toconao**, past a plantation of *tamarugo* trees which provide a tiny seed for animal pasture. A guide can be hired here to drive to **Lago Chaxa** and observe pink flamingos. The entire Salar de Atacama can be circled in a two-day trip, passing through impressively desolate landscapes and curious desert outposts.

Three kilometers (2 miles) northwest of San Pedro, at **Quitor**, are the ruins of a 700-year-old pre-Columbian fortress. This was where the native peoples made their last stand against the invading Spaniards under Pedro de Valdivia.

Thirty-two kilometers (20 miles) northeast of San Pedro are the hot springs called the **Termas de Puritama** (charge), where you will find a choice of steaming pools to wallow in, as well as a few waterfalls for a natural shower (although, annoyingly, the best pools are reserved for use of guests at the nearby luxury Explora Hotel).

Desert winds and geysers

The famous **Valle de la Luna** is about 8km (5 miles) from San Pedro. As the name suggests, this is a haunting landscape of colored gypsum, clay, and salt, without a hint of organic life to be found. The valley is at its eeriest at sunset, while under a full moon the beams reflecting off the salt crystals of the region make it a truly spectacular sight.

But perhaps the most interesting excursion from San Pedro is the one that leaves at 4am to visit the daily show of at least 100 geysers at **El Tatio**, which burst forth just before sunrise every morning. As they exit the frozen earth with strange gurgling subterranean sounds, they thrust their columns of steam high into the air. Some are wide, boiling pools, while others resemble mini-volcanoes with cones of bright yellow mineral deposits. Be very careful not to step too close to the edge of the pools; there have been some fatal accidents. The display dies down at about 10am until the next morning. The visitor can bathe in a huge pool of tolerably hot thermal waters before returning.

BELOW: the El Tatio geysers at sunrise.

Big beaches and big dunes

Traveling north toward **Iquique ⑤** takes you past numerous geoglyphs carved into the hillsides. The best collection is in the **Reserva Nacional Pampa del Tamarugal**, 48km (30 miles) south of the turning to Iquique (open daily 10am–5pm; charge). This is also the zone of nitrate ghost towns. The detour to Iquique is close to **Pozo Almonte**, 47km (30 miles) across a plateau which abruptly ends with a breathtaking view over the city. Between it and the 600-meter (1,968ft) cliffs lies a huge sand dune whose dimensions only become clear from below – this is a popular venue for sand-skiing. Iquique's golden era was the nitrate heyday from 1890 to 1920, when European opera singers appeared in the elegant **Teatro Municipal** (daily 9am–9pm; charge) and adjourned to a replica Mudéjar palace, now the **Centro Español**, across the plaza, for a late meal. After the collapse of nitrate mines, fishmeal (a fish powder used to feed livestock and farmed fish) came into its own.

The **Museo Regional** (Baquedano 951; Tue–Fri 9am–5pm, Sat–Sun 10am–5pm; charge) is worth visiting, with mummies, archeological artifacts, and a model Aymara village. The nearby **Museo Naval** on Calle Esmeralda is also worth a visit (Tue–Fri 10am–1pm and 4–7pm, Sat–Sun 11am–2pm; charge). But the main interest is in the range of stately 19th-century mansions that are kept as national monuments; many are clustered around Plaza Arturo Prat, with its clock tower and Corinthian columns. The whole center has been declared a National Monument.

About 70km (44 miles) east of Iquique is the village La Tirana, the site of the Virgen del Carmen religious festival. This annual event takes place during mid-July and goes on for a week. The festival has dance groups composed of virginal maidens and men disguised as devils. The whole experience is a compromise between Catholic rite and indigenous animist influences.

On the northern frontier

Arica ⑥ was the first port for exporting the fabulous silver wealth of Bolivia's Potosí mine. (In 1611 Potosí was the largest and richest city in the Americas.)

Day trips to the spectacular Valley of the Moon can be arranged in San Pedro de Atacama.

BELOW: the town of Putre, east of Arica.

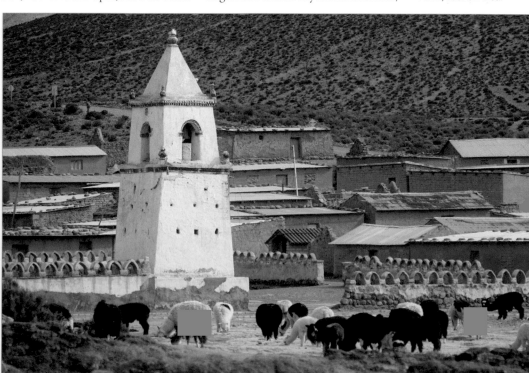

Under Peruvian rule until the 1880s, Arica is now the international link to Bolivia and Peru. Its warm-water beaches make it a popular summer resort, particularly for Bolivians. A small church in the town center was built by the French architect Gustave Eiffel, better known for his Paris tower.

The **Museo Arqueológico San Miguel** (Mar–Dec daily 10am–6pm, Jan–Feb daily 10am–7pm; charge) is 14km (9 miles) from town and has an impressive collection of sand-preserved mummies older than their Egyptian counterparts. The Azapa Valley in which the museum is located demonstrates the desert's fertility: given an adequate supply of water, brightly colored flowers grown commercially suddenly appear in the distance.

From Arica, passing the ancient geoglyphs near **San Miguel de Azapa**, and taking the inland road toward Lago Chungará, you pass through prehispanic and colonial villages with baroque churches and *pukarás*, or stone forts, used by native tribes from unrecorded times to defend themselves from invaders. As you ascend 4,500 meters (14,800ft) into **Parque Nacional Lauca**, the mighty 6,000-meter (19,700ft) high volcanoes Parinacota and Pomerape – sacred gods to the inhabitants of the high Andean plain – dominate the landscape. The ritual town of Parinacota is locked and abandoned for most of the year, but in September becomes the center for the colorful religious festivals of the Aymara shepherds in the region, who otherwise rarely show themselves.

On **Lago Chungará**, declared a Biosphere World Reserve by Unesco, wildlife teems. The large flightless *tagua-tagua* make their nests on floating reed islands; the chinchilla-like *vizcachas* with their hopping scamper could be mistaken for fleeing gray hares; the sand-colored vicuñas often tag behind llama herds; the black-and-white *piquén* (Andean geese) will show themselves far from their nesting offspring as decoys; but perhaps most famous are the pink flamingos which dwell in the lake's shallows. Covering the rocks at this altitude like a green carpet is the pungent native lichen *llareta*, which grows a centimeter a year and has been used almost to extinction for fuel farther south. ❏

DRINK

The town of Pica, southeast of Iquique, is famous for its tiny lemons – *limones de pica* – that are considered the best for making pisco sour.

RESTAURANTS

Antofagasta

Don Karl's
Antonio Toro 1093
Tel: (055) 419 401
$$$
This restaurant serves mainly German food and, with its wooden tables and benches, has a definitely German air; good service.

Picadillo
Grecia 1000
Tel: (055) 247 503
$$
Behind an unprepossessing exterior, this is comfy place for a drink or a snack; open for lunch weekdays only.

San Pedro de Atacama

El Algarrobal
Licancábur 246a
$
Set menus only at this restaurant which is a favorite with the locals.

Café Adobe
Caracoles 211
Tel: (055) 851 132
$$
Widely regarded as San Pedro's best restaurant, Café Adobe has a covered dining area around an open-pit fire and a terrace open to the desert's starry sky.

La Estaka
Caracoles 259b
Tel: (055) 851 201
$$
Adobe and ethnic textiles dominate the decor of this popular restaurant; the lunch menus are good value for money but the rest of the menu is more expensive.

Iquique

Casino Español
Plaza Prat 584
Tel: (057) 333 911
$$
This restaurant, located in the Centro Español, is worth it just for the setting, but the pisco sours are also excellent.

Arica

Café del Mar
21 de Mayo 260
Tel: (058) 231 936
$
The set lunch menu is excellent value and the service friendly; also open in the evenings for drinks and snacks.

Maracuyá
Av. Comandante San Martín 0321
Tel: (058) 227 600
$$$
Standard international fare, but good fish; the views from this open-air restaurant, especially the veranda on stilts over the sea, are lovely.

Prices are per person for a three-course meal, not including drinks.
$ = under US$15
$$ = US$15–25
$$$ = US$25–35

Ghost Towns

The north of Chile is dotted with abandoned mining towns, some of which have been preserved and are open to visitors.

The collapse of the nitrate or saltpeter market at the end of World War I was so sudden that the mining towns, which had no other reason to exist, were abruptly abandoned. A German-invented synthetic nitrate had eliminated the need for the raw material rendering Chile's "desert gold" obsolete.

Mining camps were known as *oficinas* (offices), referring to the offices of the purchasing agents, who bought everything mined within a certain radius. Virtually anyone determined and hardworking enough could be a miner, since the earliest production method consisted of simply digging up the readily visible *caliche* (nitrate ore), grinding it, and selling it at the "office." When the best ore, which had a grade of 50–60 percent, was exhausted, the office simply moved elsewhere.

More complicated processes which could utilize lower-grade ore led to more permanent settlements. These offices are identifiable by waste piles of gravel built up into cake-like constructions. Many are visible from the highway between Antofagasta and Calama, and south of Iquique. A small roadside marker gives the history of each site.

World Heritage sites

The best-preserved ghost town is Oficina Humberstone on the turn-off from Pozo Almonte to Iquique. Established in the mid-19th century, it had a population of 5,000 and provided an unusually varied existence for its inhabitants. A few tamarugo trees remain standing around the plaza, and the town's theater, including its seats, the church, and the market are still intact. The abandoned frames of workshops and homes are spread out over a large area; everything is covered with dust and battered by the steady desert wind. The air of recent habitation is genuinely spooky, as if the inhabitants had suddenly fled without warning.

In mining towns such as Humberstone everything was owned and controlled by the mining company. It built the housing, stocked the town's stores, decided who worked, for how long, at what rates, and what he did with his wages (miners were often paid in *fichas*, tokens only valid for company goods).

Nearby is Oficina Santa Laura, where a processing plant and administrative complex are preserved. In 2005, Unesco placed the two towns on its World Heritage in Danger list, citing wind damage to wooden structure and the effect of windborne salt on metal, as well as looting, as the main threats. They are open to visitors 9am–5pm (closed Mon), but guided tours are available only until 2pm.

Along the Antofagasta–Calama road just past Carmen Alto is the Oficina Chacabuco and the nearby Salinas railway station, site of an abandoned 1872 drinking-water plant which used solar energy. Chacabuco was one of the Chilean locations used in 2008 to film the James Bond film, *Quantum of Solace*.

Between Antofagasta and Tocopilla are the only functioning nitrate centers, Pedro de Valdivia and María Elena. Workers for both plants live in María Elena, which has a street plan based on Britain's Union Flag. These are both owned by the Chilean Chemical and Mining Company SOQUIMICH, which was returned to private ownership during the military regime. The nitrate market has perked up considerably with the renewed demand for natural fertilizers, and iodine can also be recovered commercially as a byproduct. SOQUIMICH is, in fact, one of the world's leading producers of iodine. ❑

RIGHT: an abandoned steam engine.

BLOOMING MARVELS IN THE ATACAMA DESERT

This mysterious, barren region of haunting beauty is home to spectacular natural phenomena and the well-preserved remains of ancient civilizations

Chile's far north is made up of barren desert and scrubland, and the forbidding high plains of the altiplano. No wonder most of the population prefer to live along the coast, in towns like Antofagasta and Iquique, famed for their architecture and expansive Pacific beaches. For the visitor, however, the mountain and desert regions present a series of awe-inspiring spectacles. The Atacama Desert is reputed to be the driest in the world, yet every decade or so a rare downpour (usually linked with the El Niño weather system) in the southern part around Copiapó and Vallenar brings dormant seeds into bloom, in a phenomenon known as "The Flowering Desert."

The oasis village of San Pedro de Atacama *(see page 195)*, dominated by the Licancábur volcano, is at the center of a region of immense geological interest, with huge salt lakes, hot springs, and unusual desert formations. East of San Pedro the terrain ascends steeply to the altiplano, where it meets Argentine and Bolivian territory. In this chilly region lie more hot springs, geysers, and mountain lakes of ethereal beauty.

More natural and geological delights lie farther north of the Atacama Desert, toward Peru, where national parks like Lauca and Volcán Isluga, and Reserva Nacional Las Vicuñas are home to a variety of distinctive wildlife.

Some hardy travelers take the train from Calama to Oruro in Bolivia. Rewards of this grueling trip include more altiplano highlights, such as the immense salt basin of Uyuni, and Lagunas Verde and Colorado.

ABOVE: Volcán Licancábur (5,916 meters/19,410ft) presides over the ancient village oasis of San Pedro de Atacama, marking the place where the flat desert meets the chilly altiplano.

RIGHT: knowledge of some of the fauna that comes into bloom in the southern Atacama Desert only every 10–15 years is very scant.

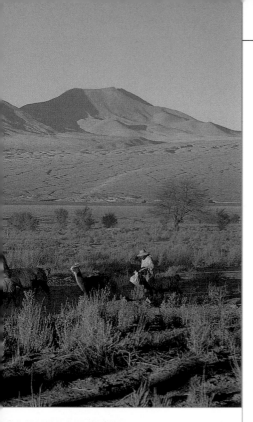

A NATURAL AND CULTURAL OASIS

The Atacama Desert has a restful quality – despite its inhospitable climate it comes as no surprise to learn that it has sustained human civilizations for thousands of years. Numerous ancient remains have been found in the area around the oasis of San Pedro, a tourist-dominated yet extremely pleasant hamlet with one of Chile's best museums, the Museo Arqueológico Gustavo Le Paige. The area's lack of rain has preserved ancient artifacts, including mummies as well as pottery, jewelry, fragments of woven cloth, and other items. It all provides a fascinating insight into what life was like before the arrival of Europeans. Also in the region is Pukará de Quitor, a 12th-century fort.

San Pedro is also a good base from which to explore the surrounding desert, with numerous tours available from the village, for instance to the Valle de la Luna, a lunar landscape of eroded salt-rock formations, the Atacama salt flat, the El Tatio geysers, and picturesque indigenous villages like Caspana, Aiquina, and Toconce.

ABOVE: flamingos are a common sight around altiplano lakes. Three species of flamingo breed around Laguna Chaxa, south of Toconao.

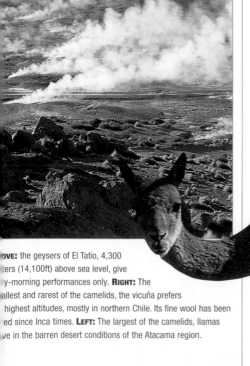

ABOVE: the geysers of El Tatio, 4,300 meters (14,100ft) above sea level, give early-morning performances only. **RIGHT:** The smallest and rarest of the camelids, the vicuña prefers the highest altitudes, mostly in northern Chile. Its fine wool has been prized since Inca times. **LEFT:** The largest of the camelids, llamas live in the barren desert conditions of the Atacama region.

JUAN FERNÁNDEZ ISLANDS

Famed as the temporary home of the real-life
Robinson Crusoe, the inaccessibility of these
Pacific islands makes them natural biospheres
replete with abundant endemic wildlife

Most people have never heard of the 18th-century Scottish sea dog named Alexander Selkirk or the **Juan Fernández Islands**, 650km (404 miles) off the Chilean mainland. Yet they are part of our popular mythology. Try to imagine being marooned on a desert isle and you will probably see a man dressed in goatskins, flintlock at the ready, scanning the horizon for passing ships. His island – unlike the barren, windswept rocks where most mariners were washed up – has plentiful wood, crystal waters, abundant food, and no wild beasts. The scene is from *Robinson Crusoe*, of course. But although Daniel Defoe set his classic novel in the Caribbean, he based it directly on Alexander Selkirk's real-life adventures on Chile's tiny Pacific possession.

The foul-tempered young Scotsman spent four years and four months on the largest of the three deserted Juan Fernández Islands. Finally rescued by a group of English privateers, Selkirk was clad in goatskins and could barely speak, croaking rather than talking. He had made himself two wooden huts with fur-lined interiors and had become incredibly fit from chasing wild animals around the rocky shores. The marooned sailor became a minor celebrity on his return home and – with the more debauched side of his character being carefully tidied up – inspired one of the most enduring classics in the English language.

The inhabitants of the Juan Fernández Islands today certainly aren't shy about this unique claim to fame. Selkirk's island was renamed **Isla Robinson Crusoe** in the mid-1970s, while another, which the Scotsman never visited, was renamed **Isla Alejandro Selkirk**. Hotel and street names in the islands' only township refer insistently to the shipwrecked hero.

These unsubtle grabs at attention might suggest that the islands are something of a tourist trap. Nothing could be farther from the truth.

Main Attractions
SAN JUAN DE BAUTISTA
EL MIRADOR DE SELKIRK
CUEVAS DE LOS PATRIOTAS
FUERTE SANTA BÁRBARA

PRECEDING PAGES:
one of Selkirk's
caves. **LEFT:**
Selkirk's rescue.
BELOW: view from
the Mirador de
Selkirk.

The three Juan Fernández Islands are believed to be the result of three separate volcanic eruptions.

Thanks to some spectacular transport difficulties, the archipelago is one of the least visited places in Chile. And while there are several fascinating excursions relating to Selkirk's adventures there, the most lasting pleasures lie elsewhere: the archipelago is a unique wilderness area, declared a Biosphere Reserve by Unesco in 1977, while its people maintain an unusual serenity and striking indifference to the lures of the outside world.

The real-life Crusoe

While Daniel Defoe's fictional hero was shipwrecked in a tropical storm (and so, in his more meditative moments, saw the Hand of God at work), the real-life mariner Alexander Selkirk could only blame himself for his predicament: Selkirk actually asked to be let off his ship in the middle of nowhere. As sailing master of the *Cinque Ports*, a privateering vessel making a circumnavigation of the globe in 1704, the quarrelsome Selkirk found himself constantly at odds with the ship's captain. Feelings finally came to a head over some poor repairs which had been made to a leak in the hull: Selkirk snapped that, if the boat was to go down, it would be without him. The captain agreed to land the Scotsman at the nearest island with a few supplies.

Selkirk stubbornly held to his demand until the very last moment. Sitting on the shore of Más a Tierra (as the island was then known), watching his former shipmates row back to their ship, the enormity of his decision struck him. Marooning was considered by pirates to be the ultimate punishment, far worse than walking the plank. A slow death by starvation or dehydration was the usual result. Most were put ashore with only their sea chest and a pistol with one ball; tales abounded of ships' crews finding a lone skeleton with a shattered skull and a rusting pistol clenched in one hand.

Selkirk is said to have plunged into the ocean and chased after the departing rowboat, screaming madly that he had changed his mind. "Well I have not changed mine!" spat the captain. "Stay where you are and may you starve!"

Goats, rats, and feral cats

This indecorous scene was the beginning of 52 months of isolation for Selkirk. He spent most of his time reading the Bible. A journalist who interviewed the Scotsman in a London tavern after his return to England noted that he believed himself "a better Christian while in this solitude than ever he was before, or than, he was afraid, he should ever be again."

Yet in the beginning, Selkirk hardly took his fate philosophically. For several weeks after the marooning, he apparently wandered the coast, wailing and staring at the empty horizon. He simply could not believe that his shipmates would leave him there to rot on the shore. It took him 18 months to accept his fate, tear himself away from the shoreline and explore the rest of his island prison. At least Selkirk was not starved for animal company. Every night he heard the "monsters of the deep" whose cries were "too terrible to be made for human ears" – which, it turned out, were sea lions that had come up to shore. Eventually Selkirk overcame his fear, and learned how to climb behind these ponderous beasts and crack their skulls with a single blow of his hatchet.

Domestic animals had been introduced during an ill-fated attempt by the Spaniards to colonize the island following its discovery by the navigator Juan Fernández in 1574. Wild goats became the Scotsman's staple food: after his ammunition ran out, he chased them on foot with a knife and became an impressive athlete. He even chased goats for sport, marking their ears as a record. However, this diversion had its dangers: on one occasion Selkirk grabbed a goat just as it was leaping off a precipice. He was able to use the beast's body to cushion his fall, but was knocked unconscious for at least a full day. After this debacle, he decided to raise goats in a compound.

Wild rats were less amusing animal neighbors, invading Selkirk's hut by night to nibble his feet and tear his clothes. The Scotsman tamed feral kittens and laid them around his bed as a defense. Apparently he also taught some of his cats and kids to dance. "Thus best we picture him," intones the

The Juan Fernández native eagle lives only on the small Isla Alejandro Selkirk. It visits the other two islands, but never settles on them; no one knows why.

BELOW: fishermen setting off from Isla Alejandro Selkirk.

early 20th- century poet Walter de la Mare, "praying aloud, singing and dancing with his kids and cats in the flames and the smoke of his allspice wood, and the whole world's moon taunting and enchanting him in her seasons."

Return to civilization

Charming as these bestial balls must have been, Selkirk did not waver in his attempts to escape the island. Every day he climbed up to a lookout to survey the horizon. On two occasions ships actually pulled into the bay and Selkirk thought himself saved – only to discover that they were Spanish barks that would have taken him as a slave to the mines of Peru if they had caught him. (On the second visit, Spanish sailors even fired on the maroon and chased him into the bushes, but were no match for Selkirk's superhuman speed. The Scotsman hid up a tree until the danger had passed.)

Finally, Selkirk spotted the English *Duke* and *Duchess* lowering anchor on the island with 50 scurvy-ridden sailors. Brought on board, the goatskin-clad Selkirk cut an extraordinary figure, but disbelievers were soon silenced when William Dampier came forward to recognize the maroon and confirm his story.

Despite romantic reports to the contrary, Selkirk appears to have had few qualms about returning to his old life of privateering and debauchery. Appointed a mate on the voyage, he took part in the pillage of various Spanish ports before returning with the profits to celebrity in London and his home town of Lower Largo in Fife, Scotland. He was no doubt gratified to learn that the captain and crew of the *Cinque Ports*, after dumping him at Juan Fernández, had spent the last four years in a festering Lima jail, having been captured by the Spanish when the vessel foundered, just as Selkirk had predicted.

Drinking and whoring soon took its toll on Selkirk, sapping his unnatural fitness. He even became sentimental for his island prison, noting to one journalist that "I am worth eight hundred pounds, but shall never be so happy as when I was not

BELOW: firecrown hummingbird.

Three-Island National Park

Except for the town of San Juan Bautista and its surrounding area, all the Juan Fernández archipelago is a vast national park that is carefully controlled by CONAF, Chile's national park service, to protect the endemic flora and fauna that put the islands on Unesco's Biosphere Reserve list. There are three official trails that visitors can take on their own but they must register at the Park administration office and, in some parts of the islands, only guided hikes are permitted. An alternative way to see the park is by boat, also visiting colonies of the native fur seal that was once close to extinction.

Plant life is unusually varied in the archipelago, with 101 endemic varieties, including a range of enormous ferns, many of which look like they belong in a Dr Seuss book, and biologists regularly turn up new finds. Of the endemic animals, the red Juan Fernández hummingbird is most famous for its needle-fine black beak and silken plumage.

CONAF spends most of its time trying to eradicate threats introduced by man: everything from mulberry bushes to the wild goats and feral cats descended from Selkirk's days. Rabbits were a problem, but they have been controlled by the simple solution of paying a trapper to catch and sell 150 a day (the islanders thought this a more humane solution than using the fatal viral disease myxomatosis).

worth a farthing." The Scotsman may have gone a little batty: he reportedly dug a cave in his parents' backyard to hide in, ran away to London with a milkmaid, dumped her, then signed on for another privateering expedition. He caught a fever in the tropics and died on board in 1723, at the age of 47. Selkirk never knew that his marooning on Juan Fernández – extended by Defoe to 28 years and with a Man Friday thrown in – would become a legend.

A remote destination

Getting to the Juan Fernández Islands today can seem as complicated as it was for Alexander Selkirk to get off them 300 years ago. Flights are generally confined to the summer months (October through April), when two companies operate the route. The frequency of flights depends, though, on demand, and getting a confirmed departure date requires luck and dedication. Even in summer, flights can be postponed for several days, depending on weather conditions.

The flights depart from Santiago's Tobalaba airport early in the morning, leaving the capital behind in a bed of smog. Two hours later, the tiny green specks of Juan Fernández appear, looking as tall as they are wide. For years it was considered impossible to build an airstrip on this rugged terrain, but in the 1970s something looking like a giant ski-jump was blasted through a far corner of the largest island. From the **airstrip ❶**, a jeep heads down a 45-degree angled road to the sea, followed by a 90-minute journey in an open fishing boat to town. On a fine day, the water is clear and blue, with schools of fish zigzagging below and the obese Juan Fernández seals sunning themselves by the shore. The boatmen often smoke succulent lumps of fresh cod caught on the outward journey and share them around with bread and water.

The town of **San Juan Bautista ❷**, where almost all of the archipelago's

600 inhabitants live, is located roughly where Selkirk spent his enforced leisure time. Set beneath forest-covered fists of stone with their peaks continually lost in gray mist, it has only a few, unpaved streets, a small museum-library, a handful of restaurants and bars, a soccer field, and one small cemetery with ship's anchors above many of the graves. With motor vehicles few and far between on the island, the only noise is the never-ending howl of the wind.

This is a lobster town and not poor, although prices of goods imported from the mainland are high. Despite the soporific calm, Bautista is crowded with monuments to war. Eighteenth-century Spanish cannons, dug up from excavations above the town, are set into the footpath, along with a series of green pillboxes built to defend the island against Peruvian warships during the 19th-century War of the Pacific. Most curiously, along the path running north from the town is a spot where famous gun shells can be seen embedded in the cliff side. They were fired by the Brit-

TIP

The El Palillo beach to the south of San Juan Bautista is the best place for swimming or snorkeling.

BELOW: fisherman in Bahía Cumberland.

ish warships *Glasgow* and *Kent* at the German cruiser *Dresden* when it tried to retire here for repairs in 1915, during World War I. The captain blew up the ship rather than surrender.

In Selkirk's footsteps

The sandalwood boom of the late 19th century totally deprived Isla Robinson Crusoe of its native sandalwood trees.

The classic hike from town follows Selkirk's path to **El Mirador de Selkirk** ❸ – the lookout used by the marooned sailor every day to scan the horizon on both sides of the island. Start early, at about 8am, to arrive before the mists roll in. The path runs through crops of introduced eucalyptus into higher forests of indigenous trees. It passes the remains of the Fuerte Santa Bárbara, an old Spanish fort built in the 18th century to ward off pirates, and a turning leading to a rock with carvings on it from 1866 – sailor's graffiti showing a ship and giant fish. The trail becomes a corridor through rainforest before revealing a knife-shaped peak.

The saddle of the mountain is the only place from which to view both sides of the island: the lush green Juan Bautista side to the east giving way to dry brown swirls and jagged peaks on

OPPOSITE: San Juan Bautista.

the northern side of the mountain. A plaque commemorating Selkirk's ordeal was erected here by the crew of a British warship in the 19th century. It has more recently been joined by a small memorial from one of the mariner's descendants from Largo in Scotland.

On the return journey, call in at the **Cuevas de los Patriotas** (Caves of the Patriots), where 300 pro-Spanish soldiers fled in 1814 after Chile's declaration of independence. Unlike Selkirk, they couldn't stand the wind and rain in their huge but damp caves, so gave themselves up. Back on the shore, a number of other caves vie for the title of Selkirk's home – although for most of the time the mariner lived in his own handmade huts.

Modern-day paradise

One of the real pleasures of any visit to Isla Robinson Crusoe is just taking a seat by the wharf and watching the world go by, sipping on a beer and chatting with the islanders. Everyone will eventually mention that Juan Fernández is a paradise. And, although the archipelago doesn't boast the swaying palms or golden sands of most South Pacific islands, it does have plenty of other elements to make it a contender: beautiful scenery, good weather, plenty of food, no crime, no poverty, no racial tensions, and no pollution.

The people of the Juan Fernández Islands are not a remote group being dragged into the 21st century, with a delicate society about to buckle under the strain. Everyone is descended from Chilean or European immigrants, and has grown up within a Western culture – albeit a detached version. The islanders take what they want from the modern world, such as medicine, music, radios, or television soap operas, and leave the rest. Perhaps that's why the half-familiar world of Juan Fernández is so beguiling: one admires the islanders' good sense but, already being a part of the outside world, can never share it.

RESTAURANTS

Lobster fishing is the principal industry in the Juan Fernández Islands which makes this the perfect place to try some. Most visitors tend to eat at their hotel, but there are a handful of restaurants in San Juan Bautista should you fancy a change, of which the following are recommended. None of the restaurants accept credit cards and, although there is a cash machine in the town, it is advisable to bring sufficient

money with you to last the duration of your stay.

San Juan Bautista

Residencial Mirador Selkirk
El Castillo 251
Tel: (032) 275 1028
$
This cosy family-run restaurant is located in an islander's house with a terrace that overlooks the bay. It serves typical Chilean dishes, including local specialties, such as freshly caught lobster and crab.

El Nocturno
Larraín Alcalde 66
Tel: (032) 275 1113
$
An inexpensive and friendly place serving snacks and homely meals that can be prepared at an hour's notice. The seafood empanadas are particularly recommended.

Prices are per person for a three-course meal, not including drinks:
$ = under US$15
$$ = US$15–25
$$$ = US$25–35

CENTRAL VALLEY

Vineyards and fruit flourish in the temperate climate of this lush, fertile region, yet until the late 19th century it marked the border of the wild, unconquered southern lands

PRECEDING PAGES: harvesting Malbec grapes. **BELOW:** traditional dance to celebrate the wheat harvest.

Running parallel between the towering Cordillera de los Andes and the lower coastal mountain range is the Chilean **Central Valley**. The area from Los Andes, just 80km (50 miles) north of Santiago, to some 500km (300 miles) farther south is the richest farmland in the country. Vineyards have been established here since the arrival of the Spanish conquistadors, and, today, wine-making for export is among its most important activities. Similarly, most of the traditional agricultural activities of the old landed aristocracy, such as growing wheat, grain, and fodder for domestic animals, have given way to the much more profitable cultivation of fresh produce for export worldwide.

Leaving the main roads, however, is to take a step back in time to a simpler, slower-paced, infinitely more relaxing era. Never is this more true than during the Independence Day celebrations held annually on September 18, which offer an inside view to festivities in rural areas throughout the country. *Fondas* or *ramadas*, outdoor ballrooms with thatched eucalyptus-leaf roofs, are erected all over the countryside. People gather from miles around to watch the competition between *huasos*, the Chilean cowboys *(see page 126)*; to dance the *cueca*, the national dance; to eat empanadas (meat and onion pasties), and to drink *chicha*, fermented grape juice.

Luxurious traditions

The busy town of **Rancagua ❶**, 87km (54 miles) south of Santiago, is as much an agricultural center as the home of miners employed in the **El Teniente copper mine**. The mine, and a heritage-listed workers' camp called **Sewell**, is at the end of the Carretera del Cobre (Copper Highway), which runs from Rancagua east and up into the mountains.

Travelers may, however, simply prefer to visit the thermal baths of **Termas de Cauquenes ❷**, 28km (17 miles)

east of Rancagua, in the Andean foothills. Used by native peoples long before the arrival of the Spanish, the first to lay claim to the medicinal waters were Jesuits. The baths were frequented by the Chilean founding father Bernardo O'Higgins during rests from his revolutionary bouts against the colonial authorities.

The construction of what is today a hotel began back in 1885. The huge high-ceilinged bathhouse with stained-glass windows leads up an enormous staircase to the dining and game-room area. Rooms and suites are set around large open gardens or at the back overlooking the Cachapoal River. The surrounding hills are filled with *peumos*, a native tree with bright red edible fruit and shiny green leaves.

In their quest to compete with the smart new boutique hotels springing up all over the country, traditional establishments such as this have used top cuisine to draw visitors. In Chile, many argue that Swiss-born chef René Acklin and his daughter Sabine have done just that at the Termas de Cauquenes. Diners at the hotel's immense restaurant are transported back a century, with its fine old furnishings contrasting deliciously with the modern fare prepared in the kitchen.

Wine country

Once back on the main highway, the next city south of Rancagua is **San Fernando**, a bustling rural center, which is gradually succumbing to the advances of shopping malls, Internet cafés, and smarter urban life. For the tourist, though, it serves simply as a reference for Santa Cruz, a charming little town 40km (25 miles) toward the coast. Laid out around a traditional Spanish-style city square (Plaza de Armas), **Santa Cruz** has, since the late 1990s, transformed itself from a quaint but lifeless colonial town into a cosmopolitan hub for travelers from all over the world.

No visit is complete without at least a night in the Hotel Santa Cruz Plaza, a restored colonial building. Its 113 rooms are extremely comfortable and it has a landscaped swimming pool and gardens and arguably one of the best restaurants south of Santiago. Its wine list is replete with the area's finest varietal whites and oak-matured reds, and tours of local vineyards can be arranged at the hotel *(see pages 103–5)*.

The town is also home to an excellent historical museum. Run by a not-for-profit foundation in a converted 18th-century estate house, the Museo de Colchagua houses the private collection of Carlos Cardoen, the hotel's owner (summer Tue–Sun 10am–7pm, winter Tue–Sun 10am–6pm; charge, except for hotel guests).

At the Museo San José del Carmen de El Huique in Palmilla, a 15-minute drive from Santa Cruz, visitors get a rare glimpse of 19th-century rural elegance as lived by the wealthy Errázuriz and Echeñique families, who settled there from northern Spain (guided visits by prior appointment only, tel: 072-933 083; Mass is said in what was the family chapel every Sunday at 11.30am and is open to the public).

Lakeside serenity

While the colonial town of Vichuquén can be reached by bus from **Curicó ❸** there is so much to see in this interesting coastal area that it's worth hiring a car. The 110km (68-mile) road that follows the northern bank of the Mataquito River from Curicó as far as Hualañé is a route of breathtaking scenic beauty, bordered by vineyards. But the cut-off route from the highway near San Fernando, through Santa Cruz, Lolol, San Pedro de Alcántara, Rarín, and the coastal town of Llico, also has its own charm, revealing rolling hills and hidden sleepy country towns.

Farther north, at the end of the main road west from Santa Cruz, is **Pichilemu**, Chile's surfing capital. This one-time rural center and fishing village has been transformed into a hip destination for surfers from around the world, most of whom stay in the beachside cabins dotting the road to Punta de Lobos and Bucalemu. Diehard surfers should ask around for details on how to reach "secret spots" farther north toward Navidad.

BELOW: Punta de Lobos beach.

The town of **Vichuquén** existed before the invasion of the Incas from Peru in the 15th century, who formed a colony there with the native Mapuches. The name of the town comes from the Mapuche language and means "the serpent lake." Time seems to have stopped some 100 years ago along its orange tree-lined streets, where unhurried locals linger along the covered wooden sidewalks. The town's museum is worth a visit.

A birder's paradise

The main attraction here, however, is **Lago Vichuquén**, just 5km (3 miles) toward the coast. Pine forests that grow in record time surround the summer houses that line the shore. Windsurfers and small sailboats cut silently across the mirror-like surface of the lake to explore the uninhabited Isla del Cerrillo that sits alone in the lake's center. There are two main hotels on the lake, both situated on the southern side. The Hotel Playa Aquelarre has spectacular views of the lake and the myriad species that make the area a birdwatchers' paradise. Binoculars and ornithological

guides are provided for guests. At the nearby Hotel Marina Vichuquén, the accent is on aquatic pursuits. There are also several camping grounds and cheaper lodgings around the southern end of the lake.

Just 3km (2 miles) north of the lake is the **Reserva Nacional Laguna Torca ❹**. The lagoon is a nesting ground for black-necked swans and another 80 or so species of exotic birds. Great blue herons hide in the reed-lined banks. The S-shaped bodies of stark, white herons wade through the shallows, while an enormous variety of ducks and the small, black *tagua* coots keep up a tremendous clatter of quacking.

After a morning's birdwatching, stop in for fresh shellfish or fried *congrio* (kingclip) at the Residencial Miramar in **Llico** (tel: 075-400 032). Returning to Vichuquén, an unpaved road forks off and runs south through a series of beachside towns famed for their seafood *picadas* (cheap restaurants). Locals and visitors alike say Donde Gilberto (tel: 075-198 3768), 7km (4 miles) before the town of Iloca, is the pick of

A blue heron in the Reserva Nacional Laguna Torca.

BELOW: surfing at Arica.

The City of Stairways

Situated at 2,000 meters (6,600ft) up in the Andes east of Rancagua, the Sewell mining town was built by the Braden Copper Company in 1905 – and named for Barton Sewell, a company executive – to house workers at what was to become the world's largest underground copper mine, El Teniente. At its peak, Sewell had 15,000 inhabitants and facilities that included its own hospital and industrial school. The timber houses, painted in vivid reds, greens, yellows, and blues, cling to the steep mountainside around a large central staircase that starts at the railway station and opens out into other stairways as it climbs, hence Sewell's popular name of "The City of Stairways".

The mine, now operated by Codelco, the state copper company, is still active, but Sewell fell into disuse in the 1970s. It was, however, subsequently renovated and declared a Unesco World Heritage Site in 2006 as an example of a company town developed in a remote and difficult natural environment. It is well worth visiting but prior planning is required. Independent visits are not allowed on the grounds of nearby mine activity and guided tours, available only on Saturdays and Sundays, must be booked through VTS (tel: 072-210 290; www.vts.cl). Tours start in Rancagua or Santiago, with lunch as an optional extra. Children under 7 years (14 if the mine is also included in the tour) and over-75s are not accepted.

Fruit-laden Lands

With its warm, Californian climate, the Central Valley provides ideal conditions for fruit-farming, one of Chile's most profitable industries.

In springtime as you drive along the Pan-American Highway south from Santiago, fields of flaming orchards perfume the air and make a brilliant display. You'll see the dark, hot pink blossom of peaches and nectarines, the lighter, rose-colored cherry trees, and the white-flowering almond, apple, apricot, or plum trees and, along the road, the huge cooling and packing plants at which the fruit is prepared for export to markets around the world.

Bounded by the Andes mountains and the Pacific Ocean, Chile is unusually free of the pests with which other countries' fruit-farming industries have to battle, and this is an asset of which it takes great care through strict phytosanitary controls at its borders.

Chile's fruit exports have grown rapidly, helped by its free trade agreements with most of the world's major economies, and reached US$3.4 billion in 2008, up from US$1.3 billion a decade earlier. And that is only fresh fruit; more fruit still is exported frozen and canned or in the form of juice.

Table grapes account for over a third of total fruit exports. Like other fruit, they take advantage of the high prices available in Europe and the United States during the northern hemisphere winter, particularly if the supermarket shelves in time for Christmas.

Increasingly, however, exporters are also targeting Asian markets, particularly China with which Chile has had a free trade agreement since 2006. In 2008, Chile's fruit exports to China rose by 68 percent to US$96 million, led by grapes, apples, and plums.

Farther south in the Central Valley, berries – principally raspberries and blueberries – are the main crop. Often grown by small producers or through cooperatives, they have brought new prosperity to once poor rural areas and, because of the damage dust does to these delicate fruits, have provided a powerful new incentive for paving country roads.

Fruit farming has also meant new job opportunities for women as *temporeras* or pickers employed during the harvest season. Some women even make a long season of it, starting with the early grape harvest in the north of the country and gradually moving south with the ripening crops.

It is hard work and the hours are long but conditions have improved. Protective clothing and proper rest periods are now more common, as are childcare facilities, while a change in regulation has allowed *temporeras* access to social security benefits.

International competition

But, although Chile is the southern hemisphere's largest fruit exporter, competition is on the increase. Over the past few years, Chile's blueberry production rose rapidly in response to high international demand but Argentina followed suit, causing a sharp drop in prices.

Peru's fruit exports have also grown rapidly in recent years and, although led by tropical fruits which Chile does not grow – principally mangoes and bananas – they include grapes and other key Chilean exports such as avocado pears and citrus fruits. It has been suggested that the two countries should, in fact, team up to supply the vast Chinese market, but this has yet to happen.

Chile is also attempting to carve out new niches for its products in international markets and, given its freedom from pests, organic produce is an obvious option. Although still small, this had been expanding steadily through to 2008, but was then hit by the economic crisis. ❑

LEFT: blueberries, a profitable export.

the bunch. It also has reasonably priced accommodations offering spectacular sea views.

Seat of Chilean independence

Continuing south on the Pan-American Highway, the town of **Talca ❺** is 60km (37 miles) southwest of Curicó. An important urban center since its founding in 1742, Talca was the traditional residence of the landed elite. The older part of town, as in most Chilean colonial towns, surrounds the **Plaza de Armas** with its jacarandas, palms, magnolia trees, cedars, and other conifers.

The **Museo O'Higginiano** (Tue–Fri 10am–6pm, Sat–Sun 10am–2pm; charge), on the corner of Norte 1 and Oriente 2, was the childhood home of the Chilean hero and father of independence, Bernardo O'Higgins. The building was also the home in 1813 of José Miguel Carrera, who presided over the first governmental junta.

Carrera declared Chile a sovereign, autonomous state in the 1812 Constitution, and also – with the help of O'Higgins – organized resistance to invading royalist troops from farther south (*see page 37*). In one of the house's many salons, Bernardo O'Higgins signed the Act of Independence. The museum also features an important collection of paintings, sculpture, historical manuscripts, and pre-Columbian artifacts.

From Talca, one of Chile's few remaining rural train services runs to Constitución on the coast. The train stops at a multitude of tiny farming communities, for many of which it is the sole form of transportation, and the 106km (66-mile) journey takes three hours, but offers a unique insight into a way of life that is rapidly disappearing.

Mexican mural

Farther south on the highway is the town of **Chillán ❻**. Repeatedly destroyed by earthquakes and rebuilt, most of its buildings are not more than 50 years old. In 1939, a night-time earthquake killed 15,000 people and destroyed 90 percent of the town. Mexico donated a school to the city as part

BELOW: the *Death to the Invader* mural in Chillán, painted by Mexican artists following the 1939 earthquake.

The Termas de Chillán ski resort on the western slopes of Volcán Chillán provides some of the continent's best skiing and snowboarding.

BELOW: Hotel Los Nevados.

of the reconstruction. The Mexican muralists David Alfaro Siqueiros and Xavier Guerrero painted representative scenes of Chilean and Mexican history there in 1941.

The Escuela Mexico (corner of Av. Bernardo O'Higgins and Vega de Saldías) still operates as a school, but staff welcome visitors who want to see the heritage-listed *Death to the Invader* mural (Mon–Fri 10am–1pm and 3–6.30pm, Sat–Sun 10am–6pm; free; currently closed for restoration and scheduled to reopen in June 2009).

The **Mercado de Chillán** (Chillán's market), on Calle Maipón between Isabel Riquelme and 5 de Abril, is the largest and most vibrant in Chile. Here you can find handicrafts from all over the country, as well as the locally made clothing that makes up the typical *huaso* (Chilean cowboy) dress: from the felt (for winter) or straw (for summer) flat-rimmed hats, and small dress ponchos in finely woven, bright colors, to the leather boots and carved wooden stirrups. The market is open every day, but is at its best on Saturdays.

Skiing and bathing on a volcano

The western-facing slopes of the **Volcán Chillán**, 80km (50 miles) from Chillán, provide some of the finest open-slope skiing in the Andes from June through October. **Termas de Chillán**, named for its famous thermal springs, is the base for the ski resort. The resort, at 1,650 meters (5,413ft) above sea level, has nine chairlifts and 32 pistes, covering a total of more than 46km (29 miles). An accomplished skier can stay on the slopes from morning to late afternoon and, as there is so much variety, need never cover the same trail twice. A series of pistes from the summit down to the wooded region around the hotel area connect to produce a 13km (8-mile) run, also the longest in South America.

After a hard day on the slopes, there is no better way to ease tired muscles than to plunge into one of the four outdoor thermal swimming pools in the Parque de Aguas. The Gran Hotel Termas de Chillán has 120 modern bedrooms, as well as sitting rooms with roaring fireplaces, three restaurants and a hot springs spa. The hotel also has six self-service apartment buildings, ideal for family groups. A short distance away is the Hotel Los Nevados de Chillán (ex-Hotel Pirigallo) while more modest hotels and guest cabins can be found in **Las Trancas** or **Recinto**, a few kilometers down the valley.

Many visitors also make the trip in the summer to hike to the geyser-like fuming springs of the thermal waters and bathe in the medicinal muds nearby. A trip in the chairlift reveals stupendous views of the towering volcanic crater and accompanying eternal snows of the Nevada de Chillán mountain range. Guided walking tours and horseback riding excursions are also available.

The road back from the Gran Hotel Termas is lined with lush forest vegetation resembling that found in the Lake District farther south. Huge old oaks join firs, pines, and the delicate, native *ñirre* trees set among giant ferns and red *copihues* – the fleshy, trumpet-shaped national flower that hangs from climbing vines.

Two kilometers (1 mile) from the hotel you can visit an enormous natural cavern, the **Cueva de los Pincheira**. This was used as a hideaway by the Pincheira brothers and their followers, a group of royalist highway robbers who ransacked the area during the struggle for independence. The colossal **Piedras Comadres**, spectacular rock walls that drop straight down from their forest-covered heights, can be seen from the road.

Before the town of **Los Angeles** ❼, 80km (50 miles) south of Chillán, the **Salto del Laja** waterfall can be viewed from the bridge that crosses the River Laja. The falls crash down some 15–20 meters (50–65ft) from two wide arches into deep, enormous pools, to be swiftly conducted into the narrow river canyon further down. The area has numerous hotels, campsites, and restaurants, some with swimming pools and other recreational facilities.

Gateway to the south

The country's second-largest city (even though, including the adjoining port of Talcahuano, it has only a population of around 500,000), **Concepción** ❽ is located some 86km (53 miles) off the

Nahuelbuta means "the big cat" in the Mapuche tongue, a reference to the puma that lives in the mountains named for it.

BELOW: Salto del Laja waterfall.

TIP

Visitors can go down the "Devil's Draught" coal mine, near Lota, in which Chile's best-known novel of mining life, *Sub Terra* by Baldomera Lillo, is set.

Pan-American Highway. It lies at the mouth of the **River Biobío**, the natural boundary between southern and central Chile, and is an important center for the country's forestry industry. Founded by conquistador Pedro de Valdivia in 1550, Concepción was the site occupied by the Real Audiencia, the political, military, and administrative center of the Spanish colony from 1565 to 1573. The location of the city was changed a number of times due to repeated earthquake devastation, particularly in the mid-18th century, and attacks from the Mapuches. Its present location was settled in 1764.

Repeated reconstruction following the natural disasters, combined with economic growth, have made Concepción a modern city with little remaining of its past glory, and many visitors would rather pass on through it.

The city's pride is the **Universidad de Concepción** campus, with its open amphitheater and central green dominated by the university's watchtower. Nearby are the marble-fronted walls of the courthouse, and the railway station,

above which is a mural depicting the history of the city. The **Casa del Arte** (Pinoteca), on the corner of Lamas and Larenas, houses an extensive collection of national paintings.

In **Talcahuano**, the battleship *Huáscar* can be visited. Captured from the Peruvian fleet during the War of the Pacific in 1879, it has been held as a trophy of the victory that added the country's northernmost provinces and their rich mineral deposits to the national territory. Worth a visit in nearby **Lota** is the park created by the Cousiño family, the original owner of the area's now mostly disused coal mines.

The Devil's Draught

One of these, the **Chiflón del Diablo** (Devil's Draught), is open to visitors as part of a tourist circuit created to help revive the formerly mining-dependent community. Visitors are lowered 40 meters (131ft) down a shaft and guided through its tunnels as ex-miners relate anecdotes about the grueling life at the coal face. Other attractions include the town's museum and the Central Hidroeléctrica Chivilingo, Chile's oldest

BELOW: the Universidad de Concepción campus.

power plant. Accommodations can be found in Lota at a number of basic, but clean and friendly, hotels.

The Viña Macul vineyard is still owned and run by the Cousiño family, who built the Palacio Cousiño in Santiago. They also founded Chile's first forestry industry in the Colcura Valley, near Lota, in 1881, to supply beams for use in their mines. Dark pine forests, a faster-growing crop than the native hardwood forests, run south along the road to Curanilahue, which is lined with timber-laden trucks. The cellulose plant for paper manufacturing in the beach resort of **Arauco** has contributed to the economic development of the zone. This industry is probably primarily responsible for the paving of the road south, which was taken by the Spanish conquerors as they explored the area between the coast and the Nahuelbuta mountain range.

Ruta de los Conquistadores

Following this so-called Ruta de los Conquistadores, one arrives in **Cañete** ❾. This town has a frontier flavor that announces the beginnings of the Mapuche lands. It was here that the Mapuche *toqui* or warrior chief Lautaro surprised conquistador Pedro de Valdivia and put a dramatic end to his life *(see page 77)*. Cañete's **Museo Mapuche** (Jan–Feb Mon–Fri 9am–7pm, Sat–Sun 11am–7pm; Mar–Dec Sat–Sun 9am–6pm; charge) displays a large range of native peoples' culture and a traditional Mapuche *ruca* (dwelling house) can be seen behind the museum.

Lodgings are available on the nearby **Lago Lanalhue** where there are a number of hotels and cabins as well as camping facilities. The summer months are ideal for activities such as windsurfing and fishing, and the lake is also used for swimming and nautical sports.

There are also hotels and cheaper lodgings in the quaint neighboring town of **Contulmo**, which was settled by Prussians in 1868. The **Grollmus** house, a large wooden dwelling built in 1923, and mill have 23 varieties of *copihue*, which bloom between March and April, and the remains of a small hydroelectric generator that used to supply the town with its lighting. ❏

RESTAURANTS

Rancagua
Termas de Cauquenes
28km (17 miles) east of Rancagua
Tel: (072) 899 010
www.termasdecauquenes.cl
$$$
The food here is a real treat and well worth the detour from the main road. Booking is advised for Saturday and Sunday lunch.

Curicó
Viña Miguel Torres
Panamericana Sur, Km 195 approximately 1km/½ mile south of Curicó
Tel: (075) 564 100
www.migueltorres.cl
$$$
The restaurant of this renowned vineyard, one of the pioneers of Chile's wine export boom, is open for lunch daily (12.30–3.30pm), but serves dinner on Fridays only.

Talca
Russo
7 Oriente 931
Tel: (071) 511 051
$$
Opened by one of Chile's most successful caterers, who is from Talca, this modern restaurant serves interesting and imaginative food. Closed in February.

Chillán
Centro Español
Arauco 555
Tel: (042) 430 920
$$
This restaurant in Chillán's Spanish Center serves hearty Chilean and Spanish dishes.

Mercado Municipal
Maipón s/n
$
For a cheap and cheerful lunch of local dishes, including the traditional *cazuela de pavo* (turkey stew), try any of the cafés around the municipal market.

Concepción
Le Chateau
Camino de Concepción a Chiguayante
(approximately 15 minutes by car from Concepción)
Tel: (041) 317 5800
$$
Traditional French fare, with good fish. This restaurant is best visited during the day to enjoy the impressive view.

Bahia de San Vicente
Caleta Lenga
$
The inexpensive restaurants of this fishing community on the Bay of San Vicente, north of Concepción, are great places to enjoy really fresh seafood.

Prices are per person for a three-course meal, not including drinks:
$ = under US$15
$$ = US$15–25
$$$ = US$25–35

THE LAKE DISTRICT

Snow-capped mountains reflected in looking-glass lakes, quaint wooden hamlets steeped in healthy mountain air, fishing ports, and old rural traditions – the Lake District is Chile's wonderland

The Lake District exercises a near-mythic fascination on Chileans. The south symbolizes everything healthy, unspoiled, and pure in Chile and its people. City folks, particularly in Santiago, look kindly on southerners as their own better selves, even while succumbing to the temptation to take advantage of their gullibility and innocence. The *huaso*, the typical small farmer, is the object of an ambiguous mix of derision and affection in Chile and, in popular folklore, he always comes from the abundant, fraternal south rather than the arid north where skeptical, wary individualism sets the tone of human relations.

Foreign visitors will be made to feel very much at home in the Lake District, where European influences of all kinds, including immigration, have long been welcomed. An early pioneer and champion of southern settlement and development, Vicente Pérez Rosales *(see page 240)*, exemplified this eurocentrism when he announced in 1854 that "the word 'foreigner' has been eliminated in Chile. It is an immoral word and should disappear from the dictionary." Pérez Rosales was not thinking of Peruvians or Brazilians or other mestizo nations – he meant the Germans, Austrians, Swiss, and Italians whose communities are still common in the south.

Unfriendly encounters

However, native Mapuche roots are still not far from the surface of south-ern Chile's collective memory. The south, where most of the country's rural indigenous population lives, was not fully dominated by the European-descended settlers until the second half of the 19th century. For example, the first European colony was established at what is now the lakeside resort center of Villarrica, and was besieged by Mapuches in a 1598 uprising, collapsing without survivors in 1602. It was not re-established until a military mission arrived in 1882, nearly three centuries later.

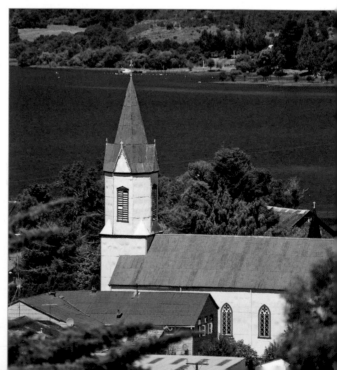

Main Attractions
PARQUE NACIONAL CONGUILLÍO
VOLCÁN VILLARRICA
PUCÓN
TERMAS GEOMÉTRICAS
FERIA FLUVIAL DE VALDIVIA
LAGO LLANQUIHUE
PARQUE NACIONAL VICENTE
    PÉREZ ROSALES
SALTOS DEL PETROHUÉ
FRUTILLAR

PRECEDING PAGES:
Volcán Osorno.
LEFT: lakeside view.
BELOW: church in
Puerto Octay.

Puerto Choque ①
Quidico ②
Lago Lleullelu
Lumaco
Paillaco
Capitán Pastene
Colpi
Quino
Traiguén
Santiago
Victoria
Selva Oscura
P.N. Tolhuaca
2890 Vn Lonquimay
Curacautín
Manzanar

Lake District

0   20 km
0   20 miles

Isla Mocha
La Araucanía
Villa Araucaria
Galvarino
Agua Santa
Perquenco
Retén Dollinco
Los Prados
Refugio Llaima
La Sombra
Termas de Río Blanco
Lonquimay
Túnel Las Raíces
Liucura
Parque Nacional Conguillío

Trovolhue
Carahue
Nueva Imperial
Cholchol
Colonia Lautaro
Cholchol
Lautaro
Cherquenco
3125 ▲
Vn Llaima
Lago Guañetué
Icalma

Nehuentué
Pto Saavedra
Almagro
Temuco
Padre Las Casas
El Alambrado
Lomacura
Melipeuco
Lago Alumine

Pto Domínguez
Imperial
Quepe
Helo Sur
Cunco
Termas de Río Blanco
Parque Nacional Lanín

Hualpín
Nueva Toltén
Teodoro Schmidt
Barros Arana
Cumuy
Gorbea
Freire
Las Hortensias
Los Laureles
Pedregoso
Allipén
Pto Puma
Lago Colico
P.N. Huerquehue
Huife
Termas de Huife

PACIFIC OCEAN

Pta Nilhue
Queule
Mehuín
San José de la Mariquina
Pitrufquén
Lastarria
Quitratué
Villarrica ④
Loncoche
Lago Villarrica
Pucón ③
El Cañi
Curarrehue ⑦
Parque Nacional Lanín

San José
Lanco
Malalhue
Calafquén
Licán Ray ⑤
Parque Nacional Villarrica
2840 Vn Villarrica
2360
Puesco
3747 Vn Lanín

Cruces
Pto Altué
205
Máfil
Huichaco
Pucono
Los Tallos
Panguipulli
Pullingue ⑥
Coñaripe
Lago Pellaita
Carrinque
Liquiñe
Lago Calafquén ⑩
Lago Huechulafquén

Curiñanco
Valdivia ⑧
Niebla
Corral
Calle Calle
Hueyelhue
Los Lagos
207
Reumén
Riñihue
Folilco
Choshuenco
Lago Panguipulli
Lago Neltume
Neltume
Puerto Fuy
Salto del Huilo Huilo ⑨
Enco
2415 Vn Choshuenco
Parque Nacional Lanín
Junín de los Andes

Chaihuín
Pta Galera
Los Ulmos
Huite
Lago Riñihue
Los Ríos
2240
Lago Pirihueico
San Martín de los Andes

Hueicolla
Sta Elisa
Pichirropulli
Rapaco
Pto Nuevo
Dollinco
Futrono
Llifén ⑫
Pto Maihue
Lago Lacar

El Mirador
La Unión
Sta Rosa
5
Lago Ranco
I. Huapi
Lago Maihue

La Barra
Trinidad
Río Bueno ⑪
Bueno
Trumao
El Crucero
Lago Ranco
Riñinahue
Lago Traful

Misión de San Juan de la Costa
San Pablo
Chirre
2240 Vn Puyehue
Parque Nacional

Bahía Mansa
Puaucho
Osorno ㉓
Remehue
Las Lumas
215
Lago Puyehue
Termas de Puyehue
Aguas Calientes
215
CORDILLERA DE LOS
Villa la Angostura
Parque

Huilma
Río Negro
Cancura
El Encanto
Lago Rupanco
Puyehue ⑬
1990 Vn Casa Blanca
Lago Nahuel Huapi
Nacional

Millantue
El Bolsón
Riachuelo
Puranque
Purranque
Piedras Negras
Puerto Rico
2190 Co Puntiagudo
P.N. Vicente
Peulla
2164 Co Torcillas
San Carlos de Bariloche

Hueyusca
Bahía San Pedro
Crucero
Corte Alto
Puerto Octay ⑲
Puerto Fonck
Las Cascadas
Petrohué
Lago Todos los Santos
Pérez
Puerto Blest ⑰
Peulla ⑯
Huapi

Teguálda
Paraguay
Fresia
Colegual
Nueva Braunau
Lago Llanquihue
Frutillar ⑳
Llanquihue
Petrohué ⑱
2852 ▲ Vn Osorno
Salto del Petrohué
Ensenada
Rosales
Villa Mascardi

Maichihue
Parga
Río Frío
5
Llanquihue
Los Riscos
2015 Vn Calbuco
Ralún

Pta Capitanes
Los Muermos
Las Quemas
Puerto Varas ⑭
Correntoso
Río Sur
Lago Chapo
Cochamó ㉑
Río Villegas

Misquihue
Puerto Montt ㉔
Chamiza
Parque Nacional Alerce Andino
Lago Tagua Tagua
En Foyel
El Bolsón

Maicura
5
Calbuco
Seno de Reloncaví
La Arena
Cta Puelche
2111 Vn Yate
2270 Co de la Torre

Bahía Maullín
Carelmapu ㉕
Pargua
Aguatao
Isla Puluqui
㉖
Vn Hornopirén 1672
Lago Puelo

Canal de Chacao
Guabún
Ancud
Quellón
Chacao
Golfo de Ancud
Isla Queulin
⑦
Cta Gualaihue
Hornopirén

In the interim, an uneasy state of semi-war prevailed. Early in the 1600s, the River Biobío (which reaches the sea at what is now the port of Concepción) was established as the frontier between the Spanish colony and native lands, but the truce was violated annually in raids from one side or the other. Spanish mercenaries fought to capture Mapuches and sell them into slavery, while the Mapuches raided to plunder cattle and other goods or to punish the invaders. Regular peace conferences between the two sides usually ended in great celebrations of feasting and drinking and vows of friendship – which would invariably last only a few months before the next outbreak of hostilities.

Finally, commerce pacified the situation. A regular trade in cattle, woven goods, knives, arms, and liquor developed, although violent outbursts between Mapuches and European soldiers, brigands, and shady dealers of all sorts continued to occur regularly. Naturally, the mestizo population grew steadily with the constant contact, and colonial garrison commanders preferred them as soldiers since they knew the area well and were notoriously impervious to hardship.

These hostilities meant that the Lake District was, until relatively recently, unexplored territory for those of European descent. Lago Colico, near Pucón, was the last of the big lakes to be discovered by Europeans, making its first appearance on maps in the early years of the 20th century. The great Lago Llanquihue near Puerto Montt was first sighted by Pedro de Valdivia in 1552, but Mapuche raids put it effectively out of bounds to Europeans until new waves of settlers began to arrive three centuries later.

Life in the outback

Chile's south is a more recently tamed version of the North American Wild West, and, in more remote areas, life revolves around horses, farm work, and social events, lubricated with large quantities of wine or *chicha* made from fermented apples. Country families tend to live off seasonal sales of milk, or a cash crop, or tourists, spending long months consuming the stores of grain they harvested themselves, while

The copihue, Chile's national flower, grows in forests from Valparaíso to as far south as Osorno. A climbing evergreen, its bell-shape flowers – beloved by humming birds – are usually red, although there is also a white variety.

BELOW: farmstead overlooked by Volcán Osorno.

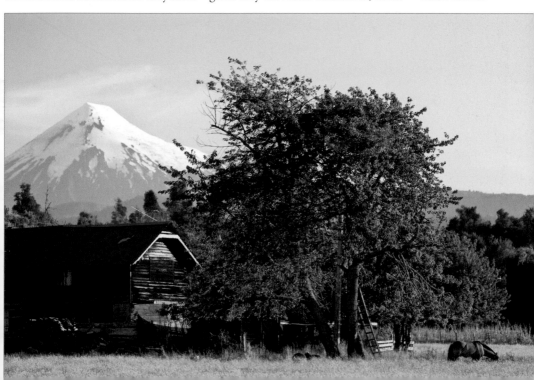

the men look for paying jobs in the larger towns and cities.

The rural areas are connected by an extensive network of local buses which transport schoolchildren, farmers and country residents returning from the larger towns with provisions. The buses are slow due to the terrain and the constant stops at every lane or farmhouse, but they are very cheap and reach many remote settlements. The first and sometimes only bus tends to leave before dawn, so it is always prudent to inquire about schedules the day before traveling. As the terrain is ideal for backpacking and hiking, Chilean youth swarm southward in the summertime, many of them spending long hours on the highway awaiting motorists or truckers who will give them a lift. Most have the barest minimum of funds and camp wherever possible.

Gateway to the Lake District

The Lake District is generally considered to begin at the Toltén River, which flows off Lago Villarrica, but this is more a result of the area's fame as a resort region than strict topographic considerations. The characteristic combination of volcanoes and lakes actually begins farther north, around the area of Parque Nacional Conguillío, northeast of Temuco. This region is home to several volcanoes, including **Lonquimay** (2,890 meters/9,480ft) which entered into full eruption in 1988 and blanketed the area with dangerous volcanic dust; and **Llaima** (3,124 meters/10,249ft), which erupted in 1994. Lonquimay means "without a head" in the Mapuche tongue, referring to the volcano's flat top.

This is also Mapuche territory – the Mapuches' ancestors used the accessible mountain passes and gathered pine nuts from the ancient *araucaria*, or monkey puzzle tree, which is endemic to the southern Andes. There are male and female *araucaria* trees – biologists can determine their sex by examining their bark. These rare coniferous trees, which take 500 years to mature fully and can live for more than 1,000 years, were endangered by logging activities until President Aylwin's government responded to environmental cam-

Chile's native parrots abound in the mountains around Conguillío and give campers a raucous early morning call.

BELOW: Lago Llanquihue.

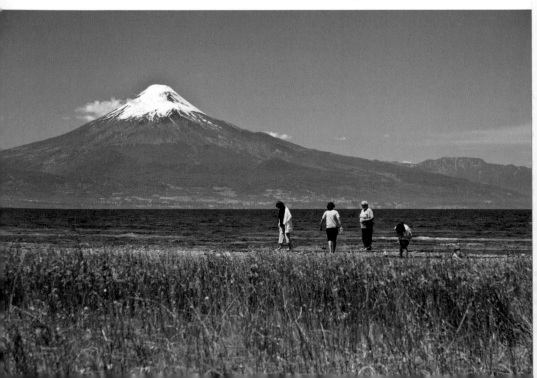

paigners and prohibited their destruction in March 1990.

Temuco, founded in 1881, following an important treaty between the new republic and the Mapuches, is now a rapidly growing industrial town, and a good base from which to explore the northern Lake District. Its **Museo Regional de la Araucanía** (Tue–Fri 10am–5.30pm, Sat 11am–5pm, Sun 11am–2pm; charge) provides information on the native people and their history. Mapuches from the surrounding countryside come to Temuco to sell their wares; the central market, although rather touristy, is a good place to buy local handicrafts and to try traditional dishes. The **Cerro Nielol** hill and forest park, where the national *copihue* flower grows in abundance, offers the best view of the city.

Source of the Biobío

The town of **Lonquimay** and the land surrounding it lie to the east of the Andean cordillera, despite the general rule that the highest peaks mark the territorial boundaries between Chile and Argentina. However, **Lago Gualletué** south of Lonquimay provides the headwaters of the important **Biobío River**, which then runs north for nearly 100km (60 miles) before turning westward toward the Pacific Ocean at Concepción (*see Central Valley map, page 217*). As this river was long considered the border dividing Spanish lands from unconquered Mapuche territory, Chile claimed the hydrographic basin.

The main road to Lonquimay passes through the **Las Raíces** (roots) **Tunnel**. This was originally a railway tunnel, built in the 1930s as part of a plan (subsequently abandoned) to connect the Atlantic and Pacific oceans by rail. The tunnel is passable in all weathers (though large icicles form in winter).

On the road to the tunnel from Curacautín there are several thermal baths, as well as the beautiful 50-meter (16ft) Princess Waterfall and two huge volcanic rocks, Piedra Cortada and Piedra Santa, which were considered sacred by the indigenous population.

Parque Nacional Conguillío can be reached from Curacautín in the north or Melipeuco in the south. Both routes skirt the snow-covered **Volcán Llaima**, and lead through virgin forests of *araucaria* and other Chilean species such as *coigüe* and *raulí*, as well as oak and cypress. Twelve hundred year-old *araucaria* trees can be seen in Parque Nacional Conguillío, which was set up in 1950. Conguillío's prehistoric feel led the BBC to film parts of its 1999 natural history series *Walking with Dinosaurs* here. The park's popularity has brought about a serious erosion of vegetation, and, in 2002, forest fires burned 1,633 hectares (661 acres) of the seldom-visited eastern section of the park.

Three tiny lakes in the park (Verde, Captrén, and Arco Iris) were formed by lava flows which blocked several rivers. The lakes are just a few decades old, and the trees that once grew on their beds can still be seen below the water. Volcán Llaima now has a small, modern ski resort on its slopes, at Los Paraguas.

A private concessionaire manages the main campsite on the shores of the

An Active Landscape

Chile has over 2,000 volcanoes, located mostly in the Andes Mountains, of which over 500 are considered geologically active and around 60 have erupted in the last 500 years. The entire country forms part of the Pacific "Rim of Fire" which stretches along the western coasts of North and South America, west to New Zealand and the western Pacific islands and up through Japan and the Kamchatka Peninsula.

Chile's volcanoes are doubly dangerous because of their eternal snows, which melt into rapid, devastating mudslides upon full eruption. The lava itself advances much more slowly but burns away everything in its path. These lava "runs" can be observed at the Villarrica and Osorno volcanoes, and you can climb the Villarrica volcano for a peek down at the magma quite near the surface. Although some of the active volcanoes are considered semi-dormant, a strong eruption can always set off a chain reaction of volcanic activity, as happened in the 1960 earthquake.

The lakes are of glacial origin, their basins carved out by advancing ice, then filled by the melting ice as the glaciers receded. There is also evidence of tectonic influence, with earthquakes causing some lake basins to sink further while newly formed volcanoes sometimes shift the course of rivers as they rise up between them.

largest lake, Lago Conguillío, as well as several log cabins in a stunning location in an *araucaria* forest. December is the best time to visit, before the Chilean summer vacation crowds arrive in January and February.

Mapuche stronghold

On the coast, west of Conguillío, is the even more isolated **Lago Lleulleu** (in the Mapuche language, a repeated word has extra importance). Aside from the tiny community at **Puerto Choque ❶**, the only civilization nearby is at **Quidico ❷** on the ocean, which is popular in the summer for its excellent seafood and windswept beach. The end of the main road is just past **Tirúa** where Mapuche chiefs once charged a toll for land traffic between Concepción and Valdivia. According to legend, the bishop of Concepción was kidnapped and held here in 1778, only escaping when a rival chief won his freedom in a game of chance.

Next to the beaches at Viña del Mar and Reñaca, the area around Villarrica and Pucón is the most popular holiday resort in Chile. The two towns are the main urban centers on the end of **Lago Villarrica**, which is dominated by the active **Volcán Villarrica** (2,840 meters/9,320ft), just an hour's detour from the north–south PanAmerican Highway. **Pucón ❸** could be called the "Viña of the South" for its success in attracting summer tourists, especially since the 1934 construction of the Gran Hotel Pucón by the Chilean State Railroad Company. (Guests arrived by train to Villarrica, then boated 25km/16 miles across the lake to their lodgings.) It is now enormously popular amongst the Chilean middle classes, who are rapidly buying up the summer condominiums along the beach. Many flock to the area in the summer months, sunbathe on the beach, take part in noisy water sports on Lago Villarrica by day, and crowd the casino in the Hotel de Los Lagos by night.

Though it has become very commercial, Pucón provides all the services a tourist could want, including an excellent variety of restaurants, bars, and discotheques, and is extremely popular with backpackers.

BELOW: the holiday resort of Pucón.

The town is also a key center for adventure tourists, and by far the most popular activity is the one-day hike to the lava-filled crater of Volcán Villarrica *(see page 121)*. An increasing variety of water sports, including rafting, kayaking, and hydrospeed, are also practiced on the Trancura River. Though the service offered by adventure travel agencies varies, most provide high-quality imported equipment and qualified guides trained to ensure international safety standards.

Skiing is available in winter at a resort owned by the Gran Hotel Pucón on the slopes of Volcán Villarrica. More relaxing activities include horseback riding, fishing, and visits to nearby hot springs and national parks.

The area around Pucón has also pioneered environmental tourism projects. **El Cañi**, east of Pucón, is one of Chile's first private parks. Its ancient *araucaria* forest growing on an extinct volcano became a reserve in 1992 with funding from Ancient Forests International and has been developed as a center for environmental education and scientific research. Though it requires a steep three-hour hike, reaching the summit rewards the climber with spectacular views of all the area's volcanoes on a clear day. Visits are best organized through the École hostel in Pucón.

Cultural resort

Numerous Mapuche communities are tucked away in the hills surrounding **Villarrica ❹**, and each summer a Mapuche cultural festival is held in the town. This includes a nightly demonstration of religious rituals. Some unusual craft work can be found among the stands, but most of the work has long been copied by artisans in Santiago and elsewhere.

One of the town's main streets is named after General Emil Koerner, the German military scientist who was hired in the late 19th century by President Balmaceda to reorganize the Chilean armed forces (he used the area for training). Koerner then betrayed Balmaceda to side with an 1891 insurrection fomented by local oligarchs *(see page 42)*. The oligarchs won, President Balmaceda committed suicide, and Koerner proceeded to

Some Mapuche families living near Tirúa scratch a living by harvesting and selling the edible cochayuyo seaweed that amasses along the seashore.

BELOW: backpacker hangout, Pucón.

Farming employs many families in the Lake District.

BELOW: tour agency in Pucón.

reshape the army along Prussian lines, a model which remains largely in force today. His prestige led to a surge of pro-German sentiment which helped to stimulate a second wave of German immigrants, most of whom headed for the newly available lands in the south.

Mountain beaches

Just a short drive from Pucón to the north and northeast are lakes Caburgua and Colico, and, in the mountains of **Parque Nacional Huerquehue**, lakes Tinquilco, Toro, and Verde. Rare outcroppings of "flywing" rock crystal usually observed only in the coastal mountain range 100km (60 miles) to the west give some of Lago Caburgua's beaches white sand rather than the usual black sand that comes from the volcanic rock elsewhere in Chile's Lake District. The lake is surrounded by densely forested hills, some areas of which can be explored on defined paths. Its waters flow underground, producing the springs at **Ojos de Caburgua**, a popular picnic spot. Access to the Huerquehue Park lakes is

a serious 5km (3-mile) climb but a small bus company, Minibuses Caburgua, operates a service that leaves Pucón approximately every 30 minutes and takes visitors right to the park entrance.

Puma live farther up in the mountains; these animals are rarely seen, but come closer to human civilization in winter when food is scarce. Pumas do not generally attack humans unless threatened, but still need to be considered dangerous animals. An 80km (50-mile) route from Caburgua's north shore through the Blanco River Valley can be hiked in about four days, ending up in the outpost of **Reigolil** (where a bus descends to Curarrehue four times a day). A traverse from **Volcán Quetrupillán** to the village of Puesco through *araucaria* forests is increasingly replacing the circuit around Volcán Villarrica as the most popular hiking route in Parque Nacional Villarrica. Local tour agencies leave hikers at the beginning of the trek, and there are public bus services back to Pucón.

South of Villarrica, a half-hour's trip

Frontier Traditions

Rural traditions persist in many frontier towns of southern Chile. Men can often be seen wearing flat-brimmed felt hats, and they are quick to invite visitors to drink a sweet wine that goes down with treacherous ease. On special occasions, a host family will kill a sheep or goat by plunging a knife into the neck and catching the blood in a pan filled with *cilantro* (coriander), where it is congealed with lemon juice to produce *ñache*, which is considered a great delicacy and pre-feast appetizer.

Grains are the traditional farm commodity, though the uncertainty of the weather makes farming risky. Potatoes are easily grown, but transport costs wipe out any chance of profit, so farmers usually consume them or use them as animal feed. Hops and sugar beet are also grown. Pasture is abundant, and many families earn a few pesos selling milk to the big dairy plants.

To fortify themselves for heavy farm work, the men breakfast on *chupilca*, white wine poured over toasted wheat, or *mudai*, a pasty, carbohydrate-rich juice made from cooked grains. Visitors should avoid giving offense by always accepting anything offered, even if they cannot bring themselves to sample it. When you've had enough, just leave the plate or glass untouched before you.

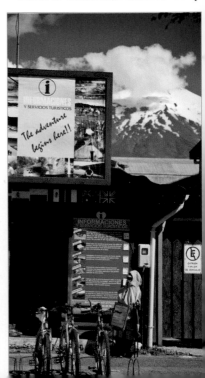

on a paved highway leads to the rapidly expanding resort of **Lican Ray ⑤** on Lago Calafquén. Wood furniture-making is becoming an important economic activity in this area, and dozens of workshops have sprung up in recent years, particularly on the road from Villarrica to Lican Ray. Farther along the lake on a newly paved road is **Coñaripe ⑥**, which retains the atmosphere of pre-boom Lican Ray. Regular buses do go this far, but Coñaripe is the end of the line before the rugged unpaved circuit around the lake, and the "back way" into Panguipulli.

Thermal baths proliferate across the area due to the constant activity in the volcanic belt that runs along the cordillera. Some, such as the **Termas de Menetué** or **Termas de Huife** farther east of Pucón are upscale commercial operations with eating and lodging facilities and bathing fixtures. Others, including the tiny **Termas de Ancamil**, just before Curarrehue, 45km (28 miles) east of Pucón, are rustic, family-run affairs where one simply descends into the cave with a candle and bathes, while the recently opened **Termas**

Geométricas, some 16km (10 miles) east of Coñaripe, have architecturally interesting wooden walkways joining the different pools.

Border activity

The town of **Curarrehue ⑦** is a typical southern frontier center, where families often have relatives on the Argentine side and travel across the border to take advantage of work opportunities. The Chile–Argentina border in the south is lightly guarded, as the mountain passes are essentially uncontrollable. During the Pinochet dictatorship, many of these frontier towns smuggled people in and out who either could not move around legally or were in serious trouble for political reasons. Cattle-smuggling into Chile from Argentina causes occasional outbreaks of foot-and-mouth disease, which cannot be controlled in Argentina's vast ranches but has been basically eradicated in Chile.

The inhabitants of Chile's Andean foothills, like those surrounding Curarrehue, are unfailingly cordial, although sometimes shy in front of strangers.

BELOW: enjoying the beach at Lago Llanquihue.

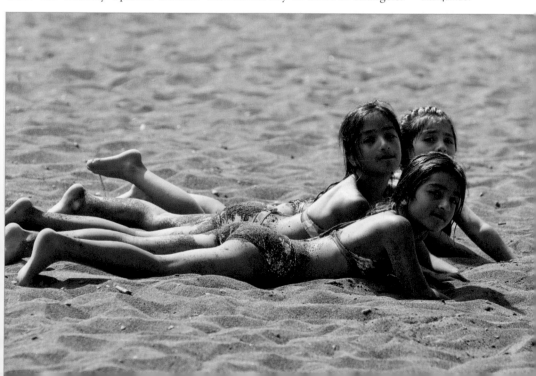

This friendly environment is not preserved, however, in the towns that have been turned into regular summer resorts. Here, the traditional generous welcome to strangers disappears behind a mask of indifference. Concerted efforts and extra-gracious greetings usually manage to break the ice, but it's worth the effort to try a visit off the beaten path.

As part of a plan to develop a tourist route, known as the Ruta Interlagos, the Chilean government has gradually been upgrading 300km (186 miles) of road south from Victoria, north of Temuco, skirting past national parks Tolhuaca and Conguillío and lakes Colico and Villarrica, before ending in Lican Ray.

A slice of Germany

Valdivia ❽ is the best example of the urban face of Chile's south: sophisticated and festive, rainy and verdant, with a palpable German influence in architecture, cuisine, and culture. Although usually treated as part of the Lake District, Valdivia is located at the crossroads of two rivers and is just a few kilometers from the sea, separated from the lakes by the coastal mountain range. The approaches to the city are marshy breeding grounds for unusual waterfowl. Named for the first conquistador to enter Chile from Peru, Pedro de Valdivia, the city was founded in the mid-1500s but had a difficult time of it for the first 100 years. It was taken over by a Dutch pirate in 1600 and, being on the Mapuche side of the Biobío River dividing line between Crown and Mapuche territory, had to await the building of fortifications in the mid-1600s to achieve a measure of security. The **Museo Histórico y Antropológico Mauricio van de Maele** (Jan–Feb daily 10am–8pm, Mar–Dec Tue–Sun 10am–6pm; charge), on Teja Island in the middle of Valdivia, is housed in an old settler's mansion and includes Mapuche artifacts and period furnishings – providing an excellent insight into the prosperous lifestyles of the 19th-century German immigrants (see page 240).

In 1960, Valdivia was the epicenter of the world's largest recorded earth-

Valdivia is home to one of Chile's oldest and largest independent breweries, the Cervecería Kunstmann. Its beer garden and restaurant on the road to Niebla is a favorite tourist attraction, although rather pricey.

BELOW: Kunstmann brewery, Valdivia.

quake, followed by a tidal wave whose effects can still be seen. Most of the old buildings were destroyed, but some European-style buildings remain by the waterfront. The **Museo de Arte Contemporáneo** (Jan–Feb daily 10am–2pm and 4–8pm, Mar–Dec Tue–Sun 10am–1pm and 3–7pm; charge), also on Teja Island, is built on the ruins of the old Andwandter brewery.

Summer explosions

Valdivia has a popular week-long summer festival in February in which musical shows are staged on bandstands along the river bank, boats parade down the river, and firework shows are presented on the last afternoon and night. There is also a film festival.

The city's long riverside walks are full of visitors throughout the season, as are the nearby beaches. The Parque Saval on Isla Teja has a riverside beach, and the nearby Botanical Garden, with many native species, is worth a visit.

A highly recommended stop is the **Feria Fluvial**, a lively fish market on the quay from which all the river cruises depart. Fat sea lions come right up into the market, but be careful; they have been known to attack passers-by.

Though swimming is possible in the rivers, most bathers head for the port villages of **Corral** and **Niebla**. Colonial-era fortresses are preserved at the latter site, which independence hero Lord Thomas Cochrane, a dashing Scots navy commander in the service of the Chilean rebels, took from the Spanish against heavy odds in 1820. For a bit of exercise, visitors can row from Corral to the tiny island of **Mancera**, Valdivia's military headquarters during the 18th century, to see its small church and convent.

River trips from Valdivia north to the Santuario de la Naturaleza Río Cruces pass through the habitat of black-necked swans to the confluence of three rivers. A few years ago, this sanctuary was the subject of a major environmental controversy when, following the start of operations at a nearby wood-pulp plant, the swans, a relatively rare South American species, started to die and many more migrated. Effluent from the plant was blamed for the disappearance of the waterweed on

The Santuario de la Naturaleza Río Cruces, just north of Valdivia, is home to an astounding variety of river birds and plant life. The area was submerged under water in the earthquake of 1960.

BELOW: fresh fish at the Feria Fluvial in Valdivia.

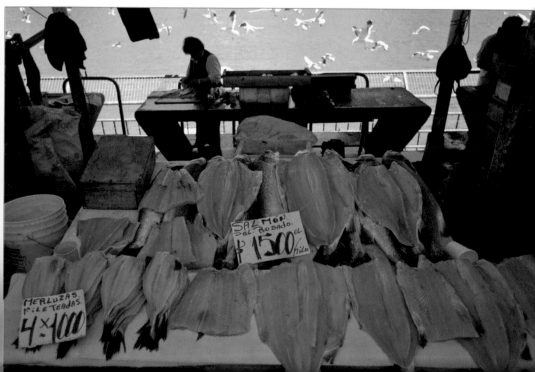

German Settlers

During the 19th century, millions of people fled famine and hardship in Europe and came to the Lake District in search of a better life.

German immigration to Valdivia occurred in two periods: a minor influx in the first half of the 19th century and the more important wave between roughly 1885 and 1910. The immigrants played an important role in commerce and industry, using technical knowledge brought from the old country. Some cultivated their new lands, although climatic conditions were not ideal. Others arrived as ironsmiths, carpenters, tanners, brewers, watchmakers, locksmiths, and tailors.

Chile in 1850 was just emerging from three decades of political anarchy and economic stagnation, and distant provinces like Valdivia were left largely to their own devices.

By 1900, a traveler claimed that upon entering Valdivia, he could not believe he was still in Chile. Many of the tradesmen had converted their shops into factories. Valdivia became Chile's prime industrial center, with breweries, distilleries, shipbuilding, flour mills, tanneries, 100 lumber mills and, in 1913, the country's first foundry. Furniture-making was stimulated by the immense availability of beautiful native woods.

The wealth of the Germans of Valdivia was legendary in Chile until their luck changed, starting with the imposition of a heavy liquor tax in 1902 at the behest of Central Valley vintners. Unfavorable trade conditions wiped out much of the leather market. A great fire laid waste to the city in 1909, while the local merchant class was superseded by mine and estate owners from farther north, closer to the byzantine politics of the capital.

Puerto Montt and Osorno

Beginning in the mid-19th century, the region around Lago Llanquihue was also heavily settled by German immigrants, who disembarked at what is now the Seno de Reloncaví. Vicente Pérez Rosales, the indefatigable promoter of colonization in southern Chile, organized a solemn ceremony to establish Puerto Montt formally with a group of the recent arrivals, none of whom understood a word of Spanish. According to an account of the ritual, led by a Catholic priest, the Protestant settlers interrupted at what seemed to them an appropriate pause with a rousing chorus of *Hier Liegt vor Deiner Majestad* (Here Before Your Majesty). Despite the idiomatic complications, Pérez Rosales's project was a success in the long run.

Osorno is well known as having been settled by Germans. However, despite the many German street names, the immigrants never actually numbered more than 10 percent of the total population of the region.

Chileans were also drawn to these new lands, generally uneducated and destitute people hoping to make a new start. The foreigners quickly established themselves as the dominant class, employing the mestizo citizens and directing economic development.

Chile's largest remaining concentration of Huilliches (southern Mapuches) is to be found in communities scattered between Osorno and the coast, around towns like Puaucho and San Juan de la Costa. Although educational and healthcare facilities have improved in recent years, this is still one of Chile's worst pockets of rural poverty. Huilliches can be seen trading their cash crops in the market in Osorno, which is a drab city compared to more prosperous and sophisticated Valdivia. ❑

LEFT: an exhibit at the Kunstmann brewery, showing how German settlers made beer.

which the swans feed. The company was forced to reduce the plant's output, prior to building a duct out to sea, and the swan population now appears to be recovering slowly. Many boats make a stop at the indigenous Huilliche village of Punucapa.

South of Corral you reach **Chaihuín**, a fishing village with what some consider to be the most beautiful, untouched ocean beach in Chile and which is developing as an ecotourism destination. Most of the original larch trees in the nearby hills have been cut and sold, but the place retains a frontier flavor.

Detours into the wilderness

The largely underdeveloped **Seven Lakes** district is among the least visited by vacationers due to a peculiar topographical layout and poor access. The district is named after seven lakes that all share the same river basin and include the large Lagos Calafquén, Panguipulli, and Riñihue, the smaller Lagos Pellaifa, Neltume, and Pirihueico, and Lago Lacar in Argentina. The lakes are generally bordered by heavily wooded cliffs with steep descents; roads are potholed and slippery at the best of times, with difficult climbs and narrow turns through the mountains, which are often impassable in winter. Low-suspension vehicles will fare worst. However, the landscapes are spectacular, and local residents will guide visitors to even more extraordinary spots. These lakes are good for fishing and exploring, but not so good for bathing as beaches are few and far between.

The circuit around Lago Calafquén is dominated by the seemingly changing position of Volcán Villarrica to the north. Finally, **Volcán Choshuenco** (2,415 meters/7,923ft) appears to the south. Recent lava flows can be observed from the highway shortly after leaving Lican Ray. From Coñaripe an alternative route leads to the small **Lago Pellaita** after a ferocious climb at **Los Añiques**. The way down leads through an agricultural valley to the Mapuche village of **Liquiñe**.

From there, it is possible to drive to **Lago Neltume** and **Puerto Fuy** ❾ on the finger-shaped **Lago Pirihueico**,

Sign outside the Cervecería Kunstmann in Valdivia.

BELOW: sign advertising a volcano hike.

*A German house in
Puerto Varas.*

BELOW: lakeside
view at dusk.

which can be crossed in two hours on a ferry boat that connects to an international road to San Martín de los Andes in Argentina.

Panguipulli ❿ (Town of Roses) was formerly the railway station that received logs dispatched from the interior via steamboats plying the lake of the same name. The construction of roads later superseded the lake transport system. The town is brilliantly decorated with rose bushes. As Panguipulli is located on the flat central plain rather than in the mountains, it tends to be hotter than other lake towns, and its beaches are somewhat less impressive.

On clear days, you should be able to make out Volcán Choshuenco, situated some 50km (30 miles) to the southeast. The volcano itself can be climbed by motor vehicle up to the refuge after a trying, 80km (50-mile) drive along the lake. To the east, about halfway to Puerto Fuy, is the **Salto del Huilo Huilo**, the highest and one of the most impressive waterfalls in Chile, which crashes down a deep vine-covered gorge into the River Fuy. Note that it is impossible to continue the circuit

around Lago Riñihue out of season (and frequently in season as well) due to a severe, 7km (4-mile) climb with terrible road conditions just after the tiny lakefront community of Enco. An approach can be made from the town of Los Lagos on the Pan-American Highway, passing through the town of Riñihue.

Fishermen's outposts

The enormous **Lago Ranco** and the smaller adjacent **Lago Maihue** have developed considerably as tourist centers in recent years. However, out of season they are very quiet. On the northern shore of Lago Ranco, the resort of **Futrono** is accessible by turning off the Pan-American Highway at Reumén. For foot travelers, buses to Futrono leave regularly from Valdivia and **Río Bueno** ⓫ all year round. Guided adventure tourism in the surrounding hills is still little developed, though Futrono has a network of rural tourism.

Many of the communities surrounding the lake originated as fishermen's hostels; a couple are now successful lodges serving upscale clients. The

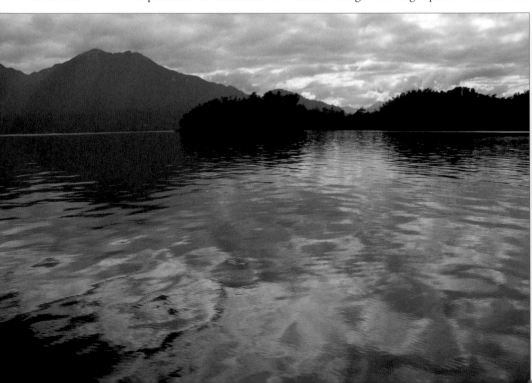

town of **Lago Ranco** itself is full of cheap tourist guesthouses. The pebble beach and a hill behind the town give fine panoramic views. A small museum (Dec–Mar daily, 11am–1pm and 2.30–7pm) on the road leading to the beach has some interesting historical items. Boats can be rented when available. Activity after dark drops off sharply except for a pair of lakefront bars, although things are livelier during the summer festival.

The most beautiful and heavily settled part of the lake lies directly east along an unpaved road to the **Riñinahue** peninsula and the Calcurrupe River near **Llifén ⑫**, where the paving starts again. The road from Lago Ranco to Llifén is dotted with colonies of new summer vacation homes and crosses **Salto del Nilahue**, a double waterfall with a tremendous, roaring flow, especially in early summer. From the bridge over the River Nilahue, a tertiary road leads to the lower end of Lago Maihue and the hamlet of **Carrán**, named for the Carrán volcano which just appeared in 1957 and last erupted in 1979.

A Mapuche community near the southeast end of Lago Maihue and within view of **Volcán Puyehue** (2,240 meters/7,349ft) to the south is said to preserve the purest indigenous traditions.

The 810-hectare (2,000-acre) **Isla Huapi** in the middle of Lago Ranco is also an indigenous colony with some 40 Mapuche and Huilliche families. Huilliches were the original inhabitants, but Mapuches from Argentina colonized the island. The penetration of evangelical groups has led many to fear the end of the Mapuche and Huilliche cultures on Huapi, but residents are not legally allowed to sell their ancestral lands which were divided and assigned to them individually under Chile's indigenous law of 1979. There are ferry services to the island from Frutono and Lago Ranco.

Lago Ranco can be completely circled crossing the new bridge over the Calcurrupe River, which replaced the old vehicle raft. A sturdy high-clearance vehicle is recommended for the unpaved stretches. The Caunahue River Canyon just north of Llifén has a dramatic view.

BELOW: en route to Puyehue National Park.

Lush forests in the shadow of the volcano

Lago Puyehue is known to many travelers since it lies along the main route to Argentina from southern Chile. In wintertime, when heavy snow covers the Andes mountains, bus and lorry traffic from Santiago sometimes has to detour nearly 1,000km (600 miles) south to this pass, which is much lower and usually remains open throughout the year. The road has excellent views of the lake from gently rolling hills, then climbs to 1,300 meters (4,300ft) through **Parque Nacional Puyehue** on the way to the famous resort of San Carlos de Bariloche on the Argentine side. The main town on the Chilean side is **Entre Lagos** (Between the Lakes) on the western tip of Lago Puyehue, a former railroad center now heavily dependent on tourism.

A detour toward Volcán Casa Blanca (1,990 meters/6,529ft) leads to the open-air hot springs at **Aguas Calientes** ⑬. The park headquarters here make a good starting point for excursions. The road leads past several small lakes, through lush virgin forest, including an unusual temperate rainforest, and ends at a ski resort on the slopes of the volcano which can be climbed more easily than Volcán Villarrica farther north. Another topographic oddity is the existence of deciduous trees (beech) at the volcano's tree-line. At the top the views are very impressive even for this region, as the volcanoes Osorno, Puntiagudo, and Puyehue can all be seen in a semicircle.

The area around nearby **Lago Rupanco** tends to be exclusive and upscale, without the ready facilities for camping and day-trips that abound around all the other lakes. Foreigners enjoy it for its extraordinary, mountain-ringed setting and superb fishing. The approach from Entre Lagos leads to a tiny settlement at **Puerto Chalupa**, which has a lovely beach. From the south, the road from **Puerto Octay** is a 25km (15-mile) drive, with no public transport service. The beautiful campgrounds along the south shore of the lake are also virtually inaccessible without a vehicle.

Lago Llanquihue is the grand-daddy of all the Chilean lakes. It is South

The Termas de Puyehue Hotel, situated within the Puyehue National Park, is one of Chile's most traditional spa resorts, offering both thermal and mud baths. See www.puyehue.cl for more information.

BELOW: Parque Nacional Puyehue.

America's fourth-largest, covering some 877 sq km (339 sq miles) and nearly 50km (30 miles) across from Puerto Octay to Puerto Varas on the south shore. The lake has an oceanic feel, with breakers that churn higher in winds or rough weather and mini-climates in its interior that keep boaters and fishermen alert. The map on page 230 shows that, except for the narrow strip of land between Puerto Varas and Puerto Montt, the lake would be part of the ocean. The enormous national park at the eastern end of Lago Llanquihue, stretching all the way to the Argentine frontier, bears the name of Vicente Pérez Rosales, the promoter of foreign immigration to the region *(see page 240)*. It was Chile's first, established in 1926.

Lago Llanquihue is one of the most visited sites in all of Chile, and tours of the district often start in Puerto Montt and then work back toward the north. **Puerto Varas** ⑭ is the main lakeside resort town. The beaches (the name of one, Niklitscheck, reflects a later immigration of Slavs, especially in the far south) run for several kilometers with rows of shops and excellent restaurants,

and plenty of nightlife. The views from Puerto Varas across to Volcán Osorno (2,652 meters/8,701ft) and Volcán Puntiagudo (Sharp-Pointed), 2,190 meters (7,185ft), are breathtaking, and summer activities abound, making it a fun place to hang out. The ease of transport and the plentiful accommodations to suit all budgets and tastes mean that all kinds of travelers gather at night to stroll the beach walks and rub shoulders.

Peak season is February; the views are just as fine in January, but the maddening *tábanos* are thickest then – irritating horseflies attracted to dark clothes and shiny objects, which love to buzz around your head in the sunshine. They don't come out in overcast weather, and since their life cycle is only a month, they disappear in early February. But before that they can easily ruin a day out.

Going east from Puerto Varas the road curves and dips, providing countless views of the lake from every imaginable angle. Winds tend to whip across even on bright, cloudless days, so the air is likely to remain cool and tempt

There are numerous lakeside towns and villages either side of the border between Chile and Argentina.

BELOW: Lakeside restaurant in Puerto Varas.

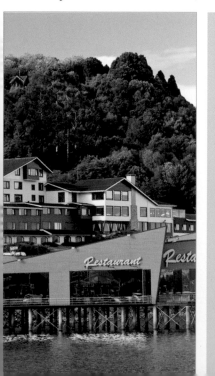

Salmon Clean-up

Over the past 20 years, southern Chile has seen the development of a new export industry – salmon-farming – and now rivals Norway on world markets. Young salmon are hatched and bred in the area's lakes before being moved to seawater cages along the coast for fattening. The industry's development has increased the number of jobs in a region where employment was previously scarce and explains the rapid growth of Puerto Montt, with its vast salmon processing plants, and Puerto Varas, where most of the industry's executives prefer to live.

But it has been bad for the environment. Once pristine lakes and sheltered sea bays have been polluted with salmon feed, antibiotics, and organic waste. A clean-up is, however, in sight.

Hit by an outbreak of ISA, a highly contagious salmon virus, which began in 2007, the industry has been forced to rethink its practices. As well as reducing the density of seawater cages – as many as a million fish can currently be being fattened in one bay – producers are increasingly starting to use on-land plants, rather than lakes, for hatching and breeding – partly because of environmental pressures but also because the contamination the industry itself has caused now poses a risk to the health of juvenile fish.

Pampering at the Termas Puyehue resort (see page 244).

BELOW: the restaurant in the Termas Puyehue.

the unwary to overdo exposure to the sun. The notorious deterioration of the ozone layer, which becomes progressively worse as one moves closer to Antarctica, contributes to the potency of the sun's rays.

Numerous *hosterías* by the lakeside provide lodging and full meals, but they can be pricey. On a clear day, residents will come down from their rural domiciles and gather in lakefront soccer fields to watch a match in the strong breeze with the sparkling water in the background. **Volcán Calbuco** (2,015 meters/6,611ft) is quite close on the right. This volcano's top was blown off in an 1893 eruption, leaving a jagged cone. About halfway to Ensenada is the **Río Pescado** (Fish River) which, not surprisingly, is famous for its good fishing.

Waterfalls in Black Rock

From **Ensenada** ⑮ most visitors head up the 16km (10-mile) spur to Petrohué, stopping to see the unusual **Saltos del Petrohué**. These are a series of oddly twisting water chutes formed by a crystallized black volcanic rock which is particularly resistant to erosion. Volcán Puntiagudo's odd shape is also due to this erosion resistance: its central core is composed of the same crystallized rock which remains unaffected while the surrounding material erodes away. The water of the Petrohué River is bright green due to the presence of algae, a phenomenon repeated in **Lago Todos los Santos** (All Saints Lake), which begins at the town of Petrohué.

From the falls to the lake the road is cut by several river beds which will rise suddenly on a warm day with melt from Volcán Osorno. Eruptions from the volcano centuries ago diverted the River Petrohué's flow from Lago Llanquihue south to Lago Todos los Santos; signs of the earlier lava flows can be observed along with strange vegetation and insect life not found even a few kilometers away. **Petrohué** itself is nothing but a lodge, lakeside campground (the fishing is said to be great), and forest service outpost, but a large modern catamaran leaves from the dock for daytrips on the lake. In the height of summer this area is plagued by two types of biting fly – the *colihuacho* and the *petro*

(Petrohué is a Mapuche word meaning Place of Petros). The only relief from these pests is to shelter in the deep shade of the forests.

Small glaciers atop Volcán Tronador, (Thunder Mountain; 3,451 meters/ 11,322ft), can be observed en route, and Volcán Osorno is even more imposing from the Lago Todos los Santos side than from Lago Llanquihue. The lake itself is narrow, with forested cliffs rising sharply on all sides. Lunch at touristic **Peulla** ⑯ at the other end is expensive. The famous **Cascadas Los Novios** (Bridal Falls) may be only a trickle if rain has been scarce, and the hamlet can be surprisingly hot. But the small beach is pleasant, and the river above is shady and fresh. Hiking excursions into the mountains from Peulla are excellent. It's possible to continue the same day to San Carlos de Bariloche in Argentina by taking the road to **Puerto Blest** ⑰, from where you pick up another boat.

The area from Ensenada north along Lago Llanquihue was covered in an eruption some 150 years ago and nicely illustrates how plant life gradually returns after destruction by a lava flow; the borders of deciduous forest are abruptly marked on either side.

Three km (2 miles) from Ensenada is the road to **La Burbuja** (Bubble) refuge on the volcano's slopes, well worth the 19km (12-mile) climb. In clear weather, the sunset seen from the top is memorable, and the local refuge/ski center has overnight facilities. The road eases down to the town of **Las Cascadas** ⑱ (The Waterfalls), but there is no public transport for this 20km (12-mile) stretch. Hitchhiking is easier in the afternoon, but never a sure thing. The road has more than the necessary twists and turns – locals explain that the original track was paid for by the kilometer, and their relatives ensured it was as long as possible.

Las Cascadas is the base for an attractive 4km (2½-mile) hike into the hills, but it's easy to get lost, so it's advisable to hire a guide from the town.

Symmetrical peak

Volcán Osorno, a perfect, snow-covered cone, dominates the view from the road. Skilled mountaineers can climb to the crater in about six hours, but quickly shifting clouds and hidden crevasses can be deadly even for the expert. Plentiful stories of people being lost there are intended to discourage freelance exploring. It is worth visiting one of the various farms set back up in the hills a few hundred meters, on the pretext of buying homemade cheese or marmalade – you should be able to get a wide vista of the lake and volcano together, and will understand why the original settlers went to the trouble of making these densely overgrown lands habitable.

Some settlers employed Chilotes, mestizo fishermen from Isla de Chiloé farther south, to help with the backbreaking labor, sometimes abusing their trust to trick them out of fair wages. One whispered story even suggests the imported workers were often "lost" in the thick jungle in order to avoid paying them anything. Settlers dragged logs or their farm produce

BELOW: flowers on the shore of Lago Llanquihue.

As you walk through the woods of southern Chile, you'll probably see a brown bird with a rust-colored breast hopping through the undergrowth; it will be a chucao, named for its distinctive call.

BELOW: the pier at Frutillar.

down to a dock to be picked up by the steamboat from Puerto Varas, sometimes going along to the town for provisions. But the frequent lake squalls could lead to financial disaster: in order to avoid capsizing, passengers would have to dump their recently bought goods overboard, package by package.

The only surviving pier from the epoch is at **Puerto Fonck** on the road that connects Las Cascadas with the road to Osorno. The long stretches of beach from Las Cascadas toward Puerto Klocker and Puerto Fonck are deserted. European settlers did not feel secure in the area until the Mapuche people were finally defeated in the late 1800s.

The Mapuche survivors were herded into undesirable lands deep in the mountains (both Andes and coastal ranges), where soils were poor and animal husbandry difficult. While the foreign and domestic settlers rushed in to conquer the wilderness, the original inhabitants suffered poverty, discrimination, and social decomposition with the attendant social ills that continue to plague these communities today.

The first tourist outpost

The idea of Lago Llanquihue as a vacation spot occurred as early as 1912 to a government functionary, Interior Minister Luis Izquierdo, who built a summer mansion on the Centinela peninsula next to Puerto Octay with a group of his friends. The house remains in use today as the Hotel Centinela. Nearby, on the northern lakeshore, **Puerto Octay ⑲** is a popular resort town, and a bit less crowded than the southern side of the lake. The road along the lake heading south toward Frutillar has more spectacular views, and some stops of interest.

The tidy little town of **Frutillar ⑳** has a famous classical music festival in the summer. It is actually two towns joined together: Lower Frutillar is 4km (2½ miles) down a steep incline from Upper Frutillar. There are more houses up above, many of which offer summer lodgings at reasonable rates. Fixed-rate taxis will ferry you up and down if the walk is too tiring. Frutillar and other towns in the area are known for their pretty shingled churches, which often appear in tourist brochures with the lake sparkling in the background.

A new road has opened up the **Estuario de Reloncaví** (Reloncaví Estuary), a finger of brackish water that connects with the Seno de Reloncaví (Reloncaví Sound). Fishing here is not what it used to be after years of commercial exploitation, but there are still plenty of unexplored inlets. This area and the region farther south are sometimes called "continental Chiloé" for the similarity in culture with Isla de Chiloé (*see page 255*). As the road winds down the glaciated Petrohué River Valley onto the east shore of the Reloncaví, the characteristic Chilote tiles begin to appear on many of the buildings. These are made from water-resistant *alerce*, sequoia-related trees that live for hundreds of years and can resist forest fires. The wood is so valuable that *alerce* stumps are sometimes harvested and split for sale.

From Ralún, at the mouth of the Petrohué, a bridge crosses the river to **Cochamó ㉑** farther south, a fishing town which has views of **Volcán Yate** (2,111 meters/6,926ft), and **Puelo ㉒**. These towns are reminiscent of the isolated communities along the Carretera Austral highway which winds through the largely uninhabited archipelago region in the far south for close to 1,000km (600 miles).

Sleepy city

Of all the southern cities, **Osorno ㉓** is the least interesting, partly due to the strange lack of street life. A business day in Osorno feels like a Sunday, and Sunday feels like a day of national mourning. The town was abandoned after the great Mapuche uprising of 1598, its inhabitants fleeing to establish protected outposts on the ocean inlets just north of Isla de Chiloé. Osorno was not refounded until 200 years later, and it is still more of a market center for country residents than an urban entity. The cattle auction is perhaps its most impressive attraction.

City highlights include the modern cathedral on the Plaza de Armas, and the **Museo Histórico** (Jan–Feb Mon–Thur 9.30am–6pm, Fri 9.30am–5pm, Sat–Sun 2–7pm; Mar–Dec Mon–Thur 9.30am–5.30pm, Fri 9.30am–4.30pm, Sat 2–6pm, closed Sun; free), with displays on Osorno's history and the German arrival. Osorno's wooden houses have sharply angled roofs to handle the rain and snow, and when the storm clouds begin to threaten, the place has the air of a city in Quebec or northern New England. The 18th-century **Fuerte Reina Luisa** fort is derelict – the one at Río Bueno, 30km (19 miles) north, is better-preserved. It has a good view of the river, also known as El Gran Río, which carries off the water of four lakes (Maihue, Ranco, Puyehue, and Rupanco) – making it the second-largest in Chile.

Southern port center

The bustling, windy city of **Puerto Montt ㉔** was connected by rail to the rest of Chile in 1912 and became the contact point for the rest of the south. It remains so to the present day, despite the loss of its railway line. It is an important fishing center; seafood at

BELOW: housing development near Puerto Montt.

the harbor of Angelmó is famous. The port was completely destroyed in the earthquake of 1960. Boats leave from here for the long, slow trip down through the southern archipelago. (Puerto Chacabuco requires 22 hours, Puerto Natales three days.) The port is protected from the strong winds by **Isla Tenglo**.

From the hills above the city there are fine views of the entire Seno de Reloncaví. Local boat trips can be arranged either in Puerto Montt or at La Arena where the estuary begins. From Chamiza, to the east of the town, it is possible to get close to **Volcán Calbuco** on the southern side of Lago Llanquihue. German settlers built an interesting Lutheran church in Chamiza next to two giant *saav* trees. **Parque Nacional Alerce Andino** has good facilities, and Lago Chapo is off the usual tourist beat. In the other direction is the port of **Maullín**, one of the few places this far south where it's possible to observe the open sea.

A peaceful rural site situated near Puerto Montt has thrown the archeological world into a frenzy, pushing back the possible date of human arrival in the Americas by thousands of years. During the 1970s, scientists discovered that the area around the Chinchihuapi Creek, known as **Monte Verde**, held human remains dating from 12,500 years ago. In 1998 more remains were found at the site, which suggest possible human occupation 33,000 years ago. There are plans to build a museum in Puerto Montt to display exhibits from the site; the local authorities have donated land, but the project has yet to raise sufficient funding.

Southwest of Puerto Montt is **Carelmapu ㉕** one of the oldest settlements, dating from the Spaniards' flight after their defeat by the Mapuches around 1600. On its rough beaches, the original wild strawberries from which commercial strawberries were developed still grow, as in many other remote places in the south of Chile. An alternative route is the road that follows the bay southwest from Puerto Montt to Calbuco. This offers distinctive views of the volcanoes toward the north. **Calbuco ㉖**, like Carelmapu, predates Puerto Montt by some 250 years. ❑

Until 1930, the little fishing village of Maullín could only be reached by boat. Its name means "full of water."

BELOW: cruise ship in Puerto Montt.

RESTAURANTS, CAFÉS, AND BARS

Restaurants

Prices are per person for a three-course meal, not including drinks.

$ = under US$15
$$ = US$15–25
$$$ = US$25–35

Temuco

Mercado Municipal
Manuel Rodríquez 960, or entrances on Diego Portales, Bulnes and Aldunate streets.
$
As in most towns in southern Chile, the market in Temuco is the best place for a cheap and cheerful meal of traditional Chilean fare amid stalls laden with local produce and crafts.

La Pampa
Caupolicán 0155
Tel: (045) 329 999
$$
Popular with local businesspeople, this steak house serves huge cuts of barbecued beef as well as some fish dishes.

Pucón

Arabian Café
Fresia 354
Tel: (045) 443 469
$
A good place for a snack of falafels or stuffed eggplant.

Hostería École
General Urrutia 592
Tel: (045) 441 675
$
The restaurant of this popular hostel is open to the public and serves excellent vegetarian food. A popular gathering place for gringo visitors.

La Maga
Gerónimo de Alderete 276
Tel: (045) 444 277
$$$
An excellent Uruguayan-owned steakhouse, which also serves grilled fish.

Villarrica

Restaurant Kiel
General Koerner 153
Tel: (045) 411 631
$$
Part of the Hotel Yachting, this restaurant serves reliable food and has great views over the lake.

The Travellers
Valentín Letelier 753
Tel: (045) 413 617
$
A lively restobar with an eclectic choice of lunch and dinner dishes. The umbrella-covered tables outside are a lovely place for a leisurely meal on a summer evening.

Valdivia

Café Haussmann
O'Higgins 394
Tel: (063) 213 878
$
The most traditional German café in Valdivia, famous for its *crudos* of raw steak paste served on toast with lemon juice and its generous sandwiches.

Entrelagos
Vicente Pérez Rosales 640
Tel: (063) 218 333
$$
Renowned for its chocolate and marzipan, Entrelagos also runs a teashop serving excellent pastries.

Perla del Sur
Avenida Prat 500

Tel: (063) 245 531
$
Located right next to the Feria Fluvial fish market and one of the best places in town to eat seafood.

Frutillar

Club Alemán
Av. Philippi 741
Tel: (065) 421 249
$–$$
An institution in Frutillar, the German Club serves hearty food and wonderful *küchen* at very modest prices. The lunch menu is particularly good value.

Guten Appetit
Balmaceda 98
Tel: (065) 421 145
$$
Overlooking the lake, this restaurant serves good food that mixes traditional Chilean fare with some German dishes.

Puerto Varas

Café Mamusia
San José 316
Tel: (065) 529 271
$
A tearoom that offers simple meals throughout the day. Also a good place for breakfast.

Ibis
Vicente Pérez Rosales 1117
Tel: (065) 232 017
$$
A good restaurant specializing in seafood. More traditional than Imperial 605, but sound quality.

Imperial 605
Imperial 605
Tel: (065) 233 105
$$$
In a beautifully restored old house, this restaurant serves simple but varied and imaginative food, with a strong emphasis on local ingredients.

RIGHT: as one of Chile's most popular tourist areas, the Lake District offers a wide range of places to eat.

ISLA DE CHILOÉ

This large, rainswept island is a culturally distinctive area with its own music, dance, and craft traditions, and a wealth of spellbinding myths and legends

Santiago

For a moment you think you've misheard, that someone has simply pronounced the word "Chile" and for some peculiar reason your ears have given it an extra "o." To some extent Chiloé is Chile in miniature, a peculiar time capsule that contains some of Chile's best and harshest traditions, shaping them into song, dance, crafts, and a mythology which has become one of the main strands of the country's national identity. Much of "Chilean" folk music and dance was born in Chiloé's gentle summer fogs and harsh winters.

December, January, and February are the better months for a visit to Chiloé, because the warmer summer weather makes it easier to travel within the main island and across to some of the smaller islands. In recent years, Chiloé has become something of a standard pilgrimage for the young and the not-so-young, so you may meet more people from Santiago than from the islands.

Chiloé's flood myth

A Mapuche legend tells the story of what may have been the formation of Chiloé as witnessed by the Mapuche and Chono peoples long before the Spanish reached the continent. It tells how the twin serpents Cai Cai and Tren Tren do battle. Cai Cai, the evil one, who has risen in rage from the sea and flooded the earth, assaults Tren Tren's rocky fortress in the mountain peaks, while the people try in vain to awaken

the friendly serpent from a deep sleep.

Meanwhile Cai Cai has almost reached Tren Tren's cave, swimming on the turbulent waters. Cai Cai's friends, the thunder, fire, and wind, help her by piling up clouds to bring rain, thunder and lightning.

Pleas and weeping don't wake Tren Tren. Only the laughter of a little girl, dancing with her reflection in the sleeping serpent's eye, arouses her, and she responds with a giggle so insulting that Cai Cai and her stormy friends fall down the hill.

Main Attractions

COSTANERA DE ANCUD
MIRADOR CERRO HUAIHUÉN
CAULÍN
CATEDRAL DE CASTRO
MUSEO DE ARTE MODERNO
CHONCHI
PARQUE NACIONAL CHILOÉ

PRECEDING PAGES:
boats at low tide.
LEFT: *palafitos*
(wooden houses),
Castro.
BELOW: Ancud.

A young Chilote in Castro, one of Chile's oldest towns.

BELOW: fishing boat, Castro.

Cai Cai charges again, all the more furious, shattering the earth and sowing the sea with islands. She makes the water climb ever higher, and almost submerges the mountain where her enemy lives, but Tren Tren arches her back, and with the strength of the 12 guanacos in her stomach, she pushes the cave ceiling upward, so that the mountain grows toward the sky. Cai Cai and her friends keep bringing more water and Tren Tren keeps pushing her cave roof higher until the mountain reaches above the clouds, close to the sun, where the evil serpent cannot reach it. Cai Cai and her servants fall from the peak into the abyss, where they lie stunned for thousands of years.

The waters gradually recede, and the people are able to return to their lands, untroubled by either of the giant serpents, who continue sleeping. However, sometimes, it is said, Cai Cai has nightmares, and an island appears in the ocean or the earth trembles a little. The legend may tell the story of an ancient earthquake which was accompanied by tidal waves and flooding, but it is also remarkably similar to scientific accounts of how the peculiar attributes of the area came about. These changes occurred gradually, over thousands of years, of course, but were no doubt punctuated with dramatic upheavals in a region which is so geologically active that even today, natural catastrophes occur every 30 or 40 years.

Birth of an archipelago

The scientists explain that over thousands of years, two giant tectonic plates forming part of the earth's crust clashed, producing the volcanoes characteristic of mainland Chile: Hornopirén, Huequi, Michimahuida, and Corcovado. During the Ice Age, glaciers bore down upon the Central Valley region, carving a gap through the coastal mountains and pushing the valley farther and farther below sea level.

When the glaciers began to melt at the end of the Ice Age, the ocean poured through the openings located at the north and south ends of what is now the main island of Chiloé, to create the interior sea that now divides Chiloé from the mainland, turning what was previously the coastal mountain range into a series of islands which now form the archipelago of Chiloé. Toward the center of Isla de Chiloé, where the lakes of Huillinco and Cucao cut partially through the island's mountain range, the land drops to sea level, and many islanders fear that Chiloé may one day be cut in two.

Chiloé's **Isla Grande** (main island) is the second-largest island in Latin America, after Tierra del Fuego. Like a great ship moored off the Chilean coast it seems to float, surrounded by several smaller constellations of islands called the Chauques, Quenac, Quehui, Chaulinec, and Desertores. Some of these islands are so close to each other they are joined at low tide. The low mountains along the west coast of the main island are nevertheless high enough to stop the damp winds blowing off the Pacific, creating a slightly drier microclimate along the interior sea, where virtually all the settlements are located.

The interior sea, generally calm – at least as seen from the shore – can be difficult to navigate, especially for the many Chilotes who still rely on small rowboats or launches. As the tides roar in through the tiny channel of **Chacao** in the north (crossed by the mainland ferry), they eventually meet and clash with the tides pouring through the channel to the island's south, creating huge whirlpools and waves that have been identified as a potentially rich source of tidal-generated electricity. In Cucao, on the Pacific coast, the difference between high and low tides is 2.5 meters (8ft), while in Quemchi it is 7 meters (23ft), because of the shallowness of much of the interior sea. These powerful tides leave shellfish and fish, a major source of food for the islanders, trapped on the beaches and in sea pools.

Lago Cucao gets its name from the "cuca" heron that frequents its shores.

The making of the Chilotes

The first known inhabitants of the islands of Chiloé were the Chonos, a tough, seafaring people who have gone down in history for the creation of the *dalca*, a small, canoe-like boat built by binding several rough-hewn planks together. For centuries, the Chonos guided the Spanish and other adven-

BELOW: the Pargua–Chacao car ferry.

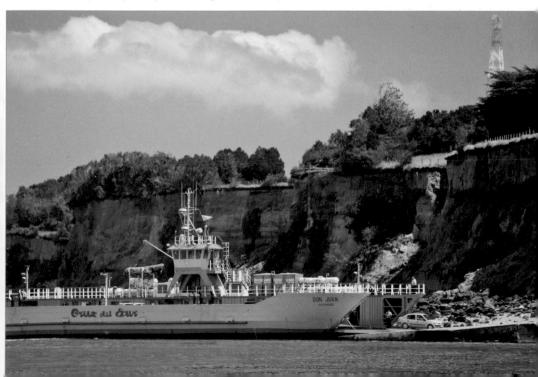

The island of Chiloé was once covered in impenetrable woods, which have gradually been cleared to make way for agriculture.

turers through the intricate channels and fjords which honeycomb Chile's southern shores. They spoke a different language from the Mapuches or Huilliches (southern Mapuche), who began to invade the islands.

These invasions forced the Chonos to migrate farther and farther south. In the 1700s, the Jesuits pushed the Chonos and the Caucahues, a separate native group who had not been integrated into the Mapuche tribe, into small reserves on Isla Cailín, south of Quellón, and later the Chaulinec Islands, where they eventually mixed with the other inhabitants. The Jesuit mission on Isla Cailín was the southernmost chapel in the Christian Empire.

When Alfonso de Camargo became the first European to see Chiloé in 1540, the archipelago's inhabitants were a mixture of Chono and Mapuche living scattered along the coast, which was at once their main highway, source of food, and the cradle for a wealth of legends and oral histories which are the backbone of Chilote culture to this day. The homes in which they lived were straw *rucas*, clustered near beaches

BELOW: Dalcahue woman, Chiloé Island.

and woods in groups of up to 400 people and known as *cabís*, led by *caciques* or chiefs. Using wooden tools, they farmed potatoes and corn in fields protected by fences which were woven using basket techniques, and they reaped the rich harvest of shellfish along the shores. They were also excellent weavers of llama wool.

Serfdom and rebellion

Thirteen years later Francisco de Ulloa's expedition formally "discovered" the islands, and 14 years after that, Martín Ruiz de Gamboa officially took possession of them, calling them Nueva Galicia. On February 12, 1567, he founded the city of Santiago de Castro and for the next 200 years the Spaniards divided up the available land – and the people living on it – in what became known as the *encomienda* system, which was a kind of serfdom. The idea was that the native peoples worked for free in order to "pay tribute" to the king of Spain. This native labor system was used in the mining of gold in Cucao, the weaving of woolen cloth and the logging of *alerce*, a tough, fine wood native to Chile (which is today in danger of extinction). In the early years, the products of Chiloé brought considerable wealth to the Spaniards who had taken possession of the land, but brought desperate poverty to its people.

In 1598, when the Mapuche communities of Carelmapu and Calbuco on the mainland rebelled against the Spanish invaders, the survivors retreated to Chiloé, where they established towns in 1602. The people of Chiloé twice joined forces with "pirates," destroying Castro with Baltasar de Cordes in 1600 and attacking Carelmapu and later Valdivia, across the channel, with Enrique Brouwer in 1643. In the centuries that followed, the Spanish and the Mapuche-Chonos of Chiloé lived in virtual isolation and extreme poverty, with occasional visits from Spanish ships sent from Lima, Peru, sometimes as many as three years apart. Despite this neglect, Chiloé became a royalist stronghold during the wars of independence in the early 19th century. The governor of Chile fled to Chiloé,

and despairingly offered the island to Britain. The offer was declined, and Chiloé surrendered to the mainland republic in 1826.

Over the centuries the two races, Spanish and Mapuche-Chono, fused, preserving much of the native languages and customs. The Chilotes all wore the same clothes and suffered the same hardships, creating a sense of social equality unusual in the Spanish Empire. Settlement continued along the coast until the early 1900s, when lands were given to German, English, French, and Spanish "colonists," and the building of a railway in 1912 between Ancud and Castro finally opened internal communication between Chiloé's two main cities.

A distinct culture

Today the Chilotes continue to be a proud, independent people, clearly distinguishable from their fellow Chileans, with their own dialect mixing influences from 16th-century Spanish with many indigenous words, and a rich tradition of music and dance beloved throughout Chile. The tragic

The curiously named Hotel Unicornio Azul (blue unicorn hotel) in Castro.

BELOW: guarding the clam catch, Ancud.

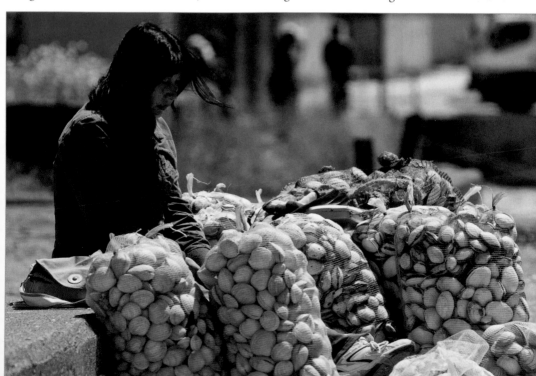

poverty of the early colonization, which forced many men to take seasonal work on the sheep farms of the Magallanes area and even in Argentina, has now given way to greater prosperity, born of tourism and the introduction of salmon farming.

The one great weakness of the Chilotes is the game of *truco*, which is played with the Spanish 40-card deck. *Truco*, which roughly translated means "trickery," is an extraordinary gambling game divided into two parts, the *envío* and the *truco* itself. The cards are half the game; the other half is the skill and imagination of the players who bluff and jest, using rhyming couplets laden with double meanings. Today, you are as likely to see a lively game of *truco* on a ship at Punta Arenas as in a Chilote bar. And the Chilotes who've gambled away a season's earnings on the sheep ranches and are unable to return home are legendary. This forced migration of working men has also given rise to the image of the Chilote family as a virtual matriarchy of distant, sometimes almost mythical men, and strong women raising their chil-

There are more than 150 churches and chapels in Chiloé. The oldest churches were built entirely of wood, using wooden plugs instead of nails, and provide some of the world's few remaining examples of 18th-century wood architecture.

BELOW: the wooden interior of the Iglesia San Francisco.

dren, their livestock and tending their crops, keeping the island alive.

A land of chapels

It was during the 200-year period when the Spanish were barred from the Mapuche lands in mainland Chile that the Jesuits began the evangelizing activities which left an enduring mark on the islands' legends and villages. Some of the most strikingly beautiful characteristics of Chilote architecture are the wooden chapels built during the Jesuits' stay, many of which survive to this day. Between 2000 and 2001, Unesco's World Heritage Committee declared 16 of these chapels sites of universal value on the grounds that they represent the only Latin American example of a rare form of ecclesiastical wooden architecture. In 2002, the tower of the chapel in Chonchi was toppled by a storm and others are in poor shape but, in early 2004, the Inter-American Development Bank authorized a grant of US$2.8 million for their repair.

The chapels, which often stood completely alone on the coast unac-

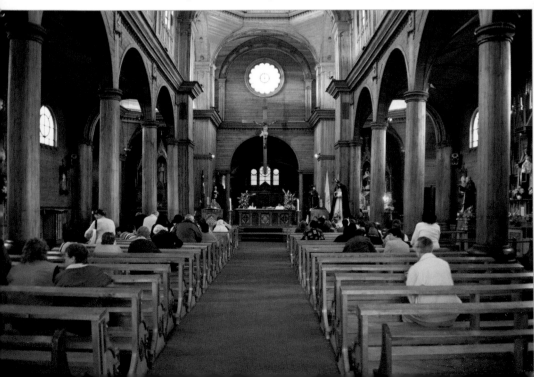

companied by human habitation, were built as part of the Jesuits'"Circulating Mission." This consisted of a boat manned by two missionaries who started their annual rounds from Castro with religious ornaments and three portable altars, complete with a "Holy Christ" to be carried during ceremonies by the *caciques* (chiefs), a "Holy Heart" to be carried by children, a "Saint John" to be carried by bachelors, a "Saint Isidore" for married men, "Our Lady of Suffering (Dolores)" for single women, and "Saint Notburga" for married women.

To this day, a *fiscal*, a sort of native priest, has the custody of chapel keys, and in August people from nearby islands gather on Isla Caguache to celebrate their religion with ceremonies similar to those initiated by the Jesuits and modified by later Roman Catholic missions. The chapel of Vilupulli, near Chonchi, continues to stand alone, with no human settlement around it, exactly as the chapels did in the 1700s. These chapels are an interesting example of the Chilotes' outstanding ability to absorb foreign cultures without los-

ing their own identity. Their design is strongly influenced by German architecture of the period, because several of the Jesuits were from Bavaria.

The *tejuelas* or wooden shingles commonly used to roof buildings throughout southern Chile, and which are one of the most striking characteristics of homes in Chiloé, were also a German idea, brought by the colonists who originally settled in Llanquihue and Puerto Montt on the mainland. The visible part of the *tejuela* is approximately a third of the total length, as they overlap so well that these buildings are extremely resistant to the heavy rains of the region. Before the *tejuelas* were introduced, Chilote homes usually had roofs of straw, similar to those of the Mapuches' *rucas*, and also extremely resistant to rain.

A tradition of handicrafts

For centuries, the women of Chiloé have spent the harsh winters producing clothing and household items. Different parts of the islands are associated with different crafts. The small town of **Chonchi** (south of Castro) is known for its woven

Castro's brightly painted cathedral was built between 1910 and 1912 to replace an early building destroyed by fire.

BELOW: Catholic festival, Castro.

*The islands of Chiloé
are dotted with small
wooden chapels, like
this one on Isla
Quinchao.*

BELOW: people on
Quellón preparing
curanto.

wool products, especially blankets and ponchos, as well as *licor de oro,* a liqueur made with saffron. **Quellón ❶** is famous for its ponchos, which are resistant to rain because the wool used for making them is raw and full of natural oils. On **Isla Lingue,** across from Achao, baskets are woven from local fibers, although some have fallen into disuse owing to the difficulty of working with them. Many of the islands' legends have been woven into decorative objects from all areas of Chiloé.

On Sunday mornings, there is a traditional market by the dock in **Dalcahue ❷,** where hundreds of craftspeople from all over the archipelago still gather to sell their wares. They also prepare traditional Chilote meals, particularly the *curanto,* a concoction prepared over a fire built in a hole scooped out of the earth, containing a variety of shellfish and meat and served with *milcao,* a traditional flatbread made with grated potatoes. The traditional woven fences of the Mapuche-Chonos can still be seen separating livestock from planted areas in some parts of the islands, and the *birloche* or *trineo,* a sled-like vehicle

towed by oxen, continues to be used on several of the smaller islands.

Keep your eye out in markets and fairs for the *almudes,* wooden boxes of a fixed size, still used to display a seller's wares. The *almud* is also a unit of measurement, and the boxes have the peculiarity of measuring one *almud* on one end and half an *almud* on the other. Their origin is Spanish. Stone mills introduced by the Jesuits can be seen in several Chilote museums, and they are still in use in some areas between Castro and Dalcahue. In February, wooden *chicha* (cider) presses are still very much in evidence, pressing the sweet juices out of apples piled in traditional baskets. Hanging in the windows of many houses you'll see woolen socks or ponchos, or other handmade items for sale. If you're lucky you may also get a glimpse of a Chilote loom, which is horizontal and nailed to the floor. It is still used by the artisans, who must kneel to work it.

Chilote sweaters are made from sheep rather than llama wool. The women shear the sheep, clean and wash the wool by hand, dye it with colors prepared from local herbs, and spin it using a simple spindle which twirls on the floor.

Holding on to the past

Chiloé is in many ways as mysterious, as long-suffering, and as contradictory as it has been for most of its history. Modern fish-processing plants and salmon farming have provided more employment. At the same time, pollution and overfishing of coastal waters are now problems. Already the *loco*, a tasty shellfish marketed abroad as abalone, is virtually extinct, and attempts to protect it have created only a thriving underground of unscrupulous entrepreneurs.

Other Chilotes have tried to eke out a living from fishing, with mixed results, and developmental agencies have created programs for improving Chilote agriculture, marketing and handicraft techniques. Even as modern factory ships sail under foreign flags, just outside Chile's 322km (200-mile) limit, the Chilotes themselves continue to live – and die – by traditional rowboats and small motor launches. Chilote culture itself – the music, poetry,

and stories – is increasingly packaged for a burgeoning tourist industry, a process which tends to create and preserve caricatures devoid of their original meaning. Like similar attempts in other parts of the world, this has harmed as well as helped the local economy.

Chilote cultural activity is on view during the Festival Costumbrista, held in the second or third week of February in Castro and other towns, and during local summer events.

Jumping-off points

Ancud and Castro, the main island's two cities, provide good bases for exploring the archipelago. Until 1982, **Ancud ❸**, which has a population of 27,000, was the capital of Chiloé. The city was an international port until the beginning of the 20th century, and it retains a peculiar mixture of traditional Chilote buildings, docks, and plazas combined with more modern signs and structures.

Ancud's central plaza is flanked by the **cathedral**, government buildings, and the **Museo Regional de Ancud**

The Sunday morning market in Dalcahue is one of best places to buy local crafts, and just beside it, there are restaurants with lovely views over the harbor.

BELOW: clothes store in Puerto Varas.

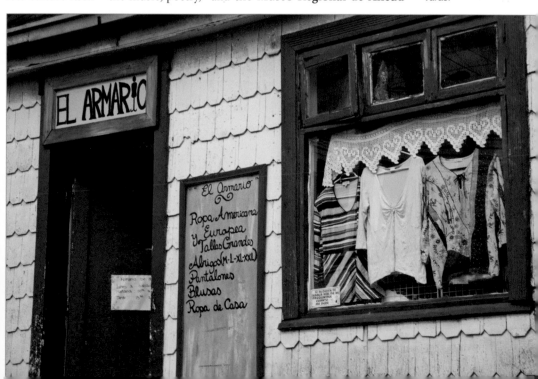

The typical Chilote boats use a cross-shaped anchor, made with a stone and two planks of wood.

(Jan–Feb daily 9.30am–8pm; Mar–Dec 10am–5pm, Sat–Sun 10am–2pm; charge), which contains exhibits about Chilote culture and mythology.

If you have a vehicle, you can enjoy a lovely drive along the **Costanera** (coast road), with a view of the Gulf of Quetalmahue. Lining the shore are the older, often impressive houses of Ancud's wealthier citizens.

The **Mirador Cerro Huaihuén** (a lookout point) affords breathtaking views of the city and across the Chacao Channel toward the mainland. By following the Costanera, then Bellavista and San Antonio northward, you'll quickly reach **Fuerte San Antonio**, which was built in 1770. On January 19, 1826, it became the last Spanish garrison to surrender to the wave of independence which had swept South America. Ancud then became the focus for colonizing expeditions aimed at southern Chile, including one that settled the Strait of Magellan in 1843. In the late 19th century, Ancud boomed with the whale and wood industries, and newly arrived settlers from Europe, primarily of German origin. However,

BELOW: *palafitos,* traditional wooden houses on stilts.

when the railway extended to Puerto Montt in 1912, Ancud lost its importance, and in 1982 the trade and shipping center Castro became the capital of Chiloé.

Near the waterfront, craftspeople set up stalls selling mostly woolen goods. At the covered fruit and vegetable market on Calle Pedro Montt – which burnt down in early 2008 but is being rebuilt – look out for the blue, black, and red varieties of potato that are native to Chiloé (*see page 94*).

An interesting side trip from Ancud is a visit to the oyster beds at **Caulín**. To get there you must travel back along the highway toward the ferry's arrival point at Chacao, and then turn left toward Caulín at Km 24, where you can enjoy fresh oysters at reasonable prices, before spending an afternoon on the beach or heading back to Ancud.

If you drive south from Ancud and then west, you'll find good fishing at the *refugio* (refuge) at **Puerto Anguay**, as well as several good places to picnic. Along the way, look out for the **Butalcura River Valley**, with great patches of dead trees in the water where the 1960 earthquake caused the earth to collapse.

Settlement on stilts

Castro ❹ has a population of about 29,000, and is located about 90km (56 miles) to the south of Ancud. Although it is technically one of Chile's oldest cities, having been founded in 1567, Castro suffered so many attacks and privations that there are few signs of its antiquity within the city itself. On the highway just to the south of Castro are *palafitos*, Chiloé's distinctive wooden homes on stilts.

It's best to see Castro on foot, strolling from the **Plaza de Armas** with its painted **cathedral** shoreward to enjoy the market area with its lively crafts fair, then back up the hill toward the **mirador** (lookout) with its statue of the Virgin and its bird's-eye view of the city's cemetery, piled high with conventional gravestones and small structures resembling houses that shelter the city's dead.

Castro's **Museo Regional** (Jan–Feb Mon–Sat 9.30am–7pm, Sun 10.30am–1pm; Mar–Dec Mon–Fri 9am–1pm and 3–6.30pm, Sat 9am–1pm; voluntary contribution), is located near the central plaza, but due to move to a new building near the port in 2010.

The plaza is also the focal point for the Festival Costumbrista, a celebration of Chilote customs, food, and crafts, which traditionally takes place in February. The **Museo de Arte Moderno** has an excellent collection of contemporary Chilean work (Jan–Feb daily 10am–6pm, closed Apr–Dec except for special exhibitions; voluntary contribution).

Set on a hill just outside the town, it also provides a spectacular view of the interior sea and of the snow-capped mountains across on the mainland. The building, built of Chiloé's traditional wood, has won architectural prizes.

Exploring the islands

From Castro you can travel up the shore of Chiloé's interior sea to visit Dalcahue, Llaullao, and, on **Isla Quinchao** (accessible by ferry), the small towns of **Curaco de Vélez**, also famous for its oyster beds, and **Achao** ❺. Achao's 18th-century church of **Santa María** is built entirely of cypress and *alerce*. Farther along the island highway is Chiloé's largest church, **Quinchao**, which was built in the 18th century and refashioned according to neoclassical ideas at the end of the 19th century. While driving around the area, keep an eye out for the traditional woven fences.

Chonchi ❻, about half an hour south of Castro, is a small town built on such a steep incline that it is also known as the "Ciudad de los Tres Pisos" (Three-story City). Local handicrafts abound, and cardboard signs advertise the famous *licor de oro*. Near Chonchi it's possible to catch a ferry to **Isla Lemuy** ❼ or head farther south to **Queilen** ❽. **Parque Nacional Chiloé** can be reached by traveling across the island toward **Cucao**, one of only two towns on the Pacific side of Isla de Chiloé. It's a good place to hike or camp, with a long and wave-pounded beach. ❏

RESTAURANTS

Apart from its hotels, Chiloé has few smart restaurants, but is full of waterfront cafés with wonderful views, that serve generous portions of freshly caught fish and shellfish. They are homely but generally reliable, and very modest in price. In some of the larger towns, there are also a smattering of New Age cafés, run mostly by foreigners. The stalls and makeshift restaurants at the Festival Costumbrista, held every year in February, are an ideal place to try local specialties such as *curanto* (meat and vegetable stew), *milcao* (traditional flatbread), and the different types of native potato.

Ancud
Mercado de Ancud
Dieciocho s/n
$
Ancud's old market, not to be confused with the covered fruit and vegetable market on Calle Pedro Montt, is a great place for a cheap and excellent fish lunch.

Castro
Feria Artesanal
Costanera s/n
$$
Castro's waterfront crafts market has smarter seafood restaurants (*palafitos*) than the market in Ancud and as a result the prices are slightly higher, although not prohibitively so.

Prices are per person for a three-course meal, not including drinks.

$ = under US$15
$$ = US$15–25
$$$ = US$25–35

Chilote Magic

Chiloé is a magical place. Gods and goddesses, ghost ships, and the lost city of the Caesars are as much a part of the archipelago as the people themselves.

Expressed in music, dance, and popular beliefs, the *Trauco*, the *Pincoya*, the *Caleuche*, and other mythical creatures haunt the forests and fields of Chiloé. Alongside them are the *brujos* or wizards, their human counterparts.

Undoubtedly, many of the mythical characters of Chiloé also serve a social purpose: the *Trauco*, for example, is a creature that is able to seduce young women by hypnotizing them with his magical gaze. Accepting the existence of the *Trauco* provides an explanation for teenage pregnancies, and the mythical creature has even been used to cover up incest. Today, when so much of Chiloé's maritime wealth is threatened by over-exploitation, these people-sized gods also serve as symbols of an ecological balance that was achieved by Chiloé's earlier peoples.

Seducer of virgins

As you walk through the forests of Chiloé, keep an eye out for the *Trauco*. No taller than a meter, this deformed, man-like creature may make his home in the fork of a tree or a small cave. He wears clothes made of vegetable fibers and always carries a staff which he knocks on the ground and against trees. His legs end in stumps, and just one look from him can kill the beholder or leave him or her mute or stupid, or with a twisted neck or a hump.

Yet, in spite of his limited physical charms, the *Trauco* enjoys considerable success with young women, whom he seduces with the hypnotic effect of his blazing eyes. To defend yourself from the *Trauco*, throw a handful of sand at him. While he's busy counting the grains, make your escape.

Another creature, the blond and beautiful *Pincoya*, slips out of the surf at sunrise and dances on the shore. When her face is turned toward the ocean, it means that abundant shellfish will soon cover the beach. If she looks inland, this means she has taken the fish elsewhere, to where there is more need for them. If you fish or extract shellfish too long from one site, she gets angry and abandons it, leaving the place barren. Legend has it that the *Pincoya* will sometimes rescue drowning sailors and leave them on the beach.

It is difficult to imagine any seagoing culture without its ghost ship, and Chiloé is no exception. The *Caleuche*, with its unlikely cargo of tragic guests caught in an eternal party, sends haunting strains of accordion music across the waves and recovers the bodies of those who have died at sea. Its crew are *brujos*, Chilote wizards with enormous powers, and it travels in a constant cloud produced by the boat itself, always at night. If caught looking at the *Caleuche*, your mouth will suddenly become twisted, your head crooked, or you'll suddenly die.

A magical city

No traveler ever sets eyes on the lost city of the Caesars, even when walking through it. A thick mist always hides it from sight, and the rivers carry approaching boats away. The lost city, with its gold- and silver-paved streets and its ability to make all who go there lose their memory, will appear only once, at the end of the world, to prove its existence to non-believers.

The city, with its enormous riches and infinite pleasures, where no one is born or dies, inspired centuries of expeditions by explorers, beginning in 1528. That was when 14 men led by Captain Francisco César, member of an advance group in Sebastian Cabot's party, ventured into the southern jungles for two months. Upon returning, they told tales of fabulous treasures, which may have belonged to the Inca Empire. The next expedition to search for the lost city started out from Castro on October 6, 1620, led by Juan Tao. This and following trips were led primarily by the Spanish and their descendants, and included the Jesuit priests José García, Juan Vicuña, and Juan Francisco Menéndez. Both the Spanish Council of the Indies and the Real Audiencia (Royal Audience) in Santiago officially authorized the search for the mystery city.

The brotherhood of warlocks

The *brujería* is a secret brotherhood of male witches organized into an underground network of councils, which meets in cleverly disguised caves, the biggest of which is in Quicaví. The members arrive disguised as birds or wearing the luminous *macuñ*, which gives them the power of flight. The *macuñ* is made of skin taken from the breast of a virgin's corpse and its light is fueled by oil taken from the bodies of dead Christians.

The apprenticeship to become a *brujo* begins at an early age, and consists of a series of increasingly cruel trials. One of the more bearable is a shower in a mountain waterfall, a ritual which is repeated for 40 nights, to cleanse away all trace of baptism. To prove that he is not weakened by sentiment, the apprentice must murder his best friend. Finally, he should dig up the corpse of a recently buried virgin and remove the skin from the breast.

Other trials include races, leaps from cliffs at night, corporal metamorphosis into animals or birds, wearing a lizard bound to the forehead (to transmit wisdom), and spending nights sleeping on a tomb in the cemetery. *Brujos* have the power to make people sleepy, to open doors, to cause illness, hair loss, or deep cuts, and to throw *llancazos* (similar to the evil eye), or to conjure up bad spells cast at a distance.

Guarding the *brujos*

The *invunche* guards the *brujos*' cave and is the product of a long and painful process: to obtain an *invunche* the wizards steal a first-born son from his parents, within the first nine days after his birth. If he has been baptized they use black magic to annul it; then they break and twist his right leg, until it rides up the back. At three months old they split his tongue and rub his skin daily with a special infusion. In the early months the *invunche* lives on milk from a black cat and later on human flesh obtained from cemeteries.

The origins of this macabre myth may be based in historical fact: the writer Narciso García Barría, considered an authority on Chiloé, relates the *invunche*'s deformities to the Inca culture. They often preferred men with some physical disability to be the guards of their temples.

Women's participation in the *brujería* is usually as a *voladora* (flying woman), for whom many of the secret practices of the brotherhood are forbidden knowledge. The *voladora* often transforms herself into a bird (the *bauda*) and serves as a messenger for the *brujos*.

The *camahueto* is a huge one- or two-horned cow-like creature that is born from the earth with such force that it leaves a small crater behind it. This creature's horns are essential to the magic of the *machi*, the *brujos*' herb doctor, who uses them to make powders which are believed to impart tremendous strength to anyone who takes them.

According to Narciso García Barría, the origins of the *brujos* may lie in an underground organization of native resistance to the Spaniards, a thesis which is supported by native Chilotes' eager participation in the attacks led by the corsairs.

In Chiloé, as in other cultures with communities of witches, the *brujería* is also the major source of a wealth of information on native herbs and medicines which are still commonly used on the island.   ❑

RIGHT: Mapuche witch doctor.

AISÉN

The gateway to Chile's far south, this beautiful region of lakes, forests, and glaciers still has a certain wilderness quality, despite the construction of the Carretera Austral road

Aisén is the hispanicized version, local folklore has it, of an English name for the area: "ice end" – the region of glaciers. English, Germans, Swedes, Spaniards, Argentines, and Chileans all did their bit to explore and sparsely colonize this spectacularly beautiful and particularly inhospitable region of fjords, glaciers and, in parts, dense forest. The early settlers at the beginning of the 20th century cleared the land they needed by burning down the woods, and several times the fires got out of control and ravaged great areas. Now, the gray, petrified remains of huge trees stick up into the sky – from the air, it looks as if a giant box of matches has been scattered over the ground.

Inhospitable frontier

The first inhabitants were the Tehuelches and the Alacalufes. The Tehuelches were nomads who lived by hunting guanacos, *ñandúes* (rheas), pumas, and *huemules* (deer), and the Alacalufes navigated the coastal channels in their light canoes. The Spanish invaders sent down a couple of expeditions in the mid-1550s to explore, to make sure that English marauders were not establishing a presence there, and – incidentally – to convert the natives to Christianity; no one bothered to try to find out how many of them there were. The Spanish were more interested, in fact, in the legendary "city of the Caesars" *(see page 266)*, said to be

hidden in the forests, with fabulous treasures of gold and jewels.

The southern coastline was not properly mapped until 1831, when Charles Darwin and Captain Robert Fitzroy navigated the area in their famous voyage on the *Beagle*, and the region's interior remained unknown for most of the 19th century.

The Chilean government only began to pay attention to Aisén when border disputes began to arise with Argentina in the late 19th century. The first attempts to settle these were unsuccess-

Main Attractions
CARRETERA AUSTRAL
MUSEO REGIONAL DE LA
    PATAGONIA
PARQUE NACIONAL QUEULAT
TERMAS DE PUYUHUAPI
FUTALEUFÚ
LAGUNA SAN RAFAEL
CHILE CHICO
RÍO BAKER

PRECEDING PAGES: San Rafael glacier. **LEFT:** farmers on horseback. **BELOW:** Puerto Aisén.

Aisén

ful. Between 1859 and 1896 four colonies were founded, two of them at Melinka and Río Álvarez, as simple trading posts for collecting and distributing seal, otter skins, and cypress wood from the area.

At the beginning of the 20th century, the first settlers made their way across the frontier at Balmaceda from Argentina. By 1907 there were thought to be 197 permanent colonizers, with their families, plus another 500-odd employees of the English-owned sheep-farming companies which had begun to exploit the region. The pioneers were naturally a hardy bunch. One government official in the 1920s tried to describe their indomitable spirit: "No incompetent or coward or milksop gives up his home and his fatherland to settle lands uncultivated before in Patagonia, isolated in these solitudes, far from the principles of all authority and justice, suffering hunger often and battling constantly against nature."

Hospitality, he noted, was one of the most developed virtues of the people of the region. "Dismount, unsaddle," the most common greeting to the stranger, was understood as an invitation to eat and stay the night. The guest's best way to repay such hospitality was "to present the most complete account possible of all events, human and divine, in the rest of the world," since other means of receiving news were non-existent.

Highway to the south

Today, the population of Aisén is just over 90,000, but many aspects of life there have not changed very dramatically from the way they were 50 years ago. The kinds of facilities that urban-dwellers take for granted – doctors, clinics, schools – are still scarce in the remoter parts of this isolated region. In recent years, salmon farming has increased in importance, providing a new source of jobs. A consortium of power companies has controversial plans to build five major hydroelectric dams on the Baker and Pascua rivers near the town of Cochrane.

One fairly recent improvement has been the completion of the **Carretera Austral Longitudinal** (to give it its official title). This is a mostly unpaved road, which runs the length of the region from Puerto Montt to Cochrane, (880km/547 miles) and on to Villa O'Higgins.

Roads already existed from Puyuhuapi to Chaitén, between Puerto Aisén, Coyhaique, and Balmaceda, and to Puerto Ibáñez, Chile Chico, and Cochrane. But the Carretera scheme, started in 1976, has successfully linked the whole region with a single north–south route to which a network of east–west roads has been added. At various points the "road" becomes a ferry from one side of a river to the other.

For the inhabitants of Aisén, the road has meant a real link-up with the rest of the country and has also become a major tourist attraction, opening up some of the most beautiful scenery on earth. The Chilean tourist office, Sernatur, distributes brochures with a description of the route, and the main stops along the way. It also has a map giving details of facilities such as lodgings, telephones, first-aid posts, and police. Information and organization are important – this is not really a suitable area to wander through without your own means of transport or a tour, unless you have all the time in the world.

Hub of the wilderness

The most central point for exploring Aisén is the region's largest town, **Coyhaique ①**. It has a population of 45,000, and, while pleasant enough, travelers generally use it as a jumping-off point for trips to remoter parts. Coyhaique can be reached by plane from Santiago or Puerto Montt, or by following the Carretera Austral south, but there are sections of the road which have no bus services. The most popular route is by ferry from Puerto Montt to Puerto Chacabuco and then on by bus.

Once in Coyhaique, take a casual stroll along Calle Prat. That's where most of the travel agents are found. You can book a tour here, or go by public transport to most parts of the recently opened south. The **Museo Regional de la Patagonia** (Mon–Fri 8.30am–1pm and 3–5.30pm; free except for groups) has a fine collection of photographs depicting the region's history, including the construction of the Carretera Austral.

Fish – mainly rainbow trout – are plentiful in all of Aisén's rivers and lakes. Boats for lake expeditions can be organized from Coyhaique, either for the day or for a few days' stay in one of the area's fishing lodges. Skiing is available, too, in winter, at **El Fraile**, 30km (19 miles) southeast of Coyhaique, and 1,000 meters (3,281ft) above sea level.

Traveling north from Coyhaique, the road runs through bright green woods of *mañío* and *coigüe*. A side road takes you to **Puerto Cisnes ②**, a remarkably well-established little settlement whose mayoress for years was a formidable Italian lady who ruled the place with a very firm hand. She was a friend and admirer, initially of General Carlos Ibáñez del Campo, and then of Gen-

TIP

Punctures are a frequent occurrence on the stony Carretera Austral, so it's wise to carry more than one spare wheel.

BELOW: boats moored in Puerto Aisén.

eral Pinochet (whose horoscope she used to tell). With the ear of both presidents she managed to get facilities in her village that many locals grumble would be better located farther up the main road, at Puyuhuapi.

On the main road just past the junction with Puerto Cisnes on the way to Puyuhuapi is Piedra El Gato, a massive boulder which had to be partly blasted away to build the road. Continuing north to Puyuhuapi, the road passes **Parque Nacional Queulat**, one of the supposed locations for the legendary city of the Caesars. Fishing, camping, and hiking are possible amid lakes and glaciers.

Northern boundary

Puyuhuapi ❸ is situated near Lago Risopatrón and has thermal springs, a luxury hotel, a garage, and a carpet factory, which turns out sturdy handmade woolen rugs. The settlement was started by four Sudeten Germans who emigrated from Czechoslovakia at the time of the Nazi invasion, and made their way to this remote spot on the other side of the world, which they are said to

have read about in a Baedeker guide.

From **La Junta ❹**, the junction of the Palena and Rosselot rivers, it is possible for experienced sailors to navigate the Palena River to the wide beaches at its estuary, at **Puerto Raul Marín Balmaceda ❺**, a six-hour journey. Beyond La Junta the road leads to Chaitén, 150km (93 miles) to the north. There are some interesting sights along the way, such as the magnificent Cavi hanging glacier, which requires a short detour and a hike.

Chaitén ❻ was largely destroyed in May 2008 when the nearby Volcán Chaitén erupted after lying dormant for over nine thousand years. All the town's 4,000 inhabitants were successfully evacuated but the town was buried in ash and houses were carried away on the vast mudslide that followed. In early 2009, the government announced plans to rebuild the town at a safer location, farther north along the coast.

Situated just north of Chaitén is **Parque Pumalín**, one of the world's largest private parks. Its owner, Douglas Tompkins, the North American conservation businessman who

BELOW: an expedition to the Pascua River.

founded the Esprit clothing chain, established the park in a bid to protect Chile's indigenous forest. Restaurant and camping facilities are available at Caleta Gonzalo. Near the border with Argentina lies the pretty village of **Futaleufú**, a popular rafting and kayaking destination.

Some 25km (15½ miles) south of Chaitén, via the village of Amarillo, are the **Termas El Amarillo** ❼ thermal springs, where you can take a warm dip.

Whisky on the rocks

Aisén's most popular attraction is without doubt **Parque Nacional Laguna San Rafael** ❽, with its magnificent glacier. The sight provoked awe and gloom in Charles Darwin when he visited it in 1831. He described the place as "sad solitudes, where death more than life seems to rule supreme." He must have seen the glacier on one of the many days of low cloud. When the sun is shining, it is an awesome spectacle, with light glinting off the aquamarine ice and the landscape alive with black-necked swans and distinctive furry beavers. Passengers are taken by rowboat or motor launch to the very base of the glacier where it meets the sea. Icebergs float by so close you can reach out with your hand and touch them. The climax of any visit is to have a whisky on the rocks, using pieces of ice chipped straight from the glacier.

The glacier can also be visited without going via Coyhaique. Several of the ferry companies in Puerto Montt run services to Chacabuco which detour via Laguna San Rafael. For those who wish to travel in comfort, cruisers such as the *Skorpios* also operate five-day trips from Puerto Montt.

Traveling south

The route south from Coyhaique to Cochrane can be done in a day through hilly country, and then past the beautiful Lago General Carrera. At **Villa Cerro Castillo** ❾, near Puerto Ibáñez, 100km (60 miles) from Coyhaique, are two famous Stone Age paintings, of which there are several in the area. A detour to **Bahía Murta** ❿, and from there a horse or boat ride, takes you to **Puerto Sánchez**, a former mining village of some 80 people, where you can see the wave-sculpted "chapel of marble" and the underground caves of the Panichine Islands.

A ferry to the other side of the lake takes you to **Chile Chico** ⓫, one of the region's earliest settlements. The area here enjoys a dry, warm microclimate, which gives the people who live here the opportunity to cultivate a much wider range of fruit and vegetables than in the rest of the region. The place has a quiet, rustic charm that can be quite beguiling. Many travelers who had planned to pass straight through to Argentina find themselves staying for several days in Chile Chico, enjoying the sunshine and taking the occasional dip in the icy waters of the lake.

A six-day boat ride down the Baker River, from **Puerto Bertrand** ⓬ to **Caleta Tortel** ⓭, offers thrills and spills. The River Cisnes is another favorite trip. All of these excursions can be organized from Coyhaique.   ❑

Aisén is a popular destination for fly fishing enthusiasts, who come for the rainbow trout.

RESTAURANTS AND BARS

Coyhaique

Casino de Bomberos
General Parra 365
Tel: (067) 231 437
$
This restaurant, run by the fire brigade, is renowned for its friendly atmosphere. Good value for money.

La Casona
Obispo Vielma 77
Tel: (067) 238 894
$
A pleasant family-run restaurant that serves traditional Chilean fare with a strong emphasis on local ingredients, including tasty lamb dishes.

Piel Rojo
Moraleda 495
Tel: (067) 236 635
$
A lively bar that turns into a disco later at night.

Restaurant Histórico Ricer
Horn 48
Tel: (067) 232 920
$
Close to the plaza, this is one of the town's oldest and most popular restaurants. The menu includes vegetarian dishes.

Puerto Aisén

Hotel Caicahues
Michimalonco 660
Tel: (067) 336 326
$
Restaurant in a hotel in Puerto Aisén, west of Coyhaique. Owned by the local municipal government, it provides simple set meals. Credit cards not accepted.

Prices are per person for a three-course meal, not including drinks.

$ = under US$15
$$ = US$15–25
$$$ = US$25–35

CRUISING CHILE'S SOUTHERN SEAS

Beyond the Lake District, Chile breaks up into a mass of islands. Boats can take you to the most beautiful, unspoiled parts that roads cannot reach

Boats reign supreme in southern Chile's inhospitable but stunningly beautiful fjord region. They are the life-support system of the area's isolated fishing villages during the harsh winters, and in summer they ply a bustling tourist trade. The main attraction is the majestic San Rafael glacier, two days by boat out of Puerto Montt. This spectacular ice wall is the destination of the luxury Skorpios cruise boats, as well as several more modest services.

Another popular trip takes passengers from Puerto Montt down to Puerto Natales, gateway to the beautiful Parque Nacional Torres del Paine. Tourist cabins are modest, but the views and the atmosphere on board more than compensate. Puerto Montt is the starting point for any journey into the fjords, including Isla de Chiloé. But if you suffer from seasickness, beware. The narrow inland waterways are glassily calm, but the Gulf of Corcovado or, farther south, the Gulf of Penas, can test even the best sailor.

Several services run from Punta Arenas to the southern tip of Tierra del Fuego. One of the best – and most expensive – is the luxurious four-day *Australis* cruise. There are also many enjoyable boat trips in the Lake District. One of the best starts from Petrohué on Lago Todos Los Santos and ends 12 stunning hours later in San Carlos de Bariloche in Argentina. (*See Travel Tips, page 331, for details of tour operators.*)

ABOVE: a trip on the Laguna San Rafael provides an unmissa[ble] opportunity to see the 30,000 year old glacier and experience[e] the surreal atmosphere of the lagun[a]
LEFT: pelicans are the constant companions of Chile's fishermen, pickin[g] up any scraps they leave behind.

ABOVE: getting up close to the San Rafael glacier. **LEFT:** Each spring, several thousand Magellanic penguins return to their breeding grounds on the Otway Sound, near Punta Arenas, where they dig burrows in the sandy shoreline.

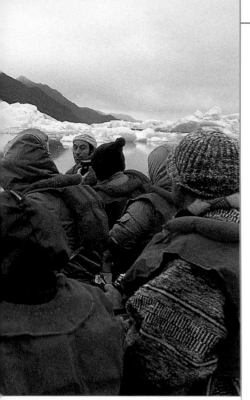

WILDLIFE OF THE FJORDS

Sea mammals such as seals and sea lions are a common sight in southern Chile's remote fjords. Like the Alacalufe Amerindians who once fished these waters, the modern inhabitants of the isolated villages dotted around the fjords still hunt and eat baby seals. In the most remote areas, you may also be lucky enough to see a blue whale. This huge animal migrates to the fjords in summer.

A sure companion for any boat trip south of Puerto Montt is the *tonina*, or Chilean dolphin. These fast-moving, playful animals usually swim in small groups and delight in chasing a boat, darting from side to side.

The steep sides of the fjords are covered with many native trees, including a type of cypress and ferns, some of them almost tree-size. The dense vegetation is also home to an enormous variety of birds, including a colorful woodpecker and a tiny hummingbird.

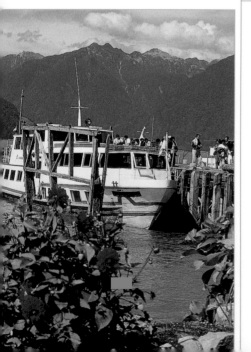

BELOW: Lago Todos Los Santos is also known as "Lago Esmeralda" (Emerald Lake) due to its striking color. Located in the Parque Nacional Vicente Pérez Rosales, it can be visited as a day trip, or en route to Argentina.

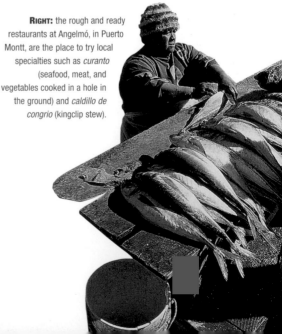

RIGHT: the rough and ready restaurants at Angelmó, in Puerto Montt, are the place to try local specialties such as *curanto* (seafood, meat, and vegetables cooked in a hole in the ground) and *caldillo de congrio* (kingclip stew).

MAGALLANES

A harsh, inhospitable territory of bleak plains, fierce winds, and wilderness areas of extraordinary beauty crowned by the rocky peaks of Torres del Paine

S tretching toward the windswept southern tip of South America, the province of Magallanes exists quite apart from the rest of Chile. The hardy people who live here consider themselves first as Magallánicos, second as Chileans – hardly surprising, considering that they cannot reach Santiago by road without crossing the border into neighboring Argentina. In order to come and go from this stormy corner of the world, you have either to travel for days by bus across the endless stretches of Argentine Patagonia, to fly direct, or to take a lengthy, rocky cruise through the icy southern seas.

The terrain of Magallanes is formidably harsh. The region is split between impenetrable mountain ranges and bleak, barren Patagonian plains. Yet these harsh physical conditions have helped form a distinct local character. "The sheer difficulty of living here brings people together," says writer Francisco Coloane, the most famous chronicler of Magellanic life. "It creates a human solidarity and sense of honor that people from the rest of Chile don't always share."

Growing in isolation

History has conspired with the tyranny of distance to keep Magallanes apart from centralized rule in Chile. The region was first developed by foreign sheep companies – mostly British-owned – which had interests on both the Argentine and Chilean sides of the

border. Magallanes soon had more in common with Argentine Patagonia than the distant world of Santiago. English was spoken more often than Spanish – followed by a chorus of Croat, Russian, and Italian, as workers arrived from all parts of the globe.

This cosmopolitan tradition can still be felt in the towns and old *estancias* (farm estates) of Magallanes, where the surnames are as likely to be MacMillan or Covacevic as anything of Spanish origin. The isolation of the south also developed its own political traditions:

PRECEDING PAGES: snowy peaks. **LEFT:** Torres del Paine. **BELOW:** tree bent by the Patagonian wind.

like the remote mining towns of the north, Magallanes has a long history of left-wing activism. Some of the bitterest strikes in Chilean history occurred in the province, and it was from Magallanes that the socialist leader Salvador Allende was first elected to Congress. Regional independence still marks its politics today, fed by a resentful belief that central government ignores the far south.

What today lures most travelers to this far end of the globe is the province's unspoiled wilderness. Much of Magallanes is made up of a jigsaw of tiny islands and channels without any permanent habitation or regular passenger services. These are the tips of underwater mountains – the continuation of the Andes range that has sunk into the icy sea – and they can only be glimpsed on rare boat journeys or from the air. Down toward the battered coastline of the Strait of Magellan are colonies of penguins, crystal lakes, trees gnarled by the ever-present Patagonian wind, and some of the most spectacular mountain scenery anywhere in South America.

Horrifying sights

Magallanes takes its name from the Portuguese explorer Ferdinand Magellan who, while working for the Spanish Crown, became the first European to set eyes upon its shores in 1520. A gale blew his fragile sailing ships through what is now the Strait of Magellan toward the ocean he baptized the Pacific. On the way a landing party stopped off near modern-day Punta Arenas, to find a beached whale and 200 corpses raised on stilts. Shuddering at the gruesome sight, the navigator hurried toward the west.

Further Spanish contact with the area was hardly more encouraging. A group of 300 conquistadors under Pedro de Gamboa tried to set up a settlement on the straits, but the savage winter drove them all to starvation. A lone survivor who had lived among the local people was found three years later by the English pirate Thomas Cavendish. For the next 250 years the region was visited by explorers, cartographers, and naturalists but few saw any reason to linger. Only in the 1830s did the Chilean government, spurred on by a wave of optimism

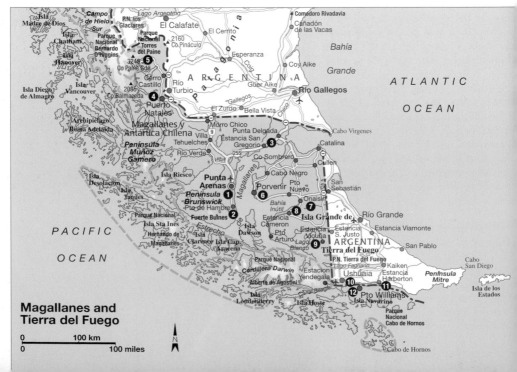

Magallanes and Tierra del Fuego

and economic expansion, cast possessive glances toward the remote south. Prompting action was the occupation of the Falkland Islands by Britain in 1833 and the lengthy explorations made in the region by the British naturalist Charles Darwin on the *Beagle*.

In 1843, President Manuel Bulnes claimed the land around the Strait of Magellan, Tierra del Fuego, and southern Patagonia. A boatload of 21 motley soldiers was sent to found Fuerte Bulnes on the straits, but the location proved to be so inhospitable that the outpost was abandoned; Punta Arenas was founded in its place five years later. This new settlement grew slowly into a town, with raids by native peoples and a bloody mutiny punctuating its early days. But Chile was forced to abandon its claim to much of Patagonia: Argentina took advantage of Chile's preoccupation with Peru and the north to take the lion's share of the south, leaving Magallanes with the border it has today.

At the end of the world

Today **Punta Arenas** ❶ is a city of some 120,000 people, the hub of Magallanes and the first port of call for most foreign travelers. Facing out across the straits, it has an almost Dickensian flavor, full of rusting corrugated iron buildings and grandiose mansions from the late 19th century. The class divisions of old are still echoed in the streets: here you can find elegant, if run-down, parlors where apéritifs are sipped with an aristocratic flourish. Sitting adjacent are seedy bars full of sailors, naval recruits, and a ubiquitous collection of weary old men – usually wearing woolen caps and tightly buttoned overcoats, huddled over their glasses of pisco and whisky, taking refuge from the biting wind.

Weather dominates the city's mood. Despite its latitude, Punta Arenas never experiences the extremes of cold found in equally remote places in the Northern Hemisphere. Nevertheless, the skies bring few comforts. Even in summer, when the sun shines for up to 20 hours a day and temperatures are moderate, the wind and rain can often make Punta Arenas seem a gloomy frontier town. But when the sun breaks through the billowing clouds, its cool air is bracing

Alcohol, introduced by whale-hunters during the 19th century, contributed to the disappearance of native communities in Magallanes.

BELOW: Punta Arenas.

and a stroll through the quiet streets can be pleasant as well as fascinating.

Memories of a golden age

Scattered around Punta Arenas are opulent monuments to a golden age when it was one of the busiest ports on earth. Its history is in many ways that of the whole far south. A series of unexpected events in the mid-19th century helped lift the town out of obscurity. The industrial age in Europe and North America was creating a boom in sea trade. The Panama Canal had not yet been thought of. Sea clippers and the new steamships making their journeys around the world – carrying anything from European machinery to Texan petroleum and Australian wheat – all had to stop at Punta Arenas, the town at the end of the world.

The boom soon made Punta Arenas the logical center for Patagonian sheep farming. In 1877, an English trader brought a flock of stock from the Falkland Islands to Elizabeth Island in the Magellan Straits. The experiment was a success, and soon other entrepreneurs were following suit. A Machia-

vellian Spaniard named José Menéndez and the Russian-born immigrant Mauricio Braun became leading figures: starting off as rivals, they were soon linked by marriage to form a Patagonian dynasty that would dominate the south for decades.

Farm administrators were brought in from Scotland, England, Australia, and New Zealand, making Magallanes, as writer Bruce Chatwin noted in his classic *In Patagonia*, look like an outpost of the British Empire. But the *peones*, farm hands who worked the land in generally dismal conditions, almost all came from the overcrowded farmyards of Chile's own Chiloé.

Punta Arenas's golden age ended abruptly when the Panama Canal was opened and boats no longer needed to travel round Cabo de Hornos (Cape Horn). Magallanes continued to be a profitable sheep region until toward the Great Depression, when a long decline began. Competition from Australia, New Zealand, and Canada squeezed Chile and Argentina from the major world markets. Many of the English managers left for their home-

TIP

A raft from Río Verde, just north of Punta Arenas, takes vehicles and pedestrians over to Isla Riesco.

BELOW: immigration statue, Punta Arenas.

land as land reform carved up the largest estancias of the south. Even Don José Menéndez decided to move to Buenos Aires. Today many of the farms are nearly bankrupt.

This downward economic spiral was only halted with the discovery of petroleum and natural gas in 1945. Oil companies stepped up exploration in the straits over the following decades, and Magallanes again prospered. Workers looking for high wages flocked from the north, while fishing also boomed, and Punta Arenas became a duty-free port. During this period, Magallanes achieved one of the highest per capita incomes in Chile, before starting to stagnate again as the oil wells dried up.

A tour of past glories

The modern center of Punta Arenas is, as it always has been, the **Plaza Muñoz Gamero** Ⓐ. Surrounded by trees and neat gardens, the plaza is dominated by a bronze statue of Magellan, looking proudly over the heroic figures of various local Mapuches, who were idealized by a sculptor after they had been largely wiped out by marauding European settlers, keen to ensure that no native would interfere with the profitable grazing of sheep. These days children pose for photographs while touching the feet of one of the Mapuche figures for luck.

Flanking the plaza are three box-like buildings – the **Hotel Cabo de Hornos**, the **cathedral** Ⓑ, and the grandiose **Centro Cultural Braun-Menéndez** Ⓒ, situated opposite the Cabo de Hornos on Calle H. de Magallanes.

Built by the Patagonian pioneer, Don Mauricio Braun, in 1905, it is rightly referred to by locals as "El Palacio" (The Palace). The mansion was designed by a French architect to outstrip the finest houses of Santiago. Marble was imported from Italy, wood from Belgium, wallpaper from France, and furniture from England.

Upon entering the mansion, visitors pass through the airy hall with classical frescos painted on its ceiling. Everything in the adjoining rooms is done

on a grand scale: the main bedroom contains a massive Louis XV four-poster bed, while the games room has a gigantic billiard table and furniture in Art Nouveau style. The salon – the most important room in the house – is crowded with gilded tables and chairs under a glittering crystal chandelier and stern portraits of long-dead family members. The walls of the dining room are covered with pressed Italian leather, while the *escritorio* (office) still contains the mahogany desk from which the fate of the south was directed.

The rest of the house's ground floor has been converted into the **Museo Regional de Magallanes** (Oct–Apr Mon–Sat 10.30am–5pm, Sun 10.30am–2pm; May–Sept daily 10.30am–2pm; charge, except Sun), with exhibits from the time of the foundation of Punta Arenas to the 1920s. The mansion was shared by the Brauns and Menéndezes after constant intermarriage linked the clans. But as land reform took its toll on their estancias and profits, the families handed over the building to the government. It became a national monument in 1974.

The hard water of Punta Arenas produces some of Chile's best beer.

BELOW: part of the Magellan monument in Punta Arenas.

The old port

Some of the oldest streets in Punta Arenas stretch down from Calle H. de Magallanes to the straits. A walk along Calle Roca takes you to the old port area, with its range of seedy flophouses, cafés, and bars. Many of the old houses made of tin and corrugated iron seem to be on the point of collapse, but these vestiges of the late 19th century give a glimpse of the bustling days of the past.

Another walk out along Calle Bories leads to the fascinating **Museo Regional Salesiano** Ⓓ (Tue–Sun 10am–1pm and 3–6pm; charge), one of the most unusual museums in South America. The Salesians are a religious order that once tried to "save" the native peoples of the region by creating missionary refuges, only to find that European clothes gave them influenza and killed the tribes as surely as the white settlers' bullets. The museum's disordered exhibits provide a fascinating insight into the lives of several groups of people whose way of life and very existence has been largely destroyed.

A room full of pre-Hispanic artifacts gives a good introduction to the four tribal groups that once lived in Magallanes. Inhabiting the barren plains east of the Andes were the fierce Tehuelches (or Aónikenk) peoples. Their impressive stature and enormous moccasins are traditionally believed to have inspired Ferdinand Magellan to exclaim "Ha! Patagón!" (big foot), giving Patagonia its name.

The travel writer Bruce Chatwin has offered a more plausible explanation, suggesting that the name came from an early 16th-century romantic story where a monster called the Grand Patagon appears. Magellan was likely to have been familiar with the tale, where the man-like creature roars like a bull, just as Magellan noted that the Tehuelches did.

Canoeing around the rough islands of the southeastern Pacific were the maritime nomad tribe the Alacalufes (Kawéskar), who hunted sea lions and dived for shellfish. Today the last survivors of this race live in the remote fishing village of Puerto Edén. The Onas (Selk'nam) hunted guanacos on the northern plains of Tierra del Fuego while the Yaghanes (Yamanas) navi-

BELOW: fishing boats in dock.

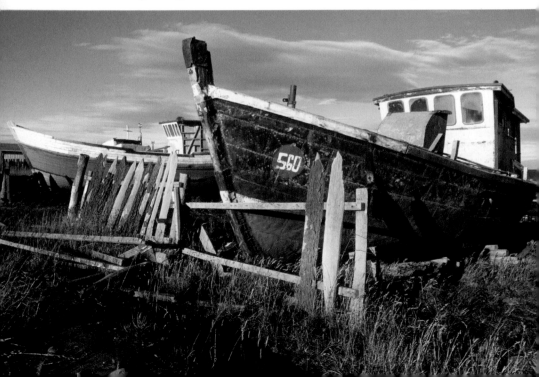

gated the icy forested islands south of the Beagle Channel. The Onas were wiped out in the early 20th century, and only a handful of mixed-blood Yaghanes are still alive.

Keep an eye out in the museum for a piece of skin and some 10,000-year-old droppings from the giant ground sloth found in the Cueva del Milodón (Milodón Cave) near Puerto Natales (*see page 291*).

Farther out along Calle Bories is the **Cementerio Municipal** Ⓔ, comparable in splendor only to the famous Recoleta necropolis in Buenos Aires. Settlers from every part of the world are buried here, as well as the victims of the many shipwrecks that occurred on this savage coast. Just off the opposite side of the road, a small shop sells Punta Arenas artisan chocolate. It's tucked away in a side street, but the friendly local people will be happy to point you in the right direction.

Penguins and crabs

An hour's drive from Punta Arenas are the famous *pingüineros* (penguin colonies) on the Otway Sound. Hundreds of these comical-looking creatures live in burrows dug into the sandy shoreline. It is possible that this was where the Italian Antonio Pigafetta, a member of Magellan's crew in 1520, recorded the first European sighting of the penguin.

The species seen here is the *Spheniscus magellanicus*, named for the straits on which it lives rather than the explorer himself. It is known as the jackass penguin on account of the odd braying sound it makes. Try to visit the *pingüineros* in a small group, since large numbers of people send the penguins scurrying away on their flippers, which they use as front legs to run on all fours. The penguins spend most of April to August at sea, heading north to warmer climates before returning from September through March to their breeding grounds here.

Some 54km (34 miles) south of Punta Arenas along the inky Strait of Magellan is the reconstructed **Fuerte Bulnes** ❷ fortress on the site of the original 1843 settlement. The highway passes the skeleton of the wrecked ship *Lonsdale* on the outskirts of town, and

Magellanic penguins heading to the sea on Isla Magdalena.

BELOW: Magellanic penguins.

some classic Patagonian scenery, but the fort itself has a disappointing Disneyland look. On the way back most tours stop at **Punta Hambre**, where the unfortunate Pedro de Gamboa tried to set up his settlement 300 years ago (*see page 282*).

The road to Argentina

Along the highway 150km (93 miles) north of Punta Arenas is the first sheep farm of the south, **Estancia San Gregorio ❸**. Built in 1878, it was taken over by José Menéndez four years later and extended to 90,000 hectares (222,400 acres). It can only be visited with the permission of the current owner, although a good deal can be seen from the road.

San Gregorio remains the classic example of the many estancias that, in the 19th century, were like small, self-contained towns. The company's own launch, the *Amadeo*, lies rusting by the shore at the estancia's entrance, where the captain decided to leave it after 50 years of service. Two railway lines ran to the estancia. In the grounds are large wooden shearing sheds, still with old faded stock awards hanging there.

After decades of grinding oppression, the *peones* became drunk on freedom. In scenes reminiscent of the French Revolution, they camped out in the mansion, put the bust of Don José in the outhouse and went through the family cellar. Prize sheep munched freely at the garden before finally being slaughtered for mutton soup. The estancia was returned to private hands after the brutal 1973 military coup. Farther along the road toward Argentina is **Fell's Cave**, where some of the oldest prehistoric human remains in the Americas have been found. It can only be visited with the help of scientists at the Instituto de la Patagonia in Punta Arenas.

Gateway to the mountains

Puerto Natales ❹, 242km (150 miles) northwest of Punta Arenas, is set prettily on the shores of the Ultima Esperanza Sound. Hotels abound, and surprisingly, in view of Puerto Natales's small size, there are plenty of places to eat, drink, and even to dance. This is

The centolla, a bright orange king crab, is one of the great delicacies of the south; they look huge and vicious but are actually rather timid creatures.

BELOW: rodeo.
BELOW RIGHT: Grey Glacier.

the place that the inhabitants of Punta Arenas come to when they want a change of scene.

The waterfront, where black-necked swans bob on the cold waves, is a lovely place to walk, while the climb up the **Cerro Dorotea** hill gives fine views of the whole Ultima Esperanza area. Just outside town there is an old meat-packing plant bought by the British after World War I. In its heyday, thousands of sheep were slaughtered here weekly for the dinner tables of Europe, and many of the steam-driven engines used then are still lying about. One sits in the main plaza.

The meatworks ensured that Puerto Natales would be a leftist town. A riot began here in 1919 when Chilote workers killed an English assistant manager, lynched three policemen, and looted the stores. But before long the government sent in the army, and 28 ringleaders were taken away, among them some Maximilianist Russians who were blamed as foreign agitators.

Puerto Natales is the gateway to some of the most spectacular sights in Magallanes. Most easily reached is the **Balmaceda Glacier** to the northwest. Boatloads of tourists leave most mornings to see this aquamarine river of ice that inches its way down from the Andes to the sea. Gigantic ice blocks crash regularly from the glacier, sending shock waves across to the boat, while powerful winds whistle through the narrow channel. Most boats pull up at a small jetty, and passengers can safely walk along paths near the side of the glacier. On the way, the jagged Torres del Paine mountain peaks can be seen on the horizon, while the channel shore is lined with waterfalls. Groups of seals and sea lions sit on rocky outcrops, while porpoises, steamer ducks, and black-necked swans can be spotted in the icy waters.

Prehistoric cave-dweller

A quite different day-trip can be made to the enormous **Cueva del Milodón** (Mylodon Cave; *see box, page 291*), focus of a scientific furore nearly a century ago and a key element in Bruce Chatwin's classic travel book *In Patagonia*.

Today, the Cueva del Milodón is a popular picnic spot outside Puerto

BELOW: Puerto Natales.

Natales. A life-size model of the mylodon, rearing back on its hind legs, has been placed at the cave mouth, but nothing else remains to suggest its past. A piece of the mylodon's skin and its dung can be seen in the Museo Regional Salesiano in Punta Arenas (*see page 286*), and there are more substantial mylodon remnants in the repository of antiquities in the British Museum in London.

From Puerto Natales, the road north continues to **Cerro Castillo** on the border with Argentina and, from there, to **El Calafate**, the gateway to Argentina's **Los Glaciares National Park**. Inexpensive bus services run regularly from Puerto Natales to El Calafate (around a five-hour trip) in summer. Rental cars are also allowed to cross the border, but, unless you plan to return to Chile, beware of a hefty drop-off charge.

The untouched wilderness

By far the most impressive sight in the Chilean south is **Parque Nacional Torres del Paine ❺** (pronounced pie-nee). Lying at the far south of the Andes mountain chain, it is one of the newest nature reserves in South America, having been formed in 1959 and only reaching its present size in the early 1970s (Unesco made it a Biosphere reserve in 1978). The uninhabited park is crowded with glaciers, lakes, and gnarled Magellanic trees, and provides some of the most magnificent walking in the world. The dramatic mountain formations are a sight that few people will forget, while the park itself is full of animals, including guanacos, flamingos, *ñandúes* (ostrich-like creatures), and condors.

Every morning in summer and several times a week at other times of the year, vans and buses make the three-hour drive from Puerto Natales to the park along a rough dirt road. The trail winds through mountain passes before descending to the foot of the Andes, providing the first view of the **Cuernos del Paine** (Paine Horns), twisted pillars of gray granite, dusted with snow and rising from the flat Patagonian plains into a sky usually full of billowing clouds.

Like everywhere else this far south, weather in the park can be unpredict-

TIP

The road north from Puerto Natales crosses the border into Argentina to the popular El Calafate tourist center on Lago Argentina.

BELOW: Lake Pehoé.

able, to say the least. The best times to visit are January to April, but even then clear skies are rare and can disappear within minutes. The famous Torres (Towers) del Paine are even more spectacular than the Cuernos, but often difficult to see because of cloud cover. The one thing that never seems to change is the gusting Patagonian wind that drives from the plains to the west.

All visitors to the park must sign on at the administration building, where the wardens (*guardaparques*) will give advice on the condition of the trails. The classic views of the park can be easily reached by road and on day-trips operating from Puerto Natales. If you want to stay in the park, advance booking is essential. There are several small hotels, including the **Hostería Pehoé** on one of the lakes and the **Posada Río Serrano**, a converted estancia (farm estate) house. Its restaurant has the obligatory log fire and stuffed animal heads, as well as sculptures made from the park's bulbous wooden tree roots. A luxury hotel, **the Salto Chico Explora,** is beautifully designed and set on the shore of one of the lakes. It runs some of the best guided tours around the park but is very pricey.

Roaming in the wilderness

Several day-trips, as well as more ambitious walks, can be made from these bases. The park has more than 250km (155 miles) of walking tracks, including the classic seven-day circuit and the four-day "W" route. Along the way are *refugios* or shelters, often primitive wood-and-corrugated-iron edifices that barely keep out the wind and rain; good sleeping bags, and cooking gear, are essential. If you plan to do the seven-day circuit or the "W" route, you should bring a tent as well, since the *refugios* can get full.

This hike starts at the administration building at the southern end of **Lago Pehoé** and gives ever-changing views of the Cuernos. The walking can be strenuous – the longest stretch in one day is 30km (19 miles). Many people make two- or three-day walks rather than the full circuit. A good compromise is to walk to the first *refugio* next to Lago Grey, camp overnight, take a day-trip to **Grey Glacier** and then walk back to the

Perhaps surprisingly, the enormous prehistoric mylodon that lived in Patagonia 10,000 years ago was a herbivore.

BELOW: the Mylodon Cave, near Puerto Natales.

The Giant Sloth Hunt

In 1896, German-born landowner Herman Eberhard found a strange 1.2-meter (4ft) long stretch of hairy skin on the floor of a cave. The following year, part of the skull of a huge mammal, a claw, and a large human thighbone were found. Before long, a scientist in Argentina had announced that the skin was from a Mylodon Listai (named after himself), a giant prehistoric ground sloth endemic to the South American continent. The bones of several mylodons had been found during the 19th century, but Listai asserted that this piece of skin was so fresh, the beast had only recently died – and a living example could not be far away.

"Positive sightings" of huge hairy beasts became the norm in the region. Excitement was sufficient in Britain for the *Daily Express* newspaper to finance a scientific expedition to search for a living mylodon. Despite hearing many ghostly tales, they found no live example (although expedition leader Hesketh Prichard's book *Through the Heart of Patagonia* became an inspiration for Arthur Conan Doyle's *Lost World* tale). Meanwhile, a team of archeologists dug away in the cave, but they found little more than huge amounts of sloth dung. Radio carbon-dating has since shown that the skin is about 10,000 years old but was perfectly preserved in the dark, damp cave.

New oil and gas exploration under private concession contracts awarded in 2007 could give the Magallanes economy a significant boost.

BELOW: guanaco in Torres del Paine National Park.
OPPOSITE: the famous towers.

administration center the next day.

Those who make the effort are rewarded with superb views of snow-covered peaks, turquoise lakes, and lush valleys. The walking trails are lined with flowers, sometimes crossing wide pasture and at other times hugging mountainsides or passing through verdant forests. The Grey and Dickson glaciers, when discovered in the wild, are somehow more impressive than others more easily reached.

Most routes in the park allow walkers to see plenty of animals, most commonly guanacos: unlike in other parts of South America, they appear unafraid of people and can be easily photographed from up close. Condors cruise between mountain peaks, hares and foxes dash about in the scrub, and swans and flamingos can be seen on many of the lakes.

Although the weather can turn from fair to foul and back again within minutes, the memories of this national park will last well after your clothes have dried out. Many people who go for a few days stay for a week: the liberating sensation of being in one of the most remote and untouched wilderness areas on earth is worth savoring for as long as possible.

The remote archipelago

The map of Magallanes shows hundreds of scattered islands stretching to the Pacific. Very few are visited, and fewer still are inhabited. A large area of the south has been incorporated into **Parque Nacional Bernardo O'Higgins** and into forestry reserves. There is little chance of visiting these wilderness areas without hiring your own boat in Punta Arenas or Puerto Natales.

For most travelers, the way of seeing these islands is to take the pricey week-long *Skorpios* cruise from Puerto Natales or to travel on the Navimag passenger boats between Puerto Natales and Puerto Montt *(see Travel Tips, page 331, for details)*. This three-day journey goes through the Estrecho Smith and Estrecho Estebán. It is not particularly comfortable unless you hire a cabin, which increases the price significantly, but some travelers are captivated by the romance of a sea voyage and the chance to watch the remote islands drift by. ❑

RESTAURANTS

Punta Arenas
Club de la Unión
Plaza Muñoz Gamero 716
Tel: (061) 242 685.
$$
Lunch in the conservatory of this old mansion on the main square is worth it just for the setting. In the evenings, try the bar in the same building.
La Luna
O'Higgins 1017
Tel: (061) 228 555.
$$
A great place for a drink or an informal meal.
Sotito's Restaurant
O'Higgins 1138

Tel: (061) 243 565
$$$
Popular with locals and a good place to try the local lamb or *centolla* (king crab).

Puerto Natales
Asador Patagónico
Prat 158
Tel: (061) 413 553.
$$
On the main square in what used to be the town's pharmacy, this is a meat-eater's choice, best known for its lamb.
Hotel Cost-Australis
Pedro Montt 262
Tel: (061) 412 000
$$$

International-style food using the best local ingredients.
Indigo Patagonia Hotel
Ladrilleros 105
Tel: (061) 413 609
$$
Imaginative food at moderate prices with great waterfront view; closed Apr–Sept.

Prices are per person for a three-course meal, not including drinks.
$ = under US$15
$$ = US$15–25
$$$ = US$25–35

THE PICK OF THE NATIONAL PARKS

With most of the population concentrated around Santiago and Concepción, the rest of Chile has some beautiful wilderness areas to explore

Almost one-fifth of Chile is protected to varying degrees in national parks and reserves. The national park service, CONAF, administers 33 national parks, 48 national reserves, and 15 natural monuments, as well as some nature sanctuaries. The first national park in Chile, Vicente Pérez Rosales *(see page 240)*, in the southern Lake District, was founded in 1926. Entrance fees contribute to maintenance and conservation work.

Chile's long, narrow geography means that its national parks are very varied. Not many people want to trek in the hot, dry desert north – the main attractions of parks like Lauca and Volcán Isluga are the wildlife and the superb scenery. These parks are best tackled in a four-wheel-drive vehicle, preferably with a driver who knows the area well. Farther south, coastal parks like the popular Pan de Azúcar give protection to sea life and are popular for camping.

Many national parks such as Nahuelbuta, Alerce Andino, and Conguillío have been created to protect Chile's native forest. Unfortunately, the popularity of Parque Nacional Conguillío, in the northern Lake District, has brought with it serious erosion.

In the far south, parks like Laguna San Rafael and Bernardo O'Higgins protect Chile's southern lakes and glaciers, while prime trekking territory is found in the magnificent Parque Nacional Torres del Paine, in Magallanes.

Finally, the archeological monuments of Easter Island are protected by Parque Nacional Rapa Nui. For more information, contact CONAF's central office, at Av. Bulnes 285, Santiago; tel: (02) 663 0000.

ABOVE: the Parque Nacional Pan de Azúcar contains some of Chile's most impressive coastline and protects a large colony of Humboldt penguins. **BELOW:** Trails go to the Petrohué Falls in Parque Nacional Vicente Pérez Rosales. White-water rafting is done on the River Petrohué.

LEFT: the *copihue*, Chile's national flower, grows on a tree ivy in the Central Valley and farther south; it is mostly red, but there is also a white variety.

THE PLEASURE OF PAINE

Parque Nacional Torres del Paine, 112km (70 miles) north of Puerto Natales in Magallanes, covers a wilderness area of 181,400 hectares (450,000 acres). Created in 1959, the park achieved World Biosphere Reserve status from Unesco in 1978, and is today one of Chile's best-known and most beautiful tourist attractions.

The park's crowning glories are the spectacular Torres (towers) and Cuernos (horns, pictured above), stark granite peaks that form part of the Paine Massif. The range continues into Argentina's Parque Nacional Los Glaciares, with the Fitzroy Range, attracting climbers from all over the world.

Parque Nacional Torres del Paine is a haven for the *ñandú* (rhea) and the guanaco, which European settlers slaughtered to near-extinction to make room for sheep but has since recovered. Used to visitors, they aren't unduly bothered by cars and it's usually possible to get quite close to take pictures. You might also see flamingos, condors and, if you're really lucky, a puma.

Most people visit in January and February but the best month is December. As well as greater solitude, it is the time when the wildflowers are in best bloom.

RIGHT: unusually for the bird world, it is male *ñandúes*, or rheas, which incubate the female's eggs and raise the chicks. When scared, they run away fast, constantly changing direction.

POLO·NORTE
16.112 Kms.

NUEVA YORK
10.778 Kms.

TOKYO
15.556 Kms.

SANTIAGO
2.555 Kms.

RIO DE JANEIRO
3.978 Kms.

ESTOCOLMO
17.223 Kms.

BERLIN
16.112 Kms.

LONDRES
15.223 Kms.

LAUTARO
1.991 Kms.

VALPARAISO
2.744 Kms.

TIERRA DEL FUEGO

The land at the southernmost tip of South America is the bleakest, stormiest part of the continent, yet it exerts a constant fascination for travelers who want to visit the last stop before Antarctica

Santiago

Lashed by wind and wild seas at the southern tip of South America, **Tierra del Fuego** exerts a perverse fascination. Despite – or because of – its desolate image, few who travel to the far south of Chile can resist paying a visit to the literal end of the earth, the last fragment of land before the treacherous, forbidding territory of Antarctica.

The archipelago's name, which means "land of fire," came from the explorer Ferdinand Magellan, who in 1520 saw smoke rising from campfires on its shores (Magellan originally called it "land of smoke", but the Spanish King Charles I thought "land of fire" might be more poetic). It took the navigator no less than 38 days to force a passage through the strait that now bears his name. Fear of returning through these waters drove Magellan's men ever westward after their captain's death in the Philippines, eventually making the few survivors of the expedition the first to circumnavigate the globe.

For centuries afterwards, Tierra del Fuego was dreaded by sailors for its frequent storms and freezing rains. Rounding Cape Horn between the Atlantic and Pacific oceans became a nautical vision of hell, as can be seen in the works of Herman Melville, Samuel Taylor Coleridge, Jules Verne, and Edgar Allen Poe. Today Tierra del Fuego maintains its sense of being a Klondike-style frontier. Despite the grisly past, the people of its remote, windswept towns have a rawness and surprising warmth toward strangers. And, most importantly for many travelers, the islands of Tierra del Fuego contain some of the last great wilderness areas on earth.

Darwin among the savages

The British naturalist Charles Darwin added a new dimension to the image when he visited Tierra del Fuego on the *Beagle* in the 1830s. He pronounced the native people, who had been living in the far south for tens of thousands

Main Attractions
CANAL BEAGLE
BAHÍA INÚTIL
ONAISIN
LAGO BLANCO
PARQUE NACIONAL TIERRA DEL FUEGO
ESTANCIA HARBERTON
ISLA NAVARINO
MUSEO MARTÍN GUSINDE
CABO DE HORNOS

PRECEDING PAGES: windswept plains.
LEFT: a long way from anywhere.
BELOW: iceberg.

of years, to be the lowest on the human evolutionary scale.

"I never saw such miserable creatures," Darwin wrote in his classic *Voyage of the Beagle*, "stunted in their growth, their hideous faces bedaubed with white paint and quite naked... Their red skins filthy and greasy, their voices discordant, their gesticulation violent and without any dignity. Viewing such men, one can hardly make oneself believe that they are fellow creatures placed in the same world... What a scale of improvements is comprehended between the faculties of a Fuegian savage and a Sir Isaac Newton!"

Darwin's verdict was to be shared by the first settlers of Tierra del Fuego. By the end of the 19th century the Fuegian indigenous people would be exterminated in one of the most extraordinary cases of genocide in history *(see page 302)*.

A fitful invasion

Although a constant stream of explorers and later whalers followed Magellan's path, European settlement of Tierra del Fuego was generally slow in coming. The Spanish had constant plans to outwit the English and Dutch pirates by setting up a naval base on the island, but the dismal conditions prevented settlement. It was not until the 1840s that Chile and Argentina both laid claim to the area, and several decades later before anybody could be convinced actually to live there. A border was drawn up; some missionaries made tentative landings; and in the 1880s the first miners arrived in search of gold.

While there were some clashes between these fortune-seekers and the indigenous peoples, the real problems between newcomers and natives did not begin until entrepreneurs realized that the Northern Plains were possibly the best sheep country in South America. On the Chilean side of the border, the first *estancia* or ranch was set up in 1893 by the Sociedad Explotadora de Tierra del Fuego, with the Russian-born Don Mauricio Braun as director general. He named it Josefina after his wife and appointed a New Zealand-born sheep farmer as manager.

The elimination of indigenous people allowed sheep farming to reach

BELOW: Ushuaia, Argentina – the world's southern-most city.

new heights. Some of the largest farms ever built were opened up on Tierra del Fuego and became enormously profitable for the mostly British-owned companies. As in the rest of Patagonia, immigrants drifted in from around the world, including a large number of exiles and eccentrics. Chilean Tierra del Fuego received an unusual number of arrivals from what was then Yugoslavia.

In modern times, the discovery of oil gave the island's economy a temporary boost. But the population remains thin. Argentina has tried to settle its part of Tierra del Fuego by making Ushuaia a duty-free zone and holiday resort, but the Chilean section remains a sleepy and undeveloped part of the country, where little seems to have changed since the late 19th century.

Exploring the "large island"

The term "Tierra del Fuego" properly includes the whole archipelago at the southern tip of South America, although the Isla Grande de Tierra del Fuego is the largest island and is usually the one referred to. It is divided between Chile (70 percent) and Argentina (30 percent), with its northern and western sections a treeless Patagonian plain and the southeastern part a lush, mountainous land full of forests and peat bogs. The Chilean section is physically the less dramatic of the two, and travelers to the island crossing over from Punta Arenas will normally want to visit both sides.

Thanks to relatively warm ocean currents, the island's weather is not as harsh as parts of Norway and Canada which lie at an equivalent latitude in the Northern Hemisphere. Even so, it lives up to its stormy reputation. A recommended time to visit is during the summer months, from November to March, when daylight lasts for up to 20 hours and the sun is relatively warm. The weather shifts erratically from cloudless sky to drizzle and spectacular rainbows, or a deluge and back again within minutes, with the only constant being a gusty wind. It is worthwhile preparing for a range of weather conditions to pass by every day.

Travelers coming from Chile usually cross the dark Strait of Magellan

Beavers, brought from Canada, have become a pest on Tierra del Fuego, damming rivers and destroying woods.

BELOW: Cape Horn.

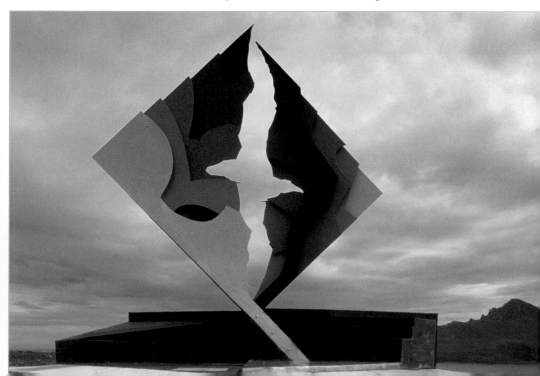

The Lost Tribes

The appropriation of their lands during the 19th century led to the persecution and demise of southern Chile's indigenous peoples.

In the mid-19th century, Tierra del Fuego was home to four native groups. The most numerous were the Onas, or Selk'nam, a nomadic race that hunted guanacos over the open plains with bows and arrows. The Haush people occupied the eastern tip of the Isla Grande, living in huts made of branches and skins. Roaming the southern islands with bark canoes and dressed in seal hides were the Yaghans. The men hunted otters with spears and Yaghan women would sometimes dive into the icy waters to pluck *centollas* (king crabs) from the ocean floor. Finally, living in the fjords of southern Chile, were the Alacalufes.

Christian missionary Thomas Bridges compiled a dictionary of the Yaghan language that shows how they ordered their harsh world with metaphors. Bruce Chatwin lists a few phrases in his book, *In Patagonia*: "mussels out of season" was a synonym for shriveled skin and old age; "jackass penguin" meant lazy; "sleet" was the same word as "fish scales."

Traditionally roaming the pampas to hunt guanaco, the Onas naturally found sheep an easy and satisfying prey. For the farm owners, stealing their property was the ultimate crime and they killed the Onas in retribution. But the Onas could not accept that the fences across their traditional lands were meant as boundaries, and continued to hunt the "white guanaco." The estancia owners hired gunmen to protect their lands and the gruesome rumor soon began to circulate that they were paid one pound sterling bounty for each Ona they shot dead (ears were supposedly demanded as proof).

The missions

Salesian missionaries argued that the native peoples could only be saved if they were transferred en masse to nearby Isla Dawson, and the estancia owners agreed to this method of removing the "pest."

Official records show that most of the people in the Dawson mission died of European diseases to which they had no immunity, but the folk memory persists of active resistance, battles, and massacres. Old-timers still tell of such gruesome characters as the Scotsman Alex McLennan, nicknamed the "Red Pig" for his face made ruddy by constant boozing. He is said to have lured families into traps by offering food, only to have his men open fire from their position in hiding. The Englishman Sam Hyslop, who boasted of gunning down 80 Onas, was finally caught by a group of Onas and flung to his death from a cliff.

Argentines were well schooled in eradicating indigenous peoples and hunts went on unrestricted on that side of the border, but the Chilean population had moments of conscience-stricken doubt. The ugly rumors, coupled with the fact that mostly women and children were being brought back from raids, caused a public outcry.

The Chilean police found a mass grave and were going to prosecute the estancia owners. But by this stage some native people were fighting back – a handful of white deaths (a total of seven in 10 years) were registered and few people raised their voices against clearing the island any longer. In the Isla Dawson mission, epidemic followed epidemic and by 1925 the last Ona had died.

The Museo Martín Gusinde in Puerto Williams (*see page 305*) documents the history of the indigenous peoples of Tierra del Fuego, while the Museo Mundo Yamana in Ushuaia, Argentina, has interesting displays depicting the way of life of the Yaghan or Yamana people. ❏

LEFT: Yamana woman near Cape Horn.

from Punta Arenas on the ferry that sails daily except Monday usually at 9am, although this can vary depending on the weather (tel: 061-218 100). Prior booking is required for vehicles. As tradition suggests, the crossing is usually a rough one, but the water is also on occasion as smooth as glass. The optimistically named port of **Porvenir** ❻ (Future) is the landing point on Tierra del Fuego, heralded by a cluster of battered fishing boats on shore and a sign that gives the distances to every point in Chile. Arica, Chile's northernmost town, is 5,300km (3,250 miles) away.

Descendants of Yugoslavs still make up the bulk of Porvenir's 4,700 inhabitants, few of whom seem to take to the streets. At weekends, it is like a ghost town. The buildings are corrugated-iron constructions mostly dating from before World War I. A wooden church steeple dominates the skyline, adding to the haunting impression. The **Museo Provincial Fernando Cordero Rusque** (Mon–Thur 8am–5.30pm, Fri 8am–4.30pm, Sat–Sun 10am–1.30pm and 3–5pm; charge) is connected to the municipal buildings on the main plaza, with historical photographs and a Fuegian mummy discovered in the nearby countryside. A waterfront stroll brings you to a lookout on the south side of Bahía Porvenir.

Into the plains

Most travelers spend one night at the most in Porvenir before heading for the open countryside. A dirt highway runs along the barren slopes of **Bahía Inútil** (Useless Bay) for 90km (56 miles) to **Onaisin** ❼, the original home of the Caleta Josefina estancia. Keep an eye out for the **Cementerio de los Gigantes**, (Cemetery of the Giants), a set of huge, regularly shaped stones scattered in the pampas. Just a couple of minutes farther south is the historic **Cementerio Inglés** (English Cemetery), where the British-born estancia workers were buried. In this windswept, forsaken spot are the graves of the few whites who fell to the arrows of native peoples at the end of the 19th century.

Along the bay 50km (31 miles) farther south is **Estancia Cameron** ❽,

Porvenir started out as a police post during the 1880s gold rush. Today, pink flamingos and black-necked swans swim along the waterfront.

BELOW: trekking the Dientes de Navarino.

founded in 1904. Nestled in a picturesque gully by the choppy gray sea and still with its original wooden buildings, the estancia was recently acquired by a Santiago-based investment group which plans to revive it as an active sheep farm.

Travelers with their own vehicles can continue along the road into the more remote, mountainous and rainy area of the island, taking their own fuel, food, and camping gear, although lodging is available on some of the estancias. **Lago Blanco**, surrounded by Fuegian peaks, is considered the most beautiful in the far south of Chile. The highway then leads south to the doorway of Chile's last estancia, **Vicuña ⑨**. A large part of this area, including forests of *lenga* (southern beech) and vast peat bogs, was donated to the New York-based Wildlife Conservation Society by the Goldman Sachs investment bank to form the Karukinka reserve, which will include a visitors' center and some sustainable tourist activities, such as trekking and birding. However, its first priority is to control the beaver population (with no natural enemies,

this imported species has multiplied rapidly, doing extensive damage by damming and diverting waterways).

From Vicuña the road returns north along the frontier. A road from Vicuña to Bahía Yendegaia, 140km (87 miles) south on the Beagle Channel, is slowly being built.

Across the border

Most travelers who come this far south will want to continue into the Argentine side of Tierra del Fuego. The easiest way is to head directly from Porvenir to the frontier at **San Sebastián**, then continue onward to **Río Grande**. This rough-and-ready oil town on the island's east coast is little more than a place to pass the night before continuing south.

On the southern coast of Tierra del Fuego, squeezed between dramatic mountain peaks and the blue Beagle Channel, is the island's largest and most attractively placed town, **Ushuaia ⑩**. Its setting is majestic, with the wicked-looking granite peak of Mount Olivia dominating the skyline. Despite the often bitter weather, this is a popu-

BELOW: woodland ponies.

lar resort town and base. Its energy and faith in progress sets it apart from other towns of the south, with new buildings being flung up everywhere amongst mud and twisted trees.

Boat trips on the Beagle Channel pass islands crowded with sea lions and penguins, or scattered with the rotting remains of shipwrecked boats. And only an hour outside of Ushuaia is **Parque Nacional Tierra del Fuego**, which preserves the sense of being at the end of the world: paths wind over spongy moss oozing cold water, past tough shrubs, thorny bushes, and trees that have grown bent 45 degrees with the prevailing wind.

A pleasant drive eastward along the Beagle Channel leads to **Estancia Harberton** ⑪, the first farm on the Argentine side of Tierra del Fuego set up by the missionary the Reverend Thomas Bridges in 1886. On a narrow peninsula surrounded by green meadows of bright flowers, the estancia is worth visiting as much for its serene beauty as its history. Guided tours are offered in both English and Spanish. Across the water are three obscure islands over which Chile and Argentina nearly went to war in 1978, until Pope John Paul II intervened and drew up a settlement.

Southernmost settlement

While Ushuaia is the southernmost town of its size in the world, the title of southernmost permanent human settlement outside of Antarctica goes to Chile's **Puerto Williams** ⑫ on Isla Navarino. Established in 1953 as a naval base, it can be reached by plane or ferry from Punta Arenas. The setting is, once again, magnificent, and there are many walks in the unspoiled countryside nearby.

Isla Navarino was home to the native Yaghan people and was first visited by the *Beagle* on its maiden journey. The captain, Robert Fitzroy, took four young Yaghans back to England for education, and returned with them on the famous journey with Charles Dar-

win. The friendliest Yaghan was named Jimmy Button by the crew. He had learned some of the manners of an English gent, but on his return to Tierra del Fuego he quickly returned to his former Yaghan lifestyle. Fitzroy had hoped that Button would be a force for "civilizing" the Yaghan people and converting them to Christianity, but the reverse proved true: two decades after his return, Button was to command attacks on the first European settlements in the area; he led the slaughter of several missionaries on Isla Picton and Isla Navarino.

Today, there are no full-blooded Yaghans, though a few mestizos live near Puerto Williams in a settlement called **Ukika**. The **Museo Martín Gusinde** (Oct–Mar Tue–Fri 9am–1pm, 2.30–7.15pm, Sat–Sun 2.30–6.30pm; Apr–Sept Tue–Fri 8am–1pm, 2.30–6.15pm; free) in the naval township, considered one of the best in the south, focuses on the history and demise of the Yaghans culture and, on the second floor, also has some exhibits about European settlement and missionaries in the area. ❏

Some estancias have been converted into fishing lodges in an attempt to develop a new tourist trade.

RESTAURANTS AND CAFÉS

Porvenir

El Chispa
Manuel Señoret 202
Tel: (061) 580 054
$
Simple dishes; popular with the locals. Credit cards not accepted.

Club Croata
Manuel Señoret 542
Tel: (061) 580 053
$$
The smartest restaurant in town, serving simple Chilean dishes. Credit cards not accepted.

Puerto Williams

Angelus Irish Coffee

Centro Comercial
Norte 151
Tel: (061) 621 080
$
Popular with locals, this coffee shop also serves simple but varied meals at lunchtime and in the evening.

Lakutaia Hotel
Seno Lauta s/n
Tel: (061) 621 721
$$$
The restaurant of this new luxury hotel, 3km (2 miles) outside Puerto Williams, is open to non-guests but must be booked 24 hours in advance.

Prices are per person for a three-course meal, not including drinks.

$ = under US$15
$$ = US$15–25
$$$ = US$25–35

EASTER ISLAND

Easter Island

Santiago

Pacific Ocean

Chile's Polynesian possession, nearly 4,000km (2,400 miles) west of the mainland, is one of the world's most intriguing islands, dominated by more than 600 giant stone statues of unknown origin

Main Attractions

AHU TAHAI
RANO KAU
AHU VINAPU
RANO RARAKU
AHU TE PITO KURA
PLAYA OVAHE
ORONGO

PRECEDING PAGES:
moai at night.
BELOW: an actor in
the film *Rapa Nui.*

T
he first inhabitants of Easter Island called their home Te Pito o Te Henua – the Navel of the World. Gazing down from one of the island's two volcanic crater rims, it is easy to see why. This tiny volcanic island, only 117 sq km (45 sq miles) in area, is almost lost in the endless blue of the Pacific Ocean. The nearest Polynesian island, Pitcairn, is 2,000km (1,240 miles) to the west; the coast of South America is some 3,800km (2,360 miles) to the east. The island has a maximum length of 24km (15 miles)

and width of 12km (8 miles). Volcanic in origin, it has several dead craters dotted over its sparsely covered surface, one of which now contains a freshwater lake. The terrain on the treeless volcanic slopes is fairly grassy, but most of the island is covered in rugged lava fields. Dotted around the coast are hundreds of caves, which were once used as refuges (in times of war) or secret burial places.

Until 30 years ago, Easter Island was visited only once a year by a Chilean warship bringing supplies. But even though few people before the 1960s could make a personal visit, Easter Island has gripped the world's imagination for centuries. One baffling image made it famous: littering the island are hundreds of giant, tight-lipped basalt statues, unique in the whole of Oceania. The tiny island and its mysterious statues have presented us with one of the most fascinating archeological riddles of all time.

How did an early seafaring people find this remote speck in the Pacific Ocean? Where did they come from? How did they transport their enormous statues, carved from a quarry in the side of a volcano, to the coast and erect them on giant stone altars? And above all – *why* did they do so?

Today, regular flights from Santiago have broken the island's isolation. People visiting Chile have the chance to see this legendary site, marvel at the remains of an enigmatic Pacific culture, and make up their own minds on the origin of the statues.

Polynesian or American?

The long-standing assumption that the first Easter Islanders were Polynesians was thrown into doubt in 1947 when the Norwegian explorer Thor Heyerdahl sailed a balsa raft, *Kon-Tiki*, from Peru to Tahiti. The highly publicized journey showed that it was theoretically possible for a pre-Inca South American culture to have colonized the Pacific.

Heyerdahl went on to spend a year digging on Easter Island, and concluded in his best-selling book *Aku-Aku* that the first islanders actually came from the Peruvian coast, fleeing the destruction of the ancient South American empire of Tiahuanacu around Lake Titicaca in Bolivia. According to this theory, the seafarers brought with them a number of American plants that are still found on the island (including the sweet potato and totora reeds), as well as their sunworshipping religion and famous skills as stonemasons. Heyerdahl argued that

they were eventually joined by a group of Polynesian settlers. The two groups lived in harmony until an eventual war finally destroyed the islanders of South American origin.

Most archeologists now discount the bulk of Heyerdahl's findings, although his groundwork is still valuable and makes stimulating reading. Nor do his theories seem so outlandish compared to an extraordinary rash of more recent claims. Crackpot visionaries have announced that the Easter Islanders were descendants of ancient Egyptians, interplanetary travelers, red-haired North Africans, or even survivors of the lost continent of Atlantis.

The Long Ears and the Short Ears

The absence of historical records on the island has fueled speculation. Almost all of the original islanders were wiped out by slave raids during the 19th century, so that by the time serious archeological work began in the 1980s the old culture was virtually dead.

According to those few surviving inhabitants who were first interviewed

TIP

Whether you're using a digital or film camera, make sure you bring extra film or batteries. Photo opportunities on the island are endless, but supplies are limited and the shops are often closed.

BELOW: restoring a
moai to its original
position.

in the late 19th century, Easter Island
was discovered by King Hotu Matua –
a name meaning "prolific father" in
Polynesian – who arrived on Anakena
beach on the island's northern coast
from a scorched land to the east. Tradition holds that 57 generations of kings
succeeded Hotu Matua until the 1680s,
during which time another set of
ancestors arrived under a chief called
Tuu-ko-ihu.

The legend goes that the two groups
were divided between so-called "Long-
Ears," who carved the *moai*, and the
newcoming "Short Ears," who were
kept in an inferior class and helped in
manual labor. Eventually the Short
Ears rebelled and slaughtered all of the
Long Ears bar one. Unfortunately, so
many different versions of this story
soon cropped up – mostly completely
contradictory – that they only added
confusion to research. Most investigators are now finding it safer to believe
that none of the versions is authentic.

Orthodox opinion now holds that
Easter Island was first populated before
AD 500 by Polynesians coming from
the Marquesas Islands, remaining in

isolation until the arrival of Europeans.
The bizarre culture was developed by
the islanders themselves, who lived in
a fairly egalitarian society dominated
by small independent warring tribes.
According to this view, 1,200 years of
total isolation allowed the creation of
a new language, of the famous statues
that still preside over the island, and of
the only writing system known in all
Polynesia and the Americas – the *rongo
rongo* script. This conclusion is far from
watertight, and most visitors to Easter
Island will want to decide the truth for
themselves.

The first European contact

The first European to stumble across
this speck in the Pacific Ocean was the
Dutch Admiral Jacob Roggeveen. He
and his crew landed and spent a day
ashore on Easter Sunday, 1722 – and
christened the island for the occasion.
Roggeveen's logbook tells how the
party anchored off the mysterious
island at dusk and were greeted by fair-
skinned Polynesians, similar to those
in Tahiti and Hawaii. Some had darker
skins, the Dutchman wrote, while oth-

ers were "quite white" like Europeans, with reddish hair.

Roggeveen records with awe that the *moai* were still standing, many up to 9 meters (30ft) tall, and with great cylinders on their heads. The inhabitants of the island, he wrote, "kindle fires in front of certain remarkably tall figures they set up; and, thereafter squatting on their heels with heads bowed down, they bring the palms of their hands together and alternately raise and lower them." The islanders kept up the ritual until dawn, when they praised the sunrise. Many of the worshippers wore long wooden plugs in their ear lobes, lengthening them to their shoulders – a practice found in much of Polynesia and also among nobles of Peru, whom the conquistadors called *orejones* or "Long Ears."

The islanders lived in long, low huts of reed, that looked strangely like boat hulls turned upward, the remains of which can still be seen. Their lands were neatly cultivated, Roggeveen noted, and "whole tracts of woodland" were visible in the distance. Examining the *moai* closely, the Dutchmen decided that they were not of stone but were modeled from a strange clay stuffed with small stones. With that curious decision, the crew rowed back to their ships and weighed anchor.

After less than 24 hours on shore, they had decided that the islanders were friendly but expert thieves, pinching a few hats and tablecloths. A misunderstanding led to one Easter Islander being shot on board their boat, followed by another dozen being gunned down on shore, giving islanders an ominous taste of what European contact would bring.

The Spaniards, English, and French

The island was left in peace for another 50 years before the arrival of a Spanish captain named Don Felipe González. In typical colonial Spanish fashion, he marched with two priests and a squadron of soldiers to a high point on the east coast, planted the cross and claimed the island for his king. The men of the island, he noted later, were naked except for feather headdresses, while women wore short cloaks around

Easter Island was given the name Rapa Nui (Great Rapa) *by Tahitian sailors in the early 1860s, as it reminded them of an island called Rapa near their home. That island is now known as Rapa Iti, or Small Rapa.*

BELOW: the almost treeless landscape of the island.

their breasts and hips. Don Felipe also observed with some interest that the islanders looked nothing like the indigenous peoples of South America, then recorded how he taught some to recite in Spanish, "Ave Maria, long live Charles III, king of Spain," before disappearing over the horizon.

Next came the renowned English navigator Captain James Cook, landing in 1774 after a journey through the Society Islands, Tonga, and New Zealand. Cook had no doubt that the islanders were of Polynesian descent, although they seemed to be few in number and living in a miserable state. Little land was in cultivation. Meanwhile, dozens of the stone statues had been overturned, Cook found, and those that remained were no longer worshipped but used as burial sites. The scurvy-ridden Englishmen were forced to leave with nothing but a few baskets of sweet potatoes – although even then they were cheated, since islanders had weighed down the baskets with stones and laid only a few potatoes over the very top.

What had happened since the days of the Dutchmen's visit? Modern evidence confirms that serious environmental degradation was already well under way on Easter Island by the time of the Dutch visit in 1722: pollen samples show that the island was heavily forested when man first arrived in AD 500, yet there were no trees left by the beginning of the 19th century. Most writers now believe that the population of Easter Island had simply outgrown its resources. The food supply began to fail, the island's forests were felled, and the soil began to erode. Without wood for canoes to escape the island, the tribes turned on one another in destructive wars: the giant statues were toppled and broken, while cannibalism became common. The resulting ruin is seen by many today as a taste in miniature of the Earth's own future, as the human race consumes the planet's limited resources with increasing voracity.

The slave traders arrive

Easter Island's internal destruction pales into insignificance compared with the devastation finally wreaked by contact with the outside world dur-

Easter Island's Polynesian heritage is celebrated in the Tapati festival, held every year from late January to early February.

BELOW: island elder relates legends using string.

ing the 19th century. Whalers and slave traders put the island on their itineraries, bringing a series of tragedies to this hitherto isolated outpost.

The most dramatic blow was the Peruvian slave raid of 1862. Early on Christmas Eve, strangers rowed ashore with brightly colored clothes and presents that enticed the islanders out to greet them. On a given signal, the slave hunters attacked, tying up those who surrendered and shooting any who resisted. One thousand islanders were kidnapped, including the king and most of the learned men, to be taken to work on the guano islands off the coast of Peru – but not before the slavers celebrated Christmas on board with rum and salt pork.

Brutal conditions at the guano mine, starvation, and epidemics had killed off 900 islanders before the bishop of Tahiti was finally able to intervene on their behalf. Of the remaining hundred who set sail for their homeland, 85 died en route from smallpox. The handful who returned brought the plague with them: by the 1870s only 110 men, women, and children were alive on Easter Island.

Following this devastation came the first missionary to the island, Eugène Eyraud. Unsurprisingly, he met a hostile reception and was forced to flee – only to return two years later with reinforcements. Many of the islanders were converted to Christianity, however superficially, over the next few years.

Chile takes over

Spain may have claimed Easter Island for itself in 1770, but the Crown hardly bothered to maintain its claim. No other expeditions were sent to the island, and with the collapse of Spanish control of Latin America in the early 1800s, the way was left open for another colonial power to walk in and take over.

As part of its 19th century burst of expansionism, Chile annexed Easter Island in 1888. The republic wanted to show off its powerful naval force and

show itself the equal of major European powers by grabbing a piece of South Pacific territory. Apart from the perceived prestige of such an acquisition, Chile saw the island as having valuable agricultural potential, and a gateway to Asian trade.

Few Chileans showed much interest in colonizing this new jewel in the nation's crown. The government found itself handing over control of the island to sheep-grazing companies – first a Chilean concern run by a Valparaíso businessman, then in the early 1900s to the British company Williamson Balfour. The Liverpool-based company used the Compañía Explotadora de la Isla de Pascua (CEDIP), leased from the Chilean government, to manage the island, and made handsome profits until their license was revoked in 1953. Islanders recall the company's rule as a time of dismal subjugation. They were effectively restricted to living in Hanga Roa, the island's only town, so that the rest of the island would be free for sheep to roam. Generally they were forced to work for little or no wages. It was during this period that immigrants

Native Easter Islander in festive costume.

The Purpose of the *Moai*

Each of the brooding *moai* was carved from the island's soft volcanic rock to the same general pattern. There are estimated to be close to 1,000 on the island: all with the distinctive heavy foreheads, pointed chins and (in all but a couple of cases) elongated ears. The hand position is typical of Polynesian carving, but the form of the figures is clearly unique. Their average height is around 6 meters (20ft). Most are male, but some are women with breasts and vulvas. While archeologists originally thought they were carved eyeless, the *moai*, in fact, had eyes: the whites were made of coral and the pupils from the glistening black obsidian that can be found everywhere on the island.

Archeologists generally agree that the *moai* were figures of deceased chiefs or gods. (A key piece of information recorded by George Foster on Captain Cook's 1774 visit was that the *moai* were often named after these dead heroes.) The eyes of the *moai* are believed to have transmitted *mana* or power to the living family chief, signifying prosperity in peacetime and success in war. At one point there were as many as 15 *moai* set up on any particular *ahu*, or platform, all glaring down from on high and sending *mana* to the family head. From this viewpoint, it is not difficult to imagine what effect a fully constructed *ahu* must have had on its family – as well as the utter devastation of morale when it was pulled down.

interbred with the remaining few Easter Islanders, leaving little trace of the original inhabitants. Three-quarters of the population in the 1930s was of mixed descent, with everyone from North Americans to Germans and Tahitians living in Hanga Roa. Many years later, when news arrived that Thor Heyerdahl had floated a raft from Peru to Tahiti, several islanders made boats to stage their own escape. Some succeeded, and guards were posted to stop the exodus.

After 1953, the island's government was given to another authoritarian hand: the Chilean navy. The islanders suffered the same humiliations as in the days of the sheep company: the inability to vote, their local language suppressed, and having to endure the navy's arbitrary and often absurd decisions.

The biggest change came in 1967, when the completion of the airport finally allowed flights from Tahiti and Santiago. The sudden possibility of large-scale tourism helped focus international attention on the island, and the Chilean government was forced to make some improvements. During the

1970s and 1980s, better water supplies, electricity, a hospital, and a school were installed. The most astonishing change to the island was the extension of its airport as an emergency landing site for the US space shuttle. Opened in 1988, the airstrip has completed the Easter Islanders' transition from the Stone Age to the Space Age.

Downtown Hanga Roa

Almost all visitors now arrive at the airport, on one of the five weekly (more in summer) LAN flights, and are greeted by their first glimpse of Easter Island's famous *moai* (statues). Rather small affairs compared to others on the island, the airport *moai* still provide a taste of the mysteries to come.

About 15 minutes' walk from the airstrip is the tiny township where Easter Island's 3,300 people almost all live, **Hanga Roa ❶**. Built around a few wide roads, with thick, heavy palm trees hanging at regular intervals, the village looks like a classic South Pacific hideaway. The pace of life is relaxed, and a speed limit of 20kmph (12 mph) is imposed on the town.

BELOW: painting event at the annual Tapati festival.

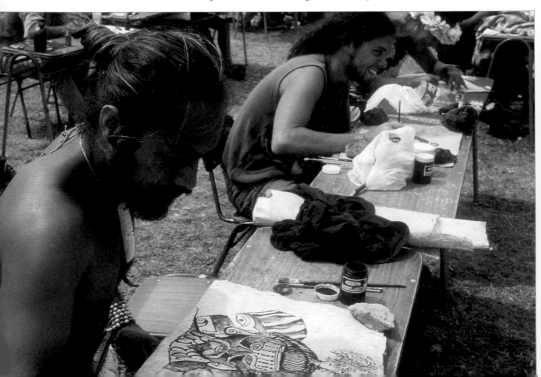

There are a handful of large hotels on Easter Island, but many visitors prefer to stay in one of the small *residenciales* scattered about Hanga Roa. Reservations are not necessary – the owners crowd around the airport gates after every arrival offering their prices. There are also some small restaurants, bars, and several discotheques.

Tourism is Easter Island's biggest industry, and many of Hanga Roa's inhabitants now make a living from selling woodcarvings to travelers, endlessly repeating the same basic forms. The best-known piece is also the ugliest: the *moai kavakava* or "statue of ribs." This human figure with a huge nose, ears, and starved physique, is said to have been first carved by King Tuuko-ihu. Apparently, the king was sleeping at the foot of a cliff when he awoke to find two ghosts staring down at him. He ran home and immediately carved their image, and islanders have followed the pattern ever since.

While one or two archeological sites can be reached on foot, the best way to explore the island is on an organized tour or by jeep (the island has several car rental outlets). Motorbikes can be hired by the hardy (anyone who doesn't mind bouncing over volcanic rock for several hours), as can horses (although these are often in poor shape) and bicycles.

Most hotel or *residencial* owners will provide information about island tours. Some of these tours are great value for money, with university-trained guides who will explain the orthodox history as well as discussing some of the wackier theories. The most important *ahus*, or *moai* platforms, can be covered in one day, and the rest in another day's tour. Certainly, if you want to visit all the sites on foot, you'd better bring a tent. Whichever mode of transport you choose, take plenty of sunblock, especially in summer, a good sun hat and a large supply of water – the tropical sun on Easter Island is notoriously fierce, yet the sea breeze can make the temperature seem deceptively cool. Mosquitoes can also be a problem so take some insect repellent.

In search of *moai* and *ahus*

One short stroll from Hanga Roa allows a pleasant introduction to what

Replica carvings of the moai kavakava *(statue of ribs) are sold in Hanga Roa.*

BELOW: meeting place in Hanga Roa.

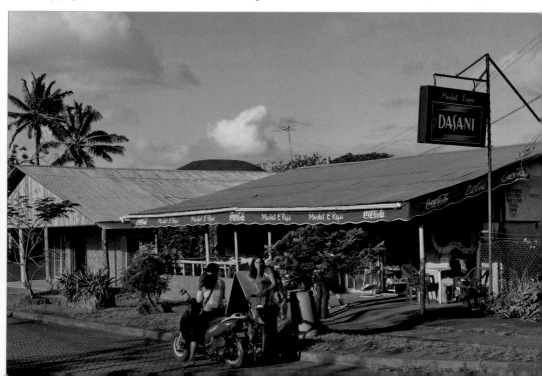

The moais' "top-knots" were made from volcanic scoria quarried at the small volcanic crater of Puna Pau, a couple of kilometers east of Hanga Roa.

Easter Island has to offer. Starting from the small fishing port, follow the coast road north, away from the shops. On the outskirts of the village, a cemetery appears. The missionary presence has ensured that the population is at least nominally Catholic, and one of the less well-known pleasures of Easter Island is visiting a Mass service on Sunday and listening to the singing.

Just past the cemetery stands one of the most photographed archeological sites, **Ahu Tahai ❷**. Here, five statues stand in a row on their *ahu* with their backs to the sea. Like other *ahu moai*, they were knocked down, probably some time during the 18th century *(see page 312)*. The archeologist William Mulloy restored them to their rightful position in the 1960s; his grave is only meters from the site. You can also see the remains of ancient boat-shaped houses. This is a favorite spot at sunset, when the *moai* are silhouetted against a scarlet sky.

Just north of Ahu Tahai is the small **Museo Antropológico Padre Sebastián Englert** (Tue–Fri 9.30am–5.30pm, Sat–Sun 9.30am–12.30pm, closed Mon;

BELOW: *moai* lined up along the coast.

charge). Exhibits include the *rongo rongo* tablets, *moai kavakava* figures, and some wonderful late 19th- and early 20th-century photographs of Easter Island's earlier inhabitants.

Having had a taste of the most accessible *moai*, your appetite will be whetted for a day tour of the island. By heading east from Hanga Roa you can follow the general chronology of the island and gain an insight into how archeologists and historians have pieced together their theories on where the Easter Islanders came from, as well as how, why, and when they carved their statues. In the process, you will probably see enough *moai* in one day to last a lifetime.

Vinapu *ahus*

From the airport, follow the airstrip southeast, then turn right past an oil depot to reach **Ahu Vinapu ❸** – probably the most important site in establishing the chronology of Easter Island. There are two *ahus* here, both of which once supported *moai* before they were toppled and broken – *moai* parts are scattered all around the site. The most

The Hollywood Take

Walking around the outskirts of Hanga Roa, you may encounter some unusual *moai* bearing a striking resemblance to some of the ancient megaliths found in Latin America. According to National Park staff, these *moai* were produced by the fertile imaginations of a Hollywood film crew, who designed them as props for the film *Rapa Nui*, which was shot on Easter Island in 1993.

Produced by Kevin Costner and starring Jason Scott-Lee, the film is a story of forbidden love in a time of war. It is set during the period of conflict between the Long Ears and the Short Ears, but also draws on stories related to the Bird Man cult *(see page 322)*. Easter Islanders, many of who worked as extras on the film, still remember its controversial shooting. Fans of the film argue that it brought money and new fame to the island; while critics that it is a travesty of their customs and that a number of authentic monuments were damaged during the shooting.

Archeologists and historians were also irritated by what they denounced as the film's gross inaccuracies. As well as its loose interpretation of the island's complex history, they complained, for example, that the scanty costumes designed for the Native islanders owed more to Maori traditions than those of Easter Island.

famous *ahu* – known as Vinapu No. 1 – contains a wall of perfectly carved and fitted stone blocks that is strikingly similar to the walls at Tiahuanacu near Lake Titicaca, Bolivia, and some of the Inca walls around Cuzco. Not surprisingly, it is a key element in Thor Heyerdahl's argument that the Easter Islanders themselves originally came from South America. Vinapu No. 2 is a much rougher version of the same model *ahu*.

Thor Heyerdahl's Norwegian expedition used Carbon 14 dating of fire remains and other materials near here to divide the island's prehistory into the Early Period (AD 400–1100), Middle Period (1100–1680), and Late Period (1680–1868). It appears that some *ahus* – including Vinapu No. 2 – were constructed in the Early Period, in the earliest centuries of human colonization, although their exact purpose is a matter of conjecture. The erection of the majority of *ahus* and *moai* belongs to the Middle Period; while the Late Period belongs to the bloody cannibal wars that probably resulted in the end of *moai* production and the destruction of the statues and their *ahus*.

Heyerdahl found that the finely worked *ahu* of Vinapu No. 1 actually predated the cruder No. 2, supporting his argument that the first inhabitants of the island were skilled South American carvers. But later archeologists have reinterpreted the Norwegian expedition's findings to show that No. 2 came first. It is now generally believed that the masonry skills of the islanders improved over many generations, and that Vinapu No. 1 is the climax of their own achievement, independent of developments in Bolivia or Peru.

Foundations of a hare paenga boat-shaped house at Ahu Tahai.

The south coast

Continuing along the southern coast of the island brings you to the most striking examples of the Late Period's *moai*-toppling wars.

Ahu Vaihú 4 is probably the most extraordinary sight along this stretch. Eight large statues have been pulled in a row from their *ahu*, looking rather forlorn with their noses in the dirt and top-knots scattered. One of the *moai* has been completely shattered. Farther along, **Ahu Akahanga 5** has four sim-

BELOW: *Te Pito o Te Henua* – the Navel of the World.

ilarly humiliated statues, with another bunch scattered from a second *ahu* across a nearby estuary. The remains of a village have been found on the hill slopes opposite – the foundations of several boat-shaped houses can be seen, as well as some round houses. Another site, **Ahu Hanga Tetenga ❻**, has been almost completely devastated and its two *moai* shattered.

The *moai* mine

From here, a dirt road runs inland toward the huge volcanic crater of **Rano Raraku ❼**. This so-called **Road of the Moai** is littered with more and more fallen giants before reaching the most impressive site on the island.

By far the most famous of the *moai* are the 70 standing sentinels embedded up to their shoulders in grass on the south slope of the volcanic crater. They lead the way to the quarry or "nursery" cut into the side of the impressive crater rim. This was where the *moai* were cut from volcanic tufa. Some 400 figures have been left there in all stages of completion, paying mute testimony to the unknown disaster that

stopped all work dead in its tracks.

A trail leads straight up from the car park to the largest *moai* ever built – a 21-meter (69ft) monolith. Leading off to the right, the trail comes to two other huge statues still part of the rock, while 20 or so more stand on the inside of the crater.

Many obscure differences have been found in the *moai* of Rano Raraku. There are several female statues among the crowd of males, while others have unusual carvings on their flanks or backs. One figure displays a rough three-mast sailing ship on its chest. A line hangs from its bow to a round figure that may be an anchor or turtle caught on a fishing line. With a little imagination, the boat has been explained as either a European ship or a large totora-reed vessel.

Also found buried at Rano Raraku by the Norwegian expedition was the unique kneeling statue, now found on the right slope of the crater, which looks like no other *moai*. Somewhat less than four meters (13ft) high, it has a rounded head and face, as well as a beard and short ears.

Moai *at Rano Raraku.*

BELOW: *moai* at Tongariki beach.

Carving from the rock

The remains in the quarry give very clear evidence on how the *moai* were originally modeled from the rock. Trenches were cut for the easy access of carvers, who chipped away until only the spine was left down the *moai*'s back. Eventually, the spine was severed and the statue was lowered by ropes to a temporary upright position on the slopes below, where it was finished off. The sheer fact that these giant figures were cut from vertical as well as horizontal rock-faces testifies to the skill of the workers, while the number of broken statues on the slopes reveal the work's danger. The tools used to carve the *moai* were small basalt picks called *toki* – thousands of them have been found at the quarry.

Thor Heyerdahl's Norwegian expedition decided to find out how long it might take to carve a *moai* by commissioning a team of islanders to work on a statue at Rano Raraku. The incident is recounted in Heyerdahl's *Aku-Aku*: the then mayor of the island brought a family team to work non-stop for three days before giving up with fingers twisted from the work. But they had begun to make an impression, and the experience suggested that it would take a skilled team between 12 and 15 months to carve a *moai* about 4 meters (13ft) high, using two teams constantly in shifts. But how did the islanders move the other *moai* to different parts of the island?

Making the statues walk

Following the coast road on to the north of the island gives you an idea of the enormous scale of the problem. Here is located **Ahu Te Pito Kura ❽** – at some 9.8 meters (32ft), it is the largest *moai* ever transported. The name means "navel of light", and the rock from which it was hewn is said to have been brought by King Hotu Matua himself.

Heyerdahl was able to convince some 180 merry dinner guests to pull one 4-meter (13ft) long *moai* across a field with ropes made from tree bark, showing that it was easier to move the statues than had first been expected. In *Aku-Aku* he suggested that a much larger statue could be pulled using

According to the Chilean government, Easter Island is at the limit of the number of visitors it can sustainably receive. However, a proposal to establish an annual cap on visitor numbers has been controversial.

BELOW: crater of Rano Raraku.

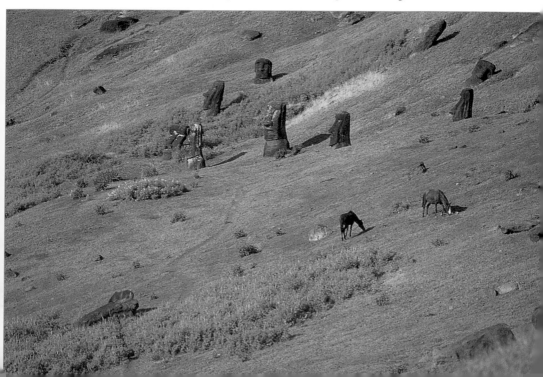

more people and wooden rollers. Others suggested that small rocks could be used like marbles to move the statues. But these theories still seem unconvincing when faced with the size of Ahu Te Pito Kura and the ruggedness of the volcanic terrain around Rano Raraku.

The archeologist William Mulloy came up with a theory that has won widespread support. First a huge forked sled (made from the large trees that tests have shown once covered the island) would be attached to the front of each statue, tied into place over the protruding belly and stuck beneath the chin. This sled protected the statue from the ground and allowed it to be moved by leverage using a bipod. The statue's own weight could then be used to help move it along in a repetitive series of upward and forward movements. While hardly foolproof (and there are numerous broken *moai* around the island), the method is at least possible. Curiously, the theory of short jerking movements recalls the islanders' own belief that the *moai* "walked" to their *ahu*.

EAT

Don't leave Easter Island without trying tuna empanadas (pasties), which are the local specialty and are served at most restaurants, bars, and even at kiosks on the street.

BELOW: local craftsman carving a Moai Kavakava.

An experiment in ancient engineering

One more baffling mystery remains: once the statues had been moved by this painstaking method, how did the islanders then erect them – along with top-knots – onto their stone altars?

When the Norwegian expedition arrived in the mid-1950s, not one *moai* was at its post on an *ahu*. All lay where they had fallen centuries before, and nobody had even attempted to move them. Heyerdahl resolved to raise a *moai* using only the materials that would have been available to the original islanders. The lone statue now standing at **Ahu Ature Huki** on **Anakena beach** ❾ was the result of the experiment that put the first *moai* upright since they were toppled.

Having dragged the *moai* to the *ahu*, Heyerdahl's team carefully worked a series of long poles underneath the statue's stomach. Three or four men heaved at the end of each pole as another man, lying on his belly, slipped small stones underneath the giant's face. Slowly the statue began to rise from the ground, supported on this

The *Rongo Rongo* script

As if enigmatic megaliths and intriguing legends were not enough, there is yet another Easter Island mystery that may never be solved: the strange inscriptions known as *rongo rongo* writing. Found on small wooden boards, this script contains 120 different figures based on "bird man" or human forms and is read alternatively from left to right then right to left. When outsiders first glimpsed the boards in 1865, none of the surviving islanders knew how to read them, the priests who understood them having perished after the Peruvian slave raids. Attempts by Russian and German experts to decipher the strange script have so far borne little fruit.

Furthermore, few scholars agree on where the writing first came from. Guesses range from the Indus Valley of Pakistan to the Andes mountain range. But other archeologists have begun to doubt whether *rongo rongo* is in fact prehistoric at all: since no similar pictographs are carved in stone elsewhere on the island, it is possible that the script is an emulation of European writing. *Rongo rongo* may have developed from observation of the Spanish treaty of annexation in 1770, possibly fixing chants into some concrete form – only to be forgotten as the island priests died in droves after they were forced to work on Peru's guano islands.

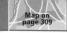

mattress of tightly packed pebbles. It took a dozen men working for nine days to get the statue on a 45-degree angle. Another nine days and it was almost upright. Finally, it slid with the guidance of ropes to a standing position. Raising a *moai* with a top-knot would have been done in the same fashion, Thor Heyerdahl argued, strapping the stone "hat" to the statue's head with ropes and poles.

Since that date many other *moai* have been restored to their *ahus*, as can be seen today. But it is still astounding to consider raising a statue on Ahu Te Pito Kura – with its top-knot it would have been a massive 11.5 meters (38ft) tall. William Mulloy estimated that it would have taken 30 men one year to carve this *moai*, 90 men two months to move it 6km (4 miles) from the quarry to the *ahu* and 90 men three months to erect it. Yet this pales in comparison with the 21-meter (69ft) monolith still being cut in the quarry when work was abandoned.

These theories of how the *moai* were moved and raised also suggest why carving suddenly ceased at the Rano Raraku quarry: the Easter Island workers simply ran out of trees. Eighteenth-century explorers had reported the island's lack of timber. It seems likely that work was abandoned when there was no wood left to take the statues from their nursery to the coast.

Golden beaches

Only 100 meters (330ft) away on the headland at Anakena is **Ahu Nau Nau** and seven more *moai*. But having viewed statues all day, it probably comes as a welcome relief to find that these last *moai* stand above the white sands of **Anakena beach**. This was the legendary landing place of Hotu Matua, the founder of the island. Many of the caves nearby are said to have been his refuge while waiting for a boat-shaped house to be built nearby.

But if you are in the mood for a swim after a hard day of *moai*-spotting, one small bay is even more appealing than the wider expanses of Anakena: nestled beneath a cliff of volcanic rock, **Ovahe Beach** must be one of the most beautiful on earth. Its sands are pure and golden, a match for any South

BELOW: stone sentinels at Anakena beach.

A wooden Christ figure, one of many impressive carvings in the Iglesia Hanga Roa.

BELOW: making traditional reed boats.

Pacific paradise, and the water is so clear that you can count your toe hairs while swimming.

From here you also have a view of the **Poike peninsula**. This area has a major place in local legend. When the "Short Ears" tired of working for their "Long Ear" rulers and rebelled, the Long Ears were said to have gathered on this peninsula behind the Poike trench. Filled with branches and tree trunks, the ditch was intended as a fiery defense rampart. But a traitor who was married to a Short Ear woman alerted the Short Ears, who slipped into the peninsula and surrounded the Long Ears, driving them into their own flaming ditch – where all but the traitor died.

Interestingly, while this had been considered a fable by most researchers, the Norwegian expedition found thick layers of charcoal and ash here. They were able to show that a great fire had occurred in the trench some 350 years before, suggesting that there may be some truth in the islanders' tales.

From here, the road through the center of the island leads past the old sheep estancia back to Hanga Roa. From the town you can make another excursion along the island's northern roads to sites like **Ahu Akivi** ⑩ and **Ahu Tepeu** ⑪. These are interesting enough sites, but they offer few surprises to those who know the rest of the island.

Center of the mysterious "bird man" cult

A quite different excursion from Hanga Roa can be made directly south to the volcanic crater of **Rano Kau**. Instead of *moai*, its interest centers on a bizarre "bird man" ritual that flourished here among the original inhabitants. It is also without doubt the most visually spectacular spot on Easter Island.

A road and path run steeply upward from Hanga Roa through typical scrubby terrain. Without warning, the enormous crater of Rano Kau appears below. It's not hard to see why Heyerdahl described it as a "giant witch's cauldron." Filled with black water and floating green fields of totora reeds, its steep, 200-meter (656ft) high wall is gently eroded on the seaward side to include a view of the Pacific. The ruined ceremonial village of **Orongo** ⑫ is perched atop this breathtaking location, with the volcano on one side and sheer cliffs on the other, dropping some 400 meters (1,300ft) down to the crashing sea. Scattered in the briny void are three tiny, craggy islands – Motu Kau Kau, Motu Iti, and Motu Nui.

Orongo is now restored and part of a specially created national reserve. Entry costs US$10 at the ranger's office. The ancient village contains a range of 53 oval buildings, constructed in the 16th century, with their floors cut into the side of the slope. Walls were made from overlapping slabs of stone, with other large slabs meeting horizontally to make an arch. The entrances are small tunnels big enough for only one person to enter at a time. But the main attraction is a string of 150 "bird man" carvings on rocks on the edge of the cliffs: a man's body is drawn with a bird's head, often holding an egg in one hand.

Archeologists know a considerable amount about the "bird man" cult as its ritual was performed up until 1862, and survivors were able to describe it in detail to later investigators. The strange ceremony is linked to the supreme deity Makemake, who is said to have created the earth, sun, moon, and stars. Makemake rewarded good and punished evil, and for centuries was considered responsible for bringing the only visitors to the island from the outside world: an annual migration of sooty tern birds.

Begun in the warring period of the 18th century, the "bird man" cult may have been an esoteric attempt to direct tribal competition toward a peaceful course. It may also have symbolized a wish to escape from the increasing horror of confinement on the island.

The quest for the first egg

The basis of the "bird man" cult was finding the first egg of spring laid by the sacred *Manu Tara* bird, or sooty tern. The chief of each tribe on the island sent one chosen servant to Moto Nui, the largest of the islets below Orongo. Swimming across the dangerous waters, the unfortunate

A variety of small sweet pineapple grows on Easter Island; look for the plantations along the road from Hanga Roa to Anakena beach.

BELOW LEFT: banana race at the Tapati festival.
BELOW: memories of the "bird man" cult at Orongo.

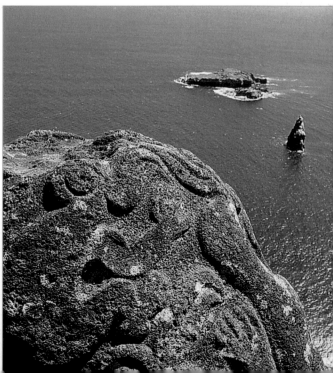

TIP

The variety of colorful fish around Easter Island makes for some great diving; this can be arranged with a number of local tour companies.

servants or *hopus* each spent about a month looking for the first egg while islanders gathered on the Orongo cliffs making offerings and prayers to Makemake. When the egg had been found, the successful *hopu* plunged into the swirling waters (with the egg apparently strapped to his forehead), swam to the mainland and climbed back up the cliffs to present the prize to his master.

The successful master would then be named the "bird man" for that year, an important status position. Strangely, the advantages which this office conferred are far from clear. The chief would have his head, eyebrows and eyelashes shaved, then his head painted red and black. His standing in the community would be increased, but for the whole of the following year he would remain in seclusion in a special house, presumably having gained the favor of Makemake.

A final verdict?

After visiting all the major sites and immersing oneself in the mystery of Easter Island, few visitors can resist making some sort of decision for themselves on the most debated question of all: did the first islanders travel from Polynesia or were they South American refugees as Thor Heyerdahl suggests, escaping in fleets of reed boats from the collapse of a magnificent Andean empire?

It is fair to say that modern archeological opinion weighs heavily against Thor Heyerdahl's dramatic interpretation. Peter Bellwood in his work *Man's Conquest of the Pacific* provides a fairly balanced summary of the latest research, arguing that while nobody can prove Heyerdahl 100 percent wrong, the chances of him being right are quite remote.

Firstly, the language of Easter Island – which is believed to have been spoken since before AD 500 – is completely Polynesian. Secondly, the skeletons found on the island are Polynesian – although they are all from the Late Period. Thirdly, there is no evidence that any portable artifacts dug up on the island came from South America, while many items are certainly Polynesian in style. Finally, the

BELOW: the beach at Hanga Roa.

posture of the *moai* can be found in the art of Polynesia as well as in Tiahuanaco-style carving from South America, and may be a common inheritance from past millennia.

But there are some points on which Heyerdahl apparently has a case. The sweet potato and totora reed are South American plants and may have been introduced at a late date, and the stone house designs found on the island recall those of Peru. However, the most surprising piece of evidence for anyone who has visited Peru and Bolivia must be the close-fitting stone-work of Ahu Vinapu No. 1, so strikingly reminiscent of Tiahuanaco and Inca work. Its date is set at around AD 600, within the classical period of Tiahuanaco culture.

Yet of the 300-plus *ahus* on the island, this is the only piece of stone-work that is reminiscent of a uniquely South American culture. So while a case for major South American migration cannot be made, it is not impossible that at some point in the remote past people from Tiahuanaco visited Easter Island.

The orthodox view of Easter Island's past can be summed up simply: Polynesian seafarers arrived between AD 400 and 500, slowly increasing in numbers and building their statues. As the centuries passed, the island's environment could no longer sustain them. They fought amongst themselves, destroyed their own achievement and left the rest of the world to puzzle over the ruins.

To some this may seem a little dull without the grand arrival of Incas or survivors of an unknown Atlantis carrying on their lost civilization. But, to quote Bellwood: "Is it not even more exciting that a group of isolated Polynesians could have evolved such a magnificent prehistoric record by using their own ideas, brawn, and procreative ability rather than someone else's? Too many anthropologists in the past have held the view that all good things come from a very few areas, and that most of these areas were inhabited by Caucasoids... The peoples of Oceania deserve the credit for their achievements, not the peoples of some imaginary Mediterranean colonial enterprise." ❏

Dwarfed by a giant.

BELOW: body painting at the Tapati festival.

RESTAURANTS AND CAFÉS

Restaurants on Easter Island are expensive, partly because most ingredients have to be imported, and variety is limited, but the fish is excellent. When you tire of lobster and tuna, try *vidriola* (amberjack), a particularly tasty local fish.

Hanga Roa
Au Bout du Monde
Policarpo Toro s/n
Tel: (032) 255 2060
$$$
A Belgian restaurant that now rivals the older Taverne du Pêcheur; live show of Easter Island

music and dancing in the evenings.
Haka Honu
Policarpo Toro s/n
Tel: (032) 255 2163
$$$
With a terrace overlooking the fishing harbor, this is a delightful place for an evening drink that also serves meals.
La Taverne du Pêcheur
Caleta de Pescadores
Tel: (032) 210 0619
$$$
A Frenchman founded and runs this little restaurant right by the fishing harbor that serves local fish as well as

classic French fare. Pricey but the food is good, although the service can be rather off-hand. Booking is advisable.
Merahi Ra'a
Te Pito s/n
Tel: (032) 255 1125
$$$
This café on the main street serves good food and provides friendly service at a modest price.

Prices are per person for a three-course meal, not including drinks.

$ = under US$15
$$ = US$15–25
$$$ = US$25–35

※INSIGHT GUIDES   TRAVEL TIPS
CHILE & EASTER ISLAND

TRANSPORTATION

GETTING THERE
AND GETTING AROUND

GETTING THERE

By Air

Except for some flights from neighboring countries, almost all international flights arrive at Santiago's modern, privately-operated Arturo Merino Benítez (AMB) airport. On entry, passengers from the US, Canada, Australia, Mexico, and Albania, which charge Chileans for tourist visas, are liable to a so-called "reciprocity tax". This can be paid by credit card as well as in cash. The amount is subject to change but, as of March 2009, was: US, US$131; Canada, US$132; Australia, US$61; Mexico, US$23; Albania, US$30.

Arriving passengers are advised to declare all food products on the form provided for this purpose on the plane. The strict checks carried out by the Agricultural Inspection Service (SAG), which include sniffer dogs, are designed to preserve Chile's freedom from agricultural pests and undeclared items, even if not specifically mentioned on the list of forbidden products (principally dairy products, meat, fruit, vegetables, and plants) may be confiscated and a US$200 fine imposed. Products that have been declared, even if considered inadmissible, are not liable to the fine, although they will still be confiscated.

AMB charges international passengers a departure tax of US$30, but this is usually included in the original price of the ticket.

From the US and Canada

It is possible to fly directly to Santiago from the US, with either

LAN International Offices

ARGENTINA
Buenos Aires: Cerrito 866, Unicenter Shopping, Cabildo 1072, Belgrano.
Bariloche: Mitre 534, Local 1.
Córdoba: San Lorenzo 309, Nueva Córdoba.
Mendoza: Av. España 1002.
Rosario: San Luis 470, Piso 7.
Salta: Buenos Aires 92, Local 1.
Tel: 0810 9999 526.
AUSTRALIA
403 George Street, Sydney.
Tel: 1 800 558 129.
BOLIVIA
La Paz: Av. 16 de Julio 1566, El Prado.
Santa Cruz: Calle Quijarro 10, Sucre, Edificio Guapay. Tel: 800 100 521.
BRAZIL
Rua da Consolação 247, 12° Andar, Conj. B, São Paulo.
Tel: 0 800 761 0056.
COLOMBIA
Calle 100 No. 8 A-49, Torre B, Piso 7, Oficina 708, Bogotá.
Tel: 01 800 956 4509.

ECUADOR
Quito: Av. La Coruña y Av. Francisco de Orellana, Centro Comercial Quicentro Shopping; Amazonas N47-205 y Río Palóra, Edificio Armonía.
Guayaquil: Malecón 1401, Piso 5; Mall del Sol, Locales 82 y 83;
Cuenca: Bolívar 9-18 y Benigno Malo; Manta: Av. 2 No. 1155, Edificio Banco Pichincha Piso 9, Of. 904.
Tel: 1 800 101 075.
GERMANY
Liebfrauenstrasse 1–3, D-60313, Frankfurt. Tel: 1805 340 767.
MEXICO
Mexico City: Ignacio Ramírez 20, Oficina 302.
Cancún: International Airport.
Tel: 01 800 123 1619.
NEW ZEALAND
Level 12A Sofrana House, 396 Queen Street, Auckland.
Tel: (64) 0930 83352.
PERU
Lima: Av. José Pardo 513, Piso 1, Miraflores; Aeropuerto Internacional

Jorge Chávez, 1er nivel; Jockey Plaza, Av. Javier Prado Este 4200, Surco; Calle Las Begonias 780, San Isidro.
Tel: 213 8200 from Lima; 0801 11234 from outside Lima.
SPAIN
Capitán Haya 1, Piso 7 28020, Madrid. Tel: (34) 902 112 424.
UK
Office 201, 77 Break Street, London W1F 9DE. Tel: 0800 977 6100.
US
Miami: Concourse A, Level 2, International Airport.
New York: ATO Terminal No. 4, JFK.
Los Angeles: 1960 East Grand Av. St 530, El Segundo CA 90245.
Tel: 1-866-435 9526.
URUGUAY
Colonia 993, Piso 4, Montevideo.
Tel: (02) 902 3881.
VENEZUELA
Av. Blandín, Centro San Ignacio, Torre Kepler, Piso 3, Of. 3-1, La Castellana, Caracas.
Tel: 800 100 8600

American Airlines (www.aa.com) or Delta Air Lines (www.delta.com), and from Canada with Air Canada (www.aircanada.com). Chile's excellent airline, LAN (www.lan.com), also has several flights nightly from major US cities.

From Europe

LAN operates nightly flights from Frankfurt and Madrid while European airlines serving Chile include Air France-KLM (www.airfrance.com; www.klm.com) and Iberia (www.iberia.com). Other European airlines, including British Airways, have connections via Buenos Aires or São Paulo.

In the UK, tickets can also be obtained through specialist travel agencies such as Journey Latin America (tel: 020-8747 3108; www.journeylatinamerica.co.uk), Cox & Kings (tel: 020-7873 5000; www.coxandkings.co.uk), and South American Experience (tel: 0845-277 3366; www.southamericanexperience.co.uk).

From Australasia

The most direct route from Australia or New Zealand is on the LAN and Qantas Airway flights from Sydney with a stopover in Auckland.

From Latin America

A number of South American airlines, including Aerolíneas Argentinas (www.aerolineas.com), Avianca (www.avianca.com), GOL (www.voegol.com), and TAM (www.tam.com.br) fly to Chile. From Santiago, there are regular LAN flights to most major Latin American destinations, and the airline also has a service to Tahiti via Easter Island.

LAN offers a South America Airpass that allows holders to purchase one-way tickets to many destinations in South America at preferential rates. This must be acquired at least 14 days prior to departure date.

By Rail

Two previous rail connections from Bolivia to Arica and Antofagasta no longer operate and there are currently no international rail links to Chile.

By Sea

Except as part of cruises, there are no boat services to Chile from other countries. It is, however, possible to cross from Bariloche in Argentina to southern Chile's Lake District by a combination of road and lake ferries (see page 331).

Transportation in Santiago

Subway: Santiago's metro is comfortable and efficient. There are four lines: one runs east–west beneath Av. B. O'Higgins and on through Providencia, while the other three link residential suburbs in the south of the city to this line. Buy tickets at the various stations – currently US$0.75 per ticket.
Buses: In 2007, all Santiago's bus routes changed in a bid to rationalize the previously chaotic situation. The new Transantiago system, which suffered enormous start-up problems and still elicits many complaints, uses smaller buses on short "feeder" routes that connect with "trunk" routes along major arteries, served by larger articulated buses, and the metro. Fares are paid using a prepaid smart card called BIP! which can be purchased at metro stations. One fare, currently around US$0.65, covers up to three connections (only one of which can be to the subway), within a 2-hour period. Maps are available at subway stations or at www.transantiago.cl (in Spanish). Watch out for pickpockets.
Taxis: Taxis are black with yellow roofs. They each display on the windshield their minimum fare and the rate per 200 meters and must also carry a license certificate. All taxis have meters that should be turned on when you enter the car, although some drivers conveniently forget. While most city taxi drivers are trustworthy, it is best to avoid those waiting outside major hotels, who often try to overcharge tourists. Women on their own at night are best advised to call a radio taxi rather than to flag one down in the street.
Colectivos: These are simply taxis that take up to four passengers for a flat rate on a fixed route. *Colectivos* are even cheaper than taxis, but the routes they take are limited. The price is usually around US$1, and the routes are similar to those of the buses. *Colectivos* are readily available, and particularly useful, at the metro terminal stations.

By Bus

There are a number of bus services from Argentina of which the most frequent are from Mendoza to Santiago and, in the south, from Bariloche to Osorno. The overland journey from Buenos Aires to Santiago via Mendoza takes about 24 hours. The crossing from Peru goes from Tacna to Arica in the far north of Chile. From Bolivia, buses take the road from La Paz to Arica and from Oruro to Calama.

By Road

The main border passes from Argentina to Chile are Los Libertadores in central Chile, Paso Jama in the north, and Cardenal Samoré in the south. However, there are also many more, some of which are not paved and are often closed in winter, including the crossing in Patagonia from El Calafate to Puerto Natales. The main road from Peru runs from Tacna to Arica while the main roads from Bolivia are from La Paz to Arica and from Oruro to Iquique, via Colchane.

GETTING AROUND

Despite its length, Chile is an easy country to explore. Santiago is its transportation hub and has frequent flights to all other major cities and some towns and, filling a previous gap, there are an increasing number of flights between provincial cities. However, apart from the last-minute deals available on www.lan.com, prices are quite high.

Excellent overnight bus services run up and down the Pan-American Highway, the country's north–south backbone, and there are also direct services from Santiago to other major cities, including a virtual shuttle service to Valparaíso and Viña del Mar. The train service that once played a key role in transportation to the south has fallen into increasing disrepair and now only reaches down to Chillán (and even in that case is prone to cancellations and delays).

The more difficult part of Chile to explore is the fjord region to the south of Puerto Montt where the only road,

Vegetarians

Non meat-eaters may face some problems when traveling with Latin American airlines. LAN provides attractive vegetarian meals – options excluding dairy products are also available – on 48-hour request. Other major airlines provide similar facilities, but smaller operators are less reliable, even if you make arrangements in advance.

the Carretera Austral, is unpaved and does not reach Punta Arenas, which can only be reached by road through Argentina. However, ferries and small planes serve this area.

To and from the Airport

Arturo Merino Benítez International Airport (tel: 02-690 1752) is 26km (16 miles) west of central Santiago. Porters are available to assist you with your luggage. A respectable tip for this service would be about US$0.50.

If you're traveling by taxi, use the official service, which has a desk just inside the arrivals exit. Plenty of other taxis moonlight at the airport, and it is possible to negotiate a cheaper price than the official service (approximately US$30), but, for the unwary, these services also have a few tricks up their sleeve. Alternatively, you can use the regular airport shuttle service, which will take you to most destinations within the city, or the bus to the subway.

The major car rental firms all have offices in the airport terminal.

Orientation in Santiago

Santiago is a sprawling city, but the city center is relatively small and easy to explore. "El centro" is roughly triangular-shaped, bounded on one side by the enormous Avenida del Libertador General Bernardo O'Higgins, more conveniently known as the Alameda, on another side by the muddy Río Mapocho, and on the third by the North–South Highway.

In the center is the Plaza de Armas, a city square common to most Spanish-founded cities in South America. Another typical feature is the grid pattern of city streets, which couldn't be simpler for your orientation – although keep in mind that the street names change on either side of the plaza.

Between the plaza and the Alameda is where the traditional hive of business activity can be found, with wall-to-wall office blocks, shops, hotels, and cinemas. Two main streets, Paseo Huérfanos and Paseo Ahumada, have been turned into pedestrian precincts to accommodate the crowds, but are still almost always highly congested. The Alameda continues eastwards into Avenida Providencia and the suburb of the same name.

Santiago's city center, especially between the Plaza de Armas and the Alameda, is incredibly hectic and congested during the working week – you'll find yourself tiring very quickly. The most pleasant time to stroll around is in January and February, when the city empties for the summer holidays, although it gets hot at this time, so don't plan to do too much.

By Air

Chile's national airline, LAN, has offices in most large towns, but attends telephone inquiries or bookings only through its national number (tel: 600 526 2000). It also has a reliable Internet booking service (www.lan.com), with tickets for collection at the airport.

Another small national carrier, **Sky Airline**, (tel: 600 600 2828) operates in Chile. Fares can be substantially cheaper than LAN, although the quality of service and punctuality tend to be inferior.

In Aisén, two local companies cover routes within the region: **Aerotaxis del Sur**, Puerto Montt, tel: (065) 252523, www.aerotaxisdelsur.cl. **Patagonia Airlines**, Puerto Montt, tel: (065) 481273, www.patagoniaairlines.cl.

Cielo Mar Austral, a tour operator in Puerto Montt (tel: 065-264010; email: cielomaraustral@surnet.cl) sells tickets for both airlines and, when demand exceeds scheduled flights, charters planes.

In Magallanes, the airline **Aerovías Dap** connects Punta Arenas to destinations on Isla Grande de Tierra del Fuego and in Argentine Patagonia. They have offices in Punta Arenas (tel: 061-616 100), Puerto Williams (tel: 061-621 051), and Porvenir (tel: 061-580 089; www.aeroviasdap.cl).

To the Juan Fernández Islands

Two airlines offer flights to Isla Robinson Crusoe:
Aero Transportes Araucania, Av. Larraín 7941, Santiago, tel: (02) 275 0363, www.aerolineasata.cl.
Lassa, Av. Larraín 7941, Santiago, tel: (02) 273 4354, www.lassahelicopteros.com.

To Easter Island

LAN has at least five weekly flights to Easter Island (more in summer). Early booking may yield one of the (scarce) cheaper tickets but, otherwise, expect to pay around US$800 return. The flight takes just over five hours.

By Bus

Chilean bus companies provide comfortable conditions for long-distance travel. The vehicles are well maintained, clean (except for the restrooms) and comfortable. They always depart on schedule, refreshments are provided on board, and smoking is prohibited.

The routes are well served, so you rarely need to book more than a few hours in advance, and the cost is low. For long trips, you have the luxurious option of traveling on a *bus cama* (sleeper bus), with first-class seating arrangements – reclining seats with lots of leg room. These buses are very comfortable and include meals, color TV, stereo headphones, and hostess service.

Make sure that you do not lose your token for any baggage placed under the bus.

Santiago Bus Stations

There are four main bus terminals in Santiago managing nearly all international and domestic traffic:
Terminal Santiago, Av. B. O'Higgins 3850, tel: (02) 376 1750, www. terminaldebusessantiago.cl.
Terminal San Borja (also known as Terminal Norte), Borja 184, tel: (02) 776 0645, www.terminalsanborja.cl.
Terminal Los Héroes, Tucapel Jiménez 21, tel: (02) 420 0099.
Terminal Alameda (Tur-Bus), Av. B. O'Higgins 3750, tel: (02) 270 7500.

Airline Reservations in Santiago

Aerolíneas Argentinas, Roger de Flor 2921, tel: (02) 210 9300.
Air Canada, Av. Andrés Bello 2687, Piso 16, tel: (02) 337 0022.
Air France-KLM, Américo Vespucio Sur 100, Of. 202, tel: (02) 290 9330.
American Airlines, Huérfanos 1199, tel: (02) 679 0000.
Avianca, Isidora Goyenechea 3365, Of. 1201, tel: (02) 270 6600.
British Airways, Don Carlos 2939, Of. 1105, tel: 800 207 207.
Copa Airlines, Fidel Oteiza 1921,

Of. 703, tel: (02) 200 2100.
Delta Air Lines, Isidora Goyenechea 2939, piso 6, tel: 800 202 020.
GOL, Aeropuerto Arturo Merino Benítez, tel: (123) 0020 9104
Iberia, Bandera 206, Piso 8, tel: (02) 870 1000.
LAN, Huérfanos 926, tel: 600 526 2000.
Lufthansa, Av. El Bosque Norte 500, Piso 16, tel: (02) 630 1655.
TACA, Dr. Barros Borgoño 105, piso 2, tel: 800 461 133.

This can be confusing, and it is important to make sure you understand from which terminal a bus will leave. Buses to Valparaíso and Viña del Mar are best caught outside the Pajaritos station of the metro (Av. General Bonilla 5600), where they leave approximately every 15 minutes. Most international bus companies depart from the Terminal Santiago. However, buses for Mendoza in Argentina depart from the Terminal San Borja. There are also *colectivos* (communal taxis) to Mendoza, departing from the Terminal Santiago.

Two main bus companies cover most domestic destinations. **Tur-Bus** (tel: 600 660 6600; www.turbus.cl) has offices at the Universidad de Chile and Tobalaba metro stations and other locations around the city. **Pullman Bus** (tel: 600 320 3200; www.pullman.cl) has offices in the Universidad de Chile, Pedro de Valdivia, Los Leones, and Tobalaba Metro stations. Again, check which station your bus will depart from.

By Rail

Sadly, rail travel in Chile is a shadow of its past glories. The remaining services cover only destinations between Santiago and Chillán in the south. There are no services to the north or the coast. All trains leave from Santiago's Estación Central.

Train timetables can be obtained and bookings made by calling tel: 600 585 5000, Mon–Sat 7.30am–9.30pm, or in person at Estación Central, Av. B. O'Higgins 3170, Mon–Fri 7am–10.45pm, Sat–Sun 7.30am–10.45pm or at the railway office in the Universidad de Chile metro station (tel: 600 585 5000, Mon–Fri 9am–8pm and Saturday 9am–2pm).

By Boat

From the Lake District south, boats become important and, particularly in Aisén, provide vital support for the local inhabitants as well as glorious trips for visitors.

Lake District

The Lake District offers dozens of spectacular boating options. The trip from Petrohué to Puella across Lago Todos los Santos is the first leg of the "Journey of the Seven Lakes," a magnificent route to Bariloche in Argentina.

The Southern Channels

A number of *transbordadores* (ferries) cross from Chiloé to Chaitén and

Puerto Chacabuco in Aisén and other ferries cross the region's fjords where these interrupt the Carretera Austral.

Navimag, operates a regular roll-on ship from Puerto Montt to Puerto Chacabuco, calling in at the San Rafael glacier, as well as a service from Puerto Montt to San Rafael and back. Tickets can be bought from their website (www.navimag.cl) or from their offices in Santiago (Av. El Bosque Norte 0440; tel: 02-442 3120), Puerto Montt: Angelmó 2187; tel: 065-432 300), Coyhaique (Paseo Horn 47 "D,"; tel: (067) 233 306), Puerto Natales (Pedro Montt 308; tel: (061) 411 421), and Punta Arenas (Magallanes 990, piso 2; tel: 061-200 263).

Skorpios (www.skorpios.cl) operates weekly cruises from Puerto Montt to San Rafael from September to May. Santiago: Augusto Leguía Norte 118, Las Condes, tel: (02) 477 1900. Puerto Montt: Angelmó 1660, tel: (065) 275 646.

Magallanes

Navimag *(see above)* also operates a weekly service from Puerto Montt to Puerto Natales, while Skorpios *(see above)* offers weekly cruises from Puerto Natales to Puerto Edén.

By Road

Car hire in Chile is relatively expensive, especially in the provinces. However, in some places, it is well worth the cost, particularly if you share expenses with other travelers. For example, in the Lake District and the Central Valley, having one's own transportation opens up many more opportunities.

Car drivers should make sure they have the original registration document of their vehicle. There are plenty of modern service stations on

Illegal Products

It is illegal to transport any type of seafood on buses. The officials of SAG (the Agricultural Inspection Service) conduct rigorous searches at all international borders and several regional borders and, depending on the area of the country, may confiscate fresh fruit, vegetables, and dairy products. SAG checkpoints are clearly marked on road maps.

the tourist routes, and fuel is about US$0.80, but varies significantly in line with international oil prices.

Santiago has a number of new high-speed roads with an electronic toll system. These can be used without the windscreen-mounted bleeper but a daily pass, available at most service stations and at main entry points to the city, should be acquired either before or shortly after using the highway.

Hertz has one of the largest car rental networks, with branch offices in most major cities. It has offices at Andrés Bello 1469, Providencia (tel: 02-360 8600), and at Arturo Merino Benítez Airport (tel: 02-601 0477) in Santiago; www.hertz.cl. Other major companies are **Budget** (tel: 02-598 3200; www.budget.cl) and **Avis** (tel: 600 368 2000; www.avischile.cl). The Automóvil Club de Chile also rents cars and has offices throughout Chile (tel: 600 464 4040; www.automovilclub.cl).

Car hire rates start at around US$50. Some companies offer weekly rates with unlimited mileage. It's worth shopping around. A substantial deposit or credit-card voucher may also be required.

See Maps *(page 348)* for where to purchase detailed road maps if you're planning to drive in Chile.

BELOW: a road trip requires preparation, but is a wonderful way to see the country.

ACCOMMODATIONS

HOTELS, YOUTH HOSTELS, BED AND BREAKFAST

Choosing a Hotel

Take Chilean hotel star ratings with a pinch of salt. In Santiago, they're generally reliable but in the rest of the country, they can be a bit haphazard. However, standards are mostly high and are improving all the time, with international chains now expanding down into the three- and even two-star market. As a general guide, three-star and up is almost always comfortable and certainly clean.

The busy seasons are the summer months (December–March) and the week around the Independence Day holiday, on September 18. During these periods, it's wise to book ahead, particularly in the Torres del Paine National Park, where there's a serious shortage of hotel accommodations, and at other popular tourist spots.

Hosterías, Hospedajes, and Residenciales

There's not much difference between *hosterías* and hotels, but *residenciales* are more basic affairs, with none of the hotel frills – usually no meals apart from breakfast and, possibly, shared bathrooms. At an *hospedaje*, you'll get a room in a private house, but standards vary a lot (they are particularly good value for money in the Lake District). Ultimately, the best guide as to what sort of stay you'll have at an *hospedaje* is the friendliness of the owner, so it is worth having a chat with him or her before making your choice.

Youth Hostels

Hostelling International (HI) has 17 hostels in Chile, including one on Easter Island, with rates starting at around US$10 for a bed in a shared dormitory. Contact HI Chile's office for more information: Asociación Chilena de Albergues Turísticos Juveniles, Av. Hernando de Aguirre 201, Of. 602, Santiago, tel: (02) 411 2050, www.hostelling.cl. There are also many other privately-owned hostels charging similar prices, such as the excellent Casa Roja in Santiago *(see below)*.

The International Student Identity Card (ISIC) is widely accepted in Chile and has discount arrangements with some hotels, bars, and restaurants.

Booking Ahead

It's a good idea to have accommodations reserved for your first night in Santiago, although a booking service is available in the airport. Contact **Sernatur,** the national tourist office *(see page 348 for details).*

ACCOMMODATIONS LISTINGS

SANTIAGO

Crowne Plaza Holiday Inn
Av. Libertador B. O'Higgins 136
Tel: (02) 638 1042
www.crowneplaza.cl
Situated close to the city center. Facilities include swimming pool, tennis courts, gymnasium, and conference rooms. **$$$$**
Four Points by Sheraton Santiago
Santa Magdalena 111
Tel: (02) 750 0300
www.fourpoints.com/santiago

Located in the Providencia district, this hotel offers most of the luxury frills but at the lower end of the top price range. **$$$$**
Grand Hyatt Santiago
Av. Kennedy 4601
Tel: (02) 950 1234
www.santiago.grand.hyatt.com
Rather out of the way, especially by public transport, but has a very attractive garden and swimming pool. **$$$$**

Hotel InterContinental Santiago
Av. Vitacura 2885
Tel: (02) 394 2000
www.intercontisantiago.com
Situated close to the main El Golf restaurant area.
$$$$
Apart Hotel Santa Magdalena
Helvecia 244, Las Condes
Tel: (02) 374 6875
www.santamagdalena.cl
Self-service flats in the El

Bosque district. Near the Tobalaba metro station and one of the city's main restaurant areas. $$$

Hotel Foresta
Victoria Subercaseaux 353
Tel: (02) 639 6261
Fax: (02) 632 2996
Located directly opposite
Cerro Santa Lucía: idyllic
views from front rooms. $$$

Hotel Orly
Pedro de Valdivia 027
Tel: (02) 231 8947
www.orlyhotel.com
Excellent value for money
at a very convenient
location in the Providencia
district. $$$

Chilhotel
Cirujano Guzmán 103
Tel: (02) 264 0643
www.chilhotel.cl
Great value at the lower end
of the top price range. On a
quiet street and with
excellent service from
owner-managers. $$$

Residencial Londres
Londres 54
Tel: (02) 633 9192
www.londres.cl
Ramshackle antique
interiors in a charming,
central location. $$

Tur Express Hotel
Av. Bernardo O'Higgins 3750, Piso 3
Tel: (02) 685 0110
www.turbus.com/turismo/turhotel/
turhotel.html
A basic hotel owned by one
of the main bus companies
and close to the Terminal
Santiago bus station. $$

La Casa Roja
Agustinas 2113
Tel: (02) 696 4241
www.lacasaroja.cl
Great atmosphere and value
for money. A good place for
backpackers of all ages. $

ABOVE: café terrace, Santiago.

THE NORTH

Arica

Azapa Inn
Guillermo Sánchez 660, Azapa
Tel: (058) 244 517
www.azapainn.cl
Located in pleasant grounds,
although some distance from
beach. Facilities include a
pool. $$$

Hotel Arica
Av. Comandante San Martin 599,
Playa El Laucho
Tel: (058) 254 540
www.panamericanahoteles.cl
Four-star hotel with a
swimming pool and easy
access to the best beaches
in Arica. $$$$

Hostal Huanta Jaya
21 de Mayo 660
Tel/fax: (058) 314 605
Email: hostal.huanta.jaya@gmail.com
In the center of town, cheap
and basic, but clean. $$

Hotel Savona
Yungay 380
Tel: (058) 231 000
www.hotelsavona.cl
Small, basic hotel near the
main square. $$

Iquique

Hostería Terrado Suites
Los Rieles 126, Penísula de
Cavancha
Tel: (057) 488 000
www.terrado.cl
Situated by Cavancha
beach, with a pool. $$$

Hotel Barros Arana
Barros Arana 1302
Tel: (057) 412 840
www.hotelbarrosarana.cl
Close to the beach, with a
pool. $$

Hotel Jham
Almirante Latorre 426
Tel: (057) 415 457
www.hoteljham.cl
In the town center, just two
blocks from Plaza Prat. $$

Hostal Cuneo
Baquedano 1175
Tel: (057) 428 654
Email: hostalcuneo@hotmail.com
Located on a beautifully
renovated street. $

Antofagasta

Hotel Antofagasta
Balmaceda 2575
Tel: (055) 228 811
www.hotelantofagasta.cl
Four-star hotel, with a pool
and excellent views of the
port and city. $$$

Holiday Inn Express
Av. Grecia 1490
Tel: (055) 228 888
www.holidayinnexpress.cl
Slightly out of the way, but
very pleasant. $$$

Hotel Diego De Almagro
Condell 2624
Tel: (055) 268331
www.dahoteles.com
A reasonably comfortable,
centrally located hotel. $$$

Calama

Hostería Calama
J.J. Latorre 1521
Tel: (055) 341 511
www.hosteriacalama.cl
Comfortable and quiet
hotel, with a good
restaurant. $$$

Park Hotel Calama
Camino Aeropuerto 1392
Tel: (055) 447 700

www.parkplaza.cl
Comfortable four-star hotel
near the airport with
excellent facilities. $$$

Hotel Universo
Sotomayor 1822
Tel/fax: (055) 361 640
Email: hoteluniverso@gmail.com
Well located. $$

San Pedro de Atacama

Explora Hotel
Domingo Atienza s/n
Tel: (02) 206 6060
www.explora.com
This hotel's all-inclusive
3- and 4-day deals include
excellent excursions to the
Atacama Desert. $$$$

Hostería de San Pedro
Toconao 460
Tel: (055) 851 011
www.dahoteles.com
Has 54 beds and five
6-person cabins, and a
swimming pool. $$$

Hostería Casa de Don Tomás
Calle Tocopilla s/n
Tel: (055) 851 176
www.dontomas.cl
New, well equipped hotel.
$$$

Hotel Tambillo
Gustavo Le Paige 159
Tel: (055) 851 078
www.hoteltambillo.cl
Basic facilities but a good
budget option. $$

Hostería Takha-Takha
Caracoles 101-A
Tel: (055) 851 038
www.takhatakha.cl
A pleasant and comfortable
place for budget travelers,

with quaint cabins and
serviced camping ground. $

Hostelling International
Caracoles 360
Tel: (055) 851 426
www.hostelling.cl
A renovated house a block
away from the plaza. Has
shared and private rooms.
$

Copiapó

Hostería La Casona
O'Higgins 150
Tel: (052) 217 278
www.lacasonahotel.cl
A small hotel close to the
center. $$

La Serena

Jardín Del Mar
Av. Costanera 5425

PRICE CATEGORIES

All prices are for double
occupancy per night with
breakfast unless otherwise
stated. Non-nationals
paying in dollars avoid the
19 percent IVA (sales tax).
$ = less than US$25
$$ = US$25–60
$$$ = US$60–120
$$$$ = more than US$120

Tel: (051) 242 835
www.hoteljardindelmar.cl
A tourist complex with 164 beds, divided between apartments and cabins (4–8 persons). $$$$

Hotel Francisco De Aguirre
Cordovez 210
Tel: (051) 222 991
www.dahoteles.com
A very pleasant old hotel with a swimming pool. $$$

Hostal Croata
Cienfuegos 248

Tel: (051) 224 997
www.hostalcroata.cl
Centrally located. $$

Valle del Elqui

The Elqui Valley has many campsites alongside the river but, during holiday periods, they are popular with young people – who go there to drink the pisco for which the valley is famous – and can be rowdy.

Hostería de Vicuña
Sargento Aldea 101
Tel: (051) 411301
A 15-bedroom hotel with an outdoor pool and restaurant. $$$

Hotel Elqui Domus
Camino Pisco Elqui–Horcón, Km 3.5
Tel: (09) 7709 2879
www.elquidomos.cl
In this "astronomical" hotel, the six tent-like rooms all have a retractable roof and telescope. $$$

Spa Cochiguaz
Parcela 8-B El Pangue, Cochiguaz
Tel: (051) 484 769
www.cochiguaz.com
Very New Age, vegetarian food only, no alcohol. $$$

Hostería Los Dátiles
Calle Prat s/n, Pisco Elqui
Tel: (051) 451 266
www.losdatileselqui.cl
Cabins for 2–5 people in an idyllic setting. No reduction for lower occupancy of cabins in summer. $$

CENTRAL CHILE

Valparaíso

Hotel Casa Thomas Somerscales
San Enrique 446, Cerro Alegre
Tel: (032) 233 1379
www.hotelsomerscales.cl
A boutique hotel in the home of an English-born 19th-century painter. $$$

Puerto Natura
Hector Calvo 850, Cerro Bellavista
Tel: (032) 222 4405
www.puertonatura.cl
This lovely B&B, with spa and massage services, was the home of the architect who designed Neruda's house La Sebastiana. $$$

Luna Sonrisa
Templeman 833, Cerro Alegre
Tel: (032) 273 4117
www.lunasonrisa.cl
A restored house with private and shared rooms. $$

Ottavia Hostelling
San Enrique 548, Cerro Alegre
Tel: (032) 233 9628
www.ottaviahostelling.com
Scrupulously clean. $$

Viña del Mar

Hotel del Mar
Av. Perú and Los Héroes
Tel: (032) 250 0800
www.hoteldelmar.cl
A luxury hotel with a casino, discotheque, and three restaurants. $$$$

Hotel Cap Ducal
Av. Marina 51
Tel: (032) 262 6655
www.capducal.cl
Built jutting out into the sea; some people love it, others aren't impressed. $$$

Hotel O'Higgins
Plaza Vergara s/n
Tel: (032) 268 2000
www.panamericanahoteles.cl
Centrally located traditional hotel. $$$

Hostal Victoria
Av. Valparaíso 40
Tel/fax: (032) 297 7370
Email: hostal.victoria@gmail.com
Large and characterful place opposite the railway station; shared bathrooms. $

Concón

Radisson Acqua Hotel & Spa
Av. Borgoño 23333
Tel: (032) 254 6400
www.radisson.cl
Fifty-room hotel with a sea view and excellent spa facilities. $$$$

Concepción

Holiday Inn Express
Av. San Andrés 38
Tel: (041) 248 9300
www.holidayinnexpress.cl
A little way out of town, but close to one of the city's best restaurants, Sólo Carnes y Aquarium; favored by business visitors. $$$$

Hotel Germania Suites & Apartments
Anibal Pinto 295
Tel: (041) 274 7000
www.hotelgermania.cl
Recently refurbished and central; good value for a family. $$$

Hotel Alborada
Barros Arana 457
Tel: (041) 291 1121
www.hotelalborada.cl
An unpretentious hotel, just off the main square. $$$

Hotel Alonso de Ercilla
Colo Colo 334
Tel: (041) 222 7984
www.hotelalonsodeercilla.co.cl
One block from the main square; average facilities, no restaurant. $$

Hotel Ritz
Barros Arana 721
Tel: (041) 226 696
www.hotelritz.cl
Centrally located and relatively cheap. $$

LAKE DISTRICT

Chillán

Gran Hotel Isabel Riquelme
Constitución 576
Tel: (042) 434 400
www.hotelisabelriquelme.cl
Facing one of the most attractive main squares, with 87 rooms and three suites, plus function/conference rooms. $$$

Hotel Rukalaf
Arauco 740
Tel: (042) 230 393

www.rukalaf.cl
A cheaper but comfortable alternative, very central and a good choice for an overnight stay. $$

Temuco

Holiday Inn Express
Av. Rudecindo Ortega 01800
Tel: (045) 223300
www.holidayinnexpress.cl
On the main road on the city's outskirts, the best place for an overnight

stopover; no restaurant, but light ready-to-serve dishes are available. $$$

Hotel de La Frontera
Av. Bulnes 733 and 726
Tel: (045) 200 400
www.hotelfrontera.cl
Just off the main square; modern, with above average facilities, including a pool, sauna, and function/conference rooms. $$$

Apart Hotel Tierra de Sur
Av. Bulnes 1196
Tel/fax: (045) 232 439

www.tierradelsur.cl
A modern hotel, with indoor and outdoor swimming pools, but no restaurant. $$

Pucón

Hotel Antumalal
1km (½ mile) outside Pucón,
Camino a Villarrica
Tel: (045) 441 011
www.antumalal.com
Small, luxury hotel where
Queen Elizabeth II once
stayed. One "royal" chalet
and 13 rooms, set in
4 hectares (10 acres) of
quiet woodland on a
peninsula overlooking Lake
Villarrica. Heated swimming
pool. **$$$$**

Hotel Del Lago Casino & Resort
Miguel Ansorena 121
Tel: (045) 550 000
www.hoteldellago.cl
A luxury hotel in the center
of town with a marvelous
view of the lake. **$$$$**

Termas de Huife
Camino Pucón-Huife, Km 33
Tel: (045) 441 222
www.termashuife.cl
Open-air thermal swimming
pools in an idyllic natural
setting. The luxury cabins all
have private thermal baths.
$$$$

Hostal La Tetera
General Urrutia 580
Tel: (045) 464 126
www.tetera.cl
Guesthouse run by Swiss/
Chilean couple. **$$**

Hostería "École"
General Urrutia 592
Tel: (045) 441 675
www.ecole.cl
Hostelling International
affiliate. American-owned
hostería with private rooms

and dorms; excellent
vegetarian restaurant open
to non-guests; "gringo"
meeting place and a source
of honest advice about local
activities and operators. **$$**

Villarrica

Montaña Mágica Lodge
Camino Internacional Panguipulli–
Puerto Fuy, Km 60
Tel: (063) 197 0122
www.huilohuilo.cl
This hotel, which forms part
of the private Huilo Huilo
Reserve, may look as if it
belongs in Disney World and
it is pricey, but the setting is
spectacular. **$$$$**

Villarrica Park Lake Hotel
Camino Villarrica–Pucón, Km 13
Tel: (045) 450 000
www.villarricaparklakehotel.cl
A lovely hotel with excellent
spa facilities, but very
pricey. **$$$$**

El Ciervo
General Korner 241
Tel: (045) 411 215
www.hotelelciervo.cl
A 12-room centrally located
hotel with swimming pool. It
also has a cabin for five
people. **$$$**

La Torre Suiza
Francisco Bilbao 969
Tel/fax: (045) 411 213
www.torresuiza.com
A popular place with
backpackers and cyclists. **$$**

Lican Ray

Nearly everything in this
holiday settlement is closed

outside the tourist high
season, which is from mid-
December to mid-March.

Hostal Hofmann
Camino a Coñaripe 100
Tel: (045) 431 109
www.mapasdechile.com/licanray/
hostalhofmann
Located on the outskirts of
Lican Ray, this hotel has the
advantage of being open all
year but it has only 5 rooms
so booking is advisable. **$$**

Panguipulli

Hostal España
B. O'Higgins 790
Tel: (063) 311 166
Email: jhrios@hotelsur.cl
Small, centrally located
hotel. **$$**

Valdivia

Hotel Villa Del Río
Av. España 1025
Tel: (063) 216 292
www.hotelvilladelrio.com
On the river across from the
center of Valdivia, with 100
rooms, cabins, swimming
pool, sauna, and tennis
court. Conference rooms.
$$$$

Hotel Encanto del Río
Av. Prat 415
Tel: (063) 224 744
www.hotelencantodelrio.cl
A new 22-bedroom hotel on
the waterfront. **$$**

Airesbuenos
García Reyes 550
Tel: (063) 222 202
www.airesbuenos.cl
A Hostelling International
affiliate. Has dormitories as
well as rooms with shared
or private bathrooms. **$$**

Ensenada

Hotel & Cabañas Puerto Pilar
Camino a Ensenada, Km 27
Tel: (065) 335 378
www.hotelpuertopilar.cl
With a heated swimming
pool, this hotel and cabin
complex offers a privileged
view of the Volcán Osorno.
$$$

Llifén

Hostería Chollinco
Camino Llifén–Maihue, Km 3

Tel/fax: (063) 197 1979
www.hosteriachollinco.cl
Gorgeous cabins, extensive
gardens, pool, and a
spectacular view of
mountain scenery and river.
Horseback riding and
fishing excursions available.
$$$

Lago Ranco

Casona Italiana
Viña del Mar 367
Tel/fax: (063) 491 225
Small lakeside hotel with
three rooms and five cabins.
Shared bathrooms. **$**

Puerto Octay

Hotel Centinela
Península de Centinela, Km 5
Tel/fax: (064) 391 326
www.hotelcentinela.cl
A peaceful setting on the
shore of Lake Llanquihue.
$$$

Frutillar

Hotel Ayacara
Av. Philippi and Pedro
Aguirre Cerda
Tel: (065) 421 550
www.hotelayacara.cl
Attractive rooms with
spectacular views. **$$$**

Hotel Salzburg
Camino Playa Maqui s/n
Tel: (065) 421 589
www.salzburg.cl
Impeccable rooms. The
restaurant is one of the
town's favorites. **$$$**

Puerto Varas

Hotel Colonos del Sur
Estación 505
Tel: (065) 233 369
www.colonosdelsur.cl
Well equipped modern hotel
facing the lake, with
swimming pool. **$$$**

PRICE CATEGORIES

All prices are for double
occupancy per night with
breakfast unless otherwise
stated. Non-nationals
paying in dollars avoid the
19 percent IVA (sales tax).
$ = less than US$25
$$ = US$25–60
$$$ = US$60–120
$$$$ = more than US$120

BELOW: relax in style at the Termas de Puyehue.

Casa Azul
Manzanal 66
Tel: (065) 232 904
www.casaazul.net
Quaint and comfortable
hostel; shared and private
bathrooms. $–$$

Puyehue

Hotel Termas de Puyehue
Close to Lago Puyehue,
Ruta Internacional 215, Km 76
(east of Osorno).
Tel: (064) 331 400
Famous "spa" facilities
include indoor and open-air
thermal swimming pools,
sauna, mud and sulfur
baths, tennis courts, and
gymnasium, with mountain
bikes, horseback riding,
fishing, and boat tours
available. $$$$
Hotel Antillanca
Centro de Ski Antillanca, Parque
Nacional Puyehue (20 km from
Ruta Internacional 215, Km 70)

Tel: (064) 235 114
www.skiantillanca.com
Modern hotel situated in
the center of Parque
Nacional Puyehue. Provides
an ideal base for trekking
and mountain climbing in
the summer and skiing in
the winter. Facilities include
a swimming pool, sauna,
gym, and conference
center. $$$

Petrohué

Hotel Petrohué
Ruta Internacional 225, Km 64
Tel: (065) 212 025
www.hotelpetrohue.cl
Attractive hotel situated
next to Lago Todos los
Santos and River Petrohué
in Parque Nacional Pérez
Rosales. Handy location for
trips onto the lake, and
white-water rafting, fishing,
and walking excursions.
$$$$

Osorno

**Hotel García Hurtado
de Mendoza**
Av. Juan Mackenna 1040
Tel: (064) 237 111
www.hotelgarciahurtado.cl
A modern hotel located close
to the center of town. $$$
Gran Hotel Osorno
O'Higgins 615
Tel: (064) 232 171
Email: hoteleraustral@telsur.cl
Situated on the main
square, with 70 rooms. $$
Hostal Bilbao Express
Bilbao 1019
Tel: (064) 262 200
http://hotelbilbao.cl
One of the better low-
budget alternatives in
Osorno. $$

Puerto Montt

Puerto Montt doesn't live up
to the south's reputation for
generous hospitality;

lodgings tend to be dowdy;
Puerto Varas *(see page
335)*, 21km (13 miles)
north, offers a much better
range of accommodations.
Gran Hotel Don Luis
Quillota 146
Tel: (065) 259 001
www.hoteldonluis.cl
This modern, centrally
located hotel has 60 rooms
and standard facilities but
only offers a snack service.
$$$
Holiday Inn Express
Av. Costanera s/n, on top of the
shopping center
Tel: (065) 566 000
www.holidayinnexpress.cl
A new centrally located
hotel. Has a cafeteria, but
no restaurant. $$$
Residencial Urmeneta
Urmeneta 290
Tel/fax: (065) 253 262
One of the better choices at
the cheaper end of the
range. $–$$

CHILOÉ

For budget accommodations
in Chiloé, the *residenciales*
or *hospedajes (see page
332)* are the best value, and
also provide a friendly
atmosphere and a place to
meet local people.

Ancud

Hostería Ancud
San Antonio 30
Tel: (065) 622 340
www.panamericanahoteles.cl
Beautiful interior of wooden
pillars supporting an
impressive cane ceiling, but
the rooms are very small.

Set on a hillside overlooking
the water. $$$
Hotel Madryn
Bellavista 491
Tel/fax: (065) 622 128
www.hotelmadryn.cl
Close to Plaza de Armas. $

Castro

The sea-end of Calle
Sotomayor in Castro is full
of guesthouses and family
homes that offer lodging at
very reasonable prices,
usually around US$10 per
person. The best plan is to
walk around, talk to the

owners, and ask to see the
rooms before making a
choice.
Hotel Unicornio Azul
Pedro Montt 228
Tel: (065) 632 359
www.chiloeweb.com/pweb/unicornioazul
Lovely hotel with a good
view over the harbor. $$$

Achao, Isla Quinchao

Hostería La Nave
Prat and Sargento Aldea
Tel: (065) 661 219
www.hosterialanave.cl
Clean hotel with a good
restaurant. It is built on
stilts over the sea in an
attractive fishing harbor. $$

Chonchi

Esmeralda by the Sea
Irarrázaval 287
Tel: (065) 671 328
www.esmeraldabythesea.cl
This Canadian-owned
hostel has both dorms and
private rooms (with or
without private bathroom).
A special attraction is
dining on shellfish raised
on the hostel's own farm.

• Santiago

You can also go fishing or
crabbing. $$

Cucao

This is a tiny village in a
beautiful setting, on the
coast near the Chiloé
National Park. There are
several *residenciales*
where visitors can stay. $

PRICE CATEGORIES

All prices are for double
occupancy per night with
breakfast unless otherwise
stated. Non-nationals
paying in dollars avoid the
19 percent IVA (sales tax).
$ = less than US$25
$$ = US$25–60
$$$ = US$60–120
$$$$ = more than US$120

BELOW: Hotel Unicornio Azul in Castro.

AISÉN

Coyhaique

Hostería Coyhaique
Magallanes 131
Tel: (067) 231 137
www.hotelcoyhaique.cl
Guesthouse in a beautiful park setting. **$$$**
Minchos Lodge
Camino del Bosque 1170
Tel: (067) 233273
www.minchoslodgepatagonia.com
A little way out of town; foreigners are charged a higher rate. **$$$$**

Puyuhuapi

Puyuhuapi
Bahia Dorita s/n
Canal Puyuhuapi
Tel: (067) 325 103
www.patagonia-connection.com
Luxury hotel in an area of unrivaled beauty, but difficult to get into, except as part of a 4-day package deal. Most people come here to relax in the thermal waters, but the hotel also organizes walks and riding excursions. **$$$$**

Parque Pumalín

The park offers a range of lodgings and campsites (see www.parquepumalin.cl). However, due to the eruption of the Chaitén volcano, accommodations are closed until further notice.

Lake General Carrera

Terra Luna Lodge
Puerto Guadal, road to Chile Chico, Km 1.5

Tel: (067) 431 263
www.terra-luna.cl
A comfortable base for hikes and fishing trips. **$$$**

MAGALLANES AND TIERRA DEL FUEGO

Punta Arenas

Cabo de Hornos
Plaza Muñoz Gamero 1039
Tel: (061) 715 000
www.hotelesaustralis.com
Grandiose block adjacent to the main plaza. **$$$$**
Hotel Plaza
José Nogueira 1116
Tel: (061) 241 300
www.hotelplaza.cl
Centrally located and comfortable. **$$$**
Hostal El Conventillo
Pasaje Korner 1034
Tel: (061) 242 311
Two blocks away from the Plaza de Armas. **$**

Puerto Natales

Hotel CostAustralis
Pedro Montt 262
Tel: (061) 412 000
www.hotelesaustralis.com
A luxury hotel on the waterfront. **$$$$**

Indigo Patagonia
Ladrilleros 105
Tel/fax: (061) 413 609
www.indigopatagonia.com
An attractive 29-bedroom hotel. **$$$$**
Hotel Juan Ladrilleros
Pedro Montt 161
Tel: (061) 415 978
www.hoteljuanladrilleros.com
Friendly; good views. **$$$**
Hospedaje Nancy
Eleuterio Ramírez 540
Tel: (061) 410 022
Popular with backpackers. **$**

Torres del Paine

Early booking is essential.
Hostería Lago Grey
Tel: (061) 410 172
www.turismolagogrey.com
Pleasant, but expensive, 30-room hotel overlooking the Grey glacier. **$$$$**
Hotel Explora Patagonia
Tel: (02) 206 6060; www.explora.com
Beautifully designed hotel;

offers all-inclusive 4–8-day deals. **$$$$**
Hostería Pehoé
Tel: (02) 235 0252
www.pehoe.com
Small hotel on Lago Pehoé; closed from May 1 to September 30. **$$$$**
Posada Río Serrano
Ruta 9 Norte, Km 339
Tel: (061) 613 530
www.posadaserrano.com
Restored estancia; one of the few cheaper alternatives in this area. **$$$**
Hotel Lago Tyndall
Sector Rio Serrano
Tel: (061) 614 682
www.hoteltyndall.cl
Hotel plus cabins and a dormitory-style *refugio*. **$$**

Porvenir

Hotel España
Croacia 698
Tel: (061) 580 160
www.hotelespana.cl

Simple, but with large rooms and impeccably clean. **$$**

Lago Blanco

Hostería Las Lengas
Tel: (061) 226 010
www.hosterialaslengas.com
On the shore of the lake; organizes fishing trips. **$$$$**
Hotel Lakutaia
Seno Lauta s/n
Tel: (061) 621 721; www.lakutaia.cl
Luxury hotel; offers a variety of excursions, including trekking, horseback riding, and sailing. **$$$$**

PACIFIC ISLANDS

Juan Fernández Islands

Some hotels can be booked through the airlines that service the island and there are a handful of moderately priced hotels and cabins.
Hostería Aldea Daniel Defoe
Larraín Alcalde 449
Tel: (032) 275 1233
Cabins in the town of San Juan Bautista. **$$**

Easter Island

Hotels are expensive on Easter Island, but there are some *residenciales* and cabins or rooms for rent, best chosen on arrival (and after inspection) from among the offers touted at the airport.
Posada de Mike Rapu
6km (3½ miles) from Hanga Roa
Tel: (02) 206 6060
www.explora.com
This beautifully designed

hotel offers only 3- and 8-day all-inclusive deals with guided excursions. **$$$$**
Hotel Iorana
Ana Magaro s/n
Tel: (032) 210 0608
www.ioranahotel.cl
Slightly more luxurious than Hotel Manutara, but a taxi ride from town. **$$$$**
Hotel Manutara
Hanga Roa s/n
Tel: (032) 255 1501
www.hotelmanutara.cl

On the edge of the main town, clean and comfortable. **$$$$**

TRANSPORTATION · ACCOMMODATIONS · ACTIVITIES · A – Z · LANGUAGE

A CTIVITIES

FESTIVALS, THE ARTS, NIGHTLIFE, SHOPPING, SPORTS AND OUTDOOR EXCURSIONS

Calendar of Festivals and Events

January
Año Nuevo en el Mar (1st) Outdoor new year celebrations and fireworks, Valparaíso.
Fiesta de San Sebastián Catholic festivity in Yumbel, south of Chillán.
Semanas Musicales de Frutillar Classical music festival on the shores of Lago Llanquihue.
Festival Folklórico de San Bernardo Folkloric music festival, Santiago.
Open-air Theater Season Various parks in Santiago.

February
Muestra Cultural Mapuche Traditional music and dancing of the Mapuches, Lago Villarrica.
Festival Internacional de la Canción International Song Festival in Viña del Mar.
Semana Valdiviana A week-long festival on the Calle-Calle River in Valdivia.
Regata de las Mil Millas 1,600-km (1,000-mile) nautical race starting from Viña del Mar.

April
Campeonato Nacional de Rodeo Chilean rodeo championships, Rancagua.
Fiesta de Cuasimodo (Sunday after Easter) Religious and folkloric festival, Santiago.

May
Labor Day (1st) National holiday.
National Holiday (21st) Commemoration of the Iquique naval battle during the War of the Pacific.
National Heritage Day Last Sunday in May.

July
La Tirana (12–16th) Native and religious festivity, east of Iquique.
Festival Folklórico de la Patagonia Folklore festival, Punta Arenas.
Industrial and Craft Fair Punta Arenas.

August
Ascension of the Virgin Mary (15th) National holiday.
Santa Rosa de Lima Celebration Pelequén, near San Fernando.

September
Independence Day (18th) National holiday.
Army Day (19th) National holiday, military parade.

October
Columbus Day (12th) National holiday.
Reformation Day (31st) National holiday.

November
All Saints' Day (1st) National holiday.
Latin American Craft and Artisan Exhibition Parque Bustamante, Santiago.
National Book Fair Estación Mapocho Cultural Center, Santiago.

December
Feast of the Immaculate Conception (8th) National holiday.
Fiesta de la Virgén de Andacollo (23rd–27th) Religious festivity near La Serena.
Christmas Day (25th) National holiday.

THE ARTS

Art Galleries

Santiago has an abundance of art galleries. The largest – and most expensive – are in the upmarket Vitacura neighborhood. These include **Galería Animal** (www.galeriaanimal.com), **Galería ArtEspacio** (www.artespacio.cl), and **Galería Isabel Aninat** (www.galeriaisabelaninat.cl), not far from each other on Alonso de Córdova, and **AMS Marlborough** (www.galeriaanamariastagno.cl), on Nueva Costanera.

In the Baquedano neighborhood, the Telefónica telecommunications company puts on interesting shows in the ground-floor gallery of its corporate building on Plaza Italia.

Many smaller and often more experimental art galleries can be found in the Lastarria and Bellavista neighborhoods. In Lastarria, take time to visit the **Museo de Artes Visuales** (www.mavi.cl) in Plaza Mulato Gil and perhaps to look at the art shops nearby on Merced. In Bellavista, by strolling around, you'll find many galleries – often shoestring ones – showing the work of younger artists.

Classical Music and Ballet

For classical music, the **Teatro Municipal** (www.municipal.cl), on the corner of San Antonio and Agustinas, offers a complete season between April and December, as well as a ballet and opera season. Tel: (02) 463 1000 for further information and tickets. Tickets are also available at the theater and in the Parque Arauco shopping mall.

The **Teatro Oriente** (www.teatroriente.cl), Av. Pedro de Valdivia 099, between Avenidas Providencia and Andrés Bello, presents overseas artists during the season of May through October. Tel: (02) 231 2173.

The **Teatro Universidad de Chile** (www.teatro.uchile.cl) in Plaza Italia houses a symphony orchestra and a ballet company, both of which offer regular performances. Tel: (02) 978 2480.

Quality recordings of international music are available at the various branches of **Feria del Disco** (www.feriadeldisco.cl), Chile's main music-store chain.

Concerts

Popular international artists and bands usually include Santiago in their Latin American tours. These concerts generally take place at one of the city's open-air stadiums and are prominently advertised in the local press. Tickets can usually be purchased quite close to the date of the event and start at around US$30 for standing room.

Dance

International dance companies sometimes visit Chile; details of forthcoming events can be found in local newspapers and on www.emol.com, the website of the *El Mercurio* newspaper.

Cinema

Santiago's traditional neighborhood cinemas have mostly been replaced by multi-screen complexes, usually in shopping malls. These new cinemas, introduced by overseas chains, have better seats and sound than their older equivalents, but the fare they show stems mainly from Hollywood; for independent films, you'll need to go to the smaller "art cinemas."

The daily papers carry complete film listings, and the *Wikén* supplement of Friday's *El Mercurio* reviews each week's new arrivals. Its critics tend to be on the conservative side. Most cinemas charge around US$7.

In the center of town, the **Hoyts Paseo Huérfanos** and the **Hoyts San Agustín** carry most of the current films. Other cinemas in the center, especially the smaller ones, tend to show soft porn.

The best of the multi-screen complexes, **Cinemark Alto Las Condes**, is in the Alto Las Condes shopping mall, while the nearby Parque Arauco mall houses another

ABOVE: Chile has a strong performing arts tradition.

complex, **Showcase Cinemas Parque Arauco**. Both of these malls are a distance from the center, on Las Condes's Av. Kennedy. There is also **CineHoyts La Reina**, a stand-alone multi-screen cinema close to the Simón Bolívar station on Line 4 of the metro.

The main "art cinemas" are **El Biógrafo** (www.transeuropafilms.cl/biografo/index.html), Lastarria 81 (tel: 02-633 4435), **Alameda** (www.centroartealameda.cl), Alameda 139 (tel: 02-664 8821), and **Tobalaba**, Providencia 2563 (tel: 02-231 6630). In the center of town, the **Normandie** (www.normandie.cl), Tarapacá 1181 (tel: 02-697 2979) is a bit run-down, but shows films that aren't often available elsewhere. Small cinemas do not usually accept phone bookings.

Jazz

The center of Santiago's jazz world is the **Club de Jazz de Santiago** (www.clubdejazz.cl) in the Ñuñoa district, tel: (02) 326 5065, but there are also good places to hear jazz in the Bellavista district, such as **El Perseguidor** (www.elperseguidor.cl), tel: (02) 777 6763. In summer, there are open-air jazz concerts in Providencia on the banks of the Mapocho River.

Museums

Santiago has many historical and arts museums, mostly in the downtown area, but by far the best is the **Museo Chileno de Arte Precolombino** (*see page 151*). Just west of downtown, the Quinta Normal Park, created in 1841, has several museums. Children will enjoy this park, particularly the steam engines and train coaches in the **Museo Ferroviario**.

Rock and Pop

Batuta (www.batuta.cl) in Ñuñoa is one of Santiago's best places for live music; it's open from 10.30pm onwards, most nights except Sunday and Monday (Jorge Washington 52, tel: 02-274 7096). In Bellavista, there are also an abundance of bars where many new groups and bands give their first performances.

Theater

There are over 100 theaters in Santiago, putting on classical, modern, or avant-garde plays by Chilean and foreign playwrights, as well as outdoor performances in several city parks during January (take a cushion and warm clothing).

Theater in Santiago has traditionally been excellent, and Chileans are very proud of it. However, the number of theaters has mushroomed over recent years, and quality now varies.

If you don't have a great command of Spanish, there are plenty of lively, comical, and expressive performances to choose from. Have a look at the busking comedians in the Plaza de Armas on weekends, an interesting place for talent-spotting.

Tickets can usually be booked by phone without payment and are held for collection until half an hour before the performance starts.

Exhibition Listings

Most of the newspapers have listings of art exhibitions. The *Vivienda and Decoración* supplement with Saturday's *El Mercurio* has the most extensive listings.

Some of the best-equipped and most reliable theaters are:

Centro Cultural Matucana 100
Av. Matucana 100
Tel: (02) 682 4502
www.m100.cl

Teatro La Comedia
Merced 349
Tel: (02) 639 1523
www.teatroictus.cl

Teatro Antonio Varas
Morandé 25
Tel: (02) 696 1200
www.tnch.uchile.cl
Used by the University of Chile theater group.

Teatro de la Universidad Católica
Jorge Washington 26
Tel: (02) 205 5652
www.teuc.cl
Run by the Catholic University and stages some of the country's best productions.

There are also a large number of theaters in Bellavista that usually present new or modern pieces.

NIGHTLIFE

Santiago

Santiago nightlife might range from backgammon in Bellavista to a concert at the Teatro Municipal or a vanguard performance at the theater. Chileans also love to dance, and many do so very well, though typically as a couple performing well-known steps.

The night starts late in Santiago. Restaurants open at eight, but don't start to fill up until ten o'clock. For the young, that's still early.

Outside Santiago

Entertainment beyond the capital is very limited, except in the summer months, when the main beach and lake resorts get into gear. But even then, don't expect live theater or good cinema. Most of the activity centers around temporary discotheques and live productions of popular television music shows. One honorable exception is the music festival that the town of Frutillar on Lake Llanquihue puts on in late January, which is of a very high standard.

Nightclubs

Don't even consider going to a nightclub before midnight or one o'clock in the morning, and be prepared to dance until dawn. Those looking for a night's dancing can try any one of a vast number of nightclubs that spring up suddenly and often disappear just as quickly. Trends change rapidly, so ask around for advice on the best and the newest places, and the age group targeted.

A favorite place for dancing is **Blondie** (www.blondie.cl), Alameda 2879, local 104, while one of the currently fashionable spots is **Subterraneo** (www.subterraneo.cl), Paseo Orrego Luco 46, Providencia.

Santiago also has a number of popular salsa clubs such as **Havana Salsa**, Dominínica 142, Bellavista, tel: (02) 737 1737 and **Ilé Habana**,

Casinos

If you're in Arica, Antofagasta, Iquique, Coquimbo, Viña del Mar, Pucón, Puerto Varas, or Punta Arenas, you might want to try the casino, which besides the usual gaming activities also provides the center of local nightlife.

Bucarest 95, Providencia, tel: (02) 231 5711.

Floorshows

Santiago takes folklore from the provinces and turns it into live shows at a number of popular, but touristy restaurants:

Los Buenos Muchachos
Ricardo Cumming 1031
Tel: (02) 698 0112
www.losbuenosmuchachos.cl
Serves typical Chilean food accompanied by a floorshow.

Los Adobes de Argomedo
Argomedo 411
Tel: (02) 222 5235
www.losadobesdeargomedo.cl
Set in a huge barn-like hall, three orchestras and a dozen dancers perform on an extendable hydraulic stage, everything from Polynesian *hulas* to Chilean *cuecas*.

La Querencia
Av. Las Condes 14980
Tel: (02) 321 5522
www.laquerencia.cl
Serves good food and the live music is great for dancing.

Pubs

The Chilean version of a pub has mushroomed in recent years, encouraged by the greater availability of imported beers and increasing prosperity.

The bars on Suecia, in Providencia, are often recommended to visitors; discard that advice – the area used to be fashionable, but has degenerated into a center for drug dealing and prostitution, and, at night, is potentially dangerous. Instead, go further up Providencia where, a few steps down Luis Thayer Ojeda, toward the canal, you'll find a branch of the traditional **Liguria** bar. Alternatively, walk down Providencia to the junction with Manual Montt. There you'll find another Liguria and plenty of other good bars, such as **Ummo** on Pérez Valenzuela.

Another alternative is Plaza Ñuñoa. This is a US$5 taxi ride from Providencia, but you'll save that on the price of your drinks. This lovely

BELOW: Santiago has bars, pubs, and cafés to suit every taste.

square is surrounded by lively bars, catering for different age groups. Nearby is the **Batuta** *(see above)*.

The Las Condes pubs are more exclusive and expensive than their Providencia or Ñuñoa equivalents, but there's more space between tables, the food is better, and the waiters are professionals, rather than students. Try **Pub-Licity** on El Bosque Norte or **Play Back Studio**, Isidora Goyenechea 2901. **Flannery's Pub** (Encomenderos 83) is popular with both Chileans and the local "gringo" community. Alternatively, move up to the Vitacura area, where you'll find pubs such as the **Dublin Irish Pub**, Vitacura 9191.

Gay Scene

In Santiago, gay bars and restaurants include **Santo Remedio** on Román Díaz 152, two blocks in from Av. Providencia (tel: 02-235 0984), and **Mundano** on Dardignac 0127 (tel: 02-777 6218) in the Bellavista area, where most bars are also gay-friendly. **Sabor** on Purísima 218 is a lesbian restaurant. Gay discotheques include **Fausto** (Av. Santa María 0832), **Naxos** (Av. Bernardo O'Higgins 776), and **Bunker**, and **Femme by Bunker** (Bombero Nuñez 159) in Bellavista. Another favorite lesbian discotheque is **Máscaras** (Purísima 129), also in Bellavista.

SHOPPING

As in most other Latin American countries, shopping malls have sprung up in Chile over the past 20 years. With department stores as their anchor, along with multiplex cinemas and food courts, they're much like malls in the United States and are where the vast majority of better-off Chileans do their shopping. Similarly, supermarkets have gradually replaced corner grocery shops, most petrol stations now have convenience stores, and strip malls, typically with a bank branch, a pharmacy and a drycleaners as well as other small shops, abound.

The range of both domestic and imported products is wide and you'll be almost certain to find anything you forgot to pack.

Fair trading is a concept that is only just beginning to gain ground in Chile but Artesanías de Chile, a foundation, with three outlets in the city, does ensure that its artisans get a proper price for their work.

Sales tax (VAT) is 19 percent and is already included in the displayed price. Under Chilean consumer law, shops must sell at the price on display so insist on your rights if it doesn't match what you're being charged.

What to Buy

Chile's rich geology provides a wide diversity of minerals for handicrafts. Most outstanding are lapis lazuli (which is found only in Chile and Afghanistan), silver, bronze, and wrought copper.

Other popular souvenirs include:
• Traditional pottery from different regions.
• The colorful attire of the *huaso* (Chilean cowboy) from the South Central Valley, some of which can be bought in local *talabarterías* (saddlers' shops).
• Leather goods, boots, and handbags, available in the high-street stores and malls of Santiago.
• The beautifully worked silver jewelry of the Mapuches.
• Chilean wine and pisco, the local grape liquor.

What Not to Buy

Pavement vendors offer a wide variety of pirated products, ranging from books and DVDs to imitation Louis Vuitton handbags. This is a thriving industry and the standard of many products is high and their prices attractive. However, buying from these vendors is, in theory, an offence – although charges are rarely pressed – and is a violation of intellectual property rights for which the US has put Chile on an international blacklist.

Where to Shop

The largest malls in eastern Santiago are Parque Arauco and Alto Las Condes, both on Avenida Kennedy while the nearby Vitacura district is the place for upscale shopping. Here you'll find names like Emporio Armani and Louis Vuitton as well as some of the city's best jewelers. For a more

Lapis Lazuli

Lapis lazuli is crafted in the workshops of Bellavista into many things, not only jewelry. The quality and value of the stone depends on the intensity or depth of the color, i.e. a very dark stone is more valuable than a stone that has a paler color.

ABOVE: woven bags for sale.

Bohemian environment, try the Bellavista district, with its craft stores, lapis lazuli shops, and tiny art galleries.

Crafts

On Santiago's Avenida Apoquindo 9085, next to the church of San Vicente Ferrer, **El Pueblito de Los Dominicos** is a collection of old-style buildings, comprising about 150 shops where more than 300 craftsmen and women work before the public. Handicrafts, antiques, and plants are for sale. At weekends there is music and dancing, and empanadas (savory turnovers) for sale. Open daily; see www. pueblitolosdominicos.com.

By far the best place to buy handicrafts in Santiago, both as regards quality and price, is: **Artesanías de Chile**, Av. Bellavista 0357, tel: (02) 777 8643, www. artesaniasdechile.cl. This shop, which also has branches in El Pueblito de Los Dominicos and in the Centro Cultural Palacio de Moneda in downtown Santiago, is run by a foundation that not only markets handicrafts, but also advises artisans on how to improve their work and obtain a fair price.

You'll also find a wide selection of handicrafts in the Patio Bellavista restaurant and arts complex, Pío Nono 40-50, tel: (02) 777 4582. Outside Santiago, the best place to shop for crafts is in local markets.

Antiques

Antique shops are plentiful in Santiago, usually grouped in specific neighborhoods. Try Avenida Brasil or in and around the Galpones Balmaceda (Balmaceda 2500), in the western part of Santiago. Centro Lo Castillo, on the

ABOVE: markets and artesan stores are a good place to find traditional handicrafts.

corner of Candelaría Goyenechea and Vitacura, is a good hunting-ground, if you prefer to go upmarket.

Shopping Malls

For clothing and more general shopping, there are several modern shopping centers, incorporating a huge number of stores.

Parque Arauco
Av. Presidente Kennedy 5413
Tel: (02) 299 0500
www.parquearauco.cl
A shopping mall, containing three department stores and more than 200 specialty stores/boutiques. Take metro Line 1 to Escuela Militar station and then the C11 service which runs from there.

Alto Las Condes
Av. Kennedy 9001
Tel: (02) 299 6965
www.altolascondes.cl
The same stores as Parque Arauco. Take a *colectivo* from the Escuela Militar metro station (there is no direct bus).

Vitacura Neighborhood

The city's most prestigious shops are located on Nueva Costanera and Alonso de Córdova in the Vitacura neighborhood, alongside art galleries, smart coffee shops, and bars. The majority of stores are open Monday through Friday 10am–8.30pm, Saturday 9.30am–2pm. The city center and Providencia are also important shopping areas.

Bookshops

A good range of English-language books is hard to find, but there are a few interesting outlets:

Librería Books, Av. Providencia 1652, Local 5. Offers second-hand English books.
Librería Inglesa, Av. Pedro de Valdivia 47; Vitacura 5950; Huérfanos 669 local 11. Classic literature and bestsellers. www.libreriainglesa.cl
Librairie Française, Alto Las Condes shopping center, local 2019, second floor; Av. Luis Pasteur 5399; Estado 337, local 22. Sells books in French. www.libreriafrancesa.cl
Books & Bits, Av. Apoquindo 6856. Sells books in English. www.booksandbits.cl

Photography

There are many one-hour or one-day photo processors along Huérfanos and Ahumada, in the shopping malls and most large supermarkets. Camera supplies are available along McIver and Merced. Harry Muller, Ahumada 312, Oficina 402, provides a camera-repair service and speaks English and German.

Jewelry and Stonecraft

For lapis lazuli in Santiago:
The main shopping area for lapis lazuli is along Bellavista between Del Arzobispo and Pío Nono, but for more upmarket products, try the Parque Arauco and Alto Las Condes shopping malls.
For copper handicrafts:
Bozzo, Av. Providencia 2231, tel: (02) 233 2393. Also in the Parque Arauco shopping mall. www.bozzochocolates.cl
H. Stern jewelry is available at the large hotels, as well as the international airport.
For silver Mapuche jewelry
The different branches of **Artesanías**

de Chile or the shop in of the Ritz-Carlton Hotel, Alcalde 15, right off Av. Apoquindo.

Department Stores

Chile has three main department stores – Falabella, Paris, and Ripley – all of which offer very similar products at virtually identical prices. They have shops in the main malls as well as in the downtown area and Providencia.

Markets

Santiago's markets are not a patch on those you'll find in provincial cities, particularly in the south. They have less atmosphere and some of the goods on display, particularly the jewelry, were probably made in China. The best, however, are the **Aldea de Vitacura**, Av. Vitacura 6840, open daily 11am–9pm; the **Centro Artesanal Santa Lucía**, just across Alameda from the base of Cerro Santa Lucía, open daily 10am–7pm; and the **Feria Artesanal Pío Nono** at the start of Av. Pío Nono in Bellavista, which is liveliest in the evenings and at weekends.

SPORTS

Spectator Sports

Certain spectator sports are overwhelmingly popular in Chile. Consider a visit to the Club Hípico, the top-class horse-racing circuit in the capital; experience the enthusiasm of 70,000 football fans at Santiago's main stadium; or enjoy the spectacle of a colorful rodeo on your travels through the Central Valley. It would be difficult to exaggerate the pride Chileans have for these sports in particular.

Horse Racing

There are races at the **Club Hípico**, Av. Blanco Encalada 2540 (tel: 02-693 9600; www.clubhipico.cl) every Monday, Wednesday, and Sunday from January to March. The less exclusive **Hipódromo Chile**, Av. Fermin Vivaceta 2753 (tel: 02-270 8500; www.hipodromo.cl), has racing every Thursday and Saturday afternoon.

The quality of horse breeding in Chile is world famous. A special tour is possible to **Los Lingues** (www.loslingues.cl), a private *hacienda* (ranch) 120km (75 miles) south of Santiago, where it is said the best horses in Chile are bred. Arrangements can be made in Santiago (Av. Providencia 1100, Torre C, Oficina 205, tel: 02-431 0510) for a one-day excursion, which includes lunch, transportation, and a horse show for around US$67 per person, but don't let them persuade you to stay overnight at the hotel; it's expensive and very substandard.

Soccer

Soccer is easily the most popular sport in Chile, attracting vast crowds, who wear their team colors, carry flags and signs, and chant all day and late into the evening. Processions of enthusiasts will come storming into the Plaza Italia sounding like a political rally. Most football clubs have their own stadiums but the most important local games and international games are played at the **Estadio Nacional** in Ñuñoa, which also has tennis courts and a cycle track.

Participant Sports

Golf

Santiago and nearby seaside resorts have some wonderful golf courses, but they belong to private clubs or exclusive housing developments and are not open to the public. Most of the city's more expensive hotels do, however, have arrangements for guests who wish to play.

Tennis

Chileans love tennis and there are plenty of moderately-priced courts. They include the **Club de Tenis y Squash Lo Cañas**, Av. Monseñor Escrivá de Balaguer 5000, Vitacura, tel: (02) 242 2121, and the **Ciudad Deportiva Iván Zamorano,** Av. Padre Hurtado 2650, Las Condes, tel: (02)

340 6300. Court rentals cost around US$15 per hour.

OUTDOOR EXCURSIONS

Chile's long sea coast and its lakes and rivers are conducive to water sports, such as water-skiing, windsurfing, rowing, white-water rafting, canoeing, skin diving, fishing, and swimming.

There are numerous quality ski resorts in the Andes mountains. Facilities include ski-lifts and luxury lodges, and many are also blessed with outstanding scenery. The same mountains challenge hikers and climbers with a choice of gentle trails or some of the most rugged peaks in the world.

For nature lovers and trekkers, the country's national parks offer a wide variety of landscapes, ranging from the desert north to the forests and glaciers of the far south. The parks are managed by the Corporación Nacional Forestal (CONAF), the national park service, and most offer camping facilities for a small charge, and some also have cabins. See www.conaf.cl (in Spanish).

Adventure Sports

A number of tour operators in Santiago specialize in outdoor activities, offering activities that range from a half-day's rafting near Santiago to longer excursions, including trekking, horseback riding and kayaking. Two of the largest and most

BELOW: trekking in Patagonia.

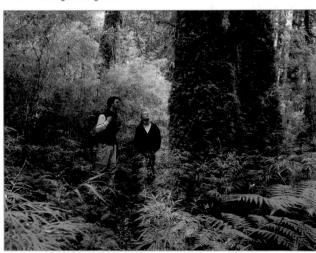

Sightseeing Tours

Sightseeing tours are best organized through tour operators in the nearest town or city *(see A–Z, pages 345–52)*. Itineraries and the sights they include are generally similar and the cost varies little.

comprehensive are:
Altué Active Travel
General Salvo 159
Tel: (02) 235 1519
www.altue.com
Latitud 90
Av. Kennedy 7268
Tel: (02) 599 4664
www.latitud90.com

Birding

Although Chile has a wealth of bird life, birding (birdwatching) is only an incipient activity and is almost always arranged by overseas operators. However, two local companies offer tours:
Cascada Expediciones
Don Carlos 3219, Las Condes
Tel: (02) 232 9878
www.cascada.travel
Agencia de Viajes Aqua Motion
San Francisco 328
Puerto Varas
Tel: (065) 232 747
www.aquamotion.cl

Fishing

The rivers and lakes of southern Chile are very popular for flyfishing and

Andean Crossing

The most interesting way of traveling to Argentina is by a combination of buses and boats, which start by crossing Lago Todos Los Santos. This journey can be made in either one or two days, finishing in Bariloche, Argentina.

there are many lodges, catering mostly for overseas visitors. Prices are high, but standards of service are excellent. They include the **Yan Kee Way Lodge** on Lake Llanquihue (www.yankeeway.com) and, further south on Lake Yelcho, the **Isla Monita Lodge** (www.islamonita.cl).

Hiking

The Torres del Paine National Park is the queen of Chile's hiking territory. Two of the companies offering expeditions there are:
Big Foot Adventure Patagonia
Bories 206
Puerto Natales
Tel: (061) 414 525
www.bigfootpatagonia.com
Patagonia Adventure Expeditions
Riquelme 372
Coyhaique
Tel: (067) 411 330
www.adventurepatagonia.com

Horseback Riding

Many tour operators offer horseback riding excursions in the Andes and even, across the mountains to Argentina, but another beautiful

place for rides is the Island of Chiloé, especially the Parque Nacional Chiloé and the beach at Cucao on the Pacific coast. Tour operators on Chiloé include:
Turismo Pehuén
Esmeralda 198
Castro
Tel: (065) 635 254
www.turismopehuen.cl
For horseback riding expeditions in the Central Valley, try the lovely **Hacienda Ecuestre La Esperanza** in Pelluhue in the Maule Region (tel: 09-9158 3467; www.haciendaecuestre.cl).

Mountain Biking

Pared Sur has many years of experience in organizing mountain bike tours in different parts of Chile and other Latin America countries. It provides bikes, although you can also use your own. Tel: (02) 207 3525; www.paredsur.cl.

Mountaineering

The best advice about mountaineering in Chile can be obtained from the **Federación de Andinismo de Chile** in Santiago (Almirante Simpson 77, Providencia; tel 02-222 0888; www.feach.cl). Their members often organize expeditions for both amateurs and professional climbers.

Paragliding

Paragliding is practiced in Chile from the far north of the country to as far south as the Biobío Region and there

are many schools and companies that offer flights. Look for operators certified by the Asociación Chilena de Vuelo Libre. Iquique in the north, and the Cachagua beach resort in central Chile are particularly popular destinations for this sport.

Skiing and Snowboarding

The main ski resorts near Santiago offer great opportunities for both skiing and snowboarding in a season that usually runs from June to September; further south, there are also resorts like Termas de Chillán and the smaller Antillanca center. A useful source of information is www.chileanski.com.

Watersports

Chile is a paradise for water sports. Pucón on Lake Villarrica is an important center but for some lovely and more unusual boat trips, try the small islands and inlets off Chiloé. Turismo Pehuén *(see above)* offers different trips each day of the week. This is also a popular area for sea kayaking. Expeditions are organized by:
Agencia de Viajes Aqua Motion
San Francisco 328
Puerto Varas
Tel: (065) 232 747
www.aquamotion.cl

White-water Rafting

The most popular rivers for rafting are the Maipo near Santiago, the Trancura near Pucón, the Petrohué near Puerto Varas and, in Aisén, the Futaleufú. Operators include:
Cascada Expediciones
Don Carlos 3219, Las Condes
Tel: (02) 232 9878
www.cascada.travel
Expediciones Chile
Gabriela Mistral 296
Futaleufú
Tel: (065) 562 639
www.exchile.com

Wildlife Viewing

Cascada Expediciones is one of a still small number of companies offering wildlife viewing excursions.

Check your Itinerary

Before you embark on a tour, check with the organizer that you will get to see everything described on the list. Plans are liable to change more frequently than printed schedules.

BELOW: zip-lining in the Cajón del Maipo.

A – Z

A HANDY SUMMARY OF PRACTICAL INFORMATION, ARRANGED ALPHABETICALLY

A ddresses

Most Chilean towns and cities are built as a grid of parallel streets, making it easy to find your way around. Street numbers – odd on one side, even on the other – progress steadily, with 100 to a block. The only complication is that the numbers can be divided when a street is crossed by a main road, starting with 1 on one side and 01 on the other. The letters s/n stand for *sin número* and are used where there is no street number in the address, usually in smaller towns.

Admission Charges

Admission charges in Chile are rarely expensive and there are mostly reductions for students and senior citizens. In some museums, admission is free on Sundays.

B udgeting for Your Trip

Since around 2004, Chile has gradually become more expensive as its currency has strengthened as a result of economic stability and the high price of copper, its main export. As a result, it is now one of the more expensive countries in Latin America. Public transport is still very cheap by European standards, and restaurant prices are moderate but hotels, in particular, have become far more expensive.

C hildren

Chileans make a great fuss of children and they are made welcome everywhere, except in expensive restaurants where they will be frowned on even at lunchtime. Menus don't usually include children's meals but efforts will be made to accommodate them. Admission for children is free or reduced-price in museums.

Climate

When to Visit
As a general rule, Chile's climate makes a steady transition from the extreme arid heat of the desert north to the bitterly cold and wet conditions of the far south. Most of the country can be visited at any time of the year, except Aisén, Magallanes, and Tierra de Fuego. In the far north, the so-called "Bolivian winter" in January or February can bring torrential rain, but usually only lasts for a few days.

The North
Rainfall is virtually non-existent in the Atacama Desert. Typical desert conditions prevail all year round, with searingly hot days and chilly nights. High winds shift the desert sands and make northern highways more dangerous for motoring. The northern skies are generally very clear,

Electricity

220 volts/50Hz is the standard current throughout the country. Chile uses the round two-pin plug. Travelers from the UK and the US will need to bring an adaptor.

CLIMATE CHART

Legend:
- ■ Maximum temperature
- □ Minimum temperature
- — Rainfall

although on the far northern coast, at Arica, there is higher humidity and frequent cloud cover. Temperatures here are less extreme, from 15°C (59°F) to 22°C (72°F). At the same latitudes, towards the Bolivian border, snow often covers the high mountain passes.

Central Valley

The area, known as the transitional zone, between Copiapó and Illapel, only receives light winter rainfall, and agriculture is therefore dependent on artificial irrigation.

Immediately south, the lush central region continues through to Concepción with higher inland temperatures and ever-increasing rainfall from north to south. The climate is idyllically Mediterranean, mild and temperate, the warmest months being November to February, when the temperatures can reach 34°C (93°F). July and August are the coolest months, with temperatures as low as 10°C (50°F) during the day. Nights are rather cool, even in summer.

The best months in Santiago are between October and April, when the days are nearly always fine – although December and January can be uncomfortably hot in the congested city center.

The summer heat is more tolerable on the coast at the famous seaside resorts, with fresh cooling breezes. The weather is excellent for skiing during the winter months at the resorts of Portillo, Farellones, and Valle Nevado, east of Santiago.

Lake District

As far south as Puerto Montt, the Lake District has a temperate climate, although heavy rain falls throughout much of the year. The temperature is cooler than in the central region, and icy winds originate from the lakes and mountains. Winter brings snow to the chalet-style resorts in the higher regions of Petrohué, Puella, and Lago Todos los Santos, and some Andean highways between Chile and Argentina can become snowbound or otherwise impassable due to fog and storms.

Chiloé

The islands of Chiloé are cold and foggy for most of the year, but for about 60 days, usually from December to March, when the sun shines, the countryside is especially picturesque. Chiloé is a particularly rainy place, especially along its western, Pacific coast.

Aisén

South of Puerto Montt, the region of Aisén has a steppe climate, with fairly low temperatures all year round. Abundant snow falls from early autumn to late spring, so the best months to visit are November to March. Summer brings beautifully crisp, clear days to the region, although cold winds and torrential rainstorms can also occur unpredictably. Worth noting is the agreeable microclimate found around the village of Chile Chico, which is suitable for growing fine fruit and vegetables.

Magallanes

In this region of glaciers and wilderness, snow covers the land in winter (except along the coastline), while rain is frequent in summer, and freezing winds of up to 80kph (50mph) are common in spring. The climate and scenery have been likened to those of Norway. It is best to visit the far south in December, January, or February, when the sun is higher in the sky and the summer average temperature climbs to 11°C (52°F).

Easter Island

This isolated Pacific Island has a semi-tropical climate throughout the year, with a particularly fierce sun that is not to be underestimated. July and August are the coolest months for wandering among the *moai*.

What to Wear

Most middle-class Latin Americans spend a great deal of their income on their appearance. Travelers aren't expected to appear as immaculately groomed as residents; however, it's sensible, especially in Santiago, to take a little extra care. You might receive better service in some establishments if you dress more formally, or if your casual wear is fairly smart. If in doubt about the dress requirements, err on the formal side. Chileans are naturally conservative dressers.

BELOW: Chiloé experiences its best weather between December and March.

ABOVE: Chile's national flag: the lone star.

Crime and Safety

Visitors to Chile, especially its larger cities, should watch out for their belongings but need not worry about their personal safety as, although theft is quite common, the rate of violent crime is one of the lowest in Latin America. In other words, just take basic precautions: watch out for pickpockets in crowded places and don't hang bags on the back of your chair in restaurants. It is also better to avoid out-of-the-way areas at night.

Customs Regulations

During your flight you will fill out a customs declaration form and supply identity details on your tourist card. The allowed quota of duty-free goods extends to 400 cigarettes, 50 cigars, 2.5 liters of liquor, and all items for personal use.

It is prohibited to import meat products, flowers, fruit, vegetables, and seeds. Most overseas visitors with "nothing to declare" find no delays in passing through customs. Chilean wine and finely crafted stones such as lapis lazuli are popular souvenirs.

D isabled Travelers

Although progress is slowly being made, Chile can be difficult for disabled visitors, especially outside Santiago. Most large hotels present no problems but not all public buildings have access facilities. New buses in Santiago have pavement-level access but, in other places and on intercity services, the steps are high (although help will usually be provided) and only some stations on the Metro, the city's subway, have access facilities. Before booking an air ticket, check the airline's policy; there have been unfortunate cases in which disabled passengers have not been allowed to board on grounds of lack of mobility or self-sufficiency.

E arthquakes

Chile is earthquake territory, and tremors, sometimes quite strong, are fairly frequent. Rule number one – don't panic! Modern buildings are earthquake-resistant – although that implies elasticity, and high floors can "swing" uncomfortably – and older buildings have already proved their capacity for survival.

In buildings: take cover under door-frames or sturdy furniture such as tables, and try to keep as far away as possible from windows or glass doors; on no account use elevators. In built-up areas: do not walk out in the street because of the danger of falling rubble, and keep clear of trees and electric cables. On country roads: avoid bridges or any elevated sections of highway.

Embassies and Consulates

In Santiago

Argentina
Miraflores 285
Tel: (02) 582 2500.
Australia
Isidora Goyenechea 3621, Pisos 12 & 13
Tel: (02) 550 3500.
Bolivia (Consulate only)
Av. Santa María 2796
Tel: (02) 232 8180.
Brazil
Alonso Ovalle 1665
Tel: (02) 698 2486.

Canada
Nueva Tajamar 481, Torre Norte, Piso 12
Tel: (02) 652 3800.
New Zealand
El Golf 99, Office 703
Tel: (02) 290 9800.
Peru
Av. Andrés Bello 1751
Tel: (02) 339 2600.
South Africa
Av. 11 de Septiembre 2353, Piso 16
Tel: (02) 231 2862.
UK
El Bosque Norte 0125
Tel: (02) 370 4100.
US
Av. Andrés Bello 2800
Tel: (02) 330 3000.

Chilean Embassies Abroad

Australia
10 Culgoa Circuit O'Malley ACT 2606, Canberra
Tel: 61(2) 628 62430
Canada
50 O'Connor Street, Suite 1413, Ottawa, Ontario
Tel: 1(613) 235 4402
New Zealand
19 Bolton St., Wellington
Tel: 64(4) 471 6270
UK
12 Devonshire Street, London W1G 7DS
Tel: 44 (20) 7580 6392
US
1732 Massachusetts Avenue, N.W
Washington, D.C. 20036
Tel: 1-202 785 1746

Etiquette

Chileans have a warm but clearly defined way of greeting. Men and women meeting, or women greeting women, will kiss one another once on the cheek. Men greeting men will always shake hands. When dealing with officials, you'll find the response more agreeable if you say *buenos días* (good day), and wait for the reply before you continue speaking. Chileans are not as

Emergencies

For any emergency services, call the following numbers:
Ambulance Service: 131
Fire Brigade: 132
Police: 133/134
Police Information: 139
Tourist Card Extension: Passport Office, Moneda 1342, tel: (02) 697 0403. Hours: Mon–Fri 8.30am–2pm.

unpunctual as other Latin Americans, but are still likely to be half an hour late for social appointments. When invited to a Chilean home, never arrive early; it's far better to be late.

G ay and Lesbian Travelers

Even by Latin American standards, Chile is still very much in the closet with regards to homosexuality. Attitudes among young people are changing rapidly, but older men particularly can be homophobic. However, there are an increasing number of gay and gay-friendly bars, restaurants, and discotheques in Santiago, especially in the Bellavista area.

H ealth and Medical Care

Chile is one of the safest countries in South America as regards health concerns. There is no malaria or yellow fever, the tap water in most cities is chlorinated, and the general standard of hygiene is high. The country is fortunate in producing an abundance of fresh fruit and vegetables in its Central Valley region, while meat products are also plentiful, thus ensuring quality foods for most people.

Precautions

Most travelers go without vaccinations. Some people have hepatitis and typhoid shots, although the possibility of encountering these diseases is remote, as long as you avoid unwashed salads. The tap water in Santiago is safe to drink, although sensitive systems should use bottled mineral water and avoid the adjustment period.

Sudden changes in diet and lifestyle often cause temporary **bowel disorders**, which are rarely anything to worry about and just a typical part of travel. The best remedy is to eat very little and drink plenty of liquid in small sips for a day or so. Tea without milk or flat lemonade are ideal. Symptoms should improve within 48 hours. If the problem lasts longer than a week, antibiotics or a visit to the doctor may be necessary.

Hot and Cold

The only other problems come from Chile's extreme climate and geography. In the Atacama Desert and on Easter Island, the heat can cause serious **exhaustion** and **sunburn**. Don't overestimate your skin's resistance. Bring sufficient water, sunscreen, a hat, and preferably sunglasses, too. Even thus prepared, the sun and heat can be trying to the

mildest of temperaments. Take things slowly and don't expect to achieve as much as usual.

In the far south, from Puerto Montt to Tierra del Fuego, the bitter cold in mountain areas and at all altitudes in winter can cause **hypothermia** to those who are unprotected: symptoms include exhaustion, numbness, slurred speech, and shivering. High winds are notorious in Patagonia, often carrying icy rain and sleet, so bring protective clothing to cover your head and body. Again, it's best to move more slowly, staying aware of your energy level. Mountain climbers should take the usual precautions.

Altitude

Though not as severe as the altitudes of Bolivia or Peru, some popular sightseeing spots in the north, and some Andean passes between Chile and Argentina, are high enough to cause slight **altitude sickness** in some people. The symptoms can become noticeable from around 900 meters (3,000ft), and include shortness of breath, headache, weakness, and mild nausea. Aspirin is one of the best remedies for mild altitude sickness. In rare cases, severe altitude sickness is indicated by dizziness and intensity of the other symptoms. The immediate treatment for this condition is to move to a lower altitude.

Medical Treatment

The Chilean national health service is generally of a reasonable standard. Hospitals have outpatient departments, which will treat visitors' accidents and emergencies, but are likely to be much busier than private clinics. Ask your embassy or hotel to recommend doctors who speak English.

Pharmacies in Chile are usually well stocked with the latest medical supplies, and most products are available without a prescription. Many pharmacies remain open until midnight, and some operate round the clock. Ask your hotel for a list of addresses. There are also increasingly popular homeopathic outlets in most cities.

Clinics in Santiago

For a private clinic contact:
• Clínica Las Condes, Lo Fontecilla 441, tel: (02) 210 4000.
• Clínica Santa María, Av. Santa María 0500, tel: (02) 461 2000.
• Clínica Alemana, Av. Vitacura 5951, tel: (02) 210 1111.

I nsurance

All travelers should invest in comprehensive travel insurance, which is available through travel agents. Check that this will cover the cost of your return flight if you're flown home in an emergency, as well as covering stolen or damaged valuables.

Internet

Internet access is ubiquitous and cheap in Chile. Even in small towns, Internet cafés abound and, in Santiago, the main shopping malls and some cinema complexes have facilities. In addition, Wi-Fi access has spread rapidly and there are, for example, clearly-marked hot spots in subway stations and Santiago's international airport. However, beware of hotel business centers which tend to charge grossly inflated rates.

L ost Property

Although Santiago's subway and airports have lost property offices, the chances are that, if you've left something behind, you've lost it. It's worth marking objects like cameras with your name and a telephone number so an honest finder can call you, but don't bother with the police station, except in small towns.

M aps

Maps are available at the Santiago office of Sernatur, the national tourist board, which is located at Providencia 1550.
• The *Plano del Gran Santiago* (city map), which can be purchased at most newsstands, shows the city center and inner suburbs, and metro lines. Outside Santiago, Sernatur branch offices can supply free city maps.
• Addresses in Santiago can be found on www.mapcity.cl, a free website, from which maps can also be printed.
• The *Gran Mapa Caminero de Chile* is the most practical map of Chile – also available at newsstands.
• Excellent road maps are available from the Automóvil Club de Chile, Av. Andrés Bello 1863, Santiago, tel: (600) 464 4040.
• Turistel is the name of a series of Chilean guidebooks (in Spanish) which contain maps, details of accommodations ranging from campsites to hotels, and other tourist information.
• Gas stations sell road maps.
• Topographical maps are sold by the Instituto Geográfico Militar in

Santiago (sales office: Nueva Santa Isabel 1640, tel: 02-410 9300).

Media

Broadcast

There are many AM and FM radio stations currently broadcasting in the country. The radio stations play mostly rock and pop music. As you would expect, the popular stations, such as Pudahuel, concentrate on Spanish-speaking singers and groups, while their upmarket competitors offer a more international variety. Only three stations – radios Beethoven, Universidad de Chile, and Universidad de Santiago – regularly broadcast classical music. For news bulletins, try either the popular Cooperativa, a stalwart that goes back to the dictatorship days when it dared say things that other stations didn't, or Radio Chilena.

If you're out in the country, listen to the local radio stations. In remote areas, people use them to keep in touch, and you'll get an interesting insight into local life.

Television

Chile has six main television channels, two of which transmit only news. Of the other four, TVN (Televisión Nacional) is state-owned, while Canal 13 belongs to the Catholic University, and the other two, Chilevisión and Mega, to local business groups. The programming of all four is relatively similar, although Mega targets lower-income groups.

Print

Chile has seven main national newspapers, as well as around 50 provincial dailies. One of the most widely read is the conservative morning daily *El Mercurio*, which first appeared in 1827. Every Friday it publishes a supplement called *Wikén* (weekend), which provides information about events in Santiago.

Other newspapers include *La Tercera* and *La Nación*, as well as two business newspapers, *El Diario Financiero and Estrategia*. An afternoon paper, *La Segunda*, circulates in Santiago and a free morning newspaper is distributed on the city's subway.

Weekly magazines include *Qué Pasa* and *Ercilla*, while *Newsweek* and *Time* are readily available in Spanish and English. In central Santiago's Paseo Ahumada, newsstands offer a wide variety of slightly out-of-date international newspapers.

Money

Money can be exchanged in hotels, exchange bureaux *(casas de cambio)*, and banks. The rate varies little between establishments, although it might not be quite as good at hotels. Banks are open to the public Monday through Friday 9am–2pm. If you have a credit card, cash can be withdrawn from ubiquitous automatic cash machines, which also take most bank cash cards.

Casas de Cambio

If you don't have a credit card, exchange bureaux are probably the best choice. They are usually found within travel agencies and are open Mon–Fri 9.30am–2pm and 3.30–5.30pm. In Santiago, exchange offices and banks are located mostly in the central business district and

Providencia, but there are also exchange offices in the main shopping malls. Money can be sent to major banks from other parts of the world with minimum delays.

US dollars are the most easily exchanged unit of currency throughout Chile. In Santiago, it's possible to exchange pounds sterling, Australian dollars, yen, and other currencies at banks, but elsewhere you'll need US dollars cash.

Public Holidays

January 1 New Year's Day
Easter Good Friday, Easter Sunday
May 1 Labor Day
May 21 Commemoration of Iquique sea battle; opening of Congress
June Monday closest to St Peter and St Paul
July 16 Day of the Virgin of Carmen (Chile's patron saint)
August 15 Ascension of the Virgin
September 18 Independence Day
September 19 Army Day with parade
October 12 Discovery of America
October 31 Reformation Day
November 1 All Saints' Day
December 8 Immaculate Conception
December 25 Christmas Day

Opening Hours

Banks are open to the public Monday through Friday 9am–2pm. Exchange bureaux are open Monday through Friday 9.30am–2pm and 3.30–5.30pm, except in the main shopping malls, where they open until 9pm and at weekends.

BELOW: shopping in Santiago.

Government offices are usually open to the public only in the mornings (8.30am–1.30pm). Other businesses are open Monday to Friday 8.30am–1.30pm and then 3–6pm.

Most **shops** in Santiago are open Monday to Friday 10.30am–7.30pm and 9.30am–1.30pm on Saturday. In the major shopping centers, such as Parque Arauco and Alto Las Condes, shops are open throughout the week, including on Sunday, until 9pm.

P ostal Services

The Chilean postal service is more reliable than that of most South American countries. Mail sent by air *(por aéreo)* takes around seven days to the US and UK or 10 days to Australia. Sea mail takes about 10 weeks. There is a daily air mail service to Europe with connections to the UK.

The general delivery service, or poste restante *(Lista de Correos)*, is located in the Correo Central (central post office) on the Plaza de Armas, in Santiago. The system is fairly well organized, although they will hold your mail no longer than 30 days before returning to sender. Opening times vary, but most are open Monday to Friday, 9am to 6pm and on Saturday morning. No offices are open on Sunday.

R eligious Services

Mass is celebrated at least once a day, and several times on Sunday, in most Catholic churches. In Santiago, a number of Protestant churches also hold services in English. These include the Santiago Community Church, Av. Holanda 151, tel: (02) 232 1113 (Sunday 10.30am), and the San Marcos Presbyterian Church, Padre Hurtado Central 599, tel: (02) 220 2228 (Sunday 9.15am).

S tudent Travelers

Holders of an International Student Identity Card or International Youth Travel Card are entitled to reduced entrance fees at most museums and discounts at some restaurants, cinemas, discotheques, bookshops, and tourist agencies. Cut-price airline tickets and more information can be obtained at the Student Flight Center, Hernando de Aguirre 201, Of. 602, Santiago, tel: (02) 411 2050.

T ax

VAT (19 percent) is already incorporated into prices displayed in shops

ABOVE: cheap hostels are a good option for student travelers.

but not always in hotel rates where foreigners are exempt. Airport tax is almost always included in the ticket price, except for an entry tax levied on visitors from some specific countries (*see page 328*). If traveling by car on Chile's main highways, make sure you have enough cash for tolls (mostly around US$4 each) and note that credit cards are not accepted.

Telecommunications

International Calls

Calls overseas can be made direct from public telephones and from call centers. You must prefix the code of the carrier you want to handle your call: there are over 30, but the largest – although not necessarily the cheapest – are Entel (its code is 123) and CTC (188). It is possible to call collect (reverse the charges), and the quality of the lines is excellent. Off-peak rates apply after 8pm on weekdays, after 2pm on Saturday, and all day on Sunday.

Faxes

Faxes are easy to send, although there is an added charge on most public fax services, which can make them quite expensive. Facilities are available at Entel and CTC call centers, in most large supermarkets, some service stations, and at photocopying shops.

Tipping

In restaurants, service is not generally included and a 10 percent tip is usual. Taxi drivers do not expect to be tipped, but it's usual not to ask for small change.

Toilets

Public toilets (*baños*) are a rarity in Chile, but bars and cafés will usually let you use their facilities. In bus and railway stations the toilets are manned by an attendant who provides you with toilet paper for a small fee.

Tour Operators and Travel Agents

Chile's main travel agents are all based in Santiago and include:
Cocha
El Bosque Norte 0430
Tel: 600 464 1000
www.cocha.com
One of the best options for booking international flights; also has offices in Viña del Mar and Concepción.

Regions of Chile

Chile is divided into the following 15 administrative regions. The capital of each region is given in brackets.
I Tarapacá (Iquique)
II Antofagasta (Antofagasta)
III Atacama (Copiapó)
IV Coquimbo (La Serena)
V Valparaíso (Valparaíso)
VI O'Higgins (Rancagua)
VII Maule (Talca)
VIII Biobío (Concepción)
IX Araucanía (Temuco)
X Los Lagos (Puerto Montt)
XI Aisén (Coyhaique)
XII Magallanes y Antártica Chilena (Punta Arenas)
XIII Santiago (Santiago)
XIV Los Ríos (Valdivia)
XV Arica and Parinacota (Arica)

Latitud 90
Av. Kennedy 7268
Tel: (02) 599 4664
www.latitud90.com
Well-organized tours, with English-speaking guides, but significantly more expensive than other options.

Turismo Mostrando Chile
Antonio Varas 175, Of. 1205
Tel: (02) 235 0624
www.turismomostrandochile.cl
This agency specializes in tours within Chile, but also offers some to neighboring countries.

La Casa Roja
Agustinas 2113
Tel: (02)696 4241
www.lacasaroja.cl
This hostel has an excellent travel agency geared to backpackers.

In Santiago, you could be blinded by the choice of tour services, but they offer basically the same tours, including a city tour, which starts from your hotel and visits many of the landmarks listed in the Places section of this book. The cost is around US$30. Night tours include a view from the top of Cerro San Cristóbal and a restaurant meal with floorshow for around US$70. There are various day excursions to Viña del Mar and Valparaíso, visiting the lush Chilean vineyards en route, which include lunch at an elegant restaurant for around US$120.

The Sernatur Tourist Office will give you a long list; some tour operators and travel agencies have offices in the main hotels.

You'll also find a whole range of tour operators in San Pedro de Atacama, most of whom also offer very similar itineraries and services.

Atacama Desert Expedition
Tocopilla 411
Tel: (055) 851 045

Cosmo Andino Expediciones
Calle Caracoles s/n, and Tocopilla
www.cosmoandino-expediciones.cl
Tel: (055) 851 069

Famous for its beaches, La Serena is also a center for visits to the Tololo, Gemini South, Las Campanas, and La Silla astronomical observatories and the Elqui Valley, renowned for its pisco (a grape-based liquor) and the birthplace of the famous poet Gabriela Mistral.

Elqui Valley Tour
Los Carrera 515
www.elquivalleytour.cl
Tel: (051) 214 846

Intimahina Travel
Arturo Prat 214
www.itravel.cl
Tel: (051) 224 350

Pucón is a resort town that comes alive during the holiday season. In summer, the tour operators run groups to the various *termas* (thermal springs), or to participate in adventure sports like white-water rafting and volcano climbing.

Expediciones École
General Urrutia 592
Tel: (045) 441 675
www.ecole.cl

Politur
O'Higgins 635
Tel: (045) 441 373
www.politur.com

Puerto Natales is the starting point for excursions to Parque Nacional Torres del Paine and also farther north to the town of El Calafate in Argentina. From Puerto Natales, regular boat trips also operate to the Balmaceda and Serrano glaciers.

Big Foot Expediciones
Bories 206
Tel: (061) 414 525
www.bigfootpatagonia.com

Estancia Travel
Bories 13-B
Tel: (061) 412 221
www.estanciatravel.com

Tourist Information

The headquarters of the Sernatur Tourist Office is located at Av. Providencia 1550 (tel: 600-7376 2887), between the Manuel Montt and Pedro de Valdivia metro stations. The office opens Mon–Fri 9am–6pm, Sat 9am–2pm. There is also a Sernatur information desk in the baggage reclaim area of the Santiago airport (open daily 8.30am–8pm) and, in other cities and towns around the country:

Ancud: Libertad 665. Tel: (065) 622800.
Antofagasta: Prat 384, Piso 1. Tel: (055) 451 818.
Arica: San Marcos 101. Tel: (058) 252 054
Chillán: 18 de Septiembre 455. Tel: (042) 223 272.
Concepción: Aníbal Pinto 460. Tel: (041) 274 1337.
Copiapó: Los Carrera 691. Tel: (052) 212 838.
Coyhaique: Bulnes 35. Tel: (067) 231752.
Iquique: Serrano 145, Piso 3, Of. 303. Tel: (057) 427 686.
Isla de Pascua (Easter Island): Tu'u Maheke and Apina. Tel: (032) 210 0255.
La Serena: Matta 461, of. 108. Tel: (051) 225138.
Osorno: Edificio Gobernación, Piso 1. Tel: (064) 237 575.
Puerto Montt: Av. X Región 480, Piso 2. Tel: (065) 259 615.
Puerto Natales: Pedro Montt 19. Tel: (061) 412 125.
Punta Arenas: Lautaro Navarro 999. Tel: (061) 248 790.

BELOW: tour agencies abound in popular destinations like Pucón.

Time Zone

From April to October, Chile is 4 hours behind GMT. From end October through March, daylight saving time is in operation and the country is 3 hours behind GMT during this period.

Rancagua: Germán Riesco 277, Of. 11 & 12. Tel: (072) 230413.
San Pedro de Atacama: Toconoa and Gustavo Le Paige. Tel: (055) 851 420.
Talca: Uno Oriente 1150, piso 4. Tel: (071) 233 669.
Temuco: Bulnes 586. Tel: (045) 211 969.
Valdivia: Prat 555. Tel: (063) 239 060.
Viña Del Mar: Quillota 72. Tel: (032) 288 2285.

Useful Websites

Basic tourist information in English can be found on Senatur's website (www.sernatur.cl), but it is not always up-to-date. A number of other websites also provide useful information for visitors to Chile in English, including:
www.turismochile.com
www.gochile.cl
www.chilecontact.com
www.chipsites.com

Visas and Passports

All foreigners require a valid identity document. While residents of neighboring countries can use their identity card in Chile, all other foreigners require passports, and a few of these must obtain visas. Countries requiring visas to enter Chile include: Russia, China, India, and some East European, Arab and African countries. It would be wise to check on the current situation before departing. All foreigners wishing to work in Chile need visas.

A tourist card is issued to all foreigners on arrival. First-time visitors from some countries are charged an administration fee (US, US$131; Canada, US$132; Australia, US$61; Mexico, US$23; Albania, US$30). The tourist card contains your identification data and is generally valid for 90 days. It is renewable for a further 90 days, though if you wish to stay longer than six months, it's simplest to take a short trip to an adjoining country and you will be issued with a new tourist card on your return. Renewal applications must be submitted personally at the Passport Office (Moneda 1342, Santiago, tel: 02-697 0403), open Monday through Friday 8.30am–2pm. The card must be surrendered when leaving the country. Don't lose it.

What to Bring

Chile is probably the most materially modern country in South America,

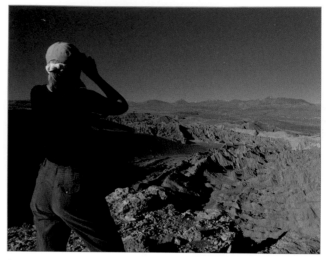

ABOVE: Chile is generally a safe place for solo women travelers.

with exhaustive shopping potential in Santiago, so if you forget to pack something, you'll probably be able to purchase it there.
• Note that foreign books, including travel guidebooks in English, can be surprisingly expensive so it is better to purchase these in your home country.
• Clothing for all weathers is necessary if you plan to tour the whole country.
• Take a first-aid kit for travel to remote areas.
• Good camping and hiking equipment is available, but the range is limited and prices are high.
• A pocket knife or Swiss Army knife might come in handy, since fruit should be peeled, or at least washed, before eating.
• Take your driver's license if you plan to hire a road vehicle.
Other useful items: a small sewing kit, a water container for walking trips, sunglasses, aspirin (often desirable in areas of high altitude), swimming costume, and protective clothing for sports and boat trips.

On the Road

If you are traveling extensively through Chile, take clothing that is most useful for all extremes of climate (see pages 345–6). Remember that southern Chile is as cold as the northern deserts are hot, so take warm socks, gloves, headgear, and a windproof and

Weights and Measures

Metric measurements are used to calculate distances and weights.

waterproof jacket. The ozone layer is particularly thin in the southern regions, so bring sunglasses, sunscreen, and headgear. Thermal underwear will come in handy if you're heading for southern regions such as the Torres del Paine National Park, Punta Arenas, or Tierra del Fuego. Travelers often prefer to buy their woolen sweaters or ponchos from artesanías in Santiago or en route, since they are very reasonably priced and of high quality.

If you're trying to cut down on shoe luggage, take some solid walking shoes that won't look too out of place in a casual restaurant. Synthetic fabrics won't crush in your suitcase, but these don't breathe as well in the hot weather. It's a good idea to use your hotel's laundering service, as cleaners tend to be less reliable and just as expensive.

Women Travelers

Providing women travelers take sensible precautions, they are as safe in Chile as in most European countries. Chilean men often stare, whistle and can make vulgar remarks, but it hardly ever goes beyond that, and stranger rape is extremely rare. The metro, Santiago's underground rail system, is safe at all hours, as are the buses, as long as you don't go off the beaten track. However, late at night, it is sensible to call a radio taxi, rather than flagging one down on the street. In remote country areas, where male alcoholism is a serious problem, a little extra care is also advisable.

LANGUAGE

UNDERSTANDING THE LANGUAGE

Of the many versions of Latin American Spanish in South America, the Chilean version is one of the hardest to understand. Chileans neglect to pronounce consonants clearly, if at all. Television newsreaders are the only exception. So Chile is not the ideal place to learn Spanish. (Best value for classes, as well as best for understanding, is probably Quito, Ecuador, if you are considering further travel in South America.) At any rate, it is much better to know a little Spanish when you arrive. English is spoken at major hotels and by quite a few Chileans, but don't count on it with taxi drivers, waiters, or porters.

Language schools, apart from advertised private tuition, include the Chilean-British Institute and the Chilean-North American Cultural Institute. The main private language schools, including Berlitz, offer tailor-made individual courses, but these tend to be expensive. Most reputable language schools ask for at least US$1,300 a week for full-day courses. Berlitz also offers a cassette that is worthwhile for beginners:
Berlitz Chile
Moneda 1160, Piso 7, Santiago
Tel: (02) 672 7639.
It may not always be essential for foreign speakers to have the correct form of address, i.e. formal or informal, or even the correct masculine or feminine conjugations, as long as you can make yourself understood. Many travelers learn Spanish to the present-tense stage and manage very well on this alone. However, in order to be well received in Chile, there are a few things worth remembering. Upon meeting someone, whether they be a taxi

driver or a long-lost uncle, you should always use the greeting, *Buenos días* (Good morning) or *Buenas tardes* (Good afternoon/evening). It is then appropriate to wait for the response before continuing your conversation. A woman is addressed as *Señora*, a girl or young woman as *Señorita* (unless she's wearing a wedding ring), and a man as *Señor*.

Basic Communication

Yes *Sí*
No *No*
Thank you *Gracias*
You're welcome *No hay de que/ Por nada*
Alright/Okay/That's fine *Está bien*
Please *Por favor*
Excuse me (to get attention) *¡Permiso!/¡Por favor!*
Excuse me (to get through a crowd) *¡Permiso!*
Excuse me (sorry) *Perdóneme, Discúlpeme*
Wait a minute! *¡Un momento!*
Please help me (formal) *Por favor, ayúdeme*
Certainly *¡Claro!/¡Claro que sí!/¡Por cierto!*
Can I help you? (formal) *¿Puedo ayudarle?*
Can you show me...? *¿Puede mostrarme...?*
I need... *Necesito....*
I'm lost *Estoy perdido(a)*
I'm sorry *Lo siento*
I don't know *No sé*
I don't understand *No entiendo*
Do you speak English/French/ German? (formal) *¿Habla inglés/ francés/alemán?*
Could you speak more slowly, please? *¿Puede hablar más despacio, por favor?*

Could you repeat that, please? *¿Puede repetirlo, por favor?*
Slowly *Despacio/Lentamente*
here *Aquí, Acá*
there *Allí, Allá, Ahí*
What? *¿Qué?/¿Cómo?*
When? *¿Cuándo?*
Why? *¿Por qué?*
Where? *¿Dónde?*
Who? *¿Quién(es)?*
How? *¿Cómo?*
Which? *¿Cuál?*
How much/how many? *¿Cuánto?/ ¿Cuántos?*
Do you have...? *¿Hay...?*
How long? *¿Cuánto tiempo?*
Big, bigger *Grande, más grande*
Small, smaller *Pequeño, más*

Greetings

Hello! *¡Hola!*
Hello (Good day) *Buenos días*
Good afternoon/night *Buenas tardes/noches*
Goodbye *Ciao/¡Adios!*
My name is... *Me llamo...*
What is your name? (formal) *¿Cómo se llama usted?*
Mr/Miss/Mrs *Señor/Señorita/ Señora*
Pleased to meet you *¡Encantado!*
I am English/American/ Canadian/Irish/Scottish/ Australian *Soy inglés(a)/ norteamericano(a)/canadiense/ irlandés(a)/escocés(a)/ australiano(a)*
Do you speak English? (formal) *¿Habla inglés?*
How are you? (formal/informal) *¿Cómo está?/¿Qué tal?*
Fine, thanks *Muy bien, gracias*
See you later *Hasta luego*
Take care (informal) *¡Cuídate!*

TRANSPORTATION ACCOMMODATIONS ACTIVITIES A – Z LANGUAGE

pequeño/chico, más chico
I want.../I would like.../I need...
Quiero.../Quisiera.../Necesito...
Where is the lavatory (men's/ women's)? ¿Dónde se encuentra el baño (de caballeros/de damas)?
Which way is it to ...? ¿Cómo se va a ...?

Telephone Calls

The area code El código de área
Where can I buy/Do you sell telephone cards? ¿Dónde puedo comprar tarjetas telefónicas?/¿Se venden aquí tarjetas telefónicas?
May I use your phone to make a local call? ¿Puedo usar su teléfono para hacer una llamada local?
Of course you may ¡Por supuesto que sí!/¡Como no!/¡Claro!
Hello (on the phone) ¡Aló!
May I speak to...? ¿Puedo hablar con... (name), por favor?
Sorry, he/she isn't in Lo siento, no se encuentra
Can he/she call you back? ¿Puede devolver la llamada?
Yes, he/she can reach me at... Sí, él/ella puede llamarme a...
I'll try again later Voy a intentar más tarde
Can I leave a message? ¿Puedo dejar un mensaje?
Please tell him/her I called Por favor avísele que llamé
Hold on Un momento, por favor
Can you speak up, please? ¿Puede hablar más fuerte, por favor?

In the Hotel

Do you have a vacant room? ¿Tiene una habitación disponible?
I have a reservation Tengo una reservación
I'd like... Quisiera...
a single/double (with double bed)/a room with twin beds una habitación individual/una habitación matrimonial/una habitación doble
for one night/two nights por una noche/dos noches
on the ground floor/first floor/top floor/with sea view en el primer piso/en el segundo piso/en el último piso/con vista al mar
Does the room have a private bathroom or shared bathroom? ¿Tiene la habitación baño privado o baño compartido?
Does it have hot water? ¿Tiene agua caliente?
Could you show me another room, please? ¿Puede mostrarme otra habitación, por favor?
Is it a quiet room? ¿Es una habitación tranquila?

What time do you close (lock) the doors? ¿A qué hora se cierran las puertas?
I would like to change rooms Quisiera cambiar de habitación
This room is too noisy/hot/ cold/small Esta habitación es demasiado ruidosa/calorosa/fría/ pequeña
How much is it? ¿Cuánto cuesta?
Does the price include tax/ breakfast/meals/drinks? ¿El precio incluye el impuesto/ desayuno/ comidas/bebidas?
Do you accept credit cards/ travelers' checks/dollars? ¿Se aceptan tarjetas de crédito/ cheques de viajeros/dólares?
What time is breakfast/lunch/ dinner? ¿A qué hora está servido el desayuno/almuerzo/la cena?
Please wake me at... Favor despertarme a...
Come in! ¡Pase!/¡Adelante!
I'd like to pay the bill now, please Quisiera cancelar la cuenta ahora, por favor

Useful Words

bath el baño
dining room el comedor
elevator/lift el ascensor
key la llave
push/pull empuje/tire
safety deposit box la caja de seguridad
soap el jabón
shampoo el champú
shower la ducha
toilet paper el papel higiénico
towel la toalla

Drinks

What would you like to drink? ¿Qué quiere tomar?
coffee... un café...
with milk cortado
milky coffee café con leche
strong fuerte
small/large pequeño/grande
with sugar con azúcar
tea... té...
with lemon/milk con limón/cortado
herbal tea té de hierbas
hot chocolate chocolate caliente
fresh orange juice jugo de naranja natural
orangeade naranjada
soft drink bebida/refresco
mineral water still/carbonated agua mineral sin gas/con gas
with/without ice con/sin hielo
cover charge precio del cubierto
minimum consumption consumo mínimo
beer hall/pub pub
discotheque disco/discoteca

nightclub club nocturno
a bottle/half a bottle una botella/ media botella
a glass of red/white/rosé wine una copa de vino tinto/blanco/rosado
beer una cerveza
Is service included? ¿Incluye el servicio?
I need a receipt, please Necesito un recibo, por favor
Keep the change Está bien, gracias
Cheers! ¡Salud!
ice cream helado
sandwich sandwich
savory turnover (filled with meat, cheese etc.) empanada

In a Restaurant

I'd like to book a table Quisiera reservar una mesa, por favor
Do you have a table for...? ¿Tiene una mesa para...?
I have a reservation Tengo una reservación
breakfast/lunch/dinner desayuno/ almuerzo/cena
I'm a vegetarian Soy vegetariano(a)
Is there a vegetarian dish? ¿Hay un plato vegetariano?
May we have the menu? ¿Puede traernos la carta/el menú?
wine list la carta de vinos
What would you recommend? ¿Qué recomendaría?
home-made casero(a)
fixed-price menu menú fijo
special of the day plato del día/ sugerencia del chef
The meal was very good La comida fue muy buena
waiter garzón/mozo

Menu Decoder

Entrada (First Course)

sopa/crema **soup/cream soup**
sopa de ajo **garlic soup**
sopa de cebolla **onion soup**
ensalada... **salad...**
mixta **mixed**
ensalada de palta con tomate **avocado pear and tomato salad**
pan de ajo **garlic bread**

Plato Principal/de Fondo (Main Course)

crudo **raw**
vuelta y vuelta **rare**
término medio **medium rare**
tres cuartos **medium**
bien cocido(a) **well done**

La Carne (Meat)

a las brasas/a la parrilla **charcoal grilled**
a la plancha **grilled**
ahumado(a) **smoked**

albóndigas **meatballs**
asado(a) **roasted**
cerdo/chancho **pork**
chorizo **Spanish-style sausage**
chuleta **chop**
conejo **rabbit**
cordero **lamb**
costillas **ribs**
apanado(a) **breaded**
frito(a) **fried/battered**
guisado(a) **stewed**
hamburguesa **hamburger**
higado de res **beef liver**
jamón **ham**
lomito **tenderloin**
milanesa **breaded and fried thin cut of meat**
pernil **leg of pork**
riñones **kidneys**
salchichas/vienesas **sausages or hot dogs**
ternera **veal**

Ave (Fowl)

alas **wings**
chicharrón de pollo **chicken cut up in small pieces and deep fried**
pato **duck**
pavo **turkey**
pechuga **breast**
pollo **chicken**
truto **thigh**
truto chico **leg**

Pescado/Mariscos (Fish/Shellfish)

almejas **clams**
anchoa **anchovy**
atún **tuna**
bacalao **cod**
calamares **squid**
camarones **prawns**
centolla **king crab**
cholgas **mussels**
congrio **kingclip**
corvina **sea bass**
jaiba **crab**
langosta **lobster**
lenguado **sole or flounder**
mero **grouper**

ostiones **scallops**
ostras **oysters**
pulpo **octopus**
salmón **salmon**
sardinas **sardines**
trucha **trout**

Verduras (Vegetables)

ajo **garlic**
alcachofa **artichoke**
arvejas **peas**
berenjena **eggplant (aubergine)**
betarraga **beets/beetroot**
brócoli **broccoli**
camote **sweet potato**
cebolla **onion**
champiñones **mushrooms**
choclo **corn on the cob**
coliflor **cauliflower**
espárrago **asparagus**
espinaca **spinach**
lechuga **lettuce**
pepino **cucumber**
pimentón **(bell) pepper**
porotos verdes **green beans**
puerro **leek**
repollo **cabbage**
zanahorias **carrots**
zapallito italiano **zucchini (courgette)**
zapallo **pumpkin or yellow squash**

Frutas (Fruit)

cereza **cherry**
ciruela **plum**
dátil **date**
durazno **peach**
frambuesa **raspberry**
frutilla **strawberry**
guayaba **guava**
higo **fig**
limón **lemon**
mandarina **mandarin**
manzana **apple**
melón **cantaloupe/melon**
mora **blackberry**
naranja **orange**
palta **avocado pear**
papaya **mountain papaya/carica**

pera **pear**
piña **pineapple**
plátano **banana**
pomelo **grapefruit**
sandía **watermelon**
uvas **grapes**

Miscellaneous

arroz **rice**
azúcar **sugar**
empanada **savory turnover**
huevos (revueltos/fritos/a la copa) **eggs (scrambled/fried/boiled)**
mantequilla **butter**
mermelada **jam**
mostaza **mustard**
pan **bread**
pan integral **wholewheat bread**
pan tostado **toast**
pimienta negra **black pepper**
queso **cheese**
sal **salt**
salsa de tomate/ketchup **ketchup**
salsa picante **hot sauce**
tallarines **spaghetti**
tocino **bacon**
tortilla **omelette**

Tourist Attractions

aguas termales **hot springs**
artesanía **handicrafts**
campamento **camp**
capilla **chapel**
castillo/fuerte **fort**
catedral **cathedral**
cerro **hill**
comunidad indígena **indigenous community**
convento **convent**
cumbre **(mountain) peak**
galería **gallery**
iglesia **church**
isla **island**
jardín botánico **botanical garden**
lago **lake**
laguna **lagoon**
mar **sea**
mercado **market**

Numbers

1 *uno*	16 *dieciséis*	101 *ciento uno*	**first** *primer(o)/a*
2 *dos*	17 *diecisiete*	200 *doscientos*	**second** *segund(o)/a*
3 *tres*	18 *dieciocho*	300 *trescientos*	**third** *tercer(o)/a*
4 *cuatro*	19 *diecinueve*	400 *cuatrocientos*	**fourth** *cuart(o)/a*
5 *cinco*	20 *veinte*	500 *quinientos*	
6 *seis*	21 *veintiuno*	600 *seiscientos*	**NOTE**
7 *siete*	25 *veinticinco*	700 *setecientos*	In Spanish, in numbers,
8 *ocho*	30 *treinta*	800 *ochocientos*	commas are used where
9 *nueve*	40 *cuarenta*	900 *novecientos*	decimal points are used
10 *diez*	50 *cincuenta*	1,000 *mil*	in English and vice versa.
11 *once*	60 *sesenta*	2,000 *dos mil*	For example:
12 *doce*	70 *setenta*	10,000 *diez mil*	
13 *trece*	80 *ochenta*	100,000 *cien mil*	**English** **Spanish**
14 *catorce*	90 *noventa*	1,000,000 *un millón*	$19.30 $19,30
15 *quince*	100 *cien*	2,000,000 *dos millones*	1,000 m 1.000 m
			9.5 % 9,5 %

mirador **viewpoint**
montaña **mountain**
monumento **monument**
Océano Pacífico **Pacific Ocean**
oficina de turismo **tourist
information office**
parque **park**
parque infantil **playground**
piscina **swimming pool**
playa **beach**
plaza **town square**
postal **postcard**
puente **bridge**
quebrada **gorge**
río **river**
ruinas **ruins**
sanctuario **sanctuary**
teleférico **cable car**
torre **tower**
zona colonial **colonial zone**
zoológico **zoo**

Traveling

airline *línea aérea*
airport *aeropuerto*
arrivals/departures *llegadas/
salidas*
bus stop *parada (de bus)*
bus terminal *terminal de buses*
bus *bus/micro*
car *auto*
car rental *arriendo de autos*
connection *conexión*
dock for small boats/large boats
embarcadero/muelle
ferry *transbordador*
first class/second class *primera
clase/segunda clase, clase turista*
flight *vuelo*
luggage, bag(s) *equipaje, maleta(s)*
next stop please (for buses) *La
próxima parada, por favor*

BELOW: safe to swim.

one-way ticket *pasaje de ida*
platform *el andén*
round trip/return ticket *boleto de
ida y vuelta*
sailboat *velero*
ship *barco*
subway *Metro*
taxi *taxi*
yacht *yate*

Addresses/Directions

a la derecha **on the right**
a la izquierda **on the left**
al lado de **beside**
alrededor de **around**
arriba/abajo **above/below**
avenida (Av.) **avenue**
calle **street**
cerca de **near**
cruce **crossroad(s)**
cruce con **at the junction of
(two streets)**
debajo de **under**
delante de **in front of**
derecho **straight ahead**
detrás de **behind**
doble hacia la izquierda/la derecha
turn to the left/right
edificio (Edif.) **high-rise building**
en **in, on, at**
en frente de/frente de/frente a
in front of
en la parte de atrás **in the rear area
(as behind a building)**
encima de **on top of**
entre **between**
esquina (Esq.) **corner**
penthouse/primer piso/segundo
piso/entrepiso/subterráneo
**penthouse/ground floor/second
floor/mezzanine/basement**
residencial (Res.) **small pension**

torre **tower**
una cuadra **a block**

Airport or Travel Agency

customs and immigration *aduana e
inmigración*
travel/tour agency *agencia de
viajes/de turismo*
ticket *pasaje/boleto*
I would like to purchase a ticket
for... *Quisiera comprar un pasaje/
boleto para...*
When is the next/last flight/
departure for...? *¿Cuándo es el
próximo/último vuelo para...?*
What time does the plane/bus/
boat/ferry leave/return? *¿A qué
hora sale/regresa el avión/el bus/
la lancha/el transbordador?*
What time do I have to be at the
airport? *¿A qué hora tengo que estar
en el aeropuerto?*
Is the tax included? *¿Está incluido
el impuesto?*
What is included in the price? *¿Qué
está incluido en el precio?*
departure tax? *¿el impuesto de
aeropuerto?*
I would like a seat in first class/
business class/tourist class
*Quisiera un asiento en primera clase/
ejecutivo/clase turista*
lost luggage office *oficina de
reclamos de equipaje*
on time *a tiempo*
late *atrasado*
I need to change my ticket *Necesito
cambiar mi pasaje*
How long is the flight? *¿Cuánto dura
el vuelo?*
Is this seat taken? *¿Está ocupado
este asiento?*
Which is the stop closest to ...?
¿Cuál es la parada más cerca a ...?
Could you please advise me when
we reach/the stop for ...?
*¿Por favor, puede avisarme cuando
llegamos a/a la parada para ...?*
Is this the stop for ...? *¿Es ésta la
parada para ...?*

Driving

Where can I rent a car? *¿Dónde
puedo arrendar un auto?*
Is mileage included? *¿Está incluido
el kilometraje?*
comprehensive insurance
seguro completo
spare tire/jack/emergency triangle
*rueda de repuesto/ gato/triángulo de
emergencia*
Where is the registration
document? *¿Dónde se encuentra(n)
el padrón/los documentos del auto?*
Does the car have an alarm?
¿El auto tiene alarma?

PLAYA APTA
PARA EL BAÑO

ABOVE: Arturo Merino Benítez airport, Santiago.

a road map/a city map *un mapa carretero/plano de la ciudad*
How do I get to ...? *¿Cómo se llega a ...?*
Turn right/left *Doble a la derecha/izquierda*
at the next corner/street *en la próxima esquina/calle*
Go straight ahead *Siga derecho*
You are on the wrong road *Está en el camino equivocado*
Please show me where am I on the map *Por favor, indíqueme dónde estoy en el mapa*
Where is...? *¿Dónde se encuentra...?*
Where is the nearest...? *¿Dónde se encuentra el/la ... más cercano(a)?*
How long does it take to get there? *¿Cuánto tiempo se requiere para llegar?*
driver's license *licencia de conducir*

Colors

light/dark *claro/oscuro*
red *rojo*
yellow *amarillo*
blue *azul*
brown *café/marrón*
black *negro*
white *blanco*
beige *beige*
green *verde*
wine *burdeo*
gray *gris*
orange *color naranjo*
pink *rosado*
purple *púrpuro*
silver *plateado*
gold *dorado*

service station/gasoline station *estación de servicio/bomba de bencina*
My car won't start *Mi auto no parte*
My car is overheating *Mi auto se está recalentando*
My car has broken down *Mi auto está en pana*
tow truck *una grúa*
Where can I find a car repair shop? *¿Dónde se encuentra un taller mecánico?*
Can you check the...? *¿Puede revisar/chequear...?*
There's something wrong with the... *Hay un problema con...*
oil/water/air/brake fluid/light bulb *aceite/agua/aire/líquido de frenos/ampolleta*
trunk/hood/door/window *maleta/capó/puerta/ventana*

Road Signs

autopista **freeway**
bajada/subida peligrosa **dangerous downgrade/incline**
calle ciega **dead-end street**
calle de un sentido **one-way street**
carretera **highway, road**
cede el paso **yield/give way**
conserve su derecha **keep to the right**
cruce **crossroads**
cruce de ferrocarril (sin señal) **railway crossing (without signal)**
despacio **slow**
doble vía **two-way traffic**
enciende luces en el túnel **turn on lights in the tunnel**
entrada prohibida **entrance prohibited**

estacionamiento **parking**
hundimiento **sunken road**
no estacionar/prohibido estacionarse aquí **no parking**
no gire en U **no U-turn**
no hay paso/vía cerrado **road blocked**
no hay salida **no exit**
no pare **no stopping here**
no toque la bocina **no horn honking**
¡ojo! **watch out!**
pare **stop**
paso de ganado **cattle crossing**
paso de peatones **pedestrian crossing**
peaje **toll booth**
peligro **danger**
pendiente fuerte/curva fuerte **steep hill/sharp curve**
rotonda **traffic circle (roundabout)**
salida **exit**
semáforo **traffic light**
trabajos en la vía **roadworks**
una sola pista **single lane**

Emergencies

Help! *¡Socorro!/¡Auxilio!*
Stop! *¡Pare!*
Watch out! *¡Cuidado!/¡Ojo!*
I've had an accident *He tenido un accidente*
Call a doctor *Llame a un médico*
Call an ambulance *Llame una ambulancia*
Call the... *Llame a...*
...police *la policía/los carabineros*
...the fire brigade *los bomberos*
This is an emergency, where is there a telephone, please? *Es una emergencia. ¿Dónde hay un teléfono, por favor?*

Where is the nearest hospital?
¿Dónde se encuentra el hospital más cercano?
I want to report a robbery
Quisiera denunciar un robo
Thank you very much for your help
Muchísimas gracias por su ayuda

Health

shift-duty pharmacy *farmacia de turno*
hospital/clinic *hospital/clínica*
I need a doctor/dentist *Necesito un médico/dentista (odontólogo)*
I don't feel well *Me siento mal*
I am sick *Estoy enfermo(a)*
It hurts here *Duele aquí*
I have a headache/stomach ache/cramps *Tengo un dolor de cabeza/de estómago/retorcijones*
I feel dizzy *Me siento mareado(a)*
Do you have (something for)...? *¿Tiene (algo para)...?*
a cold/flu *resfrío/gripe*
diarrhea *diarrea*
constipation *estreñimiento*
fever *fiebre*
aspirin *aspirina*
heartburn *ácidez*
insect/mosquito bites *picadas de insectos/zancudos*

Shopping

antique shop *antigüedades*
bakery *panadería*
bank *banco*
barber shop/hairdresser *peluquería*
beauty shop *peluquería, salón de belleza*
bookstore *librería*
butcher's *carnicería*
currency exchange bureau *casa de cambio*
delicatessen *delicatessen*
department store *tienda por departamentos*
florist *florería*
gift shop *(tienda de) regalos*
greengrocer's *verdulería*

Months

January *enero*
February *febrero*
March *marzo*
April *abril*
May *mayo*
June *junio*
July *julio*
August *agosto*
September *septiembre*
October *octubre*
November *noviembre*
December *diciembre*

hardware store *ferretería*
shopping center *centro comercial, mall*
jewelry shop *joyería*
laundry *lavandería*
library *biblioteca*
liquor store *botellería*
market *mercado*
newsstand *kiosco*
pastry shop *pastelería*
post office *oficina de correos*
shoe repair shop/shoe store *zapatería*
small grocery store *almacén*
small shop *tienda*
stationer's *papelería*
supermarket *supermercado*
toy store *juguetería*

What time do you open/close?
¿A qué hora abren/cierran?
open/closed *abierto/cerrado*
I'd like... *Quisiera...*
I'm just looking *Estoy sólo mirando, gracias*
How much does it cost?
¿Cuánto cuesta?
It doesn't fit *No queda bien*
Do you have it in another color?
¿Tiene en otro color?
Do you have it in another size?
¿Tiene en otra talla? (clothing), *tamaño* (objects)
smaller/larger *más pequeño/más grande*
It's too expensive *Es demasiado caro*
Do you have something less expensive? *¿Tiene algo más económico?*
Where do I pay for it? *¿Dónde está la caja?*
Anything else? *¿Quiere algo más?*
a little more/less *un poco más/menos*
That's enough/no more *Está bien/no más*

Days and Dates

morning *la mañana*
afternoon *la tarde*
late afternoon, dusk *el atardecer*
evening *la noche*
early morning *la madrugada*
sunrise *el amanecer*
sunset *la puesta del sol*
last night *anoche*
yesterday *ayer*
today *hoy*
tomorrow *mañana*
the day after tomorrow *pasado mañana*
now *ahora*
early *temprano*
late *tarde*
a minute *un minuto*
an hour *una hora*

Conversion Tables

Length

Inches	Centimeters
1	2.54
2	5.08
3	7.62
6	15.24
9	22.86

Feet	Centimeters
1	30.48
2	60.96
3	91.44
6	182.88
9	274.32
12	365.76

Weight

Pounds	Kilograms
1	0.45
2	0.90
3	1.36
4	1.81
5	2.27
6	2.72
7	3.18
8	3.63
9	4.08
10	4.53
20	9.07
50	22.68
100	45.36

Volume

US Pints	Liters
1	0.47
2	0.95
3	1.42
4	1.89

US Gallons	Liters
1	3.78
2	7.57
3	11.36
5	18.93
10	37.85
20	75.71
50	189.27

half an hour *media hora*
a day *un día*
a week *una semana*
a month *un mes*
a year *un año*
weekday *día laboral/hábil*
weekend *fin de semana*
public holiday *día feriado*

Days of the Week

Monday *lunes*
Tuesday *martes*
Wednesday *miércoles*
Thursday *jueves*
Friday *viernes*
Saturday *sábado*
Sunday *domingo*

FURTHER READING

Travel In Chile

Aku-Aku – The Secret of Easter Island by Thor Heyerdahl. In this sequel to *The Kon-Tiki Expedition*, Heyerdahl examines the history of the Easter Island statues.
Cape Horn and Other Stories from the End of the World by Francisco Coloane. One of many books from this author about the wonders and struggles of life in Patagonia.
In Patagonia by Bruce Chatwin. A classic and vivid account of the author's journey to the "uttermost part of the earth" in the 1970s.
The Old Patagonian Express by Paul Theroux. Theroux's account of his train journey down the length of South America is a travel classic.
Tierra del Fuego by Rae Natalie Prosser Goodall. Written by the biologist wife of the great-grandson of Thomas Bridges who set up Estancia Harberton, the first farm on the Argentine side of Tierra del Fuego.
Travels in a Thin Country: Journey Through Chile by Sara Wheeler. An entertaining and insightful account of Wheeler's six-month journey from the top to the bottom of Chile.

Fiction

Isabel Allende: All Isabel Allende's novels were written after she left Chile in the wake of the 1973 military coup, but **House of the Spirits** is set in Chile, tracing four generations of the Trueba family through the country's social and political upheavals, while ***Inés of My Soul*** is the fictional memoir of Inés Suárez, the first Spanish woman to live in Chile in the 1500s. In ***My Invented Country: A Memoir***, Allende reflects fondly but clear-sightedly on the idiosyncrasies of her home country.
Burning Patience by Antonio Skármeta. The book that inspired the film *Il Postino* weaves a story around Pablo Neruda's life and death after the military coup.
By Night in Chile by Roberto Bolaño. One of the easiest of Bolaño's novel to read, this is a satire about Chilean literature and writers.

Chile: A Traveler's Literary Companion Edited by Katherine Silver.
Robinson Crusoe by Daniel Defoe. Classic novel based on Alexander Selkirk's time on the Juan Fernández islands.

Politics and History

Chile – The Legacy of Hispanic Capitalism by Brian Loveman.
Allende's Chile by Edward Boorstein.
Pinochet: The Politics of Torture by Hugh O'Shaughnessy.
Pinochet in Piccadilly: Britain and Chile's Hidden History by Andy Beckett.

The New Song Movement

Victor, An Unfinished Song by Joan Jara. An account of the heroic folk musician's life and music written by his wife.

Send Us Your Thoughts

We do our best to ensure the information in our books is as accurate and up-to-date as possible. The books are updated on a regular basis using local contacts, who painstakingly add, amend and correct as required. However, some details (such as telephone numbers and opening times) are liable to change, and we are ultimately reliant on our readers to put us in the picture.

We welcome your feedback, especially your experience of using the book "on the road". Maybe we recommended a hotel that you liked (or another that you didn't), or you came across a great bar or new attraction we missed.

We will acknowledge all contributions, and we'll offer an Insight Guide to the best letters received.

Please write to us at:
   Insight Guides
   PO Box 7910
   London SE1 1WE
Or email us at:
   insight@apaguide.co.uk

Food and Wine

The Chilean Kitchen: Authentic, Homestyle Foods, Regional Wines, and Culinary Traditions of Chile by Ruth Van Waerebeek-Gonzalez.
Chilean Wine: The Heritage by Rodrigo Alvarado.

Poetry

Pablo Neruda – Selected Poems translated by Andrew Kerrigan.
My Life with Pablo Neruda by Matilde Urrutia.
Selected Poems of Gabriela Mistral translated by Ursula K. Le Guin.
A Translation of Alonso de Ercilla's La Araucana by Louis Carrera. English translation of the 16th-century epic poem.

Other Guides

Among nearly 200 companion books to this one are several guides highlighting destinations in this region. Titles include *Insight Guides* to *South America, Argentina, Brazil, Peru, Ecuador & the Galápagos*, and the *Berlitz Guide to Buenos Aires*.

ART & PHOTO CREDITS